W9-AEJ-839

PRAGMATISM, POST-MODERNISM, AND COMPLEXITY THEORY

A landmark and visionary book ... Doll's work, collected in this single volume for the first time, demonstrates both his scholarly brilliance and pedagogical wisdom.

Hongyu Wang, Oklahoma State University

The first volume to bring together the key works of the major curriculum studies scholar William E. Doll, Jr., *Pragmatism, Post-modernism, and Complexity Theory* provides an overview of his scholarship over his fifty-year career and documents the theoretical and practical contribution he has made to the field. The book is organized in five thematic sections:

- Personal Reflections
- Dewey, Piaget, Bruner, Whitehead: Process and Transformation
- Modern/Post-modern: Structures, Forms and Organization
- Complexity Thinking
- Reflections on Teaching

The complicated intellectual trajectory through pragmatism, post-modernism and complexity theory not only testifies to Doll's individual lifetime works but is also intimately related to the landscape of education to which he has made an important contribution. Of interest to curriculum scholars around the world, the book will hold special significance for graduate students and junior scholars who came of age in the field Doll helped create: one crafted by post-modernism and, more recently, complexity theory.

William E. Doll, Jr. is Emeritus Professor—Louisiana State University, College of Education and Adjunct Professor at University of Victoria and the University of British Columbia, Canada.

Donna Trueit earned a PhD in Curriculum and Instruction at Louisiana State University. She is co-editor of *The Internationalization of Curriculum* (1999) and *Chaos, Complexity, Curriculum and Culture* (2000). She and William E. Doll, Jr. are currently Adjunct Professors at the University of British Columbia where they co-teach graduate courses in curriculum theory.

STUDIES IN CURRICULUM THEORY

WILLIAM F. PINAR, SERIES EDITOR

For additional information on titles in the Studies in Curriculum Theory series visit **www.routledge.com/education**

PRAGMATISM, POST-MODERNISM, AND COMPLEXITY THEORY

The "Fascinating Imaginative Realm" of William E. Doll, Jr.

Edited by Donna Trueit

Routledge
Taylor & Francis Group

NEW YORK AND LONDON

First published 2012
by Routledge
711 Third Avenue, New York, NY 10017

Simultaneously published in the UK
by Routledge
2 Park Square, Milton Park, Abingdon, Oxon OX14 4RN

Routledge is an imprint of the Taylor & Francis Group, an informa business

Library of Congress Cataloging in Publication Data
Doll, William E.
Pragmatism, post-modernism, and complexity theory : the "fascinating
imaginative realm" of William E. Doll, Jr. / William E. Doll, Jr. ; edited
by Donna Trueit.
    p. cm. — (Studies in curriculum theory series)
    1. Education—Curricula—Philosophy. 2. Postmodernism and
education. 3. Pragmatism. I. Trueit, Donna, 1948– II. Title.
    LB1570.D617 2012
    375´.001—dc23   2011043933

ISBN13: 978-0-415-80873-6 (hbk)
ISBN13: 978-0-203-13897-7 (ebk)

Typeset in Bembo
by HWA Text and Data Management, London

Printed and bound by CPI Group (UK) Ltd, Croydon, CR0 4YY

With love
For Will, Sasha, and Mason
In memory of my parents,
Will and Becky
With grateful appreciation to
Bill Pinar and Donna Trueit
and
to the students who continue to inspire me.

CONTENTS

PREFACE

This volume collects the key works of a major curriculum studies scholar, William E. Doll, Jr. The main purposes of the book are to provide an overview of Doll's scholarship over his 50-year career; and to document the key theoretical and practical contributions Doll has made to curriculum studies. Of interest to scholars worldwide, the book will have special significance for graduate students and junior scholars who came of age in the intellectual field Doll helped to shape by introducing post-modernism and complexity theories. The book is intended for faculty and graduate students in curriculum studies, teacher education, and the foundations of education.

Doll's approach is primarily descriptive, although his work is based on his classroom research and teaching experiences; he takes a meta-theoretical perspective, akin to, and informed by, Gregory Bateson's: looking at a situation as always situated in a larger context and assuming dynamical forces are at play. His approach, therefore, spans the spectrum of education from elementary to advanced.

Bill Doll's intellectual trajectory through pragmatism, post-modernism, and complexity theory testifies to his intellectual work, but his intimate relation to the terrain of educational thought makes this journey much more of a pilgrimage. Through his unique insights, we can see that which sits outside the realm of conventional scholarship—and yet which has such a bearing on our work as educators.

Selected from amongst over eighty articles he has written, and thematically arranged into five sections beginning with personal reflections and ending with pedagogical reflections, the essays broadly reflect aspects of educative education that set it apart from mere factory-modeled schooling: the personal (reflections); transformation; modernist and post-modernist forms and organization; complexity; and teaching as a pragmatist/post-modernist/complexivist.

Overview

Doll's groundbreaking work has never been collected in a single volume before. The intellectual and pedagogical interconnectedness between and among pragmatism, post-modernism, and complexity theory in the context of curriculum studies cannot be more intricately demonstrated than in this book. Each section is preceded by an introduction intended to engage the reader for interaction. As a précis to the chapters, presenting merely a gloss, the writing will hopefully open a space for the reader to enter into conversation with Bill Doll's text.

There is a uniqueness to this book that comes from the interconnectedness of Bill Doll's perspectives, but there are other idiosyncrasies as well. First there is what he calls the Germanic style of his writing, adding his editorial comments within dashes in the sentence. There is the coining of new words: matrixically, scientificness, textbookize … the list goes on.

There is his abundant use of alliteration, both heuristic and playful and very memorable. In China his name is synonymous with 4 R's.

There is his tendency to honor the past by holding it close. Consequently, when he refers to Dewey, he is referring to the well worn, dog-eared, spine-broken books that line his bookshelves—underlined three or four times in some sections, in different shades of red, blue, black, green—not referring to the latterly produced early, middle or later works.

There are his footnotes. As he notes, the footnotes in his dissertation did not quite equal the length of the main text. His essay, "Keeping knowledge alive," was requested for a particular publication; when completed the editors told him to eliminate the footnotes—and there would be no endnotes either. He withdrew his essay from the book because there was no room for negotiation. A brand new journal, the *Journal of Educational Research and Development*, happily published the essay. We are grateful to Routledge for their generosity in allowing Bill's footnotes.

In editing the collection of essays we have worked to reduce the number of repetitions and redundancies that come with putting a collection of this type together; however, the great opportunity that comes from seeing someone's intellectual development over time is that one begins to see not simply sameness, but patterns. Patterns are interesting for the small variations that may lead, over time, to more obvious change. The development of his ideas over time is fascinating and conversely one is afforded the opportunity to trace themes back to early essays. Bill notes that he started to think in terms of systems while living in Redlands. In fact in "A methodology of experience, Part 1" (1972), retrospectively one sees that he is criticizing the closed system of behaviorists in education.

What Doll humbly refers to as "just silly ideas" and his "bumblings," are neither silly nor bumbling at all. Rather they are the substantive work of a modest man. Just as surely as I could never describe the echo of God's laughter (as you will note, one of Bill's favorite lines from Milan Kundera), I would never be able to describe the sound of Bill's laughter. He laughs often and loudly. He is eternally optimistic. It is the strongest recommendation I can think of for the academic work he does that he sees possibilities in any situation.

Donna Trueit

ACKNOWLEDGMENTS

As I look back on my forty years of writings, many of which are collected in this book, I am amazed not only at how much I have written but of the debt I owe to so many who have helped me as I have stumbled along my path of life, my curriculum as it were. Of the many I wish to thank, four names stand out—Steven Mann, Bill Pinar, Nel Noddings, Donna Trueit. These four have helped me shape not only my curriculum but also my *currere*. Contact with each of them, and each contact has been a lifelong one, has let me see what I did not see, devise a path I knew not existed.

My indebtedness to Steve Mann is expressed in this book. He brought to life a political/social aspect of Dewey I may otherwise have missed. His respect for me as a person has I hope carried over into the respect I wish to give to the many colleagues, critics, students with whom I have had contact.

Bill Pinar's work with and influence on me is nonpareil. We have been colleagues, friends, companions for about forty years. Our careers and, indeed, our lives have been much intertwined. His gentle but determined encouragement that I have a voice in the curriculum field that could benefit from hearing it, has inspired the writing of four books and all the essays written in my twenty-plus years working with him at Louisiana State University (LSU), and now living in the Pacific northwest. Enough other essays were written and left out of this book, that he wondered if maybe two volumes would be better than one. My production, as it were, has been influenced by his comments and his own model of super-production. Bill has also encouraged me to venture into the international field of curriculum. I am indebted to him for his founding of the International Association for the Advancement of Curriculum Studies (IAACS), and only hope some of what that organization has given to me, I have been able to return to it. Bill, may our relations together go on for the rest of our lives.

Nel Noddings, another super-producer and dear personal friend for about as long as I have known Bill, has influenced my personal method of teaching. Like others, I am admiring of the clarity of her thought, the probing of her analysis, the political and social stands she takes with gentleness but firmness. Here she has been an inspiration. I'd say a model except that in her comments on my teaching the notion of model would not be appropriate. Nel has helped me move from model to metaphor. Thank you, Nel.

What to say of Donna Trueit? Wow! First this book, and indeed other books, would literally not be without her. As an editor, now for a good fifteen years of my work, she helps me shape my thoughts, brings to my awareness that which I so often miss, and does her best with my writing. As my wife, lover, companion, we live life together and we work together. Our venture into complexity thinking is a joint project as we write and teach classes. While she scoffs at my comment that "I carry the books," she carries me. Donna helps me see aspects of relations I would otherwise not see. This is a path I continually need to retread, intellectually and personally. Thank you, Donna, not only for your help but also for your sage advice.

As would be my wont, there are three more people who have encouraged my path in directions I did not see: Zhang Hua, Deborah Osberg, and Noel Gough. Zhang Hua, encouraging our numerous visits to China, as part of that country's curriculum reform movement, has helped me see at least partially through the eyes of others. In turn, my own vision of myself and my struggle to develop a "curriculum which is dynamic, emergent, transformative, and non-linear" has become a bit clearer. Talking across cultures has helped me understand my own *currere* a bit better. Thank you, Zhang Hua, for providing this opportunity. Thank you, Hongyu Wang and Jie Yu, for helping me as I walk across the bridge (that is not a bridge) between two cultures.

Deborah Osberg, with encouragement from Brent Davis, roped me into, or steered me into, participating in the journal *Complicity*. What a realm to enter. Fascinating, editing an international journal. Here I have come in contact with writers from many disciplines with an interest in complexity, its varied definitions, and multiple uses. Deborah's polished writing, always clear and precise, has helped my own. Her struggles, with the journal, with her own writing process, and her helping young authors develop their own thoughts and expressions has been enlightening. As the journal now moves on to a new editor-in-chief, Michel Alhadeff-Jones, I look forward to Deborah's continued advice. I owe Deborah a debt of gratitude for introducing me to Paul Cilliers, an outstanding philosopher of complexity. His early death leaves the complexity field minus one of its illuminating stars.

It is hard to find words to describe my debt to Noel Gough. As with Bill and Nel, our relationship is decades old. We produced a book together, conceived and outlined while drinking wine on one our many wine country forays. For multiple summers Noel and I taught together at the University of Victoria, BC. Wine, conversation, playful proddings, and witty digs at my American love of science occurred frequently. Noel is an insightful critic and is excellent in helping me become aware of my shortsightedness; however (continuing with this metaphor), his vision for the future also coincided well with mine. It has been a joy traveling with you, and Annette, Noel.

A special place needs to be reserved for Jayne Fleener, and in doing so I move on to my colleagues and students, former and present, at LSU. Jayne was, for six years, Dean of the College of Education, a member of the Curriculum Theory Project (CTP), co-editor on the 4 C's book (*Chaos, complexity, curriculum and culture*, 2005), co-teacher with me on all our LSU complexity courses, traveling companion on our trips to China, and a warm and trusted confidant. She hosted many of the CTP social gatherings. She brought to our work on complexity, a depth of mathematics I did not have, a fine philosophical perspective, especially regarding Wittgenstein, and a critical sense to our writing and teaching. As with others it was just fun co-teaching with her. I look forward to more collaborations with her in the future.

The past ten years or so I have taught quite exclusively with others. At LSU my co-teaching was done mostly with Petra Munro Hendry, now co director of the CTP Bill Pinar and I started. Petra brings a feminist perspective to her work which I still struggle to appreciate as I should. She helped me realize the gendered, racial privilege of my rationalism; and she collaborated with me in bringing the spiritual into curriculum in our teachings—a wonderful learning experience for me. The same can be said about co-teaching with David Kirshner. He is a true mathematician and adept cognitivist. Although David's views are often quite different from my own, we truly enjoy each other's company in teaching, committee work, socializing. My insights are deepened through our work together, always a searching exploration into what is at issue.

Denise Egéa-Kuehne, once a doctoral student then a distinguished faculty member at LSU, opened my eyes and those of CTP students to the French, post-structural philosophers. This was a new world for me, one I have taken to with great enthusiasm, especially with regard to Derrida and Serres.

Wendy Kohli and Nina Asher were like co-directors to me in the Holmes Elementary (and Middle School) Education program. Each brought an enthusiasm and critical knowledge, academic and professional, to this program. Its success in integrating these two thrusts owes much to their insight and to those, particularly Thomasine Mencer and Elizabeth Willis, who took the program into the schools. It is their hard work and social commitment that has made this program outstanding.

Nancy Nelson, in the years she was with us in the CTP, brought a sense of decorum and professionalism which I had a tendency to overlook. With fondness I thank you for both.

Ann Trousdale, a children's literature specialist and close confidant, also helped develop my deepening sense of spirituality. Her spirit often infuses my writing. Ann says Grace like no other and her lovely dinner parties and lively, inspirited conversation will remain with Donna and me all our lives as cherished memories.

It is hard to find words to describe the influence our CTP doctoral students have had on me. I have learned so much with them and from them: John St. Julien,

Wen-Song Hwu, Patrick Slattery, Susan Edgerton, Laura Jewett, Mary Ann Doyle, Molly Quinn, Elaine Riley Taylor, Jeanne Robertson, Emily DeMoor, Lianfang Lu, Doug McKnight, Steve Triche, Anne Pautz, Janis Hill, Al Alcazar, Sean Buckreis, and the list goes on. All these students and more not mentioned have been with me for years, supported my efforts, and produced work of their own of which I am most proud. I am honored to know them. I'd like to pay special attention to two special groups of graduate students: the Chinese doctoral students, and the African-American students. Hongyu Wang (now an award-winning professor at her university) was my first Chinese doctoral student. She writes so eloquently on senses of self that I stand in awe. She also ushered Donna and me all over eastern China on two of our visits, tirelessly translating. Mei Wu was with us at LSU only a short time, for an M.A. and then went to study with Patrick Slattery in Texas. She is now a professor at North Texas with Sarah Smitherman Pratt, under the department chairmanship of Nancy Nelson. Lianfang Lu added immensely to our understanding of mathematics, not as an absolute, but as a product of culture, sharing her insights about the differences between Western and Eastern concepts.

The African-American students: Tayari kwa Salaam, LaVada Taylor Brandon, Nichole Guillory, Donna Porche Frilot, and Denise Taliafero Basile have sometimes together, other times separately, brought me up short with their friendly but pointed critique of my white male privilege. I have learned that the African-American idiom, "I be," instead of "I am," has connotations not found in the latter more grammatically correct phrase. I am enriched by their acquaintance and indebted to their generosity.

I have saved my last thanks to Jie Yu. Like Hongyu before her, she was at my side for many years as a graduate assistant. And like Hongyu, Jie has translated my works into Chinese, and accompanied Donna and me on three trips to China. The ongoing work she does in helping me to understand Chinese ways, her wise advice, as well as her meticulous translations, are invaluable. I am honored to have been her major professor.

The academic genealogy here is a joy to behold. There is comfort in knowing that one's ideas will sprout elsewhere. There are of course friends outside LSU who have had a strong influence on my work. Colleagues such as Bill Schubert, Dennis Sumara, Brent Davis, Barney Ricca, David Jardine, Donald Oliver (who died much too young), Chet Bowers, Janet Miller, Pat O'Riley, Peter Cole, Eero Ropo, Tero Autio, Elizabeth Macado, Ton Jorg, Lesley LaGrange, Chris Reedy, Professor Zhao, and many, many others. I thank you all. I hope in some small way these essays honor the advice and wise counsel you have given me.

Finally I wish to thank Naomi Silverman, Kevin Henderson, and the staff at Routledge for seeing this book through to print and for promoting it on a worldwide basis.

Bill Doll
September 15, 2011

PERMISSIONS

The author and publisher would like to thank the following for permission to reproduce copyright material:

Sense Publishers for Chapter 2, "A path stumbled upon," originally published in *Leaders in Curriculum Studies* (2009), and Chapter 20, "Thinking Complexly," originally published in *Complexity theory and the politics of education* (2010).

The *Journal of the Canadian Association of Curriculum Studies* for Chapter 3, "Looking back," and Chapter 15, "Prigogine: A new sense of order," both published in Vol. 6, No. 1 (2008) of the journal.

Peter Lang for Chapter 4, "Struggles with spirituality," originally published in *Educational yearning* (2002), and Chapter 8, "Beyond methods," originally published in *Passion and pedagogy* (2001).

The journal *Complicity* for Chapter 5, "Memory of a mentor," originally published in Vol. 7, No. 2 (2010), and Chapter 13, "Response to Proulx," Vol. 5, No.1 (2008) of the journal.

Wiley-Blackwell for Chapter 6, "A methodology of experience," originally published in *Educational Theory*, Vol. 23, No. 1 (1972).

Sage Publications for Chapter 10, "Piagetian thought," and Chapter14, "Modernism," both in the *Encyclopedia of curriculum studies* (2010), and for Chapter 19, "Complexity," in the *Encyclopedia of social and cultural foundations of education* (2008).

Proceedings of the 2003 Complexity Science and Educational Research Conference for Chapter 11, "Modes of thought."

National Academy of Educational Research for Chapter 12, "Keeping knowledge alive," originally published in the *Journal of Educational Research and Development*, Vol. 1, No.1 (2005) of the journal.

James Nicholas, Publishers for Chapter 16, "Post-modernism's Utopian vision," originally published in the journal *Education and Society*, Vol. 9, No.1 (1990).

New York State English Council for Chapter 18, "Complexity in the classroom," originally published in the Council's 1998 *Monograph* publication.

Association of Supervision and Curriculum Development for Chapter 21, "The educational need to re-invent the wheel," Vol. 39, No. 1 (1981), and Chapter 22, "Complexity in the classroom," Vol. 47, No.1 (1989).

Taylor & Francis Group for Chapter 23, "Reflections on teaching," originally published in *Teaching Education*, Vol. 10, No. 2 (1999).

Routledge Publishers for Chapter 24, "Classroom management," originally published in *Power, knowledge, and education in a global economy* (2000).

Grupo A Educaçao for Chapter 25, "Looking forward," originally published in *Patio-Revista Pedagogica*, February/April 2006.

East China University Press for Chapter 26, "The wisdom of John Dewey" (Da Xia Lecture, No. 87), 2010.

1

INTRODUCTION

William F. Pinar

> The concept of devising a developmental curriculum which is dynamic,
> emergent, transformative, and non-linear has ... been my challenge during
> almost all my teaching career.[1]
>
> (William. E. Doll, Jr.)

Addressing the challenge described above constitutes the 40-year ongoing project
that is the fascinating imaginative realm of William E. Doll, Jr. In the epigraph are
several of the key concepts that structure that important project: developmentalism,
curriculum, dynamism, emergence, and transformation. "Non-linear" communicates
Doll's rejection of earlier and specifically Tylerian sequenced curriculum design.
Note that it has been his experience of teaching that has provided the provocation
for Bill Doll's ingenuous scholarship.[2]

Doll begins in pragmatism, that late 19th and early 20th century quintessentially
American philosophy associating psychological development with social democracy,
political reform with scientific thinking, synthesized in the work and personified in the
character of John Dewey. Doll did his PhD dissertation research on Dewey's concept
of change, and we gain a glimpse of that sophisticated scholarship in Chapter 6. John
Dewey represents the genesis of Bill Doll's intellectual journey, a journey documented
in this indispensable collection containing essays from each period.

Dewey is a vast sea, and Doll harvested much and regularly, including most
recently and poignantly in the Da Xia Lecture presented in Shanghai in November

---

1 All quoted passages are taken from essays published in this volume.
2 On previous occasions (Pinar, 2006, 2009a, 2012) I have acknowledged the personal and
   professional significance intertwined as these have been of Bill Doll in my life; here I focus
   exclusively on his intellectual accomplishment.

2010. Especially, Doll adopted Dewey's faith in science and its methodology of experimentation. Doll characterizes Dewey's method as one of "reflection," a rigorous way of "*experimenting with directing personal experience*" "Never," Bill adds (rebuking the behaviorism of the 1960s and 1970s), was Dewey's method "the imposition of a set form." Because educational experience requires "reflective thinking," it is *both* open *and* directed. It is open in that no end is pre-set, the only end is growth, an end that has no end. It is directed in that the situation directs itself towards its own fulfillment. ... This process of going beyond is transformative.

For Dewey, Doll emphasizes, this reflective method is "one of *transformation not transmission*.""In Piaget's terms," Doll adds later, such transformation is marked by an "*elusive* process of jumping from one stage or level to the next." As that observation indicates, John Dewey led Bill Doll to Jean Piaget. Doll was not leaving one for the other. Indeed, he integrates aspects of each thinker into his post-modern view of curriculum (Doll, 1993).

Central to what Doll found intriguing in Piaget's "genetic epistemology" was Piaget's discovery that "deep seated, genomic, lasting behavior"—especially "a change of schemas or ways of operation"—did not occur through imposition as (Bill pointed out) the Lamarckians/Skinnerians believed, thereby linking the short-termism of the then contemporary behaviorism with an earlier and discredited genetics. Nor was such change "random," as "the Darwinists/neo-Darwinists asserted," criticizing in that phrase the pre-pragmatist apologists for the wealthy and powerful. Rather, such profound change occurred "via an *interaction* of environment and subject (animal/person)," accented by dynamic processes of "equilibrium–disequilibrium–reequilibration." This sequence is Piaget's of course, and what it underscores is that neither transmission nor operant conditioning accounts for significant learning, as each ignores the interactive and dynamic character of the educational process. Reflecting retrospectively (and acknowledging another important intellectual influence), Bill names both his future interest and past preoccupations when he notes that, "This interactionist approach was applauded by Ilya Prigogine, an early contributor and to chaos and complexity theories, and is much appreciated by Dewey scholars who emphasize inter- (or trans-) action as the way children learn" (Chapter 10, "Piagetian thought"). Elsewhere Doll again links his beginning—pragmatism—to where he was heading, characterizing Dewey himself as "a presager" of post-modernism, as Dewey "relied on concepts of interaction and development."

Having assimilated Piaget—incorporating that work into his "own, patterned ways of operation"—Doll moved toward post-modernism, a term he always hyphenated in order to emphasize its indissoluble link to modernism.[3] Post-

---

3 That link is not only temporal—post-modernism follows modernism—but conceptual, as for some post-modernism represents a self-reflective radicalization of modernism (Uljens, 2003, pp. 41–42).

modernism was a set of ideas that only made sense in relation to modernity, and its prefix—the infamous "post"—made clear that what is to follow is not yet fully formed, that we are only in the first stages of life after modernity. Modernity—that privileging of reason, and specifically science, over religion, coupled with the advent of capitalism (and its adversaries socialism and communism)—in Doll's lexicon specifies (in its educational usages) confidence in "linear, cause-and-effect ordering and a disregard of potentialities." For the sake of control and efficiency, as Bill's historical analysis[4]—in which he links Frederick Taylor with Ralph Tyler—makes clear, schools in America underemphasized creative potential. For a brief moment, just before the onslaught of 40 years of school "reform," the nation noticed (see Silberman, 1970).

While school reform was undermining the intellectual quality of US school curriculum, the academic field of curriculum studies was enjoying an intellectual renaissance. Animating this renaissance was the multidisciplinary phenomenon known as post-modernism, especially prominent by the 1980s. "In that decade," Doll recalls, "we came to realize that the universe in which we live is expanding at an accelerating rate." Despite the discoveries of Edwin Hubble in the 1920s, Doll notes, in education an earlier metaphysics "still formed the foundation for our epistemology, including the way we taught." Schools still sequenced curricula in "preset units," assuming a "stable IQ," and educators were enjoined to teach from a "centralized focus." Indeed, educators were pressured by curriculum reform to do so, starting in 1968 with Richard Nixon's "Back to the Basics" campaign.[5]

Why did post-modernism appeal to this sophisticated scholar of Dewey and Piaget? Post-modernism, Bill tells us, provided "a frame for bringing forth my ideas on curriculum, which up to this time had been fermenting, but not coalescing" (Chapter 2). Certainly these ideas did coalesce by 1993 in the publication of his masterful *A post-modern perspective of curriculum*. In that synthetical view—it is also "the long view," as he threads the needle from Dewey through Piaget, Prigogine, Bruner, and Whitehead—Bill characterized curriculum as rich, relational, recursive, and rigorous. With these soon to be famous 4R's, Doll "felt I had an alterative frame (not a model) to Tyler's Rationale." In *Understanding curriculum* (Pinar et al., 1995), we acknowledged this achievement (p. 503). "In recent years," Bill tells us, "I have seen the Rationale not so much as a model to be challenged but rather as an expression of a particular time, a modernist time, one now past."

---

4 As I will suggest momentarily, central to Bill Doll's intellectual journey is a strong sense of the significance of history and, more specifically, intellectual history. This affords his version of complexity theory an additional dimension of complexity, utterly central (in my view) to understanding curriculum.

5 Within school reform—that multifaceted relocation and intensification of the post-1968 conservative restoration—control is exercised through standards then testing, utilizing a tradition whose genesis Bill locates centuries earlier. Over the years, in separate papers presented at separate conferences, Bill critiqued its various rhetorical markers: "competence" and "standards" and "testing."

Post-modernism may have marked this movement from modernity and its now antiquated stability of structures,[6] but it was complexity theory that completed the journey. It is these "new sciences" of chaos and complexity that, Doll tells us, have provided "a grounding for my beliefs." Why? "In these new sciences," Doll discerns "*a sense of development that is both non-linear and self-organizing.*" This sense of development positions complexity theory as an "alternative" to constructivism (Chapter 13), "one focusing neither exclusively nor heavily on the actions of the learner but rather on the interplay of factors or forces within a dynamic, learning situation." In this concept of *interplay* the echo of Dewey is strong, as is Piaget's acknowledgement of the turbulence of assimilation.

Characterizing Doll's intellectual trajectory as moving from pragmatism and developmentalism through post-modernism to complexity theory is, I realize, too linear. Still, Bill himself invokes the image of "path"—note that he construes this path as "stumbled upon," as such acknowledgement of "arbitrariness" is not incidental to his thinking—to denote that his has been a journey from one place to another. It was during his M.A. study at Boston University, for example, Doll realized that he had come of age associating authoritarianism with spirituality. From this New England legacy he traveled a far distance, shedding an inherited sense of hierarchy in order to experience "spirit as the breath of life, that gives force, passion, and commitment to an event." What links these four is *relationality.* "We are," Bill reminds, "part of a larger ecological and cosmological frame."

Students of Doll's *oeuvre* know already this key concept of relationality. It is one of the famous four R's—recall that the others are rich, recursive, rigor—that were soon supplemented by the 5 C's of curriculum: *currere,* complexity, cosmology, conversation, and community. These partly playful lists enable "our looking at curriculum from multiple perspectives," Bill notes, here emphasizing "the interplay of the individual with the communal." Such "interplay," he reminds, "has guided much of my own teaching where the atmosphere I encourage is one not only of honoring our own thoughts and those of others, but also of bringing these ideas into experiential interactions of varied types" (Chapter 3). In this domain of ongoing pedagogical experimentalism we encounter the "fascinating imaginative realm" of William E. Doll, Jr.

Interaction—what for both Bill and for me becomes specified in the concept of *conversation*—is a key category indeed. Through dialogical encounter learning occurs, provided—in complexity theory terms—that such encounter is sufficiently *complex* to become *dynamic,* stimulating *transformation.* In *Thinking complexly* written in collaboration with Donna Trueit (Chapter 20), they explain, "*Complexity* as used in the complexity sciences deals with interactive, dynamic systems that under

---

6 Bill has never opposed structure—early on (see Chapter 3) he characterizes his view as a structuralism—but insists that structures be "worthwhile." Referencing the 4 R's, he writes: "I have come to believe there to be a certain worthwhile structure here, no matter what the structure is named." This incorporation of antecedent views accents the transformative character of curriculum.

specific and limited conditions are able to transform themselves." Note that there is no automaticity here; the teacher's reasoned and imaginative intervention is the *sine qua non* of classroom learning. Given how crucial the role teachers play is, what do Trueit and Doll advise? "Shifting one's attitude from 'reducing' complexity to 'embracing' what is always already present in relations and interactions," they suggest, may lead to thinking complexly. Such thinking characterizes learning.

Describing "thinking complexly," as a discursive practice that for themselves is "still developing … slowly being articulated … [thinking complexly] encourages us to begin to move beyond the telescopic, objective seeing of modernism. We begin to see differently," as we focus on "relations and interactions, being recursive, playing with and exploring differences, attending to intuition, abiding with mystery and ambiguity, happily relinquishing certainty." Thinking complexly enables understanding.

Understanding—also a key category for me—is, Doll explains, not "passed on" via "teaching-as-telling, but rather emerges from, is created through, interactions." Significantly, not only speech is emphasized in such an educational encounter; so is listening. "To honor interaction," Doll writes, requires "listening to both students and situations." Through such listening the teacher is able to "utilize difference," by which he means "seeing it as a positive for learning," as there is, Bill emphasizes, "no sense of self without an understanding of other." What is key, Doll concludes, is "to recognize that relationships" are profoundly (but not only) human. Indeed, "the *mysterium tremendum*" may well be, Doll suggests at one point, "the natural and innate tendency of nature to create in ever increasing complexity" (Chapter 4). Bill Doll embraces *complexity*, which signifies a

> dynamical self-organizing process within which we are embedded, embodied, emboldened. … We take this fluidity/flow to characterize, as well, a way of thinking/speaking that no longer relies on foundations and facts as the static building blocks of past intellectual thought; rather, drawing on principles derived from complexity science, we are encouraged to think of emergence as the ongoing flow of our awareness and appreciation of being-in-relation to others, the environment, the cosmos. We see these relations as systemic, networked, and patterned.
>
> (Trueit and Doll, Chapter 20)

In this passage are not only the 4 R's and 5 C's, there are the 3 P's—Play, Precision, Patterns (or Principles)—accenting "the actual integration of determinism with randomness, randomness with determinism." In such "creative tensionality" (that phrase is not Bill's but Ted Aoki's (2005a [1986/1991], pp. 161–164), whose work he regularly cites and whose achievement he has honored[7]) pragmatism,

---

7 At the 2000 LSU Conference on the Internationalization of Curriculum Studies (see Trueit et al., 2003)—organized by Bill Doll and Donna Trueit—we celebrated the lifetime achievement of Ted Aoki with a formal presentation the last night of the conference.

post-modernism, and complexity theory are interactively embedded and interrelated, thereby emerging as transformed and unpredicted events. The past, however, does not disappear into the dynamism of the present.

Historical Consciousness

>Ramus has left us a legacy to overcome, Dewey a challenge to meet.
>
>(William E. Doll, Jr.)

Doll emphasizes *conversation* as "essential" in devising a curriculum oriented "not toward testing but toward developing creative thought." To explain this insight, Doll works historically, one indispensable way of discerning "patterns" and "emergences." Demonstrating his powerful historical sense—historicity is one of the defining features of Doll's *oeuvre*—Bill returns 100 years to the genesis of pragmatism in the United States. He recalls Frederick Winslow Taylor's scheme for industrial efficiency that rationalized the subjugation of the individual to the factory system in the specification of tasks. Transferring his schemes for efficiency to education, Taylor's practice of so-called "scientific management" meant placing much greater emphasis upon planning, the "assembling of detail [that] takes place prior to the activity." Not only does the planning precede educational activity, but teaching and learning (Doll notes) also become "limited to the plan." Taylor's imprinting position in still continuing efforts to reorganize education as more efficient—in contrast to reconstructing the curriculum in intellectual terms for the sake of students' growth as individuals and citizens— does not remain static in Doll's narrative, as he then moves back several centuries, to Descartes, then forward to Tyler, devising an explanatory through line among the three.

Doll's historical consciousness, then, shifts according to his analysis, sometimes starting in the United States 100 years ago, on other occasions crossing the Atlantic and returning to the 12th century, on one occasion to the French monk and theologian Peter Abelard. What is important for Doll about Abelard is that he enables us to understand our situation in the present. What is imperative to remember today is that Abelard taught not after endless planning, linking objectives to outcomes but, significantly, via dialogue and argumentation. What happened during the intervening centuries?

To help us understand the degraded present, Doll moves to Peter Ramus, the man responsible for reconfiguring teaching as *method*, a key curricular concept that Bill Doll also links with *control* (for him, the "ghost" in the curriculum, as you will see.) What disappears alongside the disappearance of pre-modernity is dialogue, indeed orality itself, despite their utter centrality to study not only in Christian but Jewish traditions as well (Mosès, 2009 [1992], p. 175). It is this loss that imperiled the complicated conversation that constitutes educational experience, as the great Canadian political economist and communications theorist Harold Innis also knew (A. J. Watson, 2007, p. 114).

It was Ramus, Doll explains, who employed the concept of *curriculum* (in 1576) to position *sequencing* as central to learning. With sequencing established as a central and structuring feature of educational planning, "teaching now moved from laying out issues for discussion to disseminating knowledge for absorption." This is a key point, not only historically but as well in contemporary efforts to reconstruct the reality in which we find ourselves. The ancient tradition of dialogue enables students and teachers to work together, Doll explains, to "consider alternatives, question assumptions, look and listen for—and play with—differences and develop each their own critical interpretation and creative ability." Working from Walter Ong (1983),[8] Doll traces the decline of these aural and oral traditions, now devolved to decoding print on a page. In the process, he summarizes succinctly, "truth moved from the personal to the textual. Truth became depersonalized, abstracted, symbolized. Logic in all its formalism supplanted rhetoric and all its passion. The Word now was abstracted from Life. Reason became formalized" (Chapter 8).

Doll identifies Dewey as the one who relocated the authority of knowledge from logic to experience while sacrificing neither. After the displacement of "centralized certainty," he continues, "what we have left is the art of interpretation."

Teaching, then, becomes less "transmission" than it does a form of "journeying with others on a path of learning engagement and personal transformation." Linking knowing to listening to experience recasts teaching as *feeling*, what Bill characterizes as a "precognitive act." In order to teach—which, at one point, he importantly acknowledges "cannot really be taught at all"—one labors to "feel" a situation, to "sense" it at a "pre-conscious" level, then to "intuit its possibilities and parameters (or solution, if the situation contains a problem)." Teaching, then, "requires one to be attuned to the situation, to listen to it, to be immersed in it, even to converse with it." While one cannot teach such intuition, one can provide, Doll underscores, "opportunities for students to explore, to speculate, to intuit." In doing so, teachers—he emphasizes—must "listen," and not only to their students but "also to the situation in which they (students and instructor) are embedded." We can conclude that *orality* requires *interaction* which itself enables *transformations*.

Such an algorithm discloses in discursive terms the intellectual movements Doll recommends inscribing educationally through activities (see, for instance, Chapters 6 and 21). Starting from the stasis of the present moment one works one's way back (yes historically, but not only: key to this process is the dynamism of disequilibrium) into the fluidity of dialogue and argumentation that print culture and capitalism have eclipsed, reactivating each of these through enactment of Piaget's genetic epistemology, that

---

8 Associated with the so-called Toronto school in media studies (Nusselder, 2009, p. 49), Walter Ong (1983) also contributed to our understanding of the ocularcentrism of modernity (see Jay, 1993, p. 114). A student of Marshall McLuhan (Crowley and Mitchell, 1994, p. 145), Ong showed—in his study of learning Latin as a puberty rite during Renaissance Europe—how such visualism became refracted through the surface of the student body (Pinar, 2006, pp. 17–24).

"fundamentally *interactive* process of assimilation and accommodation," animated by disequilibrium, a process encouraging greater complexity. "Piaget's interactionist approach," Bill explains (juxtaposing two of the major influences in his formulation), "along with Dewey's inter- (trans) actional approach," are in fact "forerunners" to contemporary complexity theory. Complexity, Doll emphasizes, emerges "not from the elements themselves but from the interaction of the elements." Working within the "limitations of human thought," Doll suggests, complexity theory "also enables us to acknowledge unseen possibilities, inherent in any situation, as creative potential." These—working from the reality the past has bestowed through the discoveries science makes in the present—are not only main movements of Doll's *oeuvre* overall, they also enact the dynamics of his pedagogical engagement with students and colleagues. From print through dialogue to the transformation interaction enables: such "emergence" is the main marker of a transformative curriculum.

Conclusion

Due to the richness and rigor of Doll's theory of curriculum, there is no formula to follow. True, there are concepts that explain, strategies to consider, but it is to "creative potential," indeed to life itself—and not only human, as he focused for a decade on mollusks—that Doll remains acutely attuned. It is life that is characterized, above all, by transformation. Informed by evolution, history, politics, religion, Doll's very human life is dynamic, emergent, self-organizing, relational. There is a powerful multidisciplinarity to Doll's thought that both informs his theory and enacts it pedagogically, what after post-structuralism gets called "performativity." In a phrase, Bill Doll "walks his talk."

At one point (referencing Donna Trueit and Sarah Pratt), Doll specifies the political character of curriculum as also embedded in the language we use to characterize it. Such language, he notes, is never "neutral" but in fact "political" as it "advances certain frames of reference and denies or limits others." Doll's conception of the political is not limited, however, to the discursive, as he asserts that "all acts of education involving teaching are by nature political." His activism occurs through embracing complexity. "In a democratic society," he writes,

> the political purpose of education, especially liberal education, is the development of character, of judgment, of responsibility, of respect for "other." In the complex, diversified, globalized, technologically-oriented society in which we live, we believe a new set of discursive practices are needed, ones which develop, embrace, work with, relate to the complexity we find.
>
> (Trueit and Doll, Chapter 20)

I am reminded of Pasolini's positing of homologies or structural parallels between models of storytelling and models of social and economic aggregation (see Rumble, 1994, p. 211). Pasolini was asserting there are political and ethical elements of style.

As does Doll, Pasolini knew that it matters politically how you say what you say, that the domains of the discursive and political are interrelated.

Over the course of his 40-year career Doll moves from pragmatism to post-modernism to complexity theory, but he never leaves behind the constellation of ideas associated with each. Not only does each movement remain embedded in its successor—the first two are re-expressed through complexity theory, Bill's synthetical moment—but each also expresses his original reconstruction of it. Doll's genius has been to reconstruct the main moments in the 20th-century intellectual history of American educational thought—pragmatism, developmentalism, complexity theory—and in so doing lay bare the through lines that link them, creating a complex interaction among the three that transforms our understanding of curriculum from objectives to be implemented to conversation transforming how we understand—indeed, live in—the world.

Doll's originality also represents a reconstruction of his—our—generation's historical moment as that materialized in the national political situation of the United States, and particularized as a disciplinary crisis in curriculum studies. I would characterize the first—the national political situation—as, above all, characterized by an ongoing (if variegated) repudiation of the 1960s, a decade of protest, youth revolt, and political violence. While he did his undergraduate work (in philosophy and history) during the 1950s (at Cornell University), his graduate study occurred during the 1960s, taking the M.A. at (as noted earlier) at Boston University, and his PhD at the Johns Hopkins University, studying there first with Robert McClintock (whose work on study was central to mine), then with John Steven Mann (whose work was central to the reconceptualization of curriculum studies during the 1970s). Bill remembers his mentor in Chapter 2.

It was the 1960s national curriculum reform that provoked the disciplinary crisis in curriculum studies, precipitating the decade of reconceptualization, a paradigm shift reflected in the sequence of names accorded the field by the American Educational Research Association (AERA) through its renaming of Division B. That Division was named "curriculum development," but was later altered to "curriculum and objectives." Not long after, however, reflecting a field focused upon understanding, AERA settled upon "curriculum studies," its current appellation.

Doll lived through this turbulent time. As he did with pragmatism, developmentalism, and complexity theory, he was rearticulating—working through[9]—the field's main moments by incorporating the past into the present. The central position accorded the school in the field's phase of curriculum development Bill never loses; the school, and specifically the classroom, remains always in his mind's eye. Nor does he shed the traditional field's preoccupation with objectives, recasting the concept as qualities—the 4 R's for instance—that characterize a transformative

---

9 I am using the term in LaCapra's (2004, p. 45) sense: "Working through trauma involves gaining critical distance on those experiences and recontextualizing them in ways that permit a re-engagement with ongoing concerns and future possibilities."

curriculum. The past becomes present in his futuristic conception of curriculum, aligned now with breaking developments in the new sciences.

While these transformations are synthetical—in that these contain within themselves the antecedent traditions—they are also historically activated. Central to Doll's inventive intellectual strategy has been a historically informed reworking of extant intellectual movements and traditions through the juxtaposition and transformation that Piaget depicted as disequilibrium. Such reworking—working through—occurs historically as well synthetically. Doll's historical consciousness is constant, compelling him to pull on the thread of the present until it unravels, following it into the next room, the next house, the next century, until he finds what suffices as a starting-point, a heuristic that enables a narrative of understanding the present, a discursive form (e.g. narrative) he appreciates as central not only to scholarship but to science and life itself. "What is at issue here," Doll presciently understood in 1973, "is a concept of education which is different from mere training, a concept of education which is based upon man's unique powers of consciousness, reflection, symbol manipulation and the like." It is exactly these "unique powers" that become articulated—indeed activated—in the fascinating and imaginative realm of William E. Doll, Jr. Please enter through the pages ahead.

PART I

Personal Reflections

Introduction: Donna Trueit

In this section, Doll is reflective on his academic career and intellectual work. These four chapters reveal a great deal about not only who Bill Doll is—his way of being—but also about his pedagogy. The two are the same, as Nel Noddings noted many years ago when she observed Bill's teaching. She commented to him that he was inspiring and idiosyncratic, a point that Bill reflected on for years before developing the 4 R's, not as a model to be copied or followed, but as signposts for educators to use in working with their own unique situations. All this speaks of his commitment to the ideals of John Dewey. Reflection, in this Deweyan sense, is a large part of William Doll. Through reflection on a situation, in the present and in the past, one grows intellectually. This is how experience aids growth, a major theme in Dewey and Piaget.

The article that is Chapter 2 was requested by Leonard Waks (Short and Waks, 2009) as an intellectual history. In it Doll provides a personal, professional, intellectual retrospective revealing the idiosyncrasies and serendipitous influences in the course of his journey. Seeing the present not only as the result of choices directed toward an end, but also influenced by chance encounters, good fortune and playfulness.

Requested for a special issue of the *Journal of the Canadian Association of Curriculum Studies* (JCACS) on Complexity and Education, which featured a reprint of "Prigogine: a new sense of order" 25 years after it was first published, Doll recalls in "Looking back," Chapter 3, the bifurcation points that led to his developing a complexity informed curriculum.

In "Struggles with spirituality," Chapter 4, Doll ponders man's (sic) place in the world and relations to it: the anthropomorphic story that shapes modernist thoughts about religion is at odds with a spirituality which is both cosmological and ecological. Articulating a new framework for spirituality, one that honors the mysteries of life, Doll draws upon Derrida's use of *aporia* in regard to responsibility to reconceive man's relations to others as a responsibility of Being.

The final chapter in Part I is a tribute to Deweyan scholar and political activist, John Steven Mann, Doll's mentor and teacher at Johns Hopkins University. Through his relationship with Mann, Doll's idealistic view of America is opened to also recognize injustices, travesties and tragedies, developing in him a lifelong political activism in keeping with his admiration of Steve.

2

A PATH STUMBLED UPON

(2009)

In his fine and interesting entry in *Leaders in the philosophy of education*, Francis Schrag entitles his essay "The road taken." As a fellow Cornellian (1953), I believe my career is represented more by the title, "The path stumbled upon." Indeed, my first day at Cornell I fell asleep in the front row as the Dean was lecturing on the challenges we freshmen faced; and on my graduation day at Cornell, four years later, I managed to walk into the ceremony in the faculty procession line. In the years between, I stumbled into marvelous encounters with an amazing faculty (Philosophy, History, Literature), and a most interesting group of fellow students. Now, as a well-aged curriculum theorist, reflecting on my life and academic career, I believe such stumbling has merit.

I entered the field of curriculum theory unintentionally and by the back door, as I realized that philosophy—B.A. and M.A.—as a career was not for me. While Headmaster in a small, private school outside Baltimore, in the mid-1960s, I was fortunate enough to have on the Board of Directors, a member of the Johns Hopkins faculty. He suggested I try Hopkins to continue the graduate work I had begun in Denver where I was Director of Mathematics Education at another small, private school. In Baltimore, I went to see John Walton, the Chairman of the Hopkins Department of Education, a wonderful Kentuckian who read Latin and Greek as a hobby. We chatted for a while and I asked him what the entrance requirements were. He looked over my work from the University of Denver and suggested I start with a course in the history of education. I queried whether I was Hopkins material and he told me not to worry, the professors would be glad to make that clear. Later I realized that Hopkins had neither set entrance requirements, nor a set curriculum. Rather, one needed to take a course from at least four professors in the university and if one of them was willing to be my mentor then I was in; otherwise, I was out. My program of study would be worked out by my mentor and myself. My first mentor at Hopkins, Robert McClintock, had a joint appointment in History and Education. After a year he left to take a position at Teachers College (TC). I asked if I could follow him there and continue my study. "Bill," he said "TC is too professional for you; you are too much a muser to be confined to any one discipline. Stay here at Hopkins where they will honor and develop your musings." Shocked at first, I later realized the wisdom of his comment. I did stay, I did muse, and I am grateful. Hopkins in the late 1960s was an absolutely wonderful place: Jacques Derrida for lectures in the humanities; Charles Singleton on Dante; Stephen Ambrose in history (until he was asked to leave for his anti-war protests); Victor Lowe on Whitehead (most displeased that my dissertation on Dewey did not mention Whitehead—only years later did I see obvious connections: event/situation, context/experience); an Education Department that included Kingsley Price (an inspiration then and now); and a new mentor, John Steven Mann— Hopkins' first and only curriculum theorist—who let me spend my whole second year of graduate study reading in the history and philosophy of science. In my third year of study, I began serious inquiry into the writings of another Hopkins graduate, John Dewey. By now the National Defense Act was in place, distributing money to produce education scholars to combat the Russian threat. I along with others was generously provided monies for full-time academic study. Under the guidance of Steve Mann I read in and about Dewey (unfortunately avoiding Whitehead, whom Dewey said he could not understand) and took part in Vietnam War protests. To receive government monies, yearly I swore an oath that I was not a Communist (I was not) and regularly I protested the government's actions in Vietnam. Such protests slowly awakened a dormant political instinct, one I have honed, quietly, under Steve Mann's continuing tutelage.

On my doctoral committee, beside Steve Mann there were: (1) the Chairman of the Chemistry Department, (2) the Chairman of the Geology and Ecology Departments, (3) a noted philosopher, Victor Lowe, and (4) the Chair of the Education Department (who admitted me four years earlier). As was the Hopkins tradition, two members were from the department of study, and three were from outside the department. Only Steve was a curriculum theorist. The Hopkins experience of immersing oneself in the study of a subject and also roaming throughout the university (with its scholars and multiple disciplines) had a definite effect upon my subsequent career as a teacher and curricularist. Breadth and depth, *context* and *situation* (to borrow key ideas from Whitehead and Dewey) have been bywords in my own work with students, graduate and undergraduate.

The sort of insight breadth and depth bring, though, was not born of my Hopkins experience, it began in my undergraduate days at Cornell. I was naive then in my approach to philosophy and history, my chosen major and minor. Max Black, Stuart Brown, E.A. Burtt, and Gregory Vlastos, though, did have their influence on me, as did Lane Cooper in Classics and Vladimir Nabokov in Russian Literature who became a friend—he liked that I was unawed by (really unaware of) his reputation and we did share an interest in chess. While most of my Cornell professors were of serious mien, Nabokov had a playfulness about him. I responded to that. In later years, while reading Gregory Bateson (especially his work with dolphins), I began to develop, more seriously, play as a useful (indeed necessary) curriculum ingredient. Play and learning fit together nicely (as most anyone who cares for children knows). Contemporary brain research is beginning to confirm this connection. On this point, one is reminded that in the history of learning it was E. L. Thorndike who pointed out that drill on the memorization of spelling words could easily become excessive, leading to diminishing test results. Those curricularists who develop textbooks with an explicit or tacit advocacy of "time on task," could benefit from re-reading Bruner on *play*, as well as looking at the neurological research on the value of "time *off* task" (Lehrer, 2008).

Leaving Cornell in 1953, with no clear direction, I went back to Boston where I enrolled (part-time) in Boston University and took a job teaching, that I might support myself. I continued to pursue philosophy, here from a different—more humanist, less analytic—point of view. My teaching experiences, at a small, private school were eye-opening. At Boston University (BU) I came across Peter Bertocci and his sense of the spiritual, a vein I have followed via Dwayne Huebner, Gregory Bateson, and now Stuart Kauffman. In teaching, uncertified and untrained, I adopted (and was encouraged to adopt) an authoritarian role. Fortunately and most serendipitously I became aware that some of my young students (those in middle school), while not always aware of it, were categorically brighter (not necessarily more knowledgeable) than I. One instance stands out. On rainy days the school had recess inside, often we played brain-teaser type games. One day we played "monkey in the well"—here the monkey, down in the well, say 30 feet, climbs up 3 feet in the day and falls back 2 feet at night, how long does it take the monkey to climb out of the well? I needed to use my image-making skills to solve this, drawing a picture; one of my quieter, more introverted, students devised a formula. In Bruner's terms he was working at a symbolic level, I at an iconic one. I began to rethink my methods of teaching, which at that time revolved around what might well be called "teaching-as-telling."

The school I was at in Brookline, MA, sent a number of its eighth-grade graduates on to Shady Hill School in Cambridge, the one Bruner used in much of his work with young people. I joined Bill Hull, John Holt, and others on Friday afternoons when we "played with" mathematical relationships, often using Cuisenaire Rods, with middle-school youth. These were glorious communal sessions, all of us working together, infused with the spirit of serious play. I was involved in a learning community; indeed, more than learning, with its tight focus, we were studying, creating, exploring. From this experience grew my realization that teaching, not philosophizing, was for me.

Receiving my M.A. from Boston University (1960) I went west to Denver, my paternal home. Again I took a position in teaching, again in a private school, as Director of Mathematics. I also enrolled in the University of Denver's joint program in philosophy and education. Here I came in contact with my first formal, professional education courses. Regretfully, I was disappointed: I found the courses narrow, based on research that seemed artificial and stilted, and quite removed from the work the teachers, I, and the students were doing in school. At school, working with students from kindergarten to ninth grade in both mathematics and literature (a colleague and I developed a Saturday morning "Great Books" program which aired on a Denver TV station for a year or so) was a continual joy and full of surprises. Again, a community of learners (semi-scholars, maybe) was formed. The Denver High School, in conjunction with the University of Colorado, devised special mathematics courses for our middle-school graduates. By now the notion of a learning community (one which created and explored) was ingrained in my psyche. I became ready for new challenges and found one as Headmaster of the small, private school, outside Baltimore.

Here, with much help from parents and faculty, I was able to bring theory and practice into harmony, into a seamless unit. Literature (a roving library in the hallways, as well as my reading to the students during lunch hour), Art (works by local artists graced the hallways and classrooms), and physical activity (handstands in the classrooms, rope courses outside) were all integrated with the usual 3 R's. Our young fourth-grade teacher brought her guitar to class and the students sang songs (in French). We established a transition class between kindergarten and first grade allowing for flexibility in social and intellectual development. This latter drew the attention of Frances Ilg and Louise Bates Ames at Yale and was written up in the *Baltimore Sun*. A relationship was established with Goucher College, which sent some of its teacher trainees to work with us—for those volunteering we asked for a full year commitment (but not for every day). Again, we built a community.

On the intellectual side monthly seminars were established, meeting in my rented rooms (in an ante-bellum mansion). Graduate students from Hopkins, professors from Goucher and Hopkins, and teachers from the school (as they wished) discussed issues in curriculum, learning, and pedagogy. Both professors and graduate students put forth papers on which they were working. Attendance was usually six or seven. As a graduate student I had the opportunity to come in contact—in a wonderfully conversational and friendly manner—with a side of behaviorism (Skinnerian) I had previously shunned. While I did not adopt this view, too rigid and manipulative for me, I did begin to acquire the art of listening to and negotiating with those of another persuasion. This skill has served me well for over 40 years, as both a teacher and administrator. (Too many of us—teachers and administrators—do not, I fear, listen to our students.) Marriage, and encouragement from my Board of Directors to pursue academia, brought me to Hopkins as a full-time graduate student.

After Hopkins (PhD, 1972) I looked for a position in academia. My mentor at Hopkins advised against calling myself a curriculum theorist, as no such identification existed at that time. I was told to advertise myself as a "foundations" person. Steve Mann came to Hopkins from Wisconsin, where he worked with James MacDonald, who with Dwayne Huebner, was beginning to break away from the traditional curriculum view espoused by the Association of Supervision and Curriculum Development (ASCD). I joined both ASCD and AERA and attended conferences, made presentations and published. After a number of interviews, I chose to work at State University of New York (SUNY)-Oswego. The department there wanted someone with a background in John Dewey (at least one Education Department in the Midwest told me flat out they wished not to have anyone on their staff who was associated with "that Commie"). My dissertation at Hopkins was on John Dewey's Concept of Change.

My first summer at Oswego, a professor of curriculum became ill and was unable to fulfill his teaching obligation. I taught my first curriculum course. I found the textbook chosen shallow and others of the curriculum ilk the same. (In recent years I have studied a bit of the history of this phenomenon—going back to Peter Ramus in the late 16th century—and now understand better the textbook tradition that emanates from his pedagogy.) Instead I turned to the developmental writings of Piaget and Bruner, the deschooling ones of Illich, Holt, Kozol, Neil, etc., the traditional curriculum development ones of Tyler, Popham, Ausabel etc., and the theoretical ones of Steve Mann, which at that time were most confusing to Oswego teachers and teachers-to-be. My intent was to develop a conversation among these various strands. Various students read various authors and a network of ideas and issues emerged. The notion of each of us being on the same page at the same time was quite antithetical to the richness of the conversations we had. I saw myself then, as now, utilizing Dewey's notion of the teacher as a *prima inter pares* (first among equals). It was my task to keep the conversations Rich (full of possibilities), Recursive (looping back on themselves), Relational (building networks of ideas), and Rigorous. At this time these 4 R's, later developed to distinguish me as a curriculum theorist, were hardly dawning on my consciousness. I quickly became aware, though, that the "same page" mantra led to a rather boring class.

As a curricularist-by-default (and an organizer by nature), over a period of 15 years I helped Oswego develop its teacher education program and its university-wide, first two years of General Education. I also worked weekly with the laboratory school at Oswego and the Sodus, NY, School District on mathematics education. Being with the same students over a number of years was a joy and by now was a *modus operandi* for my work in the schools. Sharing an interest in both Piaget and mathematics, Nel Noddings and I started a lifelong friendship. On one of her visits to Oswego—we did, under my encouragement as Department Chair and Chair of the College Curriculum Committee, establish education conferences (really more conversations)—Nel pointed out to me that the success the students had in mathematics under my auspices was probably more idiosyncratic than "methodized."

I took Nel's comment seriously and (1) began a study of the methodization movement, and (2) in my own work as a curriculum theorist tried to encourage others to develop their own (idiosyncratic and situational) methods and not follow mine. In studying methodization I found it had, not surprisingly, a long history, going back to the Greek Sophists and their personal, often secret, methods. What did surprise me though was the bursting forth of this "methodization" (*the way*) movement in conjunction with the Protestant reformation, especially Calvin's use of the word "curriculum" (path or course) in *curriculum vitae* (path or course of life.) Followers of Calvin, notably Peter Ramus, applied the word *curriculum* (as a set method) to education, and in the early 1600s the universities of Leiden and Glasgow instituted sequential courses of study they labeled curricula. The methodization movement, and with it Ramus' concept of curriculum design and instructional pedagogy, swept across Protestant Europe and inhabited Colonial America. Harvard College in the century 1650 to 1750 used *only one* method to teach, indeed to reason, that of Ramus (Triche and McKnight, 2004). The methodization movement dominated virtually all intellectual thought in northern, Protestant Europe in the 17th and 18th centuries. John Bunyan, in *Pilgrim's progress*, says:

> For having now my Method by the end,
> So it pulled, it came, and so I penned.

René Descartes, in *Discourse on method*, says:

> I have formed a Method, by whose assistance … I have the means of gradually increasing my knowledge.

Gottfried von Leibniz, in *On the method of universality*, says:

> Nothing can escape our method … it spares the mind and the imagination; the latter, above all, must be used sparingly.

I believe it possible to see, if not a methodological through line, then at least a set of family resemblances,[1] starting with Peter Ramus' concept of curriculum ("placing first which is first, next which is next, and so on, in an unbroken progression from general to particular"), moving to Johann Amos Comenius' (1896) *Great didactic*, to the four steps of René Descartes "chain of reasoning," to the four steps inherent in Ralph Tyler's (1950) *Basic principles of curriculum*. As an alternative to this curriculum history, dominant for the past four and a half centuries, I developed a set of guidelines—the 4 R's of Richness, Recursion, Relations, and Rigor—designed not to produce a model for others to follow but to act as a guide for each curricularist (teacher, supervisor, developer) to use in his or her own idiosyncratic and situational way (Doll, 1993, 2005a, 2008a, 2008b).

---

1 "Family resemblances" is a term developed by L. Wittgenstein (1958, see pp. 66–67), related to language games, a way to escape the constraints and exactitudes of Aristotelian and Platonist "forms."

The most important aspect of my time in Oswego, though, was a serendipitous meeting with William Pinar. He was at the University of Rochester, I at SUNY-Oswego, about 90 miles apart on Lake Ontario in New York State. His friendship, maintained over 35 years, has meant more to me personally and professionally than any I have had outside my marriages, first to Mary Doll (producing son Will), and now to Donna Trueit. Bill and I both moved from Upstate in the early 1980s, he to Louisiana State University (LSU), I to the University of Redlands, in California. After a few years I followed Bill to LSU where for over two decades we were suite mates. There we formed the LSU Curriculum Theory Project (1995) and the International Association for the Advancement of Curriculum Studies (2000). We are now near one another in western Canada, he at the University of British Columbia (UBC), I (with Donna) at the University of Victoria, with occasional forays to UBC. Being around Bill, whose knowledge of curricular issues is prodigious, has inspired me to study further the history of curriculum, to develop an alternative frame to the Tyler Rationale, and to move into chaos and complexity theories, infusing these with a sense of Spirit.

At Oswego (Chair of the Education Department) my academic time was devoted to the study of Piaget and Bruner. At Redlands (Director of Teacher Education), I became serious about studying the emerging *new sciences*, particularly as represented in the works of Ilya Prigogine. My introduction to Prigogine was sheer serendipity. In one of my last weeks at Oswego a colleague remarked to me that if I was interested in Piaget I might also like to look at Prigogine. (In the latter years of Piaget's life he and Prigogine did correspond and each wrote supportive comments about the other's work.) In *Order out of chaos* (1984, written with Isabel Stengers), Prigogine draws heavily on the philosophy of A. N. Whitehead. Down the road from Redlands, in Pomona, California, is the California School of Theology with its renowned (Whitehead) Center for Process Studies. There, again serendipitously, I was introduced, via John Cobb and David Griffin, to the word and concept "post-modern." Here I finally found a frame for bringing forth my ideas on curriculum, which up to this time had been fermenting, but not coalescing. Unbeknownst to me, in my last year at Redlands (1988) I began work on my first book, *A post-modern perspective on curriculum* (published in 1993).

That year, along with various articles on the utilization of chaos (and complexity) theory in the classroom, I sent a rather long article into *Teachers College Record*. A postal clerk at TC put the lengthy article not in the box for the *Record* (which subsequently turned down the article) but in the box of Jonas Soltis for his *Advances in contemporary educational theory*. Jonas liked what I had written and asked for more. I wrote more chapters and sent the manuscript off. Reviewers liked what I said (really more what I was attempting to say) but wanted a last chapter on practical applications. Thus the 4 R's were created, and it is they that have carried this book and its ideas into different languages, many classrooms, and curriculum readers. Since the first drafts of the book did roam a bit over the intellectual landscape, as is my (musing) want, I was assigned an editor to work with me, chapter by chapter. His comment as we neared the end of this project, about four years later, was that the book would either be seminal or a bust. Fortunately, the former has been the result. The 4 R's, very popular in China, have kept the book alive for 15 years now.

The 4 R's, like much in my career, came from a union of necessity and playfulness. The editors wanted practicality. I thought I had suggested such throughout the text. I knew not more to do. The 3 R's of the 19th century—Readin', 'Ritin', 'Rithmetic, seemed an interesting play but too gimmicky. On a trip back to Oswego to give a talk at the NY State Foundations of Education Society, which I had played some part in founding, I suggested, quite tentatively, a fourth R, that of Rigor. I explained that politically this was a fine word to use, it would "get off my back" those who would/ were accusing me of being an effete, white tower academic, having no knowledge of the schools. The latter was, of course, a false accusation—since, at the time, I had been working in schoolrooms for over 35 years—but it was an accusation, nonetheless. More important, though, the notion of rigor, taken from a French post-structuralist point of view, has to do, not with exactness or hard, close analysis but with the purposeful looking for unseen, or hidden, or yet-to-emerge connections, relations, alternatives, combinations. In this sense, *Rigor* is a fine fourth R to bring out the possibilities inherent in a Rich, Relational, Recursive curriculum. With these four I felt I had an alterative frame (not a model) to Tyler's Rationale. (In recent years, as I have looked at the history of Modernism, I have seen the Rationale not so much as a model to be challenged but rather as an expression of a particular time, a modernist time, one now past.)

By the time the post-modern book was finished I had joined Bill Pinar at LSU. Here, working with doctoral students, ones who could study full-time, Bill and I formed a marvelous cadre of students and professors, all involved in the Curriculum Theory Project. These colleagues—after a few years of study the doctoral students were colleagues—inspired me to study curriculum as I had not studied it before. Patrick Slattery encouraged me to develop even further my curricular thoughts on the post-modern. With Stephen Triche, I delved into the history of curriculum and its origins. Molly Quinn (and Professor Petra Munro Hendry, with whom I co-taught many "pragmatism" classes), helped me bring forth my interest in spirit and the spiritual, which I now characterize along with Science and Story, as one of the 3 S's. Professor Nina Asher, following Professor Wendy Kohli, joined with me in administering a small, experimental teacher-education program integrating professional school experience (a full year of internship in the schools) with solid academic study. Sarah Smitherman Pratt, Laura Jewett, and Donna Trueit, helped me appreciate Gregory Bateson's sense of play, difference, contextualization, and the spiritual. In working through Bateson's ideas, I began to envision a new epistemology, one based on reflexivity (Doll 2005a, 2008a). Fridays were teaching days for me: in the morning I, along with others—at times we had almost as many professors as students with us—studied philosophers, historians, anthropologists. Then we went to lunch together—Friday Friends it was called. In the afternoon Wendy, then

Nina, and I would work with the Holmes interns, helping them connect the ideas of Dewey, Gadamer, Heidegger, Homi Bhabha, Serres, etc. with their own teaching practices (Monday–Thursday), thus enriching those experiences as well as gaining new insights into concepts of curriculum. By now I had expanded the 4 R's to include the 5 C's of curriculum as: *currere*, complexity, cosmology, conversation, and community. (Obviously one can think of curriculum in a number of ways, I chose five to produce a 3:4:5 right triangle, most Euclidean and modernist, hence reminding me of the arbitrariness of my own work). The richness of the Holmes experience proved invaluable to a decade of interns who have gone on to solid teaching careers. With Hongyu Wang (and Professor Denise Egéa Kuehne) I was introduced to French intellectual thought, particularly Jacques Derrida, Michel Serres, and Bruno Latour. Hongyu, a student of Professor Qiquan Zhong and a colleague of Professor Zhang Hua of East China Normal University, also started us—myself, Donna, the LSU Curriculum Theory Project—on our journeys to China.

Donna Trueit encouraged me to complete co-editing with Noel Gough (of Australia) *Curriculum visions* (2002). She, along with strong encouragement from Bill Pinar, then provided the impetus to continue the international thrust, co-editing (with myself and Hongyu Wang), *Internationalization of curriculum studies* (2003). I readily joined Bill and Donna in their interest in looking at curriculum from an international perspective. Donna and I traveled to Finland twice (2002, 2005—the latter as a Fulbright Senior Scholar), and to China three times (2000, 2003, 2007). These two countries provide interesting contrasts to American school education. Finland continually ranks high (often highest) in international school competitions but does not emphasize such—reading, and even science, seem to be part of the fabric of their culture. China, of course, is noted for its ability to turn out students who rank high on all sorts of tests, a part of their culture for over a thousand years. Neither culture though involves *conversation* (one of my 5 C's) as part of its curriculum or instructional modes. Repetition and recitation yes, recursion and conversation, no. As Donna and I strive to develop the notion of conversation as essential for a curriculum oriented not toward testing but toward developing creative thought, two nations strong in testing have the greatest interest in our work. This is not to say good test scores are neglected but rather that a primary focus on test scores (as in "No Child Left Behind") limits creative potential. Finland, and certainly China, recognize this.

Sarah (Smitherman) Pratt with her interest in mathematics prodded me to delve deeper in chaos and complexity theories. With Sarah's help and that of our newly arrived Dean, Jayne Fleener, our AERA Special Interest Group: Chaos and Complexity Theories flourished, and led in 2004 to my editing, along with Jayne, Donna Trueit, and John St. Julien, the book, *Chaos, complexity, curriculum, and culture* (2005).

My work now is focused on developing an epistemology that integrates Science, especially the new sciences of chaos and complexity, with Story, especially narrative inquiry, and with Spirit, that ineffable quality which gives vitality to any situation (this volume, Chapter 11).

Science has been the guiding paradigm in Western culture since the time of Copernicus, Kepler, Galileo, and Newton. The new sciences of chaos and complexity show us a different world, indeed a different universe, from that seen by these past thinkers. Order is no longer seen as set, simple, imposed; rather order is seen as being entwined with a bit of chaos and emerging from the interactions of elements present in any situation, especially a dynamic, ongoing, changing one. Teaching (and curriculum design) from this perspective becomes—not the imposition of set materials in a unilateral manner, but rather—a process of exploring, creating, developing with students and faculty; indeed, *studying* an issue, experiment, or idea.

Story, with its origins deep inside a culture, represents that culture in a way science with its more formal, rational, and logical way of seeing never can attain. Story has a personal truth to it, it strikes one not as provable but as verifiable in one's own experience. As experience it is always interpreted in light of who and what we are. Such personalness brings into play the hermeneutic tradition—articulated well by Ted Aoki and now by David Jardine, both of whom draw on Heidegger and Gadamer. Reading these two philosophers and their educational interpreters brings forth a new way to look at curriculum and instruction. Asking students to articulate what they see, hear, and read, and to listen to the interpretation of others opens a dialogue (Trueit would say conversation) that provides an opportunity for the *new* to emerge. If we ask where the *new* comes from, the answer lies in interpretative inquiry; inquiry where we and the "other," no matter what or who the "other" may be (person, idea, fact, culture) come into interactive play.

Spirit is the hardest to frame, yet in many ways is the most important of the three. At a somewhat superficial and elemental level, one can associate science with the quantitative in education and story with the qualitative. This dichotomous split, even when combined to minimize the split (a qualitative–quantitative research project), lacks a sense of spirit. It is Spirit as the breath of life that gives force, passion, and commitment to an event. It is something one feels, not something one defines or frames. Spirit (along with the spiritual, the sacred—not necessarily the religious) is what gives a situation, as George Santayana (1968) points out, not only its vitality but also its integrity, its honesty, its truthfulness. Personally I find spirit in John Dewey's sense of *situation*, in Joseph Schwab's *deliberation*, in Stuart Kauffman's *order*, in Gregory Bateson's *difference which makes a difference*, and in Michel Serres' *teaching as an act of humility*.

In the years I have left as a scholar of curriculum I hope to stumble along in search of an epistemology wherein Science and Story are infused with the Spirit of the Yet-to-Be.

3

LOOKING BACK TO THE FUTURE

A RECURSIVE RETROSPECTIVE

(2008)

I, a new Canadian resident, am indebted both to Deborah Osberg and the Canadian Association for Curriculum Studies for honoring me with a retrospective on my work in the curriculum studies field. This is not something I ever expected, especially back in the 1980s when I began searching for a *new curriculum model* to the one then prominent, the Tyler Rationale (1950). At the time I was much engaged in reading Jean Piaget, and while I had great difficulty with the usual American interpretation of his work—"ages and stages"—I did feel his biological sense of cognition (Piaget, 1971a) and his actual work in the fields of biology and zoology provided a framework the Rationale did not consider. This framework, that of an organism's inherent self-organizing powers,[1] became clearer to me as I was introduced to Ilya Prigogine and his work on *becoming*. As I noted in my 1986 article (this volume, Chapter 15), I found a strong connection between Piaget and Prigogine and bringing this connection to the fore, with the paradigm in which it is encased, could "stand as an alternative to the measured curriculum"—that which the Rationale had become. Only later, due to the personal insight of Sherrie Reynolds, did I realize that in his late writings, those with Rolando Garcia (1989, 1991), did Piaget express his belief in and support for the work Prigogine and his colleagues were doing.[2]

---

1   N. Katherine Hayles (1983) does a fine job of explaining the difference between the 19th century's concept of *élan vital* (vital ardor) as an (animated) living force within the cosmos but still separated from the cosmos, and the 20th century's sense of a dynamic cosmos wherein subject and object are not split (Introduction).

2   The journal, *Advances in Chemical Physics*, has devoted a Special Edition to the work of Ilya Prigogine (Vol. 135, 2007) and his influence on the fields of chemistry and physics. This edition is comprehensive and invaluable to anyone interesting in delving deeply into the sort of paradigm Prigogine developed. An earlier and more critical but still complementary view can be found in N. Katherine Hayles' *Chaos bound* (1990).

Reading in the history of curriculum at the same time I was reading Piaget and Prigogine, I became aware that the measured curriculum[3] was not an invention of Ralph Tyler, although he certainly emphasizes measurement in his work on the Eight-year Study. The dominance of measurement as a way—indeed *the* way—to assess the efficiency, hence validity, of a curriculum has roots deep in American industrial, psychological, social, and educational thought in the time period between the American Civil War and World War I. Tyler, thus, is more a culminating than seminal figure. While the American psychological, behaviorist movement had a number of sources for its origins (Green, 2007), Frederick Winslow Taylor's "time and motion" studies with pig-iron carriers at Bethlehem Steel Company, in the 1890s, became a Holy Grail. America, during these years, was not only inspired by, but actually defined by Taylor and his scientific efficiency movement (Kanigel, 1997).[4] As Robert Kanigel points out, Louis Brandeis wrote the introduction to Taylor's *Scientific Management* (1947 [1911]), Walter Lippman saw "the scientific spirit" ushering in a new sense of democracy, and Antonio Gramsci "embraced Taylor's ideas." Factory workers around the world, though, uniformly rejected the Taylor Plan.

While clergymen measured the efficiency of their sermons (Callahan, 1962), Joseph Mayer Rice, the physician who exposed the dreadful plight of schools in major American cities during this industrialization period, said the remedy for all of America's school ills lay in "the measurement of results in the light of fixed standards" (1969a [1914], p. xv).[5]

The euphoria which surrounded Frederick Taylor and his work on scientifically measured efficiency—the University of Pennsylvania awarded him an honorary doctorate for his labors in bringing the "system out of disorder" in the American workplace—led me to believe that seminal as was Taylor and his empirical results, something more lay behind America's euphoria with measurement. Hence, Rice's statement about education needing to be assessed via measurement and fixed standards, while a natural corollary to Taylor's work, also showed a deeper commitment to framing curricula in set, linear, sequential steps, validated in terms of results which could be scientifically measured.

Prigogine's own recognition and approval of Piaget's work can be found in his article "Physique et metaphysique," in *Connaissance scientifique et philosophique*. Bruxelles: Academie Royale des Sciences (1975, pp. 312–316).

3   A. W. Crosby gives a fine historical account of how Western society became a "measurement" society: *The measure of reality* (1998). For measurement in education, see S. J. Gould, *The mismeasure of man* (1981).

4   My exploration of this phenomenon can be found in my essay "Beyond methods" (2002a; this volume, Chapter 8).

5   This sense of emphasizing results is, I believe, an unfortunate corollary of what might be called "vulgar pragmatism": looking at results as their "cash value"—in William James, colorful but easily misinterpreted phrase. Pragmatism, *the* American philosophy, integrates product with process; product alone is a vulgarization of the concept. Of the many books and articles on pragmatism I recommend Dewey, 1971 [1933]; Biesta and Burbules, 2003; Hendley, 2006; Biesta, 2010.

One line of research led me back to Pierre Simon (Marquis de Laplace), to Henri de Rouvroy (Comte de Saint-Simon), and to Auguste Comte, all who applied Isaac Newton's scientific theories to social issues. Each took Newton's mathematization of physical Nature—Newton specifically states that his conjectures on the principles framing natural philosophy (gravity being the chief one) are expressed in mathematical terms only [*Philosophia naturalis principia mathematica* (1962 [1729])]— and applied it to social situations. Laplace believed he had a method for predicting all future events in the cosmos; all one needed was to acquire the necessary facts (or variables) and then, putting them into a linear, cause-effect chain, prediction became certain. Trying to get these variables to stay stable was what caused mathematicians (Poincaré) and physicists (Heisenberg) such difficulties in the early part of the 20th century. Obviously Laplace's cosmos was not a dynamic one, for in his grand design there was no instability problem: the universe was stable. Saint-Simon and Comte saw a new (industrial and technocratic) age adawning in the early 1800s, one wherein a "new breed of men would arise, 'engineers, builders, planners'" (Doll, 1993, p. 21). This new breed would no longer work *with* nature but would improve, control, *civilize nature*, using the new device of scientific measurement. Progress seemed not only possible, but inevitable. Precision, A. N. Whitehead says (1967a [1925]), is key to this measurement method; precise precision one might say.

Another line of research, directly connected to schooling and education, took me back to Peter Ramus, Johann Amos Comenius, and Puritan institutions on both sides of the Atlantic (Doll, 2005b). The inquiry is into the development of the word curriculum (as a path to be followed), on the presenting of that path (a chart or map or course of study) in linear steps, and of "giving" (laying out) knowledge to the learner in a direct, didactic, textbook fashion.[6] Ramus is the first to capitalize on using the Latin word curriculum in an educational sense. As a schoolmaster, as well as a university (Regius) professor, he wanted to keep teaching simple and basic: "the one and only way Aristotle teaches." As such he acquired the sobriquet of "the greatest master of the short-cut" the educational field has known (Craig, quoted by Ong, 1983 [1958], p. 3).[7]

Further study on the methodizing of knowledge has helped me see that Ramus, foundational as he was, was not alone (Doll, 2005b; this volume, Chapter 8). Rather he belonged to a huge methodization movement in the 16th, 17th and 18th centuries. John Bunyon was part of this movement, as were both Francis Bacon and René Descartes. The philosopher Gottfried Leibniz says, "Nothing can escape our method ... it spares the mind and the imagination"; the latter especially "must be

---

6   I am indebted David Hamilton (1989, 1992, 2003) and to two of my former students, Stephen Triche and Douglas McKnight (2004), for their historical research of this time period, on which I have drawn heavily..

7   In his "The enchanted glass: The Elizabethan mind in literature" (1935) Hardin Craig says Ramus's pedagogical simplification of the works of Aristotle "exemplifies an assertion of the rights of the practical as opposed to the theoretical and points the way to Bacon and Descartes" (in Ong, 1983, p.145).

used sparingly" (1951 [1674]). The work of Taylor in industrialization and Tyler in education are but two aspects of a broad and deep movement—*methodization* (with its corollaries of standardization and measurement)—which has shaped the West's intellectual discourse for the past four to five centuries.

General intellectual awareness in the 20th century that the universe is dynamic and emergent, not stable and stationary—as methodization, standardization and measurement require—helped Prigogine posit a new paradigm. This paradigm he says is built around the concept of the universe being an open, not a closed, system.[8] Prigogine makes much of the open system, closed system distinction, as do I in my post-modern book (1993). Basically a closed system, such as a thermostatically controlled heating/air-conditioning system, works toward a pre-set goal, one set in advance. Equilibrium or equilibrated balance is the desired state. Perturbations or movements "off the mark," are regarded as disruptions, negativities to be corrected. Such systems emphasize *setness, stability, simplicity.* In metaphorical, or metaphysical, terms they emphasize Being not Becoming. In thermodynamic terms—Prigogine was a chemist (Nobel Prize, 1977)—a closed system, such as a steam engine, is able to *transfer* energy—here from the boiler to the movement of gears. Such a system, though machine oriented, can *only transfer.* It cannot *transform.* (It is worth noting how mechanized is our language of education, and how transference oriented are its assumptions.)

Open systems by their very nature are transformative, as in atomic reactions, or in all life. Open systems replace setness toward a predetermined goal with dynamic change, stability with emergence, and simplicity with complexity. Such systems are process oriented, since they are always in process, the process of transforming the somewhat "chaotic" into the orderly. The Prigogine (and Stengers) book is entitled (in English) *Order out of chaos* (1984). As I have said before, "open systems require disruptions, mistakes, perturbations" (Doll, 1993, p. 14). These are the "stuffs" process systems transform. If no messy, chaotic, fuzzy "stuffs," then no transformations. As a curriculum theorist, I saw the need to have a curriculum filled with *richness*—that is, to have "the 'right amount' of *indeterminacy, anomaly, inefficiency, chaos, disequilibrium, dissipation, lived experience*" (p. 176). The key, of course, to this sense of a curriculum which can be both transformed and transformative—to student and teacher— is the notion of "right amount." Too much fuzziness, messiness, or chaos and transformation will not occur; but without these disequilibria, as Piaget (1977a) says, there is no development: "However the nonbalance arises, it provides the driving force of development. ... Without the nonbalance [disequilibrium] there would not be increasing reequilibration" (p. 13).

Devising a developmental curriculum which is dynamic, emergent, transformative, and non-linear has attracted me and been my challenge during almost all my teaching career. As I have said so many times, the sort of linear, sequenced developmental frame

---

8   In addition to Hayles (1990), see my "The arrow of time" (2008a) on Prigogine and his project.

often attached to Piaget's name is not the sort of development frame I have sought (Doll, 1993). Recent emergence of the "new sciences" of chaos and complexity have provided a grounding for my beliefs. Here not only Prigogine and his colleagues have been helpful, but so has been Stuart Kauffman (1993, 1995, 2000) and his colleagues at the Santa Fe Institute. In these new sciences it is possible to see *a sense of development that is both non-linear and self-organizing.* This fits nicely with what we are learning about the human brain and how it works (BrainConnection.com). Following this line of reasoning, it seems to me that a quality curriculum—one which *enhances* a learner's own way of development and at the same time *transforms* that way so that one learns with depth and breadth—can be structured along the lines of Richness, Recursion, Relationship, and Rigor. It is hard for me to say where these 4 R's came from. Obviously there is a bit of playfulness here in my naming these four, nor can I argue that it is these precise four which are needed to produce a quality curriculum—one enhancing and transformative. Yet, over the years I have come to believe there to be a certain worthwhile structure here, no matter what the structure is named.

In reading, yet again—recursion if you will—N. Katherine Hayles' (1990) exploration of Prigogine's fundamental insights, I find myself more and more agreeing with Prigogine, and with Stuart Kauffman too, that any system which is to be developmental, in a dynamic sense, must be "dissipative." That is, the system needs to operate in an environment rich enough (but not overly rich) in material that "waste" is part of the emergence process. The waste in such a system is a necessary and needed waste, as the system works both to enhance and transform itself.[9] Such a view challenges the whole efficiency movement which has captivated American curricular and instructional thought for well over a century (Doll, 2002b), exemplified by Jean-Jacques Rousseau's remark that to gain time, one must often waste time; and by A. N. Whitehead's admonition to "throw ideas into every combination possible" (Whitehead, 1967b, p.2). It is this I mean when I talk of a Rich curriculum, one filled with just the right amount of problematics, perturbations, and paradoxes that prod.

Recursion, the second R, is quite explanatory in its name—a looping back to what one has already seen/done, to see again for the first time. Such a non-linear revisiting, this time with new eyes, has been a key part of my modus operandi ever since I wrote my book on a post-modern sense of curriculum (1993). Jerome Bruner, the father of the spiral curriculum, has often commented that a curriculum not recursive hardly deserves the name curriculum. Recursion, in the mathematical sense of iteration, is a key feature of all non-linear equations (Doll, 2008b). The

---

9 This argument lies at the heart of Stephen Gould's "An earful of jaw" (1990), talking of how in evolutionary terms the ears of humans came from the jaws of fish. The efficiency of this transformation occurred via the excess (hence wasted) amount of jaw the fish provided. The notion of waste being part of an efficiency process is not a modernist concept.

act of recursion destroys linear cause–effect sequencing so uniformly accepted in our instructional practices. Developing a non-linear approach to both curriculum design and instructional practice is a challenge in and to our modernist oriented society. A rich curriculum is, I believe, a *sine qua non*, a necessary starting point, for any curriculum designed to loop back on itself, and thus, in both seeing what was not seen before and in integrating the original seen with the just seen, able to bring forth the new. Such an integrational view is compatible with and informed by the work of Gould, Kauffman, Prigogine, as well as by the American pragmatists, especially Charles Peirce and his sense of a *logic of relations* (1992 [1898]).

Relationality is the "glue" (of connections) which holds any system together, which makes a system a system. The oft-shown Lorenz attractor (Doll, 1993, front cover) is one such illustration; another is a collection of illustrations of the synapses in a brain under activity (see Brainbow.com). Relations are what Whitehead calls the "really real"; it is not things or objects but relations that are real. Born 1931, into a generally modernist world and educated in a rational/analytic frame, it took me years to understand that it was not solid, massy, hard atoms that were the really real, but relations themselves. Recent pictures of the atom[10]—more space than anything else—and readings and ponderings on Whitehead have helped me understand the reality of relations. Bruner's 1986a essay, "Two modes of thought" which influenced my thinking only many years after I first read it, explicated in my 2003 paper ("Modes of thought"), helped me understand that a good curriculum design would counter-play the rational/analytic with the non-rational/experiential. Here I take the view that it is not so much an integration of these two modes of thought as it is the counter-playing of one against the other in a dynamic manner which is important for the development of the new. Donna Trueit's persistent question of "Where does the new come from?" (2004, 2005b) has inspired and informed my thinking for almost a decade now. Her answer of "from conversation," i.e., interaction and relations, is an idea worth exploring. Here I also applaud William Pinar and his use of the word in his recent series of books, Complicated Conversations.

Rigor, as the fourth R, came to me as I tried to be both a bit less cute with the 3 R's. While Whitehead spends much time on the need for rigor in the traditional sense (Doll, 2005a), he also combines it with romance/play and generalization/abstraction. These latter qualities, quite marked in the human species, combine with rigor to remove it from the static rigor mortis frame into one where the new and the creative can emerge. As an example, when I was teaching elementary school (back in the 1960s) my fourth grade students knew their multiplication tables at least through 20×20. They did not, though, memorize 400 separate facts; instead they found patterns which they played with and abstracted: 6×17 is double 3×17, itself 30 plus 21; or 6×17 could be "seen" as 6×15 (itself 60 plus 30, or 3×15 doubled)

---

10 The journal *Discover* (June, 2007) has an interesting article by A. Stone on imaging the atom (first done in 1969) and a picture of silicon atoms. They look quite different than the "planetary" models we are used to in textbooks.

plus 2 × 17 (34). All this led to a playful/abstractive sense of working the numeration system in countless ways. Needless to say, the students enjoyed math, scored well on tests, and acquired the ability to be inquisitive, interpretative, imaginative. This same sense of rigor integrating play with precision and principles (abstractions) came forward in these same years when a teacher colleague and I ran a Saturday morning Great Books program on the local TV station with eighth graders. Here we followed not the prescribed script from the Chicago Great Books program but chose our own books and had spontaneous conversations (two teachers, eight eighth graders) about what interested us in the books and why. Again, through such "conversations" all ten of us learned, all ten of us contributed and, in Whitehead's sense, knowledge was kept alive.

Rigor can also be looked at in a post-structural, Derridean sense; that is in exploring the possibilities that exist or can exist in any current situation, event, teaching moment. How can we look at what we are doing, at what is happening, in a different sense? What happens when we look at adding 2, 3, 4 in terms of multiplying the middle term (3) three times?[11] What happens when we look at a story, not in terms of its "main idea" but in terms of various characters in the story— their feelings, their perceptions, their (possible) ideas and values? Tom Stoppard's *Rozencranz and Guildenstern are dead* (1968) comes to mind here. While one does not expect second grade students to produce such a work, they can be amazingly creative when one frees them from the fetters of a traditional focus and asks them to use their imaginations (Greene, 1995). No teachers I know do this better than the Galileo Group of David Jardine, Patricia Clifford, and Sharon Friesen (2003, 2006).

In regard to this post-structural sense of rigor, I am much attracted to the work of Michel Serres, who had Ilya Prigogine and Isabelle Stengers write a postscript to his *Hermes* (1983) collection of essays. Following from Serres, himself a "chaotician" (Serres and Latour, 1995 [1990]), I have become interested in the social/political thought of Bruno Latour, a younger scholar much influenced by Serres but also carving out his own directions (2004, 2007). While I was influenced early on by the political activism of Steve Mann, I am now drawn to William Pinar's social/political work.

In our *Curriculum visions* book (2002), born of many hours of post-AERA conversations as we traveled southern Georgia and northern California, tasting pecans and wine, Noel Gough and I took different but complementary directions in our Introductions: his is more personal and political; mine is more historical and speculative. Noel in his Introduction makes the point that any future vision must not neglect our present vision, but rather needs to emerge from our current critical engagement with the present, and that our "'seeing' is determined by where we

---

11 One could, of course, use any three sequential numbers. Those of 3, 4, 5 fit in well with a right triangle, itself half of a square as well as introducing the famous Pythagorean theorem of the square on the hypotenuse. For more exploration here see Crosby (1998) and Livio (2003).

stand and how we frame our fields of visualization" (p. 8).These themes he revisits in
the book, particularly in his essay "The Long Arms of Globalization." Here, drawing
on the writings of Jacques Derrida, Sandra Harding, Ursula LeGuin, as well as his
personal teaching experiences in South Africa, Noel describes and fights against the
"cultural imperialism and colonization" that results from globalization.To move away
from the imperialism inherent in globalization, Noel gives the name *Transnational*
to the journal he edits for the International Association for the Advancement of
Curriculum Studies (IAACS).

My own Introduction, "Ghosts and the curriculum"—read by, elaborated on,
critiqued, and played with by all the essayists—sees the "Ghost of John Dewey
hovering over the American curriculum" (p. 23) with the ghost of John Calvin
haunting, influencing, controlling, the curriculum we in North America and
Western Europe practice today. As I say at the end of my essay, what unites the
curriculum of the Calvinist Ramus with that of the objectivist Tyler is the sense of
certainty each espouses:"Both curricularists were part of the paradigm that believed
[to draw from Richard Rorty, 1989, p. 76] that if it did 'not have all the answers,' at
least it had the 'criteria for the answers.'" (p. 53)

John Dewey, of course, believed that a fixation on certainty, a *Quest for certainty*
(1960 [1929]), underlay our current metaphysical malaise; itself born of a fear
of change, a desire to unite ourselves with that which "is antecedently fixed in
existence" (p. 205). Such a desire manifests itself today in many classrooms: in a
focus on "facts,"[12] on set procedures, on rigid rules. In breaking away from this
centuries-long tradition, I (again, playfully) proposed our looking at curriculum
from multiple perspectives: those of *currere*, cosmology, complexity, conversation,
community.The first (*currere*) and last (community) of these most arbitrary five, is
intentional to emphasize the interplay of the individual with the communal.This
interplay has guided much of my own teaching where the atmosphere I encourage
is one not only of honoring our own thoughts and those of others, but also of
bringing these ideas into experiential interactions of varied types.When possible, the
south Louisiana tradition of eating together becomes part of our LSU curriculum
experience. Also, classroom doors here are always "open," and other professors,
former students, students from other classes, visitors are welcomed in to share and
add to the richness of the current conversation. The goal, here, is not to develop a
unified focus but rather to develop a network of connected and interconnected
thoughts. I see my task, as a teacher (one of many teachers in the class), as helping
all of us weave a tapestry or construct a network/matrix of the many strands and
loops "floating" around the classroom. Understanding is thus not "passed on" via
teaching-as-telling (Trueit, 2007;Trueit and Pratt, 2006), but rather emerges from,

12 We think of facts as being certain and "hard." In reality the concept came into being
   when Francis Bacon, wanting scientists to distinguish between the real/exact and the
   speculative/imagined, decreed that any bit of knowledge agreed to by twelve respected
   men (jurors as it were) would be considered a "fact."

is created through, interactions. Needless to say, my studying in the fields of chaos, complexity, and (open) systems has been invaluable; and here I owe a great debt to Brent Davis and Dennis Sumara for their encouragement, leadership, guidance. The Complexity Science and Educational Research (CSER) conferences they initiated and the journal *Complicity* that Brent started (in collaboration with Renata Phelps) have been an intellectual stimulus to my own scholarship and teaching habits.

Using *currere* (the personal) and community (the social) as brackets for an arbitrary and playful 5 C's, in my introductory essay, I then filled in the space between the brackets with cosmology, complexity, conversation. In searching for a new model, I thought that if our cosmos is creative in its Being, should not our curriculum be such also; if we now envision our learning habits as being complex, should not our curriculum reflect this complexity; and if, as Richard Rorty says (1979, pp. 171, 319), after we abandon the foundational and are left with conversation as our hope for a better future, should we not utilize this device in our teaching? In doing this I wished to open up our definition/sense of curriculum.[13] One such opening began (Doll and Gough, 2002, footnote 30) when I pondered the notion of adding Spirit to the S's of Science and Story. These three S's, especially that of Spirit, have occupied much of my curriculum thinking in the past few years. Finding this spirit is a difficult challenge; for it is not an object, which science studies, nor can it be shown graphically or symbolically, as can story. What we are studying though is always a situation, an event, an idea, a particularity and that situation has its own spirit. To know a situation we need to "plunge into the situation" (Dewey, 1958b [1934]), struggle with it, explore it in depth, *be* in it, intuiting, feeling our way around. Ephemeral, floating, even haunting, Spirit carries a situation along, impregnates it with life, vitality—even with integrity, values, aesthetics. (More on the 3 S's in Chapter 11.)

As many have shown (see especially, Davis and Sumara, 2006) what is so different about this current paradigm is that although, in a sense, we are always inside the situation we are studying we are not *simply* inside it. There is no outside, nor inside; thus the notions of external/objective or internal/subjective are quite literally, *meaningless*. The same is true of quantitative and qualitative; their split is arbitrary. Every measurement is based on some arbitrary assumptions, "stories" if you will.[14] Every qualitative experience is bounded, held in, shaped by our culture, language, past experiences. Whatever we study then, experiment on, write, draw, graph, picture—in short, *represent*—is always incomplete, and open to further revision, development, interpretation.

That which is incomplete is not closed, it is open—to new possibilities, to revisions, to a "growth" (a word and concept Dewey was fond of emphasizing).

---

13 Ted Aoki (2005b) makes an important distinction between "curriculum-as-plan"—which as teachers we plan to use in our classrooms—and "curriculum-as-lived experience"—which we indeed do use (often unconsciously) in both classrooms and life.

14 Kanigel (1997) brings out this point forcefully with his story of the *arbitrariness* of Frederick Taylor in his development of "standards." See "Beyond methods" (2002a, this volume, Chapter 8).

That which is incomplete, though, is also potentially capable of being wildly rhizomatic—unbounded, unstructured, even formless. Therefore curriculum designs and instructional strategies, if they are to be useful, need to lie in that space created by the dynamic interaction of the closed with the open (or in the interplay of the scientific with the storied, with the spiritful). In a sense we, as humans, need a "reality," or a worldview, wherein we continually strive for closure, but hope against hope (even pray) that such closure is never achieved. In this interactive or "third space,"[15] dynamically formed by the tensioned interaction between the open and the closed, lie the connections, nodes, attractors which give birth to the new.

Such a "model" is hardly what most would call a model. Models in the traditional (modernist) sense are things—objects, diagrams, etc. Here the model is an ongoing process. It needs a rich set of interacting factors for its beginnings, and recursions, relations, and rigor as it develops. As a curriculum theorist and practicing teacher I will continue my work on the philosophical, physical, and practical aspect of this new "model."

---

15 A number of authors have written about the "third space," notably Homi Bhabha and Michel Serres. I like best Hongyu Wang's treatment of it in her *Call from the stranger on a journey home* (2004).

4

STRUGGLES WITH SPIRITUALITY

(2002)

> As the archeology of our thought easily shows, man is an invention of recent date. And one perhaps nearing its end.
>
> (Michel Foucault)

We humans have always known our personal and physical existence to be temporal—we are born, live, die. This is what it means to be an individual human being. But we have not thought of our species—*Homo sapiens*—in the same temporal terms. Even with our acceptance of Charles Darwin's thesis that humanity is an evolving form—"descent with modification" is his way of phrasing (1964 [1859])—we have not seriously considered that our species evolution might be into extinction. We have, of course, worried about the nuclear destruction of life but even in this catastrophe we have assumed some life forms would live—eventually to transform themselves into the human. Again, the species as species has not been considered as evolving toward extinction—yet this is a natural consequence of the life process.

Entropy, the other dominant E of 19th century—in its popular form the cooling of the sun and hence the dying of our solar system—is quite universally accepted.[1] Yet we have almost never put these two E's—evolution and entropy—together to recognize that it is not unnatural to consider not only ourselves but also our species as temporal, maybe even "nearing its end." If our solar system is temporal why should life on one of its planets not also be temporal? In fact, how could life on a planet in the solar system be, if the system itself dies?

---

1 While entropy is almost universally accepted—Arthur Eddington (1928) says it occupies "The supreme position among the Laws of Nature" (p. 74)—it does have a history originating in 19th century mechanical, closed systems. Thus, some scientists have at the very least raised fundamental questions about it. See for example, Ilya Prigogine and Isabel Stengers (1984); my own book (1993); Paul Davies (1995); and George Johnson (1996).

For centuries we—in mainstream Christian and modernist traditions—have operated (theologically at least) on the assumption that God is securely fixed in "His" firmament with the Devil located in "His" hell. Both figures have been portrayed as male and very, very permanent. Our cosmology, if not our science, has been based on this idea of permanence. Nature is—by *its* very nature—permanent, simple, and, as Isaac Newton said, consonant and "conformable to Herself" (1952 [1730], p. 397). In fact, Newton's "law of gravity," that mathematical formula ($F = G\frac{m_1 m_2}{r^2}$) which describes both falling terrestrial apples and revolving planetary spheres, shows just this conformity: *one* law uniting the whole universe, as Pierre Simon de la Place said, with Newton being "the most fortunate of all men" for he had discovered this law (in Burtt, 1955[1932], p. 3l). Before Albert Einstein, gravity was *the* organizing law of the universe—entropy being a dissipative not organizing law.

Einstein (most unwittingly) destroyed this concept of a universe consonant, conformable, simple. While he was indeed, "the last great Newtonian," it is his theories which have helped others (us) see a subatomic world filled with millions of weird "objects," some of them "living" for only billionths of a second; and his theories have also helped us "see" a celestial world filled with black holes, exploding stars, bursting galaxies, and tumultuous new creations. In fact, we now see ourselves not as "Lords of the Universe," but as accidental inhabitants of a rather tiny planet, located "on the edge of a humdrum galaxy among billions like it, scattered across a vast megaspace" (Kauffman, 1995, p. 4).

How does all this scientific thinking, based as it is on a fundamental acceptance of change, influence our thinking about God, religion, spirituality, based as they are on a fundamental acceptance of permanence? We have here, Jacques Derrida would say, an *aporia*—a basic contradiction, an essential opposition. Already we have lost Hell—few find it a reality—and with the loss of Hell has come the lessening of the persona of the Devil and of his evil power. What for the Puritans was reality, is for us, three centuries later, mythic. The representation of Hell which Dante gives us in his *Divine comedy* (1915 [early 14th century])—nine levels or circles of damnation lying deep in the bowels of the earth's fiery, volcanic core—is now seen only as mythic, and not a very appealing myth at that. Scientifically we now realize that Hell will ultimately "freeze over." Hell freezing over! It will happen, and in less geologic time than we might realize. Our sun is likely beyond the halfway point in its own temporal existence—metaphorically it is into middle-age, maybe even advanced middle-age (P. Davies, 1995, p. 63). As it continues to age, the earth's crust will harden, ice, and its volcanic core (hell) will indeed freeze over.

Theologically we may be ready to accept the non-existence of Hell and the Devil. Both appear far less in our contemporary church sermons than they did in the sermons or Jeremiads of the Puritans. The Devil is now seen to reside more within us than as an active deity in his own right. If God is not dead, I think it fair to say the Devil is.

God may well be dead in the sense in which Frederick Nietzsche pronounced him dead[2] but He is certainly not dead in people's minds. Religion in its traditional sense is much alive, albeit maybe not well. Our theologic thinking here is not ready, I believe, to accept a non-existent (really non-anthropomorphic) God. We still accept a theology that sees God rooted permanently in His Heaven, itself located high in celestial space. If Hell has gone, Heaven remains. But where is Heaven? The celestial and magnetic blue we take to be Heaven with its puffy, white clouds is, we now know, a thin layer of atmosphere surrounding our planet. A unique surrounding? Our planet is of course but one of nine in our solar system, while the solar system is itself located in a thin galactic band we call the "Milky Way." How many galaxies are there—is billions too large or maybe too small a number? How about billions of billions? As for our uniqueness (an arrogant thought) in this vast vastness, what will speculations about past life on Mars do to it? *Are we alone* (in the universe) (P. Davies, 1995)? Did life exist at one time on Jupiter's moon, Europa?

What do such musings/speculations/theories/facts do to our concepts of God, salvation, permanence in Heaven? Is the God who inhabited Mars—a warlike God I assume—still alive? As the solar system darkens and deadens, will God still be "there"? Where? What is it like to conceive of a God ruling over a "dead" universe? Does God like the dark? Let there be Light! Where? Or will God leave this solar system, maybe this galaxy and move on to others? Was the creation of this system and us a mere whim, our species no more than "randomness caught on the wing"?—to use Jacques Monod's colorful phrase (1971, p. 98). Finally, what does it mean to our contemporary concept of Christianity to realize that the permanence we had assumed to underlie our religion and spirituality does not exist?

The argument I am making here is that our accepted concepts of God, religion, spirituality assume a type of permanence—a cosmology of permanence as it were— we no longer find valid. Our scientific theories have changed to accept change as a fundamental feature,[3] our theological theories have not so changed. Our science is post-modern; our theology is modern. What will a post-modern theology/spirituality look like?

If we consider that our theology, religion, spirituality are rooted strongly in modernism, we might legitimately consider that our theology, religion, spirituality

2   For a good analysis of what Nietzsche meant by his famous remark, and ways to interpret it, see Mary Elizabeth Quinn (1997, Ch. 2). See also Martin Heidegger, on whom Quinn draws (1977 [1954], Part II).

3   I realize this statement can be taken (1) as a deification of science, and (2) as part of that broad historical tradition—one C. A. Bowers (1993, 1995) rightly rails against—which has equated science with change and both with progress. While I approve of science, change, and progress, I do not wish to imply a simple relationship here nor an automatic one. Science is but one and only one of the three S's—Science, Story, Spirituality—framing my pedagogy. Change can be, obviously, for the poorer as well as for the better; and "progress" has brought with it much that is destructive as well as much that is constructive. The relationships among science, change, progress is complex and fragile.

have been and are anthropocentric and anthropomorphic—we have created and centered "God" around "Man"[4]—in "our image and likeness." The God of our Judeo-Christian representation is humanly male—as a loving Father, as Moses, as Christ.

Can we accept a non-anthropocentric view of God, religion, spirituality, theology? What will happen to these words and the values they represent if we do not? Here lie my struggles with spirituality. These struggles, of course, carry over to my concepts of teaching and curriculum design, areas I have devoted my professional life to exploring and areas I believe will be strongly affected by our general (albeit slow) move from an anthropocentric sense of spirituality to one more cosmologically and ecologically oriented. I firmly believe a new sense of value must be found but that this new sense cannot be rooted in an individualistic or humanly skewed frame. We are part of a larger ecological and cosmological frame—a frame Gregory Bateson (1988 [1979]) calls "mind," with us and our minds as subminds. As do Bateson and Thomas Berry (1988b, 1992), I believe our theoretical, theological, and operational frames need to focus on the universe itself and *its* ways of operating. The universe has its own patterns, and as Bateson says, they "connect." The patterns do connect into a unified whole. Further, Bateson argues, "If you fight the ecology of a system you lose—especially when you win" (in Berman, 1981, p. 257). Too much of our fight this century has been a fight of us against nature and the more we have won, the more we have lost.

To move from the personal and social to the ecological and cosmological, means, in an epistemological sense, to move toward thinking in a relational way. It is the relations between and among objects that becomes the focus (Whitehead, 1967a [1925], 1978 [1929]; Bateson and M. Bateson, 1987; Bateson, 1988 [1979]; Berry, 1988b, 1992; Bowers, 1993, 1995). The patterns exist not in the objects but in the relations among the objects. It is through the relations among the objects, particularly their differences, that we begin to understand the objects themselves—those temporary permanences we call facts. A sense of the sacred arises—a *mysterium tremendum* (to borrow from Mary Elizabeth (Molly) Quinn, 1997)—when we look at the complex of relations we find in nature and at the power and generativity of the process of creation. When we shift our gaze from the particular to the interconnected and to the generativity of all life and creation, a sense of awe arises. It is this focus, rather than our own personal salvation, I am advocating we adopt—a focus on the "pattern which connects," rather than on the individual objects connected.

Such a shift in focus lets us see the order in nature (complex), the symmetry (recursive), and the balance (dynamic). In a sense Newton was right, nature is conformable to herself, but it is not a simple conformity nor a stable one. It is the conformity of a system continually transforming itself, regenerating itself, creating itself. The process [of creation] is the reality, says Whitehead, and we are, as says

---

4   Margaret Wertheim notes that Laplace, following Newton, believed an "Intelligence" could predict all future events if it had the exact state of the universe now. Wertheim wryly notes that this "Intelligence" seemed much like a "super version of (Laplace) himself" (1995, p. 145).

Bateson, the active Creatura within the process. There is no outside/inside; all is one—a dynamic, turbulent, ordered/chaotic process of connecting patterns. In such a process, stochastic Bateson (1988 [1979]) calls it, change is fundamental, even foundational; but it is change which operates through the dynamic interaction of stability and flexibility intertwined (Kauffman, 1995; Doll, 1998a). God is now no longer a person but a word we apply to the *mysterium tremendum* of this creative process. "His," "her," or "its" reality lies within the pattern of interconnections. Indeed, "God" may even be the pattern of patterns or the creativity of creating patterns.

Traditional theology has not seen God within this patterned fabric but rather outside the fabric, the creator of the fabric. Being outside, "He" has been permanence in opposition to change; not permanence through change nor permanence entwined with change. The either/or morality of a system where the permanence (God) lies outside the system is a morality based on power. He (and now she) who has the most power becomes the determiner of the rules. While we have clothed this determiner of rules in religious and/or traditional garments, the validity or sacredness of the rules has really been determined by the power the determiner has held. "Power is power only when and only so long as it remains power-enhancement and commands for itself more power" (Heidegger, 1977 [1954], p. 78). The history of the Christian/Catholic church is a living example of this (Wertheim, 1995). "Christianity," says Derrida "has not yet come to Christianity" (in Quinn, 1997)— the Spirit of Christianity has not yet infused Christian organizations.[5]

The question of values (morality) is, I believe, the most important question we as a society (or collection of societies) face today. Certainly it is an issue receiving a lot of attention in educational, social, religious circles. Many want or believe we can (re)institute the "values" we had or did not have in the past. This, though, cannot be done. As Douglas McKnight (1997) has clearly shown, our country's social values and educational institutions (especially its public schools) were organized around Puritan-Protestant concepts.[6] America grew and as these concepts attained fulfillment they also became dissipated. Their very success led to their being assumed and hence to a loss of their driving force. As Bateson says: any attempt to maximize a single variable within a system (including purposive rationality) will force the

---

5   This statement by Derrida is appropriated from the (martyred) Czech philosopher Jan Patocka and appears in Derrida's *G.o.D.* (1995 [1992], p. 28). For myself, the comment while accurate institutionally should not be considered to denigrate the millions of wonderful persons—female and male—who have and are working within the Spirit of their religion and religious feelings. The compassion humanity does currently display owes much to these people.

6   This comment is not meant to overlook the contributions to our American culture and community made by Native Americans, Afro-Americans, Spanish-Americans, Huguenots, Chinese-Americans, Cajuns (to name but a few ethnic groups). However, the dominant power within the American culture was formed in the northeastern part of the United States where Puritan-Protestant values reigned supreme and where the American public school movement received its origins and from which it still acquires much of its driving force.

system into a "runaway" state, capable of destroying itself and its environment (in Berman, 1981, p. 256). The Puritans did try to maximize their single view of life and its way. In fact, as McKnight (1997) says: the Puritans believed that via "correct moral thoughts [they] could arrive at right moral action and [hence] change the terrain of the world" (p. 47).

In the middle of this century, Martin Heidegger saw that we in the West had lost our souls and human values,[7] not so much to technology (the subject of his essay, 1977 [1954], Part I) as to *our* hopes and aspirations for technology. Technology lies, of course, at the heart of the Industrial Revolution; itself and its "new breed" of man—the engineer—forming the social hope for the Enlightenment. Heidegger points out, in "The question concerning technology" (1977 [1954]), that in this too exalted hope, we have separated means from ends—envisioning technology merely as a device separated from its underlying essence. We have believed we can control technology—a "neutral" tool—for our own (good) ends. This was our justification for the atomic bombs dropped on Japan. The result of this "*mentalité*" has been our becoming subservient to (or "enframed" by) the essence of controlling. Our being is now wrapped up in control—*to be* we need to be controlling. We accept the controlling mode, an off-shoot of *praxis*, as the way to be. As we control, we accept the idea of control and become, ourselves, controlled.

This is the same argument I am making regarding theology. As we have separated ourselves from God, placing "Him" outside and us inside, we have become susceptible to an inferior-superior, competitive enframing. Our values are, and have been for centuries, ones of "winning" our salvation. This has made us competitive with the very "others" we so desperately need for our understandings of self. In this power game, we, as a species, are bound to lose. Our evolution to extinction may happen naturally and slowly; our movement to extinction may happen sooner because we misunderstand what it means to be a human species.

Our past, competitive, individualist values we cannot recover, nor should we wish to do so. We need another enframing, a brand new paradigm, or as Thomas Berry says "a new story" (1988b, p. 123, *passim*). For Berry, the new story is the old, old one of the universe. It is also a radical story, for as Berry says, "We must go far beyond any transformation of contemporary culture. We must go back to the genetic imperative from which human cultures emerge" (p. 207). We need to go back to the "primordial experience" of creation to focus on an "all-pervading mysterious energy" and awaken ourselves to "an awesome universe filled with mysterious power" (p. 24)—the *mysterium tremendum* Quinn develops so well.[8] This shift is away

---

7   An ironic comment considering Heidegger's own loss of soul, both to the Nazis and to an etherial idealization of the ancient Greek concept of *poiesis*. See Richard Bernstein's analysis of this in Chapter 4 of his *The new constellation* (1992).

8   The *Oxford English dictionary* (OED) attributes the English use of this phrase to J. Harvey in his translation (Chapter 4) of R. Otto's *The idea of the holy* (1923 [1917]). The OED definition (*tremendous mystery*) expresses the "overwhelming awe and sense of unknowable

from the "anthropocentric life attitude which has been our story for so long" (p. 67) in favor of an even older (but not developed in Western thought) life attitude present in cosmological creation. We are part of that creation and have our role in it.

This creative process Berry believes is neither determined nor random. Its essence lies in the act of creation itself (p.199). Bateson, a scientist not a theologian, sees the creative process as the actual integration of determinism with randomness, randomness with determinism. This integration he calls "The Great Stochastic Process" (1988, Ch. 6). Whitehead says simply, "It lies in the nature of things that the many enter into complex unity" (1978 [1929], p. 21). All three agree the process to be one where creation is emergent—the universe coming out of itself—in a mysterious but natural way.

Stuart Kauffman (1993, 1995) also sees the process as emergent and natural—one that can be seen in DNA replicating itself and studied through the use of computers and the patterns developed over time as randomness is iterated upon itself over and over. Whether the computer situations Kauffman develops of order emerging from randomness is a valid example of DNA replicating itself is an open—maybe even personal—question. Using this as a model (or a metaphor) for *all* creation is even more speculative. But in this analogic process Kauffman is moving from the known and manipulable (computer programs) to the *mysterium tremendum* of all creation. I do not believe Kauffman is trying to find the essence, origin, or source of the *tremendum*. I do not envision him trying to see into "the mind of God" but rather to show analogically that a connection might be made between the order which arises spontaneously (under certain constraint conditions) in computer programs and the creative order we find in our universe. Will other universes have different orders?

For me, as I interpret Kauffman, the mystery of how order arises (spontaneously not by imposition) remains a mystery. It is not defined, merely shown—along with its constraint conditions. In Whitehead's terms "it lies in the nature of things that the many enter into complex unity." (Whitehead, 1978) Or as Paul Davies (1995) has suggested, there may well be an innate tendency in nature to evolve more complex structures, what he calls the "law of increasing organized complexity" (p. 103). Again, this may well be the *mysterium tremendum*—the natural and innate tendency of nature to create in ever increasing complexity.

---

mystery felt by those to whom this aspect of God or being is revealed" (*Oxford English dictionary*, 1989, Vol. 10, p. 173). J. Derrida in his *G.o.D.* (1995 [1992], Ch. 3) calls it a "frightful mystery, a secret to make you tremble," and, playing off the idea of tremble not tremendous, takes the origins back to Søren Kierkegaard (1983 [1843]) and his "Fear and trembling," itself coming from St. Paul (*Holy Bible* (1963): Philippians 2:12) and his exhortation for Christians to "work out your own salvation with fear and trembling." I prefer the OED thrust which I find akin to William James' sense of an "unseen spiritual order," (1956 [1897], p. 52) and to Paul Tillich's (1957) reference to the *mysterium tremendum* as "a presence which remains mysterious in spite of its appearance, and exercises both an attractive and repulsive function on those who encounter it" (p.53).

What is our responsibility, our morality in the tremendousness of creation? As educators do we bear any special responsibility?

A God disappears, Divinity remains.

(Paul Tillich, 1957, p. 18)

Responsibility is the state of being responsible (Latin, *respondere*), answering to, being accountable for, usually to another (*Oxford English Ddctionary*, 1989, Vol. 13, p. 742). Even a cursory look at contemporary society shows that traditional senses of responsibility, authority, morality no longer hold. "Kids just don't respect anymore," they do not "respond" as we (in power) believe they should. The prevalence of such comments shows that many, too many I fear, wish us to return to a past (real or imagined) where the Puritan-Protestant ethic dominated. Not only can this not be done, the very concept of responsibility inherent in this ethic may well be not thought right through.

Responsibility as we have envisioned this concept has essentially been responsibility *to*—an Other, a God, an Ideology, a Tradition. It has been responsibility to that which lies above or beyond us in our mundane being. This sense of responsibility, which Derrida (1995) calls "sacrificial responsibility" (p. 76, *passim*), is "the most common and everyday experience of responsibility" (p. 67). It is in many ways a "monstrous" responsibility, for its relationship—of us to other—is a power relationship, one of us subjugating ourselves to the Other and hence willing to sacrifice ourselves and our loved ones to the demands of the Other—just as Abraham "sacrificed" Isaac, or as God sacrificed His Only Begotten Son. It is this sense of responsibility, "our most common and everyday experience of responsibility," Derrida feels we have "not thought right through."[9]

The responsibility of sacrifice, of subjugation is monstrous, not only in the acts it honors—everywhere, everyday—but also in the moral justification it gives to those acts. We not only kill, we explain (justify) such killing with a term like "cleansing"— in our Puritan-Protestant heritage, a term of purity and morality. Remember that the Puritan trial for witches was "dunking"; reminiscent of baptizing, of washing, of cleansing. Cleansing and words like it are not mere language plays; they represent a morality that hides immorality, a responsibility that justifies irresponsibility. We firmly believe our cleansing to be justified and moral.

Can we begin to develop a "new responsibility"—one announced by the *mysterium tremendum*? (p. 28). The *mysterium tremendum* is, of course, undefined and undefinable. But associated historically as it has been with a fear-inspiring (fear-demanding, fear-requiring?) Christian God, it has overtones of dread in it. I use

---

9 I borrow this phrase from Derrida (1995, p. 32) who borrows it from Patocka. I approach my own attempts at "thinking right through" my next comments with trepidation. Still I feel an obligation (responsibility?) to begin such a venture. I ask the reader's indulgence and welcome comments. The issues I'm about to raise are important ones, I believe.

the phrase in a different manner, however: not in regard to the dreadful but to the awe-full—to the awesome and mysterious creation present in all life; a mysterious creation we continue to explore. Instead of fear I replace awe.[10] I'm using this phrase to mark the awesomeness I believe we feel as we look upon acts of creation—human, ecological, cosmic. These are awe-inspiring not fear-inspiring acts, although fear is latently present in observing the intricacy, complexity, power of creation. But fear is not the dominant emotion; nor is it intended to be. Whereas many of the acts God commits in the Bible are, I believe, so intended.

In this new frame, responsibility takes on a different meaning. It is no longer responsibility *to*—a power relationship which allows for the legitimacy of irresponsibility under the guise of responsibility, i.e. following other's orders (p. 85)—but a responsibility *of*. This of is not a responsibility to another, as a self, it is a categorical responsibility which comes with the concept *of being,* with being in life. Derrida talks of "relation without relation" (p. 78). For me, this is relation *per se*, not relation to (another) but relation of (being). Relation *per se* is relation (or responsibility) that comes with living, conscious living; it is the relationship/responsibility we have in being. It is a categorical not personal relationship. As categorical, it removes the power play inherent in traditional relationships—i.e. in my being "responsible" when I follow the orders of those more powerful than I.

Operationalizing this new responsibility requires me to make a (free) choice; my actions owe allegiance to no other. I am free to be responsible or irresponsible. The choice I make—and it is I who must choose—is dependent only on my sense of being, not on my obligation to an other. Hence I have a "relation without relation," I am responsible without sacrificing myself or my being to the other. I am freely responsible and within this "free" responsibility there lies the possibility of new possibilities.

The contradiction inherent in this position (the aporia Derrida recognizes so well) is that this ideal can never be. On the one hand, an ethics of obligatory sacrifice is no ethics at all, and on the other hand, an ethics which has no relations is (or easily can be) an "ethics" of selfishness. Again, hardly an ethics. Yet, the possibility inherent in this intriguing impossibility is inspiring.

---

10 "Awe" does indeed have a sense of fear associated with it in its dictionary definitions. In fact, in old English awe (aye or aege) is synonymous with fear—"immediate and active fear; terror, dread" is the way the OED phrases it. However, over the centuries awe as a word has moved into "reverential or respectful fear" or subduedness in the "presence of supreme authority … or mysterious sacredness." Finally it becomes "solemn and reverential wonder, tinged with latent fear, inspired by what is terribly sublime and majestic in nature" (*Oxford English dictionary*, 1989, Vol. 1, p. 831). This latest sense is the one Harvey (Otto, 1923 [1917]) uses, referring to the "overwhelming sense of unknowable mystery." The tremendousness of this mystery appears both revealed and yet hidden the more we understand the universe's "design."
A final understanding (a Theory of Everything—TOE) is, of course, quite contrary to what I am both describing and arguing for in the *mysterium tremendum*.

My position in being-in-the-world then, as I see it, is that of being free to be irresponsible and freely choosing "the other" course, that of responsibility. I make this choice not out of personal concern for the other—hence obligating myself to the other and the other to myself—but because I am. Because I am *of being*.

With an arrogance known only to fools, I now rush in to the aporias of life that Derrida illuminates darkly. I believe our spirituality must be, not an infusion of Grace or Spirit from outside, but a relationship of being we develop, with awe and reverence toward all creation. This relationship is, I further believe, without relations to any particular "other," but is a relationship of being, one we hold as we (freely) choose responsibility. In this "free" choice lies one of life's paradoxes.

Recognition of this paradox is an educational mission. The complexity of this paradox is not easily seen; yet if not seen, our sense of responsibility is no more than a subjugation of weaker to stronger. If we are not to accept this power relationship as responsibility, if we wish a sense of spirituality that enhances rather than subjugates, that opens new possibilities, then we need not only education but a new vision of education. Education in the sense I am considering is education which focuses on *our being*—on our engagement with life as this is manifest in humanity, the world, the universe, the cosmos. Such an education does struggle with the spiritual, and is infused with the spiritual at the same time it infuses the spiritual with us. This is an education which questions the being of all we hold sacred while at the same time manifests a faith that such questioning will lead us to the sacredness of being.

So begin my struggles with spirituality.

5

MEMORY OF A MENTOR

JOHN STEVEN MANN

(2009)

In the fall of 2009, in the month of October, John Steven Mann, passed from this life. With his passing went part of my soul. Steve was my doctoral mentor; but more, he was a teacher who helped me shape my views not only on education, but also on life. The values I hold today were brought forth and refined in those years we spent as I worked on my Ph.D.

Steve came to Hopkins, in the late 1960s, as its first and only curriculum theorist, a title I proudly wear today. In some ways Steve and I came together by accident: he needed students, I needed a mentor, my former mentor having left Hopkins for the professionalism of Columbia. I was told by Robbie McClintock not to follow him there. I was a muser and Hopkins was the place where I could muse. Steve not only let me muse, he encouraged it, he gently guided me in it. We read together the writings of a former Hopkins graduate, John Dewey. I read my writings to Steve and he read his to me. Often, too often, I would read a page or two of what I had written and stop cold. "This is not very good," I would say. Steve would reply, "You needed to write this, Bill." He never went beyond that simple phrase, but the implication was definitely there: good writing is an emerging process. Failures are not simply failures, they are part of a reflective process. Ever so slowly my writing improved, although it was, still is, Germanic. With my sense of musing it was a close call (other graduate students took bets) as to whether the Notes in my dissertation would outnumber my text in terms of pages. Ultimately text won as I had only 150 pages of endnotes.

In my second year of doctoral study, I told Steve I wished to read in the history and philosophy of science. Steve gave me his library carrel key and said, "Go read." At the time Thomas Kuhn was the rage with his concept of paradigm change. After a longish, still Germanic, paper on Kuhn, which did draw some attention (even if never submitted for publication), I started my dissertation on Dewey's concept of change.

In subsequent years, change was a theme in my readings of Piaget, Bruner, Prigogine, Whitehead. Today, almost four decades after my leaving Hopkins, it is change that attracts me to the new sciences of chaos and complexity. I now call myself both a curriculum theorist and a complexity theorist. Steve, I am sure, approves.

The late 1960s was also a time of strong social change. With a background in the Ethical Culture School (New York City) and the University of Wisconsin, Steve had strong political and social views. A firm believer in the American ideal of government—one of Dewey's main works is *Democracy and education* (1966a [1916])—Steve understood the difference between democracy as an ideal and the realpolitik activities of representative government. Naively, I did not. To me our government was the epitome of all that was good and just in American society. In retrospect, I believe Steve saw his task not as telling me to recognize the error of my ways but of helping me broaden my awareness. I am grateful for this approach, and hope it is now part of me. Gradually I, along with hundreds of thousands of other college students, became aware that what the US government was doing in Vietnam and in the southern states of our country was a travesty on democracy and a tragedy on justice. I, like others, marched in protest. Although Steve approved of my actions, he also wanted his more radical groups to listen to my more moderate comments. While I never took Steve up on this offer, I did begin to adopt an attitude of listening to the other. Of entering into conversation, not dialogue. What moderate success I have had as a teacher, administrator, school board member, I attribute to the idea of "conversing with the other." Steve's own conversations moved from academia to union worker to real estate salesperson in a small New England town, to political volunteer (2008). At that time, he started reading the history of the American Constitution—a fascinating read. Toward the end of his life he asked me how one could include such readings in high school civics courses. As a Deweyian, he believed one should immerse oneself in what one was studying. The recent travesty and tragedy of the Bush presidency takes on a new light when set against the tumultuous times that gave birth to the American constitution.

Jacques Derrida makes the point that unless we can converse with death (*The gift of death*, 1995 [1992]) we really cannot appreciate life. Steve met death honestly. We emailed a lot about death and its relation to us. As an ethical culturist Steve believed that "when it is over, it is over." As a heretical Catholic, I share the same view. He asked me if my religion helped mitigate that fear—it does, it doesn't. As the cancer grew in his body, he became weaker and weaker; the messages fewer and fewer. I wrote, he did not reply. One day his daughter called me to say "My father has died. He wanted you to know."

Indeed my own life is richer for his presence. I pray his spirit will guide me when I cross over from life to death. Thank you Steve.

PART 2

Dewey, Piaget, Bruner, Whitehead
Process and Transformation

Introduction: Donna Trueit

William E. Doll's interpretations of Dewey, Whitehead, Bruner, and Piaget influence his curriculum theorizing—each in various ways contributing to the idea of learning as a transformational process in an evolving world. Doll's view that curriculum needs to develop as an interplay between and among learners, their experiences, and their culture comes forward in the grouping of essays which are also necessarily critical of a pre-set, standardized, goal-oriented curriculum such as that promoted by Ralph Tyler in the Tyler Rationale. In contrast with modernist accounts of an objective reality based on a stable world/cosmos, Doll's premise is a creative universe. Deriving from his deep, close readings of these "fab four," Dewey, Whitehead, Bruner and Piaget, themes that endure in Doll's work, developed and revisited throughout his career are: play, control, method, transformation, spirit/spirituality, creativity. There are eight essays in this section, written between 1972 and 2008, drawing on Doll's intellectual heroes. He also has his whipping boys, like Ramus, Taylor, and Tyler, influential characters who sit at critical bifurcation points in modern history and who, in Doll's writing, take the fall for the consequences.[1]

"A methodology of experience, part I" is the first major article following from his dissertation, published as the lead article in *Educational Theory*, in which Doll criticizes the prevailing model of education based on the Tyler Rationale. First situating the development of behavioral objectives historically and philosophically,

---

1 Whipping boy, according to the OED, is a "boy educated together with a young prince or royal personage, and flogged in his stead when he committed a fault that was considered to deserve flogging. Hence *allusively*."

Doll then refers to Joseph Schwab's Deweyan influenced reform of higher education, asserting the importance of practical experience in education—missing in most educational settings.

"Developing competence" is a condensation of three major papers ("Play and mastery", "A structural view of curriculum", and "Curriculum and change: Piaget's organismic origins" in which Doll deals with a distinction between competence and performance. In so doing he is countering behaviorist views that focus on performance (correct response to behavioral objectives) over students developing cognitive skills. Presenting three views of competence, in this chapter, those of Chomsky, Piaget, and Bruner, Doll claims a pedagogical field rich enough to support a new model of education for which he provides an example.

In "Beyond methods," providing rich historical insights into the development of a modernist reliance on method, a preplanned, controlled, standardized approach to activities—the one best way—out of which derive "teaching methods" for the transmission of knowledge, Doll sets the stage for Dewey's revolutionary approach to education, one that presents a very different method: the transformation of experience through reflective thinking. Dewey's experimental method encourages learners to do, to experience, to reflect, to interact, and to seek the problematics and possibilities inherent in a situation (*an* experience).

"Crafting an experience" is a note written to the students in a graduate seminar on pragmatism and spirituality. Doll provides his interpretation of the transformation of general experiential activity into "an experience," also enacting another Deweyan principle of articulating ideas in your own words, to make ideas your own.

In America, Piagetian thought is often associated with "ages and stages" and his vast corpus of biological work was relatively overlooked. Doll's close reading of Piaget's biological studies provided another way to conceive transformative development which, as Doll explains, needs to proceed as the child's own cognitive structures develop, moving through stages of equilibrium, disequilibrium and reequilibration, stressing interaction as key to transformation in cognitive growth (or learning).

Long inspired by Jerome Bruner's corpus of work, and particularly his essay, "Two modes of thought" (science/narrative; quantitative/qualitative), in Chapter 11 Doll pays homage to, and builds upon, Bruner's essay, developing the 3 S's—science, story, spirit—symbolized by a stylized heart representing the dynamic aliveness of good curriculum. In introducing a third (spirit) to Bruner's two (science and story), Doll complicates the relations between these elements, making connections to complexity theory (dynamical self-organizing systems) and to Michel Serres' use of a third space, both of which complicate the reductionism of modernist epistemologies.

"Keeping knowledge alive" deals with A. N. Whitehead's three modes of teaching/learning—romance, precision, and generalization and the dynamic interplay among them. Doll questions again the fundamental assumptions of traditional teaching and learning methods, making connections between Whitehead's own experiences of schooling and the development of his educational philosophy to provide direct pedagogical implications from Whitehead's abstract thoughts. Harkening back to a theme that runs through Doll's work, play is essential to keeping knowledge alive.

Chapter 13, written as a response to Jerome Proulx's (2008) article concerning differences between constructivism and Maturana and Varela's theories of cognition, is intended to continue the conversation, bringing forward a connection Doll made many years earlier between Piaget and Prigogine, a connection subsequently made by Prigogine himself. In his time Piaget was unable to fully articulate the dynamic process he envisioned (intuited?) in the transformational growth of children's cognitive development. Prigogine recognized Piaget's genetic epistemology as an open systems approach, one that emphasizes the interactions between organism and environment (à la Maturana and Varela) and cognitive schema transformation.

6

A METHODOLOGY OF EXPERIENCE, PART I

(1972)

Behavioral Objectives

During the decade just ended, the 1960s, behavioral objectives has probably been the most talked about subject in curriculum theory. In the early 60s it was common—with the advent of programmed instruction—to see such objectives as yet another panacea for America's educational ills. However, in a few years there appeared a number of critics questioning both its theory and practice. Today it is usual for symposia, journals, etc. to present the case in a pro–con format; in short, the bloom of enthusiasm has worn off, leaving for substance an unresolved but intriguing issue. That issue, simply put, is whether or not educational objectives should be framed exclusively, or even primarily, in behavioral terms. Behind this, of course, is another question, whether or not education itself should be goal oriented. The first question is concerned with the yea or nay of framing objectives behaviorally; the second, with objectives themselves.

One of the advantages advocated by those who favor behavioral objectives is that such a framework is more beneficial to both the student and the teacher by focusing attention on the learner's performance rather than on the teacher's. As Popham (1969) says:

> Precise objectives stated in terms of measurable learner behavior make it infinitely easier for the teacher to engage in curricular decisions. The clarity of precisely stated goals permits the teacher to make far more judicious choices regarding what ought to be in the curriculum.
>
> (p. 40)

Not only does this quote assume (probably validly) that there is a certain amount of precision gained by framing objectives behaviorally, but it also assumes, tacitly but definitely, that the whole notion of objectives implies predetermined and externally imposed ends—it being the teacher who determines "what ought to be in the curriculum." In fact I believe it fair to say, and shortly will attempt to prove, that behavioral objectives is a sub-category of the rather general notion that the process of education is best affected when means are separated from ends. It is this larger concept which is of interest to me; that is the idea of objectives themselves, regardless of the various adjectives attached, i.e. educational, instructional, behavioral.

Although the phrase "behavioral objectives" is itself rather new—having obtained popularity only in the past two decades—many of its basic aspects are as old as education itself. In terms of 20th century American education it is possible to find many of today's ideas operant in the writings of such pre-1930 authors as Bobbitt, Bode, Pressey. In terms of manifestations of behavior there is a tradition which goes back to the turn of the century and the "new psychology" of Watson, Thorndike and Judd. Finally the writings of Ralph Tyler span a period of 40+ years. Thus behavioral objectives does have a history and while Eisner (1967a) has done a good job in beginning to uncover it much work needs to be done. However, such an approach is not the one of this paper. To the extent that this paper is concerned with a historical focus on behavioral objectives it is from the year 1950 when Tyler published the syllabus for his course Education 360, *Basic principles of curriculum and instruction.*

This work, somewhat a landmark in its field—at least to the extent that it has served as a focal point for all subsequent proponents (and opponents) of behavioral objectives—is basically: "A rationale for viewing, analyzing and interpreting the curriculum and instructional program of an educational institution" (p. 1).

Toward this end Tyler's rationale is concerned with providing answers to "four fundamental questions":

1 What goals should a school seek?
2 What means should it use?
3 How should these means be organized?
4 How should the effectiveness of these means be evaluated?

A glance at these four shows three of them to be concerned with means and one with ends. Actually this is a bit misleading, for the first question is more concerned with how a school goes about choosing its goals than with the statement of what specific goals are in a school's best interests. As Tyler says, "in the final analysis objectives are a matter of choice," choice of the teachers, the administrators, the program developers—of "those responsible for the school" (p. 3)—but not of the students. To be prepared for this choice Tyler thinks the curriculum developer should be informed about the various alternative viewpoints of progressive and essentialist education as well as with various psychological, philosophical, and sociological theories of man. However, he has no preference for any specific one of these theories over another. Rather Tyler is concerned with the way the chosen goal is framed; his commitment is to framing all goals behaviorally.

> Objectives are sometimes stated as things which the instructor is to do ... but they are not really statements of educational ends. Since the real purpose of education is not to have the instructor perform certain activities to bring about significant changes in the students' patterns of behavior, it becomes important to recognize that any statement of the objectives of the school should be a statement of changes to take place in students.
>
> (p. 28)

Thus it can be seen that Tyler's monograph on the basic principles of curriculum and instruction is essentially a monograph on methods of implementing objectives already chosen. Within this methodology there are two assumptions operating. The first is that all education must be goal oriented; the second is that goals expressed in a behavioral manner can be more efficiently implemented than those expressed in other manners. As can be seen from the last quote this second assumption is one for which Tyler offers some support; namely, that objectives framed behaviorally are easier to evaluate, allow for individual differentiation, for more precise and specific formulation, and finally emphasize learning more than teaching. However, the first assumption, although prominent, is not supported. Tyler begins his monograph, on page three, with a lament that "many educational programs do not have clearly defined purposes," and then goes on to assert that while an unusual teacher may "do excellent educational work" without a "clear conception of goals" such goals are a prerequisite for any curriculum which is to be planned "systematically and intelligently." Beyond this assertion no further support for his position is given, the logic and inherent rationality of the position being simply assumed. A close reading of the monograph though reveals a key element in the assumption; namely, that ends are to be predetermined. In talking of the Deweyan idea of a learning experience as the resulting interaction between the learner and the external environment, Tyler says: "The teacher can provide an educational experience through setting up an environment and structuring the situation *so as to stimulate the desired type of reaction*" (p. 41; emphasis added).

Ironically this last quote is very non-Deweyan for it places the ends of the activity prior to and outside the activity itself. It is this separation of means from ends which forms the central focus of my criticism of behavioral objectives, while it is the integration of means with ends which will form the focus of my methodology of experience. Before going on to those sections of this paper, however, I would first like to make some overall comments on the pros and cons of behavioral objectives as each has developed in the literature.

Essentially it can be said that four categories of people could benefit from a behavioral approach: curriculum theorists, curriculum developers, teachers, and students. The theorists benefit by being able to approach education in a more systematic and planned manner, constructing taxonomies and hierarchies of learning. The taxonomies of Bloom (1956) and Krathwohl et al. (1964) as well as the structured hierarchy of Gagne (1965) are evidence of this trend. The developers of curriculum benefit from the "systems" approach, whereby feedback, testing, and measurement all become important. The work of Mager (1962) and Popham (1967) is illustrative of this trend. The teacher benefits by being able to integrate objectives with instruction more precisely than was possible before. She, or he, is also able to individualize the instructional program with varied objectives for each learner. The use of programmed instruction is illustration of this trend. Finally there is the student. It is assumed he will learn better (and more) when informed as to the goals desired of and for him. As Krathwohl says (Ryans and Krathwohl, 1965): "Students tend to concentrate on what counts. ..." If the student is informed ahead of time as to "what counts" then indeed he can, and it is hoped he will, concentrate better. At least his focus will be narrowed.

This statement by Krathwohl and similar ones by Popham (1969) and Tyler (1964)—all concerned with advantages to the student of his being pre-informed as to the goals and results expected of him warrant further attention. First of all the notion of the student being able to make an active contribution to the process of selecting objectives is almost totally absent prior to the mid-1960s; and even in the three works just cited the idea of a "student point of view" is most minimal, as well as new. Second, the consideration given to the student—and certainly behavioral objectives, especially in the writings of Ralph Tyler, has given a lot of consideration to the student—has been more negatively than positively oriented; that is, his contribution to the theory of behavioral objectives has been mostly through his lacks, needs, wants, or gaps. As Tyler says: the use of the word "need" often, "... represents a gap between some conception of a desirable norm, that is, some standard of philosophic value, and the actual status" (1950, p. 6).

Therefore, in determining behavioral goals it is first necessary to find "the present status of the students," and then compare that status "to acceptable norms in order to identify the gaps or needs." Third, the student's role in the actual carrying out of the objectives has been more that of passive receiver than of active creator; that is, the student has been expected to receive habits, training, enculturation, and indoctrination before he is considered to have a valid point of view or be allowed to function as an active agent.

Educators have often referred to the above as the shoehorn concept of learning; John Dewey has emphasized the static view of knowledge such a concept implies; and Herbert Kliebard has pointed out that while educators might have been willing to accept such a view of, and role for, students in the 1950s it is hard to see them making the same acceptances in the 1970s. For myself, I am reminded of Arthur Lovejoy's observation that virtually all past systems, social, political, educational (Lovejoy pays particular attention to the founding of the American Constitution) have been predicated on the assumption that man's human nature is essentially evil. Given the opportunity to be his own person man will inevitably and predictably cause chaos and holocaust. The traditional way to overcome this Augustinian and Calvinistic view of man's nature has been to: (1) indoctrinate man from an early age on, (2) submit him to the guidance of those who are "right," or more knowledgeable, (3) create systems of government and structures of life where controls and checks prevent him from being his own agent, or in modern terminology from "doing his own thing." Evidence that this view of human nature is still active in modern day society can be found fictionally in William Golding's *Lord of the flies* and factually in Herbert Kohl's *Thirty-six children*. While it would be absurd to say that behavioral objectivists hold such a view of human nature, it is possible to find marked similarities between this view and the attitude objectivists display towards student points of view. The attempt here is not to find a nefarious, and not so subtle, way of discrediting behavioral objectives and objectivists, but rather to call attention to the point that Eisner has recently been making; namely that there is a definite, if tacit, connection between behavioral objectives and historically established philosophies—both of education and of man. Those connections need to be explored, by the behavioral objectivists and by others. The next Part on means and ends will attempt to explore one such connection.

To those who find behavioral objectives objectionable (and by now it's obvious I must be classified in that group) one of the most common specific criticisms raised is that of manipulation. The argument runs that the more a methodology is designed to produce specified forms of behavior then the more is that methodology advocating manipulation. As Arnstine (1964) has pointed out in his article on programmed instruction—the catalyst which threw behavioral objectives into such prominence—the manipulation of people is not only contrary to American ideals about the way a democratic society should function, but is also contrary to the accepted notion of the way education should function within such a society. As he says: "If this [the shaping of human beings to predetermined ends] were really the way in which Americans wanted their children to be educated, then this nation would be indistinguishable from any other totalitarian society" (Arnstine, 1964, pp. 338–339).

A second objection, similar to the first and arising from it, is a much harder one to focus. It can be found in Bruner's statement (1961) that the art and technique of inquiry can be developed only by engaging in inquiry; in Macdonald's statement (1965) that objectives can be known in any real sense only after completion of the act of instruction; and in Eisner's point (1967a) that the predetermination of objectives ignores the very heart of the interactive process, namely the continual grouping and regrouping of elements within both the environment and the learner. I would like to frame all of these statements within the general structure Dewey develops concerning the logical and psychological organization of subject matter. The former is the organization of relationships within a discipline and between disciplines into as structured, ordered, and logical a manner as can be devised at any given time. The latter is the organization that exists between these logical relationships and the individual's own thought constructs. As Dewey says: "There is a strong temptation to assume that presenting subject matter in its perfected form provides a royal road to learning" (Dewey, 1966a [1916], p. 220).

This is the difficulty with programmed instruction, or even with textbook instruction. However, there is also another temptation for all goal-oriented educators and that is to assume that the psychological organization can be done, or made more efficient, if one individual does it for another. But the very nature of the concept requires that the individual do his own organizing. Not only is there no royal road to learning, neither are there maps which the individual must merely memorize.

What is at issue here, of course, is a concept of education which is different from mere training, a concept of education which is based upon man's unique powers of consciousness, reflection, symbol manipulation, and the like. The challenge then, to those who hold this concept of education, is to devise an educational methodology which is based on the individual's own assimilation of experience but which will not prescribe what those experiences are to be; a methodology which will have within it relationships between the logical and the psychological, but which will not impose the former on the latter. This is what the methodology of experience I am to propose later is designed to do; but first I would like to devote a Part to means and ends, for it seems to me that this is the very heart of the behavioral objectives controversy and also the origin from which any new methodology must emerge.

Ends and Means

Behavioral objectivists feel, as Popham (1969) has pointed out, that ends should be separated from means in as clear and distinct a manner as possible. Further they see the two as having quite different functions within an educational system, and see the success of that system lying in the clear, specific, and behavioral description of those functions. Many of the quotes already given provide support for the foregoing statements, but for emphasis a few more will be given here:

> It would seem obvious that ends must be specified if any appropriate choice is to be made of means.
>
> (Louise Tyler, 1969, p. 100)

> ... the determination of what the instructional goals should be is essentially a curricular, not an instructional, decision. The purpose of goal-referenced instructional models is to achieve more efficiently whatever goals have been selected.
>
> (Popham, 1969, p. 38)

All aspects of the educational program are really means to accomplish basic educational purposes.

(Ralph Tyler, 1950, p. 3)

When one specifies explicit ends for an instructional program there is no necessary implication that the means to achieve those ends are also specified.

(Popham, 1969, p. 47)

In all of these quotes there is either an explicit or tacit assumption that ends should be separated from means and determined prior to any decision about means. As Louise Tyler (1969) says there is a basic need to pre-specify objectives, a need which by its very rationality seems obvious. In fact it seems so obvious—as Robert Guttchen has pointed out in his article on Dewey's differences with Mill over the separation of means from ends—that we naturally assume the categories of means and ends to answer not only a genuine psychological need, but also to lie "at the core of any notion of rational as well as moral activity."

What could be more common and commonplace than the idea that men seek ends and that when they go about this rationally, they draw upon their best knowledge so that the means that they use will be most likely to assure success?

(Guttchen, 1969, p. 28)

John Stuart Mill felt the logic of this position to be obvious and devoted the last chapter of his sixth book on *A system of logic* to its exposition. The heart of this "Mill model" on the separation of ends from means lies in the following paragraph:

The relation in which rules of art stand to doctrines of science may be thus characterized. *The art proposes to itself an end to be attained, defines the end, and hands it over to the science. The science receives it, considers it as a phenomenon or effect to be studied, and having investigated its causes and conditions, sends it back to art with a theorem of the combination of circumstances by which it could be produced.* Art then examines these combinations of circumstances, and according as any of them are or are not in human power, pronounces the end attainable or not. *The only one of the premises, therefore, which Art supplies is the original major premise, which asserts that the attainment of the given end is desirable.* Science then lends to Art the proposition (obtained by a series of inductions or of deductions) that the performance of certain actions will attain the end. From these premises Art concludes that the performance of these actions is desirable, and finding it also practicable, converts the theorem into a rule or precept.

(Mill, 1965 [1843], pp. 139–140; emphasis added)

Bypassing for the moment the difficulties of style and wording[1] the main ideas of Mill can be expressed sequentially as follows:

1   Art proposes an end.
2   Science supplies a formulation of means.
3   Art judges the means practicable or not.
4   If practicable, Art converts the formulation into a rule of action.

Just how strong a separation Mill envisioned between means and ends becomes evident a few pages later when he says: "But though the reasonings which connect the end or purpose of every art with its means belong to the domain of Science, the definition of the end itself belongs exclusively to Art, and forms its peculiar province" (p. 144).

One of the difficulties with such a separation is that it puts the ends, to use Mill's phrase, in "a class by themselves"; it separates the "ought" proposition from the "will" propositions and removes the former from all empirical validation. Thus the ends, the very basis of the whole structure, are often no more than mere personal preferences and unassailable by the empirical evidence accumulated; for such evidence deals strictly with the means, not with the ends. This problem has been recognized by both Tyler and Mill, and each has attempted the same solution. Mill says (p. 145) that everyone framing ends must be prepared to justify his approbation in terms of "general premises," which general premises form the Doctrine of Ends and are universally recognized by all rational men. Tyler (1950, pp. 3–6) recognizes that "in the final analysis objectives are matters of choice," but also believes that certain "acceptable norms" exist. However, as Kliebard (1971) has pointed out, this phrase masks a very elusive concept: just what are these norms, and to whom are they acceptable? Much the same sort of analysis can be made of other behavioral objectivists. In fact, in general the removing of ends to a separate class by themselves gives to these ends a special status since they are now no longer required to prove themselves in the arena of justifiability. Often such categorization serves as a shield behind which exists an individual's most cherished, unexamined, and unproven prejudices.

The exclusive status of ends is, however, not the main objection Guttchen or Dewey would bring to the Mill model; their prime objection centers around the very rationality of the model. As Guttchen says, "[That] the bright lights of rationality

---

1   For Mill, Art is basically modes of action—practical action—while Science is modes of logical organization, or categories, or principles. Thus Mill says: "Art in general consists of the truths of science, arranged in the most convenient order for practice, instead of the order which is the most convenient for thought. Science groups and arranges its truths so as to enable us to take in at one view as much as possible of the general order of the universe. Art, though it must assume the same general laws, follows them only into such of their detailed consequences as have led to the formation of rules of conduct … " (p. 149).

and moral action shine where ends are clear and means are well chosen...[is] one of the grandest oversimplifications that men, as well as most philosophers, have ever entertained" (1969, pp. 29–42).

The rationality of clear ends and distinct means is really an *ex post facto* rationality; it is the result of a construct man has placed upon his completed actions as a simplification of what he would have liked those actions to have been. There is in such a construct all the logical value a simple and idealized structure has; but as an account of how man psychologically approaches, or even frames, problems it is woefully inadequate. Individuals—at all levels of intellectuality—approach their problems much more in the manner of a man stumbling (sometimes quite skillfully) "from pillar to post," than in the manner of a man working "with a clear blue-print in hand." Modern philosophers of science such as Thomas Kuhn, Michael Polanyi, and Stephen Toulmin have, in recent decades, been emphasizing this same point in regard to the work of scientists. They say that intuition, imagination, perseverance, commitment to another field or idea, and in-depth knowledge of at least two fields are some of the characteristics of those who make scientific advances. Bruner, of course, made such thinking quite central to his argumentation in *The process of education* (1960).

In the above there is a strong resemblance to what Eisner has been saying about teachers not using educational objectives. This fact may mean that the objectives have not been clearly enough defined, as the objectivists would argue; but it may also mean that objectives themselves are not useful devices for planning action. As Eisner says, following James Macdonald:

> The ends achieved are not preconceived but reflected upon in retrospect rather than in prospect. This, I believe, is what most teachers do in the process of curriculum development and what I suspect most of those reading this article do.
>
> (Eisner, 1967b, p. 279)

There is also a strong similarity with Kliebard's query that: "One wonders whether the long-standing insistence by curriculum theorists that the first step in making a curriculum be the specification of objectives has any merit whatsoever" (Kliebard, 1971, pp. 269–270).

Kliebard makes this query because while he realizes the key to Ralph Tyler and behavioral objectivists in general is the clear formation of objectives, he also realizes that Tyler's elaborate scheme for determining objectives is really no more than an assertion that objectives ultimately originate in value positions. This is, of course, to say so little about the process of selecting objectives, especially when there are a variety of value positions, as to be virtually meaningless.

The issue in contention here is that of objectives themselves. In the history of Western thought there has been the long-standing tradition that the goals and purposes of man's activity must lie outside that activity; that life itself is a preparation for something else. Around this "something else" there has existed a halo of rationality, clarity, definiteness, intellectuality and abstractness; in fact, these qualities might be said to define the limits of the theoretical as opposed to the practical. Educationally this has meant that goals and ends have been predetermined, either by God for his subjects, or by the priest for his people, or by the teacher for his students. Within this framework ends are drastically separated from means; they are, as Guttchen has said and as Mill has demonstrated, in a class by themselves. However, there are a number of people in a number of fields who are quite dissatisfied with this general framework. For them ends need to be brought into a closer and more integrative relationship with means. Thus in the writings of Eisner, Kliebard, Kuhn, Macdonald, Toulmin, etc. one can see echoes of the model Dewey proposed as an alternative to Mill.

The Dewey model, such as it may be—for Dewey's ideas on ends and means have not received the attention Mill's have, and hence don't warrant the label "model"— is probably best expressed in the following quote from *Human nature and conduct:*

> Our problem now concerns the nature of ends, that is ends-in-view or aims. The essential elements in the problem have already been stated. It has been pointed out that the ends, objectives, of conduct are those foreseen consequences which influence present deliberation and which finally bring it to rest by furnishing an adequate stimulus to overt action. Consequently ends arise and function within action. They are not, as current theories too often imply, things lying beyond activity at which the latter is directed. They are not strictly speaking ends or termini of action at all. They are terminals of deliberation, and so turning points in activity.
>
> (Dewey, 1957 [1922], p. 207)

Dewey then goes on to say that many theorists agree in placing ends beyond human activity, even though they disagree as to what those ends are. Hence many critics of Mill and the utilitarians while denying pleasure as the "outside and beyond" goal, nevertheless feel it necessary to have some goal "to induce action" and in which action will terminate. This, of course, is reminiscent of Tyler and other behavioral objectivists who proclaim the value of such outside and beyond goals, but sidestep the issue of what those goals are, or should be.

The problem, as Dewey sees it and as can be determined from the above quote, revolves around the distinction between ends-in-themselves and ends-in-view. The ends-in-themselves (or fixed ends) view assumes that ends are separate from, and both prior and superior to, means. Thus "the relation of ends-means is unilateral, proceeding exclusively from end to means." This means that all aims or purposes are directed and controlled by the end, with only those aims that coincide with the end having any validity. Such a concept of activity gives the teacher, or the program planner, a certain moral superiority that the participator in the activity never can have. Further, Dewey says the setting up of prior ends, with the justification of action as a means to that end, leads to narrowness. It leads to narrowness because: "Fixed and separate ends reflect a projection of our own fixed and non-interacting compartmental habits. We see only consequences which correspond to our habitual courses" (p. 215).

Dewey then goes on to give the example of generation after generation of people being shown targets which they had no part in constructing, and being continually urged to shoot; they would eventually gather the notion that "the targets existed in order that men might be forced to be active." But activity (including learning as well as throwing or shooting) is natural to man; the targets (varying from generation to generation, or from individual to individual) are constructed and placed by man in order that he can do his activity better. Thus, ends are "turning points in activity," not termini of activity.

Finally Dewey says that the doctrine of fixed or predetermined ends: (1) diverts attention from the examination of consequences, and (2) hinders the intelligent creation of purpose. It does the former by emphasizing, not the ends themselves, but the degree of efficiency with which the ends are achieved. In short, the correlation is between the ends and the means, not between the ends and their consequences. In regard to the second point—the intelligent creation of purpose—Dewey says that such creation can occur only when the individual has the opportunity to formulate his own purposes, act upon that formulation, and receive the consequences thereof. But a fixed ends approach emphasizes not the process of creation, but rather the product.

All of this is reminiscent (to me at least) of Guttchen's point that the Mill model is essentially a production—or thing—oriented one; of R. S. Peters' remark that to be educated is not to have arrived at a certain place, but to travel with a different view; and of Eisner's distinction between defining an objective and establishing a direction. Dewey's ends-in-view framework, of course, is designed to do the latter. Ends in this sense arise out of natural effects or consequences: they are the result of acts which at first are just hit or stumbled upon, but which upon reflection are desired for themselves. Thus, ends become projected or probable consequences, not removed from the activity in question, but turning points in that activity. As Dewey says:

> Men shoot and throw. At first this is done as an "instinctive" or natural reaction to some situation. The result when it is observed gives new meaning to the activity. Henceforth men in shooting think of it in terms of its outcome; they act intelligently or have an end. Liking the activity … they not only "take aim" … but they find or make targets at which to aim. This is the origin and nature of "goals" of action. They are ways of defining and deepening the meaning of activity. Having an end or aim is thus characteristic of present activity.
>
> (1957 [1922], p. 209)

For Dewey ends are quite different, and serve a very different function than for Mill, Whereas Mill sees ends existing outside activity, Dewey's idea of ends as turning points in activity places them integrally within the continuum of human experience. To develop these ideas in a model then it is necessary first to explicate Dewey's concept of experience, for it is within this framework that he places his famous dictum that all ends are but means to further ends.

A Methodology of Experience

Simply stated, Dewey's theory of experience is that in all ordinary occurrences there is a certain quality which pervades the situation, and which the individual first becomes cognizant of in a non-cognitive manner. That is, the immediate or primary qualities of an experience are felt or had; they are not intellectualized. Reflection, however, is itself a natural trait and once the quality becomes felt it is also then the subject for analysis and scrutiny. This cognitive aspect of an experience is what adds depth and meaning to the experience, transforming the situation from a mere occurrence to an experience—in the sense of "Have I just had an experience!"— and also laying the foundation for an increased quality when a new, but similar, experience occurs. Thus a man sipping wine first has a sensory awareness of the experience, either liking or disliking it. After reflection, analysis, comparison, and repeated tastings, new meaning is infused into the original experience. When he next tastes a similar wine—no experience had can be exactly re-had—the quality of that experience will be greater than the quality of the previous experience.

In a sense this theory of experience is Dewey's complete cosmology; that is, his philosophy, his psychology, his educational and social theory can all be placed within this framework. Educationally this means there is no end to education beyond itself, no purpose to growth other than more growth, and every end itself becomes a means to a further end. Dewey illustrates this in his chapter on "Aims in education," wherein he describes his own conception of aims, as well as his differences with the Mill model. He says:

> ... the aim of education is to enable individuals to continue their education— or that the object and reward of learning is continued capacity for growth .... [W]e are not concerned, therefore, with finding an end outside of the educative process to which education is subordinate. Our whole conception forbids. We are concerned with the contrast which exists when aims belong within the process in which they operate and when they are set up from without.
>
> (Dewey, 1966a [1916], p. 100)

When the latter occurs—when aims are predetermined and by others—then some (notably the student or learner) will find their aims "determined by an external dictation," and existing as a "means to more ulterior ends of others." However, when they are not set up from without then "they arise from the free growth of the individual's own experience," and can truly be called personal.

For Dewey this point about the learner formulating his own ends or aims is a very key one; it not only lies at the heart of his subordination of teaching to learning (that is, more emphasis on the psychological than the logical) but it also lies at the heart of his concept of experience. Dewey sees learning as a natural and important by-product of human activity; as such it is the activity, not the learning, which provides the basic framework. If the human is naturally inquisitive, reflective, and organizing then the emphasis in education should be on the patterns of inquiry, reflection, and organization, not on the products. Production, knowledge, learning are but by-products of the active process of inquiry; and this process of inquiry, since it is natural, cannot efficiently and should not morally be determined by one for another. As Dewey says:

> From one angle, almost everything I have written is a commentary on the fact that situations are immediate in their direct occurrence, and mediating, and mediated in the temporal continuum constituting life-experience. I have pointed out that one person cannot communicate an experience as immediate to another person. He can only invite that other person to institute the conditions by which the person himself will have that kind of situation the conditions for which are stated in discourse. Even if this difficult condition is fulfilled, there is no assurance that any one will so act as to have the experience. The horse led to water is not forced to drink.
>
> (1939, p. 546)

A system of education, then, based on an individual's personal experience should be one which allows the individual the opportunity to develop freely those experiences within a social context. This last phrase—develop those experiences within a social context—is most important, for experiences *do* need to be developed: they do not come into existence full-blown, and they do not receive meaning in isolation from other people. The development of experience requires dialogue and discussion.

The challenge then is in creating an educational structure wherein each individual can develop his own experiences. This structure should not be so rigid and pre-planned that the individual has little chance to do his own development, but neither should it be so loose and flexible that development is not encouraged. In regard to the evils of a rigid structure Dewey has this to say:

> The vice of externally imposed ends has deep roots. Teachers receive them from superior authorities; these authorities accept them from what is current in the community. The teachers impose them upon children. As a first consequence, the intelligence of the teacher is not free; it is confined to receiving aims laid

down from above. Too *rarely* is *the individual teacher so free* from the dictation of authoritative supervisor, textbooks on methods, prescribed courses of study, etc., *that he can let his mind come to close quarters with the pupil's mind*, and the subject matter. This distrust of the teacher's experience is then reflected in lack of confidence in the responses of pupils. The latter receive their aims through a double or treble external imposition, and are *constantly confused by the conflict between the aims which are natural to their own experience* at the time *and those in which they are taught to acquiesce.* Until the democratic criterion of the intrinsic significance of every growing experience is recognized, we shall be intellectually confused by the demand for adaption to external aims.

(Dewey, 1966a [1916], pp. 108–109; emphasis added)

In regard to setting up a structure which allows, and encourages, development from within, Dewey, of course, favors the scientific method or what he called the creative use of intelligence. This is essentially the formulation of hypotheses, the observation of results produced in the light of those hypotheses, and the reformulation of other hypotheses. Within this procedure the consideration of probable consequences in relation to those actually produced, and the consideration of various alternatives are both very important. The individual learns not merely by planning, but by checking the plans made with the results produced; and a variety of alternatives not only gives a better base for comparison but also makes unexpected but often needed readjustments possible. Again as Dewey says—in a very Schwabian type of phrase: "Where only a single outcome has been thought of ... one only steams ahead toward the mark. Sometimes such a narrow course may be effective. But if unexpected difficulties offer themselves, one has not as many resources at command ..." (1966a [1916] p. 103).

The foregoing remarks about creating educational procedures based on the development of experience where ends arise within the activity, and where actual consequences are continually being checked with planned or probable consequences brings to mind Thomas Kuhn's observations about the nature of science. Kuhn, in his book *The structure of scientific revolutions* (1962), points out that textbooks present the progress of science as orderly and cumulative; that is, one disclosure leads inevitably and logically to the next. However, Kuhn says, such an ordering is an *ex post facto* ordering and in reality scientific progress is a very halting and stumbling thing, filled with periods of crisis and doubt, and finally based more on personal commitment than on any other one factor. The prime example Kuhn gives is of Copernicus' commitment to the harmony and beauty of neo-Platonic mathematics. According to this commitment the epicycles of Ptolemy were too unharmonious to be real, and so Copernicus made other postulates—notably a moving earth and a stable sun. Copernicus' immediate successor, Kepler, shared his commitment but those who next followed were far more interested in the results of Copernicus' and Kepler's theories than in the commitments which caused those theories to come into being. Thus they took these original ideas and tested them under a tremendous variety of circumstances. In these testings the original theories were changed, modified, altered, and continually reworked. It is in this stage, between Galileo and Newton, when an idea was accepted, but also tested under new and novel circumstances, that Copernican astronomy made its biggest advances. The point that Kuhn makes from this is that science makes progress *from*, but not necessarily *toward*.

> The developmental process described in this essay has been a process of evolution from primitive beginnings—a process whose successive stages are characterized by an increasingly detailed and refined understanding of nature. But nothing that has been or will be said makes it a process of evolution toward anything.
>
> (1962, p. 169)

This idea could easily be applied to Dewey's concept of personal experiences. Growth in such experiences proceeds from commitment out into the complexities of the subject being studied: a move not toward a predetermined goal but from the simple to the complex, from the gross to the refined, from the psychological to the logical. This, however, is not the method of the Mill model nor of behavioral objectives. The teaching of subtraction to elementary school children can be taken as a case in point. There the usual method is for the teacher, or textbook writer, to choose a particular way and then have the child drilled in as many examples as possible. But it would be possible for the child to devise his own method and then test that method in a variety of cases. Over a number of years—say second grade through fifth—the class, or individuals, would develop a number of methods, each one applicable to certain cases, but no one universally satisfactory. Indeed this is just the case: in a decimal system no one method of subtraction works efficiently in all cases: ones, zeroes and nines all cause troubles. Here the student would not only gain a facility with subtraction, but he would also gain insight into the logical complexities of algebra and number theory, all through the development of his own experiences. The same case can be made for the reorganization of those studies such as literature, composition, and history which involve a greater reliance on value judgment. In place of wrong answer difficulties, one could substitute peer group opinion and consensus. All of this is a fine lead into Schwab.

In his most recent writings, notably *College curriculum and student protest* (1969) and *The practical: A language for curriculum* (1970), Schwab has been advocating the development of college curricula in accord with the structure of the practical rather than with the structure of the theoretical. The Deweyan distinction is essentially a plea for making active, particular problems the center of inquiry rather than the "construction of taxonomies," "pursuit of global principles," and "search for stable sequences." Schwab shares with Dewey a basic distrust of the theoretical as an *ex post facto* reconstruction; hence, although such a reconstruction is logical and orderly, it is also quite irrelevant to the actual processes of inquiry that brought about the result. As Schwab says:

> The subject matter of the theoretic is always something taken to be universal or extensive or pervasive and is investigated as if it were constant from instance to instance and impervious to changing circumstances. The most obvious examples are: mass, equivalence, time, igneous rock, homo sapiens, electrons etc. The subject matter of the practical, on the other hand, is always something taken as concrete and particular and treated as indefinitely susceptible to circumstance, and therefore highly liable to unexpected change: this student, in that school, on the South Side of Columbus, during the mayorality of Ed Tweed etc. ....This is to say that theoretic problems are states of mind. Practical problems, on the other hand, arise from states of affairs in relation to ourselves.
>
> (1969, p. 3)

Schwab would like to make all education—especially formal schooling—practical in the sense of dealing with these particular and personal states of affairs. However, he—again like Dewey—does not see the immediate experiences of the student as valuable without development.

The method of development he advocates is that of putting the student in very direct contact with the problems and practices within a field. Towards this end he advocates that students sit in (listening *en masse*) on faculty meetings, board of directors meetings, scholarly seminars, etc. He advocates that they be given varying degrees of responsibility—including heading committees, marking papers, drawing up courses, etc.—and be required to experience the results of the actions they take; their responsibilities should be neither sham nor token. Finally, he advocates that their courses be structured so that they come into contact in a personal manner with conflict, compromise, and complexity. What Schwab wants to do here is create a sense of community where ideas and personality will come into open conflict, but where compromise will also emerge; this he feels can be accomplished if education divorces itself from rigid principles and deals eclectically with particular problems. Once students realize the complexity of problems and once administrators and faculty are held accountable to the general community for both their actions and their stated thoughts, then Schwab believes such compromise will become natural. More importantly Schwab believes compromise, that is community participation and decision, to be the essential ingredient in future social progress.

Throughout all of Schwab there is a definite emphasis on education (schooling) as the development of experience, not as the place or means by which information gets transferred from one to another. In fact, information itself is but a means to practical decision making; and hence, education should be so structured that decisions can grow from personal and practical experiences. Within such a concept of education ends cannot be imposed from the outside but indeed must emerge from the actual process of decision making.

Summary and Conclusion

In this paper I first analyzed some of the issues surrounding behavioral objectives and then placed that analysis and the issues involved within the larger framework of ends separated from means (the Mill model). While there is a rather natural rationality to this model Dewey showed deficiencies in it and presented another model, that of ends arising from within activity. I then used this framework of Dewey's to develop an alternative to behavioral objectives, an alternative in which the goals, activities, and behaviors of the student are not determined *for* him, but rather *by* him. In this model it is the process of experiencing, in the sense of both doing and receiving the results of doing, which becomes foci.

Indeed there needs to be more work done on this model than I have presented here. For one thing, Dewey's concept of inquiry and his theory of knowledge are both important, but too complex for this paper; for another, a more detailed study of ends and means needs to be undertaken; and for a third, there needs to be developed a stronger connection between Dewey's concept of experience and the theories of modern philosophers of science. However, it appears to me that even with these projects unfinished it is possible to see within this paper the outlines of a very real and very viable alternative to behavioral objectives. If a new era in curriculum is to occur, it may well be along the lines presented here.

7

DEVELOPING COMPETENCE

(1984)

In keeping with the theme of this conference—that of reassessing competence—I would like to argue that competence can and should be developed in the schools, and that the curriculum design needed for such development will be radically different from the performative one now in use. I will begin my argument by recapitulating the competence–performance distinction I've made elsewhere (Doll, 1977) and then move on to an analysis of the competence concept in Chomsky, Piaget, Bruner. I will conclude with curriculum recommendations, including an outline of the model I believe should be employed for developing competence. I am excited about the possibilities such a model holds for American schooling but pessimistic about its adoption.

All of us in education are, of course, knowledgeable about the now-waning competency-based education movement. This movement was—I like to put it in the past tense—but another variation of the knowledge-copy view of learning which dominated American schooling and curriculum during so much of the 20th century. Others at this conference have and will continue to draw connections between this view of learning and the industrial–mechanistic society in which we live. For myself I wish only to point out that the competency-based movement equated, wrongly, competence with performance, and in so doing did disservice not only to the word and notion of competence, but also to a very exciting idea which I believe holds great pedagogic potential.

It hardly seems necessary today to cite examples from the competency movement equating competence with performance, or to state that the movement was a part of a broader behaviorist–positivist perspective. However, lest some be unaware of these connections let me cite two quotations. Both come from the Hall and Jones (1976) book, *Competency-based education: A process for the improvement of education*. With a title like that and carrying an imprimatur from Robert Howsam, it is obvious the authors believed strongly in the movement and its efficacy. The first quotation comes from a Part analyzing the foundations of the movement and states that "the prime characteristic of competency-based education is an emphasis on specification of learner outcomes in terms of behavioral objectives" (p. 6).

The second quotation defines competency as "a statement that describes the observable demonstration of a composite of the specific skills" (pp. 29–30). The sentences following this second quotation state that competency (a word which in this form bothers me) is "a description of performances," performances that somehow are "integrated" with "a set of related skills and knowledge." This quotation shows that at the very time leaders in the movement were equating competence with performance they were also realizing that competence was somehow not merely performance; that it was at least "a composite ... greater than the sum of the individual skills" (pp. 29–30).

The words themselves—competence and performance—are, as any etymological dictionary will show, and as I've argued previously (Doll, 1977), of quite different origin and have different thrusts or senses. Performance refers essentially to a "doing," particularly to a "doing" which is "completed, finished, achieved." It originated as a word to distinguish between promises made but not completed and those completed. Hence, performance is a task finished. It carries no judgment of value as to how well the task is done, just that it is done. Competence refers essentially to a state of being or to a capacity. One who is competent is one who has a certain "fitness, sufficiency or aptitude"; or to take the word's Latin derivation, a competent person is one who possesses a certain confluence, "symmetry, conjunction, or meeting together" of powers which allow him or her "to adequately deal with a situation." In short, performance is the outward and public manifestation of underlying and internal powers. The problem, of course, lies in determining just what these powers are, and in determining the relation which exists between them and their performance manifestations. Unfortunately, these powers cannot be determined directly, but must always be inferred from observable performances. The simple solution, which certain radical behaviorists like Skinner have taken, is to deny the efficacy of the competence concept and to work exclusively at the level of performance. Those in the competency movement have not, to my knowledge, made such a strong theoretical statement; but they are operating out of a similar framework. That is, they are simplistically equating competence with performance and assuming that those who perform well are competent and those who perform poorly are incompetent. This is evidenced in their development of performance checklists as indicators of competence. But as Chomsky (1964) has said:

> A person might memorize the performance table and perform on various simple-minded tests exactly as the performer who knows the rules of arithmetic, but this would not, of course, show that he knows these rules ....

> The deeper question concerns the kinds of structures the person has succeeded in mastering and internalizing. ... For anyone concerned with intellectual processes ... it is the question of competence that is fundamental. Obviously one can find out about competence only by studying performance, but this study must be carried out in devious and clever ways, if any serious result is to be obtained.
>
> (p. 36)

As a structuralist I agree with Chomsky that there are internal structures of competence underlying performance, and I wish to argue that a curriculum model based on this assumption will be more exciting and productive than the current performance model. Evaluation of this model will require the "devious and clever ways" Chomsky mentions, for competence cannot be assessed easily or directly from performance. As Nel Noddings (1980) points out, performance is neither a necessary nor a sufficient criterion for competence. Yet the two are related, and to possess or pursue one without the other is to possess or pursue little.

Chomsky

Noam Chomsky has undoubtedly done more than anyone else to illuminate the competence–performance distinction. In doing so he has been operating on at least three levels: that of linguistics, that of rules, and that of humanness. Each of these levels gives a sense of competence that cannot be found by taking performance at its face value. Linguistically, Chomsky has been impressed with the fact that mistakes in performance are not necessarily mistakes in competence. A stutterer may well know the rules of grammar, or a concert pianist may well give a poor performance, because of fatigue, nervousness, or other personal factors. Of even more import for Chomsky is the fact that in their grammatical development young children acquiring a native language evidence both a type of logic and a sense of generative creativity in their mistakes (i.e. the boy "runned" the dog). Further, all children, regardless of experience and genetic inheritance, go through this process. Thus for Chomsky there must be some sort of innate patterning, universal to all people, underlying language acquisition. This innate or deeper patterning is far more important, Chomsky believes, than the experience–response patterns behaviorists rely on so heavily.

This structural patterning is indicative, Chomsky (1968) believes, of some principle other than the behaviorist ones of associations and experiences operating when an individual speaks. This principle he calls "mind," and for its history he refers back to the Cartesians of the 17th century.

> The Cartesians tried to show that when the theory of corporeal body is sharpened and clarified and extended to its limits, it is still incapable of

accounting for facts that are obvious to introspection ... In particular, it cannot account for the normal use of human language ... [nor can it explain] the basic properties of thought. Consequently it becomes necessary to invoke an entirely new principle—in Cartesian terms to postulate a second substance whose existence is thought.

(p. 6)

This new principle has a "creative aspect" to it, and can be found in "the distinctively human ability to express new thoughts" and to understand new thoughts, all "within the framework of an 'instituted language'" (p. 6). This framework, Chomsky believes, is formed by the grammar rules underlying a language. Knowledge of these rules is knowledge of the language's competence or structure, and individuals display this competence when they perform with language. But since performance brings in many factors other than competence, what is important in performance is not the "correctness" or "incorrectness" of the performance, but the connection between the rules and the performance. Chomsky's reason for emphasizing the rule–performance connection is that he believes the correctness of a performance to be cultural and hence arbitrary, while the rule–performance connection he believes to be universal, innate, and indicative of the very essence of human thought. In this generating aspect of linguistic competence, humans are displaying the nature of mind.

> The most striking aspect of linguistic competence is what we may call the "creativity of language," that is, the speaker's ability to produce new sentences, sentences that are immediately understood by other speakers although they bear no physical resemblances to sentences which are "familiar."
>
> Normal use of language involves the production and interpretation of sentences that are similar to sentences that have been heard before only in that they are generated by the rules of the same grammar.
>
> (Chomsky, 1966, p. 11)

Young children acquire this competence or knowledge of rules at a very young age and without specific training. Once acquired they are able to convey to others thoughts, feelings, judgments, and perceptions of a subtle kind (Chomsky, 1975, p. 4). Thus the real power of a language, or of a person, lies at the competence level. This competence allows one to generate an infinite variety of sentences from a finite set of basic structures and rules. The educational task then, as Chomsky has been saying, is to get beyond performance to competence.

In working at this second level—that of the universality and power of rules—Chomsky has posited a specific attribute to human beings, the ability to understand and generate language. On one hand this ability is language specific, on the other hand it is reflective of the more universal powers of the human mind. At the language level Chomsky believes humans are "wired," or genetically programmed, to understand a language. Fancifully Chomsky calls this ability a Language Acquisition Device (LAD), or a "black box." However, at another level this language ability is not language specific, but is indicative of those more universal traits of thought called mind. Thus, Chomsky (1975) speaks of a vision competence and a mathematics competence. As he says: "[L]anguage is a mirror of the mind in a deep and significant sense. It is a product of human intelligence, created anew in each individual by operations that lie far beyond the reach of will or consciousness" (p. 4).

All this leads to a third level in Chomsky's competence–performance distinction. Quite simply Chomsky (1977) believes there to be something unique about the human species:

> Any objective scientist must be struck by the qualitative differences between human beings and other organisms, as much as by the difference between insects and vertebrates. Even the most superficial observation suffices to show that there are qualitative differences between humans and other complex organisms which must be explained.
>
> (p. 75)

This explanation will come only when we are willing to posit the notion of mind and to study this notion in terms of the competence which underlies human acts. It is this knowledge which is of most worth.

Piaget

In the Part just finished I tried to show that Chomsky's notion of competence introduces qualitative distinctions between competence and performance, and that competence while taking a particular form in regard to language is also indicative of more universal powers of human intelligence, those we call mind. In reintroducing mind as a concept for serious study, Chomsky is urging us to look beyond the performance level of human actions to a deeper, structural, more generative level. The pedagogical corollary to this, of course, is that as educators we should pay more attention to competence (and mind) than to performance (and behaviors). For competence is the well-spring of all action, although not easily discovered in such action.

In this Part I should like to look at Piaget's view of competence, particularly as this relates to the biological model of change he proposes. In so doing I am asking you (reader and listener) to throw away previous conceptions about Piaget and to consider him in a new light. First I will ask you to transpose those things Piaget calls "structures-of-the-whole" into a notion of competence as abilities underlying (and partially controlling) performance. This is necessary because Piaget does not concern himself directly with the word competence, but his notion of structures-of-the-whole is essentially a competence notion. Second, I will ask you to consider

Piaget not just as a child psychologist, but as a broad-based intellectual—a scientific philosopher, if you will—who began his career in biological science and whose recent work, from *Biology and knowledge* on, has come back to this origin.[1] This shift is necessary if we are to understand not only what Piaget is saying about cognitive development in children, but also his basic assumptions underlying those sayings. In short, Piaget's own structure is a biological one. One key quote should bring both of these points in focus. "My one idea … has been that intellectual operations proceed in terms of structures-of-the-whole. These structures denote the kinds of equilibrium toward which evolution in its entirety is striving … (and whose) roots reach down as far as biological morphogenesis itself" (Piaget, 1976, p. 136).

I will deal with structures-of-the-whole first, and then with Piaget's biological model of change, or development.

The idea of structure is an important one for Piaget, and it is one which separates him so definitely from those psychologists labeled behaviorists. These behaviorists—J. B. Watson, E. L. Thorndike, B. F. Skinner, etc.—in their desire to make psychology "scientific" adopted the model used by the physical sciences in the 19th century. In this model only the observable and measurable is dealt with, and then in a manner where the complex is reduced or factored into the simple. In aggregate the parts are assumed to equal the whole, and the whole is assumed to be divisible into its parts. Behavioristic psychology, in order to be scientific also, adopted this model without question. It decided to deal only with the events that were observable and to isolate the independent variables of human behavior in a reductionist and atomistic manner. Educationally this model advocated that children be taught discrete behaviors, and assumed that once these behaviors were learned they would form themselves into an overall developmental whole. To behaviorist psychologists the concept of structures as organizational patterns (of the mind) underlying and controlling behaviors was, and is, anathema. But for Piaget these structures are very much a reality, and all learning must be framed in structural terms. That is, it is structural patterns or schemas which control learning, and "not vice-versa" (1976, p. 76).[2]

The four main structures, those which dominate the intellectual development of the child, and which Piaget labels structures-of-the-whole, are the sensory-

1 Piaget's two most important works in this area are his magnum opus, *Biology and knowledge* (1971a [1967]), and his follow-up work *Behavior and evolution* (1978). It is also interesting to note that in his Foreword to *The essential Piaget* (Piaget, 1977b, edited by Gruber and Voneche), Piaget states that he "was extremely happy not to appear only as a child psychologist." He then goes on to say that this period was for him "only a link between biological adaptation and the analysis of that higher form of adaptation which is scientific thought." Gruber and Voneche then devote, appropriately, the first Part to Piaget's early biology writings.

2 The quotation runs: "In other words, learning is subordinated to development and not vice-versa …" He then goes on to say that while it is indeed possible to teach individual learnings, three questions must be asked: (1) Is this learning lasting? (2) Is it transferable? (3) How does it relate to other learnings?

motor, the pre-operational, the concrete operational, the formal operational. Each of these structures has its own mode of operation—action, representation, relations, systems (to oversimplify a bit)—and while the child is in a particular stage these structures govern his actions, his perceptions, his thoughts. As Piaget (1977b) says:

> ... [the child] cannot proceed in any way he likes. He finds himself, as it were, in a field of force governed by the laws of equilibrium, carrying out transformations or operations determined not only by occurrences in the immediate past, but by the laws of the whole operational field of which these past occurrences form a part.

(p. 473)

In simple terms development explains learning more than learning explains development. And while Piaget does not use the word competence here these structural levels are competence levels. Each level has its own competence pattern, and these patterns underlie behaviors in much the way Chomsky's rules underlie performance.

The foregoing has been a simplified view of Piaget's stage theory, that for which he is famous in America. However, the question of how a child or adolescent moves from one stage of competence to another—in short how competence is developed— has not been answered. For this it is necessary to go beyond Piaget's stage theory to his biological model of change. In simple terms change can be looked upon as being internally or externally directed. That is, change can be seen as proceeding according to some sort of inner, genetic, innate mechanism, or it can be seen as emanating from the environment and then passed on to, or copied by, the organism. Historically the former has been known in biological circles as preformation. It was a popular doctrine in the 17th century when it was commonly believed that the image of a person could be seen in the male sperm. In recent years the doctrine has received renewed emphasis with the concept of DNA containing all the genetic codes an individual would possess in his lifetime. The other view, an environmental one, has been championed by Lamarck and Darwin.

In its extreme form, one attributed to Lamarck, the environment causes the organism to make changes, and these changes are then passed on genetically in a direct manner to succeeding generations. In its less extreme form, that attributed to Darwin, and that which Piaget comes closest to adopting, the environment provides the trigger or motivation for change, but the change itself is an internal or genetic occurrence.[3]

---

3 The only review of Piaget's biological thrust that I have found is by Sophie Haroutounian (1979). There she labels Piaget's position as essentially Darwinian: this would be correct if one were to neglect Piaget's own alternative—neither Darwinian nor Lamarckian. Although Piaget lays out his position frequently and carefully, many prefer to place him in an either–or dichotomy.

This environmental view of change is one Piaget adopted early in his career. In 1918, the year he took his doctorate in natural science, he states: "The heredity of acquired traits is experimental fact" (1977b, p. 40). But he rejects the Lamarckian version as putting too much emphasis on the environment, and he rejects the Darwinian version, especially the neo-Darwinian, for unjustifiably emphasizing the elements or randomness and competition (or struggle) in the organism's internal adjustments to the environment. For Piaget there is an internal sense of *telos* or purpose in an organism's interaction with its environment,[4] and there is a sense or harmony, or integration, among the various systems in an organism, and between these systems and the environment. Thus instead of accepting either a Lamarckian or Darwinian form of environmentalism Piaget proposes a third way (or "tertium quid") of dealing with change. In this view it is not the internal or the external which receives emphasis, but the interaction between them. The heart of this alternative is the notion of autoregulatory systems maintaining an equilibrium or a balance both among themselves and between themselves and the environment. As Piaget (1971a [1967]) says: "Life is essentially autoregulation ... [and there is need for] a third solution which is cybernetic and is, in effect, biased toward the theory of' autoregulation" (p. 26). And: "... the central problem of contemporary biology [is] the question of equilibration or autoregulation" (p. 10). This notion of equilibration or autoregulation, framed as it is within a view of biological systems, is what underlies Piaget's view of development, including knowledge construction and his recommendations for education.

This alternative view of change, with its emphasis on autoregulation, can be found in Piaget's earliest writings and has remained with him. When he was working on his doctorate at the University of Neuchatel, studying the mollusks of Valais, one of the issues was whether the mollusks of the deep waters were of the same or of a different species from the mollusks of the shallow marshes— eating, breathing, food gathering habits of the two being quite different. Piaget argued that the two were of different species, but that each had evolved from a common ancestry, and that in time and with the right conditions either could evolve into the other.[5] The "right conditions" were those of autoregulation, where the mollusks would be able to integrate their new habits of breathing and food gathering with some of their old (or "natural") habits. In short there must be a balance between old habits, or behaviors, and new ones in such a way that harmony among the mollusks' systems and subsystems is preserved. Piaget (1977a) says:

> Time alone will have a real effect. Moreover, it is not the factors which must be new, but the ensemble of factors, their relationships, their synthesis. In other

4 This sense of *telos* or purposeness in the organism is brought out strongest in Piaget's *Behavior and evolution* (1978)
5 See Part 1, Early biology, in *The essential Piaget* (1977b), pp. 3–22.

words a new species is from its beginnings, not characterized by its properties, its acquired characteristics, but by its tendencies …

(p. 4)[6]

This model of change is central to all of Piaget's thinking. He believes it applies to human cognition as well as to lower order biological organisms. This is not to deny the major structural differences between humans and invertebrates, but it is to say that while the structural forms are different the process of change each undergoes is similar. Thus in later writings, in describing the development of thought, Piaget argues that the process is still autoregulatory. Specifically he asserts that development occurs when (1) an individual establishes an equilibrium with his environment, so that he is comfortable with his own ways of operation and can (at least tacitly) understand those operations. Then (2) a disturbance must be introduced to unbalance this equilibrium. Finally (3) a new, higher level, equilibrium must emerge, resolving the conflict or imbalance. This balance–disturbance–rebalance process is akin to John Dewey's transformation of experience, and even to Thomas Kuhn's paradigm change. As Piaget (1977a) says of the process:

we can observe a process [hence the term "equilibration"] leading from certain states of equilibrium to others, qualitatively different, and passing through multiple "non-balances" and reequilibrations.

(p. 3)

It is worthwhile to note that however the nonbalance arises, it produces the driving force of development. Without this, knowledge remains static. But nonbalance also plays a release role, since its fecundity is measured by the possibility of surmounting it, in other words, of reaching a higher equilibrium … Without the nonbalance there would not be "increasing reequilibration."

(p. 13)

It is via this process of change that Piaget believes individuals move from one level or stage of competence to another. The curriculum implications inherent in this view are, of course, radically different from the ones now in practice. The teacher must help the student, and give the student time, to establish an equilibrium with the curriculum. Then that equilibrium must, gently but definitely, be disturbed. Finally a synthesis must be produced where a new, higher level, equilibrium is established. This equilibrium–disturbance–reequilibrium process is labeled by Piaget "equilibration," or "reequilibration," to distinguish the process of movement from the static state of balance. The teacher's task is to bring this process to fruition and consciousness,

---

6 In this quotation, notice not only the words *ensemble*, *relationships*, and *synthesis*, but also the emphasis on tendencies as opposed to properties. This is but another variation on the competence–performance distinction I've been making.

without destroying its naturalness. Or as Nel Noddings (1974) has said:"The aim of instruction becomes the transformation of cognitive structures not just the mastery of a task" (p. 360).

Bruner

While Jerome Bruner does not directly draw on Chomsky or Piaget for his own view of competence, he does raise (and extend) issues they raise. Thus when Bruner is discussing the role of culture in assessing differences among peoples, his argument rests heavily on the type of competence–performance distinction Chomsky makes. And when he talks of "competence motivation" he is alluding to the same sort of internal drive Piaget is when he speaks of biological homeorhesis. Bruner's view of competence then brings forward some of the key aspects of Chomsky's view and of Piaget's view. This is especially true at the pedagogic level.

In his essay "Cultural difference," (in Bruner, Jolly, and Sylva, 1976) Bruner raises the competence–performance distinction to counteract the notion that Blacks or minority students who perform poorly in school are therefore incompetent. In doing so he "extends" the competence–performance distinction by asserting that the teacher's task is: (1) to find a performance outlet suitable for an individual's competence to emerge and (2) to help that individual transfer his or her competence–performance skill in one area to another area. The "deficit hypothesis" of the 1960s argued that those groups which showed linguistic or intellectual differences as categorized by standard testing or usage were evidencing a deficit—a deficit which could be made up by nutritional additives and intellectual stimulation. Bruner was bothered by the arrogance of this "difference is deficit" hypothesis and drew heavily on the work of William Labov, and others, to show that the performance differences among groups were more indicative of differences in social contexts than of underlying competence differences. In making this case Bruner brings to mind Chomsky's assertion that many factors other than competence come to play when an individual expresses his competence via performance. And Bruner also draws on the "linguist's assertion that languages do not differ in their degree of development," possessing instead a "functional equality" (pp. 454–455). Differences that do exist then are superficial, performance differences governed by the situation or culture in which the language is developed. As Bruner says:

> The crux of the argument … is that those groups ordinarily diagnosed as culturally deprived have the same underlying competence as those in the mainstream of a dominant culture. The difference in performance being accounted for by the situations and contexts in which the competence is expressed.
>
> (p. 458)

In making this assertion Bruner is not only reminding us that "it is difficult if not impossible to infer competence directly from performance," but he is extending the notion of competence by saying that competence needs to have a performance outlet, and the teacher's task is to find that outlet. Not only should the teacher find a performance vehicle for the expression of competence; he should also help the individual transfer the competence–performance relation he has from a task he knows and can do to one he does not know and cannot do. In this way competence will be developed by extending it from one social milieu (or performance framework) to another.

Indeed this is quite a different role for the teacher from the traditional behaviorist one of presenting material in a clear, concise, and logical way. But then as Piaget says, the knowledge–construct view of learning is different from the knowledge–copy view.

Bruner's other use of competence, that coming from Robert White's (1959) article, "Motivation reconsidered: The concept of competence," also presents some definite pedagogic principles, and is compatible with Piaget's notion of homeorhesis. In the Piaget Part just read the difference between equilibrium, as a steady state, and equilibration, as an ongoing process, can be described as the difference between homeostasis and homeorhesis. In simplified terms homeostasis is that internal balancing of systems and subsystems within an organism that keeps the organism in harmony with its environment. Homeorhesis is the progressive balance-disturbance-rebalance process whereby an organism (or individual) attains control over its environment. One of the balances Piaget (1977a) is talking about in his system of balances, or "hierarchy of regulations" as he calls it, is the balance between homeostasis and homeorhesis (Ch. 1, especially p. 21). In more general terms this is a balance between an organism's desire or drive to be comfortable with its environment and an organism's desire to conquer or control its environment.

This sense of balance between the stable and the dynamic has similarities with Bruner's balance between internal and external motivations; and the notion of homeorhesis as a driving force to control the environment is similar to White's concept of "competence motivation," which Bruner uses heavily. White's argument is that if one wishes to view motivation in terms of drives and reinforcement then it is necessary to posit another drive for humans—the drive to deal effectively, or to control, the environment. As White says:

> I shall argue that it is necessary to make competence a motivational concept; there is a "competence motivation." ... It is directed, selective, and persistent, and it continues not because it serves primary drives ... but because it satisfies an intrinsic need to deal with the environment.
>
> (1959, pp. 317–318).[7]

---

7 Also, White quoted by Bruner (1973, p. 407).

Bruner goes beyond this notion of White's by arguing that there are "forms of activity … [which] develop the competence motive … and make it the driving force behind behavior" (1973, p. 407). In short, competence as ability to control the environment is natural, but can and should be developed. The first principle for development is to maintain the nature of this internal drive. Competence is its own reward, and should not be obliterated or lessened with too many external rewards. The balance, or essential tension between internal and external motivations, should always weigh in favor of the internal, and work to develop the internal. The second principle for development is that growth in competence occurs via the balance–disturbance–rebalance process Piaget describes. To quote Bruner: "I am convinced we shall do better to conceive of growth as an empowering of the individual by multiple means for representing his world, multiple means that often conflict and create the dilemmas that stimulate growth" (1973, p. 323).

A Competence Model

In the foregoing Part I have had two aims. The first has been to separate competence from performance, lest we confuse one with the other. I have tried to show that the words have different meanings, thrusts, histories. My second aim has been to show that in the idea of competence their lies a pedagogical field rich enough to support a new model of education. This model would provide a direct challenge to the behaviorist one which has dominated American schooling for the past century. The behaviorist model comes essentially from an empiricist or positivist paradigm. In this paradigm there is no need for mind, behaviors alone are adequate; or, if one insists on positing mind as an organization of habits, this mind can be seen as a "blank tablet" ready to receive the impressions experience and schooling provide. The learning theory is associationist with a strong predilection towards stimulus–response techniques. The whole is always considered equal to the sum of the parts, thus allowing for the factoring of the whole into discrete units, with the assumption that once the units are mastered then the whole, naturally or automatically, takes shape. Performance becomes the goal, the product, and the process in this model.

The competence model not only assigns a very different role to performance—as an entry point for the study of competence—but brings with it, or arises from, a different set of paradigmatic assumptions. The overall framework is a rationalist one, positing the existence of mind, and seeing all behaviors as interpreted by or screened through this mind. Development occurs, not by direct associations, but in terms of structural patternings. Those things which can easily be assimilated into existing structural levels are learned without much struggle; other things which are not assimilated are either ignored or act as catalysts to disturb the old equilibrium and reestablish the new. This process is equilibrative and forces a good deal of interaction between teachers and students, and among both groups. Goals are not so much firmly pre-set as they emerge from the interaction and reflection on past and immediate past experiences. The whole is not considered as merely an aggregation of parts, but it is believed to have a structure and unity of its own. This unity, in terms of a person or a field, lends direction and coherence to activity. These three—mind, equilibration, holism—form the heart or foundational base of the competence model. I will not elaborate on these three, although much work needs to be done with them, but rather will refer the interested reader to my paper, "A structural view of curriculum" (Doll, 1979). Nor will I elaborate on the five pedagogic principles of action, skills and structures, role of contrast, play and mastery, development of experience, which I have also described elsewhere (Doll, 1979, 1980). Rather I will turn to personal experiences working with primary-grade children both in and not in a structural curriculum. My intent is to make practical my foregoing remarks by focusing on curriculum development, and to highlight some differences between a structural curriculum and a non-structural or traditional one.

I became interested in this project of curriculum development when, a few years back, I read David Olson's (1970) *Cognitive development*. There he shows, quite dramatically I believe, that in teaching young children (4 to 7 years of age) to do a set task (placing checkers in a diagonal sequence) it makes no difference whether the teaching model is a traditional–performance one or a structural–competence one. However, in asking them to extend their learning, either in terms of time or in terms of transfer to other tasks (here placing the checkers in the other, or opposite, diagonal), the teaching model makes an enormous difference. One example: in a traditional group, none out of 14 children (0/14) was able to transfer the skill of checker placement along one diagonal (/) to the opposite diagonal (\). Whereas 12 out of 14 children (12/14) in the structural group did it the first time. Examples like this intrigued me and my graduate students. Thus some of us set up the Oswego-Sodus Structural Arithmetic Project.

The Project began with a number of primary school teachers (K-3) in Sodus, New York, and has now been expanded to include a primary group at the SUNY-Oswego, Swetman Learning Center. The heart of the Project is to develop a curriculum and teaching methodology based on the notion that the student and the field each possess structures or types of competence. As Bruner (1960) says, the task is to bring these two structures together:

> ... at each stage of development the child has a characteristic way of viewing the world and explaining it to himself. The task of teaching a subject to a child at any particular age is one of representing the structure of that subject in terms of the child's way of viewing things.
>
> (p. 13)

The device we use for developing the students' structures, particularly those structures relating to arithmetic, is a sense of patterning. The whole curriculum-teaching part of the Project is built around patterning: copying patterns, building patterns, extending patterns, and finally transferring and transforming patterns.

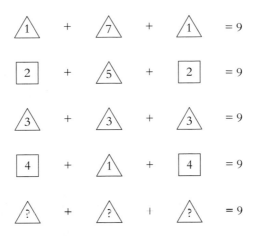

FIGURE 7.1 Numbers, shapes, and patterns

Kindergarten children work with a simple ABAB pattern. First graders examine the relations between ABAB and BABA, or AABB. Second graders build all the possible combinations—six—of ABAB, and begin to notice the concept of closing the system. Third graders compare the ABAB system with other systems such as ABCABC.

Traditional skill work with adding, subtracting, multiplying, and dividing is also put into this structural or competence framework. Thus the kindergarteners begin— with the aid of rods, cubes, blocks—simple addition and subtraction combinations. First graders relate addition and subtraction, multiplication and division as opposites, and explore non-traditional combinations, $(2 \times 5) -1 = \Delta$

Second graders look for structures within groups of numbers (see Figure 7.1).

Third graders analyze these combinations in terms of operating systems—(3×3) is a perfect square, the (2×5) combination requires a negative one (-1), or the introduction of subtraction. They also manipulate the symbols within the system for their purposes—12×15 being transformed to 6×30, or $101 - 49$ being changed to $102 - 50$. Throughout this work with numbers in terms of patterns, there is the assumption that children do have minds, competence, organizing abilities. The pedagogical task is to develop these abilities so that, over years, the child becomes aware of these abilities (his competence) and gains insight into the way a field is structured (its competence).

It is too early to make any definitive remarks about the success of the Project in developing competence. Years of longitudinal study and numerous case examples will be necessary before such statements can be made. But some personal, preliminary observations appear in order. The children like the program very much—the challenge is both exciting and rewarding. The teachers find that curriculum construction gives them a new feeling about teaching. It is hard to imagine that any

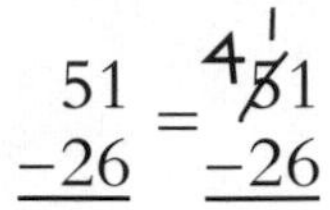

$$\frac{51}{-26} = \frac{4\overset{1}{\cancel{5}}1}{-26}$$

FIGURE 7.2 Cross out, borrow, and subtract

of them will adopt the common practice of turning pages in a text or workbook. The experimental groups are outperforming the control groups on virtually all (but not all) measures of performance testing.

I would like to close this paper with a counter-illustration, one taken from my work with my own son, age seven, who goes to a traditional school in the town in which we live. Here much of the second grade arithmetic curriculum has been devoted to learning how to subtract one two-digit numeral from another. The process of "borrowing" has been the culmination of the curriculum. The beginnings were started in early October, after a month of review addition, with drill on the subtraction "facts"—1 minus 0 through 19 minus 9. The second step was to introduce subtraction of two digit numerals from two digit numerals, with the subtrahend *always* smaller than the minuend (i.e. 56 − 23, not 51 − 26). In fact, at the time the comment was frequently made that "a larger number cannot be taken from a smaller." The third step was to introduce "regrouping," one ten being converted to ten ones (97 always become 80 + 17, never 100 − 3, nor 95 or 75 plus 2 or 22. The fourth step was "to cross out, borrow and subtract."

During all this time, and the process took months, from October to March, each segment was isolated from the other. Thousands of separate examples were done, but never was subtraction related to addition, never were the children shown the difficulty involved in 51 − 26, and never was regrouping explained in terms of need. The textbook, and this almost totally controlled the curriculum, merely presented the procedure and asked the children to copy. Neither the structures of arithmetic nor the child's own competence motivation were ever brought forward as pedagogical devices. The result of all this was that at the end of Easter vacation, when Will had some make-up work to do, he could neither solve 72 − 17 nor make an appropriate beginning. He sat trying to remember. After a time lapse I suggested he forget how he had been "taught" and try to figure out the example any way he could. "I could add," he said. "OK. Add!" "Three plus seventeen equals twenty and fifty ... two more equals fifty ... five!" "Can you do another?" "Sure!"

I conclude with this example to bring home, again, the point that children do have minds; but the performance model used in the schools does not recognize this point. It seems doubtful the schools will give up their performance model and adopt a competence one, but the model is there for those wishing to develop and use it. And I believe it has exciting pedagogical possibilities.

8

BEYOND METHODS

(2002)

> The idea that ... we can substitute "method" for deliberation ... is just wishful
> thinking.
>
> (Richard Rorty)

To say that method forms the heart of teaching is to state the obvious. However, in
so stating we are also raising questions—an activity Martin Heidegger (1977 [1954])
says constitutes "the piety of thought" (p. 31)—regarding not only the nature of
teaching and method but of education and teaching as well. Method currently lies
at the heart of our educational enterprise: its shapes our textbooks, our curriculum
plans, our ways of teaching, and our ways of teaching teachers how to teach. A
teacher-education program without "methods" courses is not a teacher-education
program, just as a textbook without methods of teaching-the-text is not a textbook,
and just as a lesson plan without a methodology is not a lesson plan. In short,
method becomes the *sine qua non* of all teaching—a truism which would bring a
smile and nod from Peter Ramus (1515–1572), who four centuries ago began our
contemporary concept of what it means to teach a curriculum by "methodizing" it.
Peter Ramus (Petrus Ramus in the Latinate) was the first and undoubtedly greatest
methodizer who ever lived. But before going into Ramus' methodizing and some of
its underlying assumptions, especially those regarding how methodizing has shaped
not only our concept of teaching but of teaching as well, I'd like to look at the legacy
this methodizing movement has left on the 20th century—a legacy with which we
are all familiar. Sometimes, as John Dewey has reminded us, the familiar is so familiar
we need to step back and look at it again, maybe to see it for the first time. The
concept of method enframes not only our educational thought but our scientific
and social thought as well. In fact, as Jerome Bruner (1986a) states, method as an

orderly way of thinking—scientific, rational, efficient—has become paradigmatic (p.13) for Western, 20th century society. Jacob Bronowski (1978) points out that the "naturalness" of this method's cause–effect procedure, hence its reductionism and predictability, is so strong that "we really cannot conceive of another way of thinking—it has become our natural way of looking at all problems" (p. 59).

It is common for us in America to ground this "scientific" way of thinking in Frederick Taylor's work with time-and-motion studies in the 1890s at a steel plant in Bethlehem, Pennsylvania. Obviously this focus is too narrow, as we can see from John Dewey's own adoption and development of method to fit his view of pragmatism. As I hope to show in my own explorations of method, its roots go back many centuries, at least to Ramus and Ramism. Thus, the line from Ramus to Tyler, if not direct, linear, and causal, is one we can trace without too much freehand artistry. In this picture, Taylor still occupies a prominent if not progenitor role, and his work remains foundational, especially for educators and curricularists immersed in the Frederick Taylor–Ralph Tyler rationale. Direct links are easily made, I believe, between Taylor's sense of method and the four-step procedure Ralph Tyler developed in the late 1940s and early 1950s for designing a good curriculum. This Taylor–Tyler axis is the one which continues to orient our educational planning today. It is one I believe has outlived its modernist usefulness and needs replacing in our post-modern age (Doll, 1993, 1998a, 2000).

Frederick Winslow Taylor: A Crusader

Frederick Winslow Taylor (1856–1915) burst, as a comet, on the American scene in the late 1890s, burned brilliantly for a short time in the Progressive Era, and went into oblivion as World War I began. However, his effect has been indelible—not only is he still considered to have had more effect on the American industrial scene than "John D. Rockefeller, Andrew Camegie, Alfred P. Sloan, Thomas Edison and Henry Ford" (Kanigel, 1997, p. 10), but Taylorism and the Taylor system have become "part of our moral inheritance." It is not uncommon for French encyclopediasts to divide their study of work organization into two broad periods—*Le period pretaylorienne, and Le taylorisme*. As Robert Kanigel has said in his biography of Taylor—*The one best way* (1997)—in virtually all the areas of modern life that Taylor touched, the economic, social, intellectual, psychological (and we may certainly add educational), "Taylor is the gold standard against which all else must be compared, the natural benchmark" (p. 9). He is "the father of 'scientific management,'" a phrase he had inscribed on his tombstone.

What he did, at the Bethlehem Steel plant, Machine Shop No. 2, in the summer of 1898 was to change the method of men working from day laborers to piece-workers, from working together as a yard gang at a set wage, then $1.15 per day for loading 92 pound pig-iron bars on railroad cars, to piece-work based on the number of bars moved. What he accomplished was to revolutionize American industry and its way of manipulating men, for his "method"—the Taylor method—was to use time-and-motion studies for outlining and controlling in great detail every step, every movement the men were to make. As he said to Henry Noll (the laborer he referred to in his writings as Schmidt, who was "so stupid ... that he nearly resembles an ox"), "a high priced man has to do exactly as he's told from morning till night ... right straight through the day. And what's more, no back talk" (in Doll, 1993, p. 41). Here lies the key to Taylor's system: fit the person to the job—Schmidt was ideal for grunt work—and then push that person (or material if one were designing tools for the person to work with) to the limit. Finding this precise limit or precise perfection was what Taylor took such pride in, what constituted the "scientific-ness" of his work. With both tools and men he often took them to the breaking point. Indeed while Schmidt was held up as the ideal "high priced man," one capable of earning not $1.15 per day but $1.71 per day (for increasing his production 400 percent), Schmidt was also a unique ideal: the only one of the work crew Taylor and his stopwatch team originally selected who could continue with the grueling pace of 1100 liftings–steppings–loadings, in precise fashion, of the 92 pound pig-iron bars per day. Of the 30 men selected for stopwatch study, 10 were chosen, 5 of these came for the final timings and only Schmidt survived the first week, only he continued to load the railroad cars at a rate of just over 45 tons per day—an increase of approximately 400 percent. From this data, Taylor then ("scientifically"?) set "the standard" at 45 tons, per man per day, resulting in pay of $1.70 a day. While this "standard" remained out of reach for most laborers, a sizable number of piece-rate workers were able to load the railroad cars for about 5 cents per ton, down from the 10 cents a ton of the former day workers. Management was happy with the increased profit. Taylor and his crew of stopwatch timers ("analysts") were hailed as messiahs of American industry.

Such personal fame was short-lived. In two years the yard crew of unskilled laborers at Bethlehem Steel plummeted from 600 to 140. These surviving 140 constituted the "finest body of picked laborers that the writer [Taylor] has ever seen together" (Kanigel, 1997, p. 323). However, it was the "other" class of men, the 460 who no longer worked at Bethlehem, that caught the attention of Congressman William Wilson, a former coal miner from central Pennsylvania, and now Chairman of the House Committee to Investigate Taylor and Other Systems of Shop Management. They tangled. Taylor eloquently described his vision of providing prosperity for all Americans, workers and managers. Wilson wanted to know what "the system" did to those who were not "first-class men." Neither was able to talk to the other. On the third day of committee hearings, after eight hours of grilling, Taylor erupted emotively and began shouting and denouncing those who could not or would not see his vision. He believed ardently that what Schmidt did, all could do with proper management and motivation. The "others" were, as he put it, "birds who could but would not sing"; they did not deserve attention. About midnight on January 30, 1912, Wilson ended the hearings. Taylor left a broken man, rested in the Mediterranean for a while and died a few years later, not yet 60 years of age.

Today Taylor is considered part of that fascinating and contradictory movement called the Progressive Era. If to Wilson and others he was a destroyer of souls, he was to himself and to a great many others the workingman's dearest friend, the Great Harmonizer, the epitome of what it means to be American. One European declared on Taylor's death: "The Taylor System is to Europe not only 'an American lesson,' it is *the* American lesson." Taylor saw this lesson and its moral in terms of realizing that the individual must be subjugated to the system. As he said in *Scientific management* (1947 [1911]): "In the past the man has been first. In the future the System must be first" (in Kanigel, 1997, pp. 11, 19).[1]

I would like to look, with some care, at three aspects of this system: its "method," its concept of "standard," and its "scientific-ness." Its method is reminiscent of René Descartes' 17th century search for "rightly conducting reason and seeking truth in the sciences" (1950 [1637], pp.11–12) and presages Ralph Tyler's 20th century listing of four criteria for developing a good curriculum (1950, pp. 1–2). The details of Taylor's method—his principles to which management was to pay attention—I have already listed and will merely relist. They are, like Descartes' and Tyler's methods, four-square:

- First, a science for each element of a man's work must be developed to replace the old rule-of-thumb method;
- Second, the workmen must be scientifically selected and trained, not left to their own methods;
- Third, attention must be given to insure all of the work being done is in accordance with the principles developed;
- Fourth, an equal division of the work and the responsibility must be drawn between management and the workmen.

(In Doll, 1993, p. 41, from Taylor, 1947 [1911], pp. 36–39)

In looking at this concept of method, a number of issues stand out. One is that this method requires planning, one might even say pre-planning; that is, great attention, precision, assembling of detail takes place prior to the activity. This is seen in both Descartes' method and Tyler's.[2] The activity, the experience—moving pig-iron, or

---

1   It is this almost messianic commitment to the concept of system which personally links Taylor with Ramus and Descartes. Such a commitment may well be a strain in Western intellectual thought, running all the way back to that great systematizer, Aristotle. It is a strain which forms part (but only part) of my own cosmological beliefs.

2   Tyler's four criteria for a good curriculum revolve around the (pre) selection of (1) goals, (2) experiences, and (3) the organization of the experiences. These three are then (4) assessed to be certain the (pre) chosen purposes are "being attained." Descartes' four steps for directing "reason in its search for truth" are (1) to admit to the mind only that which is self-evident, (2) to break all into small pieces, (3) to think in an orderly (linear) fashion, and (4) to review all the preceding, that "nothing, be omitted." What unites these foursomes are such activities as preselecting, linear organizing, separating ends from means, centralizing control, and

learning from a curriculum, or thinking rational thoughts—does not form the basis for the plan but rather is shaped by the plan. The plan precedes the activity; the activity is limited to the plan. Control lies with the planner, it is not dissipated throughout the experience. By now, we may seem so comfortable with this concept of method as (pre-) planning that anything else seems "unnatural." Yet, Dewey points out (1957 [1922]), wisely I believe, that all plans and ends are really "ends-in-view," they arise from activity, they do not precede activity (p. 209). To conceive of and to do otherwise is to straightjacket both the plans and the activities. As he says, "A true aim is thus opposed at every point to the aim which is imposed. ... The latter is fixed and rigid. And in education, imposed aims are responsible ... for rendering the work of both teacher and pupil mechanical and slavish" (1966a [1916], p. 110).

Imposed aims or goals, of course, concentrates control—all control lies with planners. To Taylor this *concentration of control* seemed quite natural[3] and was most important. In fact, it was all important, the "most prominent single element in modern scientific management" (Taylor, 1947 [1911], p. 39). Taylor would brook "no back talk," workers and managers were to be categorically separated with the workers (students for us) to receive "in writing and in detail" every day "not only what is to be done but how it is to be done and the exact time allowed" (p. 39). While a direct translation of such a methodology to today's schools would be a caricature, it is part of our school heritage and in decades not too far past was a definite reality (Doll, 1993, Chapter 2). Today, the strong separation of students from teachers and of teachers from administrators, with the former subservient to the latter remains. If there is a ghost in the curriculum, and I believe there is (Doll, 2002b), it is *control* and the fear control has brought with it.

Much of the reform movement in today's schools centers around the issue of where control should lie: with the managers/bureaucrats who do the (pre-) planning; with the workers/students who do the experiencing; or with the teachers/parents who act as intermediaries between the decision makers and those who have decisions made for them? Dewey, with his own brand of Congregational idealism, had faith that control could reside in the situation itself (1966a [1916], p. 39); it need not be

---

placing all within a closed, stable system. Tyler (1950) assumes this notion of a closed, stable system—one in "equilibrium" whose "tensions are to be relieved"—in his discussion of the educational purposes "schools should seek to attain" (p. 5).) For more on the comparison of these foursomes see Doll, 1993, pp. 26 ff. and 52 ff. See also the Kliebard–Hlebowitsh debate on Tyler's rationale (Kliebard, 1995).

3   Kanigel (1997) points out that the idea of being in control was part of the Taylor family inheritance—it was their right. Father quietly assumed control of that around him, as did both of his sons. However, I wonder if the concept of where control should be concentrated was a theme running through American society in the post-civil war era. Control and its concentration seem to have been an important part of Progressivism. Steven Selden (1999) points out that the eugenics movement in early 20th century America—a movement which certainly feared the loss of its members "rightful" control—was an integral part of Progressivism (pp. 25–27). I wonder, too, about Pragmatism's relation to issues of control. Control and Progressivism (progress) is an issue I believe warrants further study.

imported. It could be inherent in the activity of people doing, sharing, reflecting *together*. As he says, "*Common experience* is capable of developing from within itself methods which will secure direction for itself and will *create inherent standards* of judgment and value" (1958a [1929], p. 38, emphasis added).

Such a radical, indeed, heretical statement could become meaningful Dewey believed—that is acquire life, spirit, vitality—only if we first developed a philosophy or "theory of experience" (1963 [1938], Chapter 3), and with it a methodology, not of imposition but of experience (Doll, 1972, 1973).[4]

Dewey's use of the phrase "inherent standards" in the foregoing quotation is interesting, for he assumes that acceptable criteria can be developed within the situation of experience itself. Taylor, living in the same time period—they were both born in the latter 1850s—saw standards only in external, impositional terms. Taylor's view has definitely prevailed, as is evident in the "standards movement" of today; the concept of standards arising from within the activity itself is, often, quite unthinkable. Standards are to be imposed or set out by those knowledgeable, those in power. Yet in a post-modem frame that pays attention to the concept of self-organization (Capra, 1996; Kauffman, 1993, 1995), the concept of standards being imposed is meaningless. Standards, along with goals and aims, emerge; they are not imposed. The "standards" movement of current educational thought is firmly rooted in 19th century, modernist thinking.

The word *standards* is worth a closer look, as is Taylor's use of the concept. The word comes from the common Roman *estend-ere* or Latin *extend-ere,* meaning to "stretch out or extend" (Kanigel, 1997, p. 504). The earliest use was as "a flag or standard," a rallying point and inspirational guide that extended above the heads of troops in battle. Its next use, about three centuries later, in the 1400s, was either as "an authorized exemplar of a unit of measure or weight" or—similarly—as "a recognized exemplar of correctness, perfection" (Kanigel, 1997, p. 505). This sense of extending a criterion of correctness or perfection is one Taylor used in his work with Noll ("Schmidt")—again, of the 30 men chosen, only Noll was able to keep up the grueling pace of 92 pig-iron loadings per day, day after day. Once Taylor found a man who could work at this pace, he then set this "definite level of excellence" as a "prescribed ... measure of what is adequate" (Kanigel, 1997, p. 505). Within this one definition we have the sort of split that has bedeviled the concept of standards for centuries. It is considered as an "exemplar of correctness, perfection." Noll did

---

4   Currently there has reoccurred a debate about the need to "practicalize" the curriculum (Wraga, 1999; Hlebowitsh, 1999). As Dewey points out (1966a [1916], Ch. 20) such a dichotomy (between theory and practice) produces "one sided meanings" (p. 136), an evil that has beset Western thought for thousands of years. "Practical activities," he says, "*may* be intellectually narrow and trivial; but they *will* be in so far as "... they [neglect the intellectual] (p. 273). Intellectual activities alone are but games, useful possibly in themselves, but, for pragmatist Dewey, never acquiring meaning until carried forward into activity. The issue of theory versus practice is the false issue. How these two interact is the practical problem we need to face. This is our challenge as educators.

move 45 and 3/4 tons of pig-iron daily and thus the "standard" Taylor set (arbitrarily, as Kanigel points out (1997, pp. 319–323)) was 45 tons. Yet, just as all the men were to meet this exemplary "standard," so does the word carry the meaning of "a normal uniform size or amount; a prescribed minimum" (Kanigel, 1997, p. 505). So the 45 tons that Noll alone could do was both *exemplary* and *normal*: an exemplary and a minimum amount. No wonder over 75 percent of the men lifting pig-iron before Taylor came, left during his time there. And no wonder it was this "other class of men," the non-first-class men that Wilson wanted to know about. This aporia about standards plagues us today; they are exemplars of excellence, all are to attain; they both describe the minimum and weed out the weak (except, of course, in Lake Wobegon where "all the children are above average"). In our modernist frame, we use standards as rallying points around which all are to gather—only those birds who won't sing fail to come, for there are no birds who, with proper motivation, cannot sing. Scientifically (eugenically?) Taylor had no use for these birds, "this other class."[5] In a post-modern frame, this either/or, aspire to/all attain concept is neither right nor wrong, it is just meaningless—for the creation of judgments and values lies inherent within the process and activity of experience itself. We have indeed moved beyond modernism and its methods. Taylor would just not understand.

In that blusterous era following the civil war and taking its cue from the Englishman Herbert Spencer—who believed the "Knowledge of Most Worth" to be Science and only Science, for it indeed is "the best preparation for all orders of activity" (1929 [1859], pp. 84–85)—America fell in love, indeed idolized what it called "Science." Science and its methods of (super) orderly activity brought time and motion under control. No longer wild or capricious, these two were harnessed for work and "man's" benefit. *Scientific management*—the title of books by both Frederick Taylor (1947 [1911]) and Joseph Mayer Rice (1969a [1914])—became the mantra of progressivism. Even John Dewey succumbed to its allure. Popular magazines ran features on scientific management in the home, in the church, in daily living—often broken down to tenths of a percent as to how efficient one was. One aspect of this "efficiency craze" was the establishment of "Housekeeping Experiment Stations" where women were admonished to stop "soldiering" on the job, encouraged to become "part of a great factory for the production of citizens," and told to discover the "principles of domestic engineering" (Haber, 1964, p. 62).

Frederick Taylor, the self-confessed "Father of Scientific Management," was born in Philadelphia, in the post-civil war era, the steaming and throbbing heart of American industrialism. Baldwin Locomotive Works built and shipped worldwide,

---

5   The "scientificness" of the eugenics movement is explored well by Steven Selden in his
    Inheriting shame (1999). The play on the word "bird" is symptomatic, I believe, not only of
    Taylor but also of the times. The evolutionary–empirical–eugenics movement, so much
    in the air then, was much influenced by pigeon and animal breeding. The origin of the
    eugenics movement in America arose from a eugenics section of the American Breeders
    Association in the early 1900s (p. 4 ff.). Again, the tangled relationship among science–
    eugenics–progressivism is worth further exploration.

30-ton, hulking steam engines, the symbol of industrial America (Kanigel, 1997, p. 97). The son of a prominent, wealthy, and influential Philadelphia family, he traveled widely in Europe as a beginning teenager, entered Phillips Exeter Academy where he achieved consistently top grades in the then required subjects of Latin, Greek, and mathematics but did not graduate; he achieved honors on the Harvard Entrance Examination but chose instead to become a patternmaker apprentice at Ferrell & Jones in 1874—to work, hard and honestly, getting his hands dirty with the "regular employees" (pp. 106–109).[6]

As a youth, Taylor helped found the Germantown Scientific Society—really a group of his young buddies. As a patternmaker apprentice and then machinist, Fred Taylor had no real interest in the mechanical, but as a budding young "scientist" he had tremendous interest in mathematics and precision. From his travels in Europe as a teenage boy, he read books on mathematics and kept detailed notes about money, time, distance, and the technical aspects of how salt was mined in Austria (p. 105). This interest in precision became an obsession with him. As one colleague remembered:

> Fred was always a bit of a crank in the opinion of our boyhood band, and we were inclined to rebel sometimes from the strict rules and exact formulas to which he insisted that all of our games must be subjected.
>
> (Selden, 1999, p. 104)

Frederick Taylor's "scientism" was a combination of precision, hard work, subordination of self to system, and an almost fanatical devotion to pushing men and materials to their limits. He did this with Noll, and in the development of drill bits of high-speed steel that could cut through metal four times faster than those existent. Taylor felt these limits which he found were scientific laws, all "wrapped in the flag of mathematics" (p. 332). Once these "laws" were found, Taylor felt it his moral obligation and holy mission to impose them as the standard on all with whom he came in contact.

In this short précis of Taylor's scientism—his metaphysical absorption into a procedure—I do not wish to suggest there was nothing of what others would call scientific in what he did. Such would be untrue. Taylor collected and analyzed mounds of data, and he did develop useful tools—steel bits, shovels, etc. However, arbitrariness and personal passion played important roles in his view of what constituted a scientific method.[7]

---

6   This four-year, machine shop apprenticeship—not uncommon for young Philadelphia men, in this age of steam and steel, regardless of their family wealth—left a lasting impression on Taylor, one that increased as time went on. In later years, he not only glorified this experience repeatedly—"to do monotonous, tiresome and uninteresting" work, gave a man "character" (in Kanigel, 1997, p. 139)—but insisted that those men he chose as his confidants "needed to get their hands dirty" (p. 330).

7   Taylor's relation to limits, laws, standards is most curious. He truly seems to have believed that he was working scientifically and he did indeed gather mounds of data. But his relation

If Frederick Taylor is known to us as the Father of Scientific Management, it is John Dewey, three years his junior, who is known to us as "the father of scientific method." In his 1997 [1910] book Dewey outlined the famous five steps of this method: (1) *feeling of* a problematic situation, (2) *definition* of a problem, (3) drawing up of an *hypothesis,* (4) formal *reasoning, (5) testing* of the hypothesis by action (p.72 ff).[8] The effect this method has had on the bereft social sciences, including education, cannot be overemphasized. It has become the school procedure we use in telling students how to think and that we use in teaching ourselves how to go about this telling. The method is ubiquitous, it dominates our school procedures from kindergarten through doctoral degrees.[9] Dewey, though, was a stern father. He did not want his thoughts about "method" to run rampant. As he says: "To suppose that students can be supplied with models of methods to be followed in acquiring and expounding a subject is to fall into a self-deception that has lamentable consequences." And, "Imposing an alleged uniform method upon everybody breeds mediocrity in all but the very exceptional" (1966a [1916] pp. 172–173).

---

to that data was, at times, most arbitrary—i.e. his decision to pay Noll approximately 50 percent more salary for increasing production about 400%, or his decision that a "first-class man" could load pig-iron on a daily routine of 45 tons, extrapolated from the time it took a yard gang of Hungarian workers "running full out" to load one flatcar (14 minutes) minus, a mystically chosen, 40 percent. This goal of 45 tons he set for the yard workers to attain, a goal that only Noll achieved consistently. Kanigel questions whether Taylor really did develop "A Science of Work ?" (p. 325), and wonders where Taylor found some of the "wildly artificial figure(s)" he used (p. 319).

8   The phrasing Dewey used in outlining these steps was revised, in substance, in 1971 [1933], pp. 106 ff, see also 1966a [1916], p.163).

9   For Dewey, this method—really that of reflection (1971 [1933], Ch. 7)—is always a method of *experimenting with directing personal experience.* It is *never* the imposition of a set form. There is, Dewey says, "a strong temptation ... to present subject matter in its present form ... as a royal road to learning" (1966a [1916], p. 220). Such a mistake, of course, not only assumes the present form to be the perfected form but deprives the student of the very activity one is trying to develop: it confuses the products of science with the methods of science and eliminates or at least hinders the student from "learning the scientific way of treating ordinary experience."

This sense of treating ordinary experience—life activities—in a "scientific" way is important for Dewey. As Morton White (1973, Ch. 11) so astutely points out, for Dewey this is a way of helping students see and achieve further connections (growth) emanating from the experiential connections they have already made. Its aim is to help the student develop his or her own thinking, "to free experiment" from the twin evils of cultural imposition and the "purely personal" (Dewey, 1966a [1916], p. 226). In this sense, Dewey saw the scientific method—that of guided inquiry—as a new and revolutionary advance beyond the medieval and classical thought we have been caught in so long. Dewey saw this method as truly the opportunity for *activity* (experience) *to direct itself towards its own end* (p. 24). This statement—activity guiding activity to its own end—is the essence of Dewey's Chapter 3, "Education as direction," in his *Democracy and education* (1966a [1916]). It is unfortunate, but understandable given the tremendous influence of Ramism on American education, that the power and spiritfulness of this statement have been neither understood nor appreciated by the majority of those holding social power.

Dewey is not opposed to method though, far from it—method forms the heart of his procedures for logic, experience, reflection. What he does object to—and vehemently—is the concept and practice of *mechanizing method,* itself a line which runs from Peter Ramus to Ralph Tyler. For Dewey, methods cannot be pre-set, they are derived from direct and current observation of the situation at hand and are used to direct that situation (to its own end) and to harness its energies or spirit (p. 167). When methods are separated from subjects, from the experiences which give rise to them, they acquire a "mechanical uniformity" and lose their role in expanding the experience they are designed to direct. Then "methods": "have to be authoritatively recommended to teachers, instead of being an expression of their own intelligent observations" (p. 168). Such a separation of methods from persons is just what happened and intentionally so at Bethlehem Steel. Taylor did not want his men to think; in fact, "first-class" men did not think; rather, they did what they were told. In this manner, they and their experiences would be controlled. Here lies not only the ghost in the curriculum but the secret heart of scientific management.

Both Dewey and Taylor, again contemporaries in the tumultuous era when America was coming of industrial age, recognized that method was key to growth and development. Taylor wished to develop a better society for all through production of material; Dewey wished to develop a better society by having people enrich and deepen their experiences, aesthetically and spiritfully. These are quite different goals and the methods used to achieve these goals are themselves different. Obviously these differences play themselves out in the type of education (and its concomitant concept of learning) each would embrace.

I will explore first the schooling education we have known since the time of Peter Ramus and then look at an alternative to it, the aesthetic and spiritful education I believe Dewey and others advocate. To understand Ramus and his legacy it is also important to understand his times and how he related to those times.

Ramus and his Legacy

Ramus was definitely a 16th-century individual (1515–1572). Caught up in the Protestant Reformation, a French Roman Catholic with Protestant sympathies, he lost his head—his life!—in the St. Bartholomew's Day religious massacre in Paris when students broke into his University of Paris rooms, and severing his head from his body, threw the former out the window. Stephen Toulmin (1990), the historian and philosopher of science, sees the time period 1550 to 1650 as one of tumultuous social and intellectual change in Western Europe— revolutionary changes of government in Germany, France, and England, with concomitant changes in demographics, the shattering of the feudal system, Roman Christendom, Aristotelian logic, science, and metaphysics. Along with this went major changes in teaching. Modernity and methodization both arrived during this

100 year period.[10] Since I have dealt with modernity elsewhere (Doll, 1993), I will concentrate here on teaching and the methodization movement: Ramus and the Ramism which followed.

Prior to Ramus' re-presenting of the logic (really rhetoric) of that fascinating medieval figure Peter of Spain—medical doctor, logician, Pope John XXI—in his *Dialectic* (first done in 1543), teaching had been done via dialogue. This dialogue was at times a conversation, at other times a formal disputation between student and master. Abelard's 12th century *Sic* and *Non* (Yes and No) is a fine example of this: contrasting arguments, requiring the students to figure out contradictions for themselves. Such dialogue/disputation was hallowed as a *methodus* (or "the way") in Ramus' day. To the dismay of his colleagues, Ramus changed the form of all this. He developed a new way to present "the way." His new methodology—and his change did develop into this—assumed the young teenagers of the time wanted to acquire a product easily, not labor endlessly with a process. So Walter Ong titles one of his books, *Ramus, method, and the decay of dialogue* (1983 [1958]). Ramus' "method," wildly popular and controversial in its time, captured the allegiance of Puritan England, influencing especially the writings of John Milton, and sailed across the seas to Puritan New England, where its "superficial simplicity" was most attractive (p. 30).[11]

In the 16th century, the young teenagers Ramus taught as principal of the Collége de Presles were forced to memorize immense and unconnected details of Latin grammar (one needed to know this grammar to read the texts then existent). For "logic," really the categories needed for rhetorical disputation, the teenager and pre-teenager memorized symbolic "cards"—much like Tarot cards still used today—a man holding three sheaves of wheat stood for the categories "What? What kind? and How many?" while little birds (propositions having no common term) flew overhead. As Ong says, "With such pictures in mind, the little boy—however

---

10 Toulmin (1990, Ch. 1) places modernity's arrival in the years 1600 to 1650. I like 1543, the date of Copernicus' *De Revolutionibus* (1976 [1543]). Alfred North Whitehead (1967a [1925], Ch. III) prefers 1642, the date of Galileo's death and Newton's birth. All these dates fall in the mid-16th to the mid-17th century, the time of the beginnings of the scientific revolution.

11 Perry Miller in his history of "the New England mind" pays a lot of attention to Ramism and its connection to Puritanism. In his *The New England mind: The seventeenth century* (1939) he says "Ramism ... exercised the decisive role in shaping New England thought" (p. 116; emphasis added). This role was in helping students understand how to read and interpret the Bible. For this, Aristotle's logic and its system of classifications was used. What Ramism did, again as Craig (1952/1935) points out, was to make Aristotle "practical"—removing most of the Aristotle from Aristotle's categories and doing only the "application." Dewey well recognized the difficulty with such an extreme position—that of "one-sided meanings" and wished to "escape the alternatives of an academic and aloof knowledge and a hard, narrow, and merely 'practical' practice" (1966a [1916], pp. 136, 137). Dewey wanted a third way, an "alternative" to the "either/ors" of theory/practice, child/curriculum we have known for so long. I believe the "practicalizing" movement, again raising its head in educational thought, needs itself to be rethought.

weak his Latin—can remember what Peter of Spain [and his 'logic'] is all about" (pp. 58–59). A number of social and pedagogical points stand out here: (1) Latin was the only language in which academic books were printed; the late 19th century's myth of Latin "strengthening the mind" is an abstraction from a very concrete and practical Renaissance activity; (2) the youths Ramus taught were 8 to 16 years of age, hardly mature in their thinking; (3) the Latin and logic they handled were extremely simple and consisted almost entirely of memorizing rules and categories. In short, while *methodus* was designed to teach one to "think," the preparation needed for that thinking was memory and rule bound. In fact, the concept of *school thinking* that we have inherited from medieval times is still very much bound up in memory and rules. Developing a school or curriculum functionalism for thinking that involves personal deliberation, reflection, action, choice—one that Dewey stressed so much (1966a [1916], Chs 11 and 12)—is a very real struggle for curricularists and educators today.

Ramus was a schoolmaster (head of the Collége de Presles) not a scholar—albeit he had pretensions to the latter, being also a Regius professor. As a schoolmaster and textbook writer, he set out to simplify (but not categorically change) the memorization and rule learning procedures his boys needed to accomplish for their study of "logic"—really memorization of stilted forms of rhetorical disputation. Ramus did this simplification (shortcutting it was called) by drawing on the wizardry of moveable type which allowed him to produce a "visual noetic." Into this visual frame—similar to the chart bracketings used today for match play in sports events such as tennis and basketball—Ramus felt one (preferably himself) could place all knowledge. These chartings would break any subject into its dichotomous parts and further reduce the parts into smaller and smaller dichotomous but hierarchically connected parts. Whereas our sports chartings move from the many to the one (a winner), Ramus' knowledge chartings moved from the general one to the particular many. A Ramist chart (Figure 8.1) is the first one (1576) to use the word *curriculum* in the sense of formalizing or sequencing educational order.[12]

In charting knowledge in this manner, Ramus—in the interest of pedagogical expediency—"dissociated knowledge from discourse" (Ong, 1983 [1958], Preface). Teaching now moved from laying out issues for discussion to disseminating

---

12 The word curriculum which means racecourse was used by Calvin in *curriculum vitae* (course of life) and was adopted by Ramus and others to order studies in a sequential manner. Prior to Ramus, studies (and indeed the serving of food) were not organized sequentially. The approach was more like a smorgasbord (to keep the food metaphor). (See Doll, in Pinar, 1998, Ch. 14.)

Ong (1971) points out that Ramus' "itemizing approach" (p. 180) to organization, consisting both of visual charting and precise time for tasks (p. 152)—is natural for our modernist, industrial world but revolutionary for the 16th century's feudal world. The training devices Taylor developed so precisely, Ramus started in teaching young boys the rudiments of learning. Ong's book *Rhetoric, romance, and technology* (1971) is quite fascinating in connecting Ramus' procedures to our modernist, commercial, industrial world.

TABVLA ARTIVM, QVAS IN
hoc Volumine coniunximus.

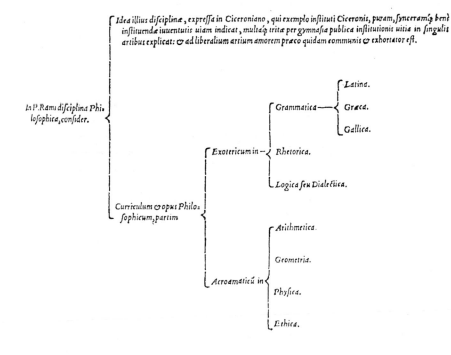

Source: P. Ramus, *Professio regia*, Basle, 1576.

FIGURE 8.1 Ramist map of curriculum

This diagram is the first to use the word curriculum in the educational sense of ordering courses. It is a chart made by Johann Thomas Freige, a Swiss printer, four years after Ramus' death and comes from his *Professio Regia*. Professio Regia, Ramus' title as a Regius or King's Professor, is the name Freige gave to the collection of Ramus' schoolboy lectures, which he, Freige, compiled after Ramus' death. The chart shows in visual form the general educational philosophy of Peter Ramus; "A Table of the Arts" he calls it, with "infinite examples from Cicero," Ramus' favorite rhetorician, and the curriculum study of the *trivium* and the *quadrivium*, "to well instruct youths and for experts for school learning." The original is in the Glasgow University Library Special Collections (Mu3 6-b. 19) and is used with their permission.

The methodization movement went well beyond teaching, of course. It lies at the heart of Descartes' (1950, [1637]) whole epistemology and is rhapsodized by Leibniz in his multiple comments on method. For example, in his "On the method of universality" (1951 [1674]) Leibniz says, "Nothing can escape our method ... it spares the mind and the imagination: the latter above all must be used sparingly" (p. 4). I suspect that comments like this were instrumental in encouraging Paul Feyerabend to write his *Against method* (1988). See particularly his comments in his Introduction where he talks of "Ideologies which use the name of science" (p. 4).

knowledge for absorption. And the form of this laying out, this "method of teaching" via "the arrangement of various things brought down from universal and general principles to the underlying singular parts" was to "place first that which is first in the absolute order of knowledge, that next which is next, and so on" in an unbroken progression" (Ramus, 1569 edition of the *Dialectic,* in Ong, 1983 [1958], pp. 245, 248). Ramus, like Taylor and Tyler who were to follow him in this concept of method as a *routine of efficiency,* never seems to have realized that the absolute order of knowledge he so revered was *his* order of knowledge—just as personal as Taylor's "standards" or Tyler's "philosophic screen."

Stephen Triche, in Chapter 2 of his dissertation, "Reconceiving curriculum" (2002), traces the methodization movement in schooling from Ramus' "visualist noetic" through Francis Bacon's "literate experience" and Johann Amos Comenius' "didactic" to Rene Descartes' "method for rightly conducting reason," and to the English and American Puritans' concept of "simple order." As this movement progressed over the centuries, teaching took on an ever increasing didactic coloration and became ever less exploratory, provocative, dialogical, or experiential. Its thrust was schoolbookish, designed to present elementary material to be absorbed in an efficient way by boys 8 to 16 years of age. This is the tradition of teaching we have inherited from our forefathers.

John Dewey's Reaction

This tradition of teaching, more monological than interactive, didactic than dialogical, bothered John Dewey immensely; not, by the way, as Philip Jackson (1998, Chapter 4) points out, that Dewey himself practiced the dialogical (except rhetorically while lecturing). Dewey's bother was pedagogical but less a practical pedagogy than a pedagogy which had epistemological and axiological roots: teaching in a methodized way removes the experiences of the learner, the learner's very being from the learning process. For Dewey, this dichotomous separation of teaching from learning was unacceptable. Dewey did not see the one subservient to the other but saw the two as interactive complements of each other. His famous phrase regarding such unnatural separation is that the child and the curriculum (the learner and that taught) exist not as categorical separates but "as two points on a single line" (1990, p. 189), each receiving its meaning in relation to the other. For Dewey, knowledge did not exist independently of human experience, it was rather *the by-product of humans reflecting on their experiences,* trying to solve the problems they found in the real world of living. His relation to science was not as a panacea of procedure but as living experimentation. Dewey believed that knowing came through acting reflectively, and he liked the public, observable acting inherent in science as a method. He felt this method separated our epistemology, our way of knowing, from medieval procedures. As he says, "the [new] methods of science ... are nothing but experimentation [inquiry] carried out under conditions of deliberate control. ... Experience then ceases to be empirical and becomes experimental ... by which activity [human doing] is made fruitful in meaning" (1966a [1916], pp. 272, 276).[13]

Walter Ong, in his final chapter of *Ramus, method, and the decay of dialogue* (1983 [1958]), argues that as the form of knowing in the medieval and post-medieval ages moved from the aural and oral to the literary—with the invention of printing, especially moveable type—so truth moved from the personal to the textual. Truth became depersonalized, abstracted, symbolized. Logic in all its formalism supplanted rhetoric and all its passion. The Word now was abstracted from Life. Reason became formalized. In contrast to this tendency, Dewey wished to base his philosophy (really his whole worldview) not on logic—his "logic" is a "warranted assertability"—but on human experience. He believed, as I've already quoted, that *"common experience is capable of developing within itself* methods which will secure direction for itself and will create inherent standards of judgment and value" (1958a [1929], p. 38; emphasis added).

Dewey believed that experience—really the experienced situation—could develop itself via integrating action with reflection. Dewey calls active experience the primary form with reflective experience the secondary form (1958a [1929], pp. 4–5; and 1966a [1916], p. 140). It is the wholistic combining of these two, *emotive doing* and *reflecting* intelligence, which excites Dewey. He develops this idea in various passages in *Democracy and education* (especially in Chapter 11, p. 150 and Chapter 12, p. 163), and, of course, makes his famous plea for an operable theory of experience in *Experience and education* (1963 [1938], Chapter 2). However, as James Garrison (1997) and Philip Jackson (1998)—leading revivalists of the "new Dewey scholarship"—note, the best development of experience occurs in Dewey's *Art as experience* (1958b [1934]). There he has a chapter on transforming experience or turning our everyday doings into *an* experience—doings reflected upon, directed, developed.

He begins this chapter by stating that experience in its usual sense is no more than everyday doings, events, happenings, "sufferings" (p. 3). The use of this word, suffering, is interesting; Dewey will return to it later when he wishes to move beyond an inchoate, unconscious, experiencing to experiencing which has an aesthetic quality to it. This he defines as being *an experience*. This spiritful sense of experience—one

---

13 The issue of "deliberate control" is delicate. Control of a certain amount—which elsewhere (Doll, 1993, 1998a) I've called "just the right amount"—is needed for freedom to be productive; but too much control fetters freedom. Regretfully, the use to which we in education have put the scientific method and its sense of control has been more on the side of fettering than of freeing. The issue of control being dissipated throughout the situation, not imposed from either its center or outside, is not well understood.

Dewey's notion of method here as guided inquiry is close to the ancients—especially Socrates'—concept of *methodus*. Again, look at what Dewey has to say in *Democracy and education* (1966a [1916]) about method—reflective thinking—as the relationship between the intellectual and the practical (Ch. 20, especially).

filled with the dynamic vitality of living—is aesthetic, and "involves a suffering, that is consistent with, indeed a part of, the complete perception that is enjoyed" (p. 41). It is this aesthetic quality which brings experience to life, which "rounds out an experience into completeness and unity" (p. 41). A few pages later, Dewey develops this theme of aesthetic experiencing even more when he says that "the undergoing phase of experience" involves not only suffering but surrendering—a surrendering to the power and force of the experience:

> To steep ourselves in a subject-matter, we have first to plunge into it. [We need to let it] overwhelm us … to bear us down [as we become passionately immersed]. [But at this very moment, when we are about to be overwhelmed], we must summon energy and pitch it at a responsive key in order to take in [the experience].
>
> (p. 53)

What different blood runs through the veins, and what a different spirit inhabits the minds, of Peter Ramus and John Dewey. For Ramus, knowledge can be universally codified (by him) before students interact with it, and learning occurs in a direct causal relation to how "clearly" the codified knowledge is presented. For Dewey, knowledge is a result, indeed a by-product, of individual's active engagement with and reflection on personal experience. Learning emerges from this reflective interaction: through reflection, people (students and teachers) learn and learn how they learn. Ramus has left us a legacy to overcome, Dewey a challenge to meet.

A Method?

The concept of method has a long history, going back to the ancient *Greek methodia (methodus* in Latin). Educationally, it has been associated with the idea of ordering learning—by those outside the immediate learning process—in a sequential, one-best way. This tradition stretches all the way from today's current behaviorally oriented processes back to Galen's training of physicians. Teaching in this frame has, basically, been that of imposing a pre-set order on those *doing* the learning. Ramus, the pedagogue most famous and most responsible for framing and disseminating this concept, not only ordered, charted, and sequenced the knowledge and skills young boys were to acquire, but also detailed the time and way they were to proceed with this acquisition. [He bragged that his 15-year-old youths had acquired university training by the time they left his college.] In a number of ways Petrus Ramus seems to have been a forefather to Frederick Taylor: both meted out strong punishment towards those who did not follow their prescriptions precisely, both were skill rhetoricians, and both were, to use Taylor's phrase, "manipulators of men." Those critical of this methodizing concept see it as manipulative, impositional, closed, destructive of imagination, nonhumanist, simplistic, and to use Dewey's phrase having "lamentable consequences." Those supportive of this methodizing concept see it as scientific, efficient, socially productive—"reasonable" is the sort of phrase, if not stated, implied.

Dewey has a quite different idea as to what method was about—the same might be said of his concepts of science, teaching, learning, knowledge, efficiency, a moral society, and so on; but here I will deal only with method. For Dewey, method is a procedure; but one different from that which runs from Ramus to Tyler. Dewey sees this method as one of *transformation not transmission*. As such, he begins with the experience of the learner not with the "logical" knowledge base of those imposing/teaching. For Dewey, teaching was not didactic imposition but communal (conjoint is a word he often used) development. The experiences of the immature are to develop, grow, be transformed by interaction with peers and adults. This is an all-share process.

The development of experience is not a willy-nilly process; its method (that of reflective thinking) is *both* open *and* directed. It is open in that no end is pre-set, the only end is growth, an end that has no end. It is directed in that the situation directs itself towards its own fulfillment. (With the emergence of complexity theory, see Kauffman (1993, 1995), this is less of a startling statement than when Dewey first made it.) For a situation to be so directive it needs to be rich in problematics (but not too rich) and filled with possibilities (but not too filled). We as interactors in the situation need to "plunge" into it—approach it aesthetically and spiritually—to actively search for the possibilities that exist in the situation. Alfred North Whitehead's admonition to "throw ideas into every combination possible" (1967b [1929], p. 2) is most appropriate here. Teaching now becomes less a process of efficient transmission and more a journeying with others on a path of learning engagement and personal transformation.

A Pedagogic Creed

In a reflective relationship between teacher and student, the teacher does not ask the student to accept the teacher's authority; rather, the teacher asks the student *to suspend disbelief in that authority*, to join with the teacher in inquiry into that which the student is experiencing. The teacher agrees to help the student understand the meaning of the advice given, to be readily confrontable by the student, and to work with the student in reflecting on the tacit understanding each has (from Doll, 1993, p. 160).

9

CRAFTING AN EXPERIENCE

(2004)

As Deweyans know, experience is the centerpiece of Dewey's philosophy and pedagogy. As important as experience is, however, and much as we teachers may want to "give an experience" to our students, we cannot do so. The best we can do, in Philip Jackson's felicitous phrase (1998) is help them do their own "crafting of an experience" (p. 122). In Dewey's own words (1966a [1916]):

> No thought, no idea [indeed, no experience] can be conveyed as an idea [or experience] from one person to another. When it is told [or so conveyed, given] it is, to the one to whom it is told another given fact, not an idea [or experience].
>
> (pp. 159–160)

The person having the experience must do the experiencing for him/herself: "The beholder must create his own experience" (Dewey, 1958b [1934], p. 54).

So, if we cannot "give" an experience to a person, how can we help a person to craft his or her own experience? Jackson, along with James Garrison (1997), turns to Dewey's aesthetic for an answer. This aspect brings forth a picture of Dewey we often miss. From Peter Ramus in the 16th century to Ralph Tyler in the 20th, the teaching aspect of education has been caught up in the maelstrom of "methodization."[1] The consequences of this movement have been "lamentable"; for, as Dewey (1966a [1916]) says: "To suppose that students ... can be supplied with models of method to be followed ... is to fall into a self-deception that has lamentable consequences ... [ones] which breed mediocrity in all but the very exceptional" (pp. 172–173).

---

1 For more on this movement see Doll and Gough (2002); Triche and McKnight (2004) and Trueit (2005b).

What to do then? Again, how do we help students craft experiences? Dewey's (1963 [1938]) answer, one both Jackson and Garrison espouse, is to "plunge into" the aesthetics of the experience at hand, to "undergo," to "suffer," to "absorb," and be absorbed into the experience (pp. 48, 56). Dewey has another wonderful quote about this activity: "[It is not easy] to understand the intimate union of doing and undergoing. … The esthetic undergoing phase of experience … involves surrender. But adequate yielding of the self is possible only through a controlled activity that may well be intense" (p. 52).

That is, as we "plunge into" subject matter, "we must summon [our] energy and pitch it at a responsive key in order to *take* in" (p. 53; emphasis in original) and be taken into the depth of the experience we are experiencing. It is this process of interactive doing, undergoing, and responding which turns experience into *an experience*. And this experiencing has an aesthetic, qualitative, intuitive, felt, creative—even spiritual—side to it. Again, to quote Dewey (1966d [1948]): "Denial … of all inherent longings and aspiring tendencies … remove[s] nature and natural science from contact with poetry, religion, and divine things" (p. 69). Crafting as experience, then, is something each person must do individually, but as teachers we can help. We can encourage students to "plunge into" subject matter, to see, feel, experience its aesthetic qualities—to explore the *spirit* of the subject at hand, as it were. And, in this process, as the experience begins to "overwhelm them," the students need to summon their own creative energy and thus help direct the experience to "its own end" (1958b [1934], p. 43), thereby *crafting an experience*—unique yet universal.[2]

2 *Experience and nature* (1958a [1929]) is one of Dewey's more important philosophical texts while *Experience and education* (1963 [1938]) is one of his more important pedagogical texts. Both of these call for and begin the development of a theory of experience. This development was never brought to fruition by Dewey, a point Philip Jackson brings out nicely and timely in his *The philosopher's task* (2002).

10

PIAGETIAN THOUGHT

(2010)

Jean Piaget (1896–1980) was one of the 20th century's most influential educational theorists, with a particular emphasis on how children learn. He was not just a learning theorist though; he was also—and indeed, foremost—a philosopher and logician, theoretical biologist, developmental psychologist, and cognitivist. His magnum opus is *Biology and knowledge* (1971a [1967], followed by his *Behavior and evolution* (1978 [1976]). In these, he lays out his "genetic epistemology," where he talks of the process of cognitive development in terms of transformations. These transformations hold importance for curricularists.

For Piaget, transformative development in humans (children especially) was development that moved actions (and reactions to actions) from one stage or level to a new, higher stage or level. Such a hierarchal process was allied with (and indeed may have been heavily influenced by) his Ph.D. study on how mollusks (snails) reacted to a change in their environment. Piaget observed the snails did not react immediately to a change in environment; rather they *assimilated* the environmental change into their own, patterned ways of operation. At a certain, undetermined point, though, enough environmental change encouraged the mollusks to *accommodate* themselves to the environmental change. This assimilation/accommodation process, *interactive* by nature, became the heart of Piaget's epistemology. He called it "genetic epistemology," referring to the fact that behavior, especially, deep-seated, genomic, lasting behavior (a change of schemas or ways of operation), could not be imposed as the Lamarckians/ Skinnerians believed, nor was it random as the Darwinists/neo-Darwinists asserted but would develop via an *interaction* of environment and subject (animal/person). This interactionist approach was applauded by Ilya Prigogine, an early contributor to chaos and complexity theories, and is much appreciated by Dewey scholars who emphasize inter- (or trans-) action as the way children learn (Dewey, 1960 [1929]).

Piaget believed that children's learning is organized around their ability, over time, to develop logical and abstract thinking—for him (as a logician) the epitome of adult thinking. His stages (really *schemas* or ways of operation) are: sensorimotor (0–2 years) where the child coordinates bodily reflexes; *preoperational* (2–6/7 years) where the child focuses on self; *concrete operational* (6/7–11/12 years) where the child/youth begins to develop a systems view, becoming aware of more than self but limited in this thinking to concrete instances; and *formal operational* (11/12 years and more) where (ideally) mature, abstract, rigorous, logical thinking becomes operational. The sense of "progression" in this process captivated American audiences, especially childhood teachers and theorists. "Developmentally appropriate practices," became a mantra for childhood educators. Childhood educators found themselves caught—they wanted to use operations which fit the stages the child was in; parents and often administrators want to "aid" the child to move through the stages quickly. The American way, as Piaget labeled it, was to move children as quickly as possible through the stages. Piaget, though, with his firm grounding in a biological, interactionist process—one where the genome has its own ways of operation, and maintaining his theory of genetic epistemology, affirmed that one could not "teach" a child out of one stage and into the next. Movement of this sort happens not by force or even by enticement but when the child's cognitive structure "desires" such a change. The transformation happens individually, unspecified, and "tout ensemble."

This sense of a sudden, total change of schemas/worldviews/ways of operation/ structures is much akin to the work being done in complexity studies at the Santa Fe Institute, especially by Per Bak and Stuart Kauffman. Piaget's interactionist approach—a tertium quid alternative to both (behaviorist) imposition and (benevolent) neglect—can be seen, along with Dewey's inter- (trans-) actional approach as a forerunner of the complexity theory approaches being developed today. Curricularists utilizing the insights of complexity theory believe meaningful, lasting learning occurs not by imposition (direct instruction), nor randomly (benign neglect); rather it occurs as the result of an interactive, creative, and dynamic tension occurring between subject and object, self and other, person and environment.

Within his genetic epistemology, Piaget labels his interactionist approach Equilibration. Here a child or young learner "seeks" a harmony within the operatory schema s/he is using. This zone of comfort is disturbed either by chance or pedagogical design and a sense of disequilibrium sets in; through the active process of assimilation/accommodation a new, more comprehensive (and logical) stage/schema emerges. Equilibration occurs as the original stage/schema is re-equilibrated. Regrettably, few educators have seen the importance of this process. To quote one, though: "By far the most important of Piaget's many original concepts ... the keystone that holds together—both logically and psychologically—the edifice of his theory" (Furth, 1981, p. xiv).

While in this process, it is disequilibrium that is "the driving force of development," there is overall a sense of active seeking, of *purpose* that Piaget posits to mollusks and humans. In one of his last writings, a book done with and finished by Rolando Garcia, Piaget explores this notion of *purpose*. Piaget believes that from an early age (when the child can distinguish relations) the young child is purposeful in his actions—s/he not only acts but acts with *intentions*. The "illogic" adults find (and are often frustrated by) in a child's operations are, from another point of view, the child's way of operating within his/her schema in a purposeful way. Over time these operations become more and more "logical."

For curricularists, the art is one of looking at not only the child or learner's actions but also ferreting out his/her intentions. Further, it means allowing/encouraging the child/learner to utilize well the power of the schema present while also providing at the right time and in "just the right amount" those perturbations necessary for new and more comprehensive schema to emerge. Such is the legacy Jean Piaget has left us.

11

MODES OF THOUGHT

(2003)

Science
Logic/
Reason

Story
Culture/
Person

Spirit
Life/Breath
"Vital Integrity"

Mysterium Tremendum

FIGURE 11.1 Doll's 3 S's: Science, Story, Spirit

Science/Logic/Reason		Story/Culture/Person
Substance/Truth/"Reality"	[Deals with]	Pattern/Experience/Relations
Precision/Definiteness/Exactitude	[Honors, Utilizes]	Metaphor/Allegory/Interpretation
"Proves" (QED)/Probes	[Method]	Narrative, Verisimilitude
Objective/"Real"	[Frame]	Subjective/Experiential
Sciences/Mathematics	[Disciplines]	Humanities/Arts
Quantitative	[Research Procedures]	Qualitative, Layered
"One-eyed Reason"	Difficulties	Solipism

A third space—one that honours, utilizes the ineffable, the aesthetic, the creative, the passionate, the awe-inspiring. Its method is one of "engaging"—engaging difference with a sense of passion, play, reverence, respect. Its difficulty is *ideological enslavement*.

The foregoing "open heart" has been inspired by Jerome Bruner's essay, "Two modes of thought" (1986a). This essay contrasts in a complementary way the scientific with the storied (which Bruner calls "narrative"). This complementary split of modes of thought and thinking is often considered in terms of the quantitative (science) and the qualitative (narrative or story). For years, as I have pondered the quantitative– qualitative distinction, I have felt a certain something was missing: a sense of the spirit which lies in that "third space" (Serres, 1997 [1991]) both separating and uniting "science" and "story." Thus, I write this essay in my attempt to find that "third space," and the creativity I believe lies there. Such a struggle also helps me understand better both science and story—the two modes of thinking that have so far dominated educational theory and practice. In my development of this essay I will draw heavily upon Jerome Bruner and upon the one he draws on, Wolfgang Iser. I will also draw upon Alfred North Whitehead and the complexity theorists who follow in his footsteps. For spirit, I am much influenced by the writings of Dwayne Huebner (1999), one of the fathers of curriculum theory. The ghost of John Dewey hovers over all (Doll, 2002b), and the writings of Michel Serres are never far from my thoughts. I ask all readers, especially those in Canada and China who subjected themselves to earlier and far more incomplete versions of the argument, to aid me in my quest. This quest is to find the spirit of creativity which I believe lies (often hidden, often yet-to-be-born) in every situation.

Bruner's essay is one I consider seminal. In it, he proposes that we consider the scientific–logical–rational mode of thinking as but one—i.e. not *the only*—way of thinking, of ordering experience, of viewing "reality." This "logico–scientific" mode he calls paradigmatic: one which has dominated Western intellectual discourse since at least the time of the 17th century and its scientific revolution. Its virtue is that of dispassionate, verifiable analysis, of "logical proof, sound argument, and empirical discovery guided by reasoned hypotheses" (1986a, p. 13). Being paradigmatic—the dominant, if not "only," way to think well—we assign the title "good" to this way of thought. When we hold up the ideal of "good" teaching, or "good" thinking, or "good" research, we are espousing the scientific, logical, rational. To use the phrase "Research tells us …" is to grant moral authority and approbation to an issue. Strong as this mode is, and as much as it has accomplished, it still *lacks heart*. Bruner says it is "heartless," seeking "to transcend the particular by higher and higher reaching for abstraction." "In the end," this mode *disclaims in principle any explanatory value at all where the particular is concerned*" (p. 13; emphasis added). It is, of course, the particular, the experiential, the personal which story brings into play. Story (or narrative) Bruner says, "is built upon concern for the human condition," *l'affaire humaine*.

Alfred North Whitehead, mathematician, philosopher, and educator, was also both awed and bothered by the revolution in thinking the scientific–logico– rational has wrought. Like Bruner, he sees this mode of thought as paradigmatic, dominant since the scientific revolution of the 17th century. He calls this thought, "the greatest single intellectual success which mankind has achieved" (1967a [1925],

p. 46). This mode of thought introduced empiricism and induction and helped humankind get away from the "unbridled rationalism" of scholastic–Christian thought (p. 39). Scientists began to observe, but they made a fatal error in believing that what they observed—"stuff, or matter, or material" (p. 49)—was the really real of reality. The concept of the perceiving organism, the individual and his/her powers (of abstracting, creating, imagining) was subjugated to the concrete. In becoming supreme, the concrete, in itself "dead," lifeless," "barren," "inert" (Whitehead, 1967b [1929], Ch. 1), and "meaningless" (1967a [1925], p. 54), took on a role it could not maintain. It usurped the role of the human and his/her ability to perceive, to sense, to abstract, to create. The perceiving individual, in all his/her sensuousness "feels" a situation and in this feeling actually brings the situation into being. The human affair for Whitehead, then, becomes one of each person interacting with the environment and in the interaction reality is born. Reality for Whitehead is not made up of material "stuff" but is a process, an interactive process between "mind and nature" to use Gregory Bateson's (1988 [1979]) phrase. Abstraction, that which the human mind does so well (Whitehead, 1967a [1925], p. 55), is necessary for all thought (p. 59). But to abstract only, to try to think without focusing thought on the "brute" facts nature lays before us (p. 17) is, as Bruner notes, to transcend the particular, to leave it, rather than to transform it. Transformation is a developmental process. For Whitehead, this process is itself reality, and any situation in this process has a certain vibratoriness: it comes into being, establishes itself (temporarily in a nexus of connections) and (like subatomic particles) fades out of existence. To quote Whitehead himself:

> [W]e shall conceive each primordial element as a vibratory ebb and flow of an underlying energy or activity. … Accordingly there will be a definite period associated with each element; and within that period the stream-system will sway from one stationary maximum to another stationary maximum.
>
> (p. 35)

All this is to say that each element (or occasion) is always involved in a nexus of connections—cultural, historical, personal. This nexus (or relationship) forms a horizontal and vertical network, a three-dimensional web, as Serres (1991 [1983]) so dramatically shows and Fritjof Capra (1996) illustrates. It is horizontal in that any current set of connections can interact (abductively) with another set of connections. It is vertical in that a particular set of connections (or elements within the set) will have past histories and future possibilities. Such a system frame is quite different from the "simple location" of an atom (or fact) isolated by itself. Again, to quote Whitehead: "The idea of simple location is the very foundation of the seventeenth century scheme of nature." The character of simple location is that "a particular material body" exists in space and time (or space-time) in a particular way: "It is just there, in that place … there is nothing more to be said on the subject." He goes on to say, "I shall argue there is no element whatever which possesses this character of simple location" (Whitehead, 1967a [1925], pp. 49, 58). Instead of simple location (isolated facts), Whitehead proposes a cosmology or metaphysic based on complex connections and dynamic (or vibratory) relationships. No object is unto itself; each is embedded, each is contingent. He believes such a metaphysic should form the *heart* of both our view of reality and our educational programs. Discrete facts in and of themselves are quite useless; however, facts embedded in a matrix of relationships provide us with the "richness" (Doll, 1993, Ch. 7) necessary for knowledge and knowing to transform themselves via creative development built upon creative development, upon creative development. This process is much akin to Dewey's (1966a [1916], Ch. 4) sense of growth and to Stuart Kauffman's (2000) sense of a new, open-ended (not closed) thermodynamics.

It seems quite natural to me that Prigogine and Stengers (1984) draw on the philosophy/cosmology of Whitehead for the metaphysics of their view of complexity theory. With his strong interest in the quanta and awareness of how the biological (with its development of the organic) would change 20th century intellectual thought, Whitehead is a natural to claim the title of Grandfather of Complexity Theory.

While Bruner and Whitehead agree that the scientific–logico–rational for all its strengths is just one way of knowing, a way most limited in the current century, it is Bruner who develops *l'affaire humaine*, not Whitehead. This is not to say that Whitehead neglects the human, far from it. His whole notion of *misplaced concreteness* is based on our human ability to abstract—to abstract qualities or patterns we see/create, and then to reify them into material "things," thus misplacing concreteness. To quote Whitehead: "We have mistaken *our* abstraction for concrete realities" (p. 55; emphasis added). It is this overemphasis on the (mistaken) reality of the concrete which leads, Whitehead believes, to our exaggerated emphasis in education on the factual, overlooking our human ability to deal with "brute" facts in a contextualized, imaginative, playful manner. This narrowness of thinking Whitehead calls "one-eyed reason" (p. 59) and its effects have been devastating in the educational, social, and political arenas.

A more "binocular" view of thinking (Bateson, Ch. 3) would be to combine the analytic with the aesthetic, the normed with the narrative, the quantitative with the qualitative, the proven with the personal, the scientific with the storied in a dynamic dance of the Yin and the Yang. It is in this dance, this movement that I find space for spirit. But before moving into the search for spirit, I'd like to focus on the storied and the role Bruner and Iser see it playing in the broadened concept of education I am laying out. Whereas the scientific–logical "attempts to fulfill the ideal of a formal, mathematical system of descriptions and explanations," the storied or "narrative is built upon concern for the human condition" (Bruner, 1986a, pp. 13, 14) with all its multifarious twists and turns. Four centuries ago, Giambattista Vico (1668–1744) commented upon this difference between the analytic and personal by saying:

Indeed, were you to apply the geometric method to life, 'you would succeed only in trying to be a rational lunatic,' steering in a straight line amid life's curves, as though caprice, rashness, chance and fortune held no sway in human affairs

(1988 [1710], p. 98; Vico quoting Terrence, *Eunuchus,* pp. 62–63).

It is life and its complexity of personal experiences that story brings forth. Story proves nothing and attempts to prove nothing. Rather, it wants to subjectively draw the reader into its world and convince him or her of the validity of that world via the "lifelikeness," or "verisimilitude" of the experience the reader has in engaging the "text." Further, the openness of the text, its uncertainty, is what gives the story power. As Iser says, "It is the element of indeterminacy that evokes the text to 'communicate' with the reader" (in Bruner, 1986a, p. 24). Here the text induces (even seduces) the reader to participate in the story's unfolding, as the text "allows a spectrum of actualizations to emerge." In this way, tapping into a "psychic reality," meaning comes through performance not proof (pp. 24, 25).

It is the "performance of meaning" which is so exciting about story and which gives it such curricular and educational power. The reader (of fiction or non-fiction) participates in evoking meaning from the text. Meaning is co-created, as the text and the reader perform their duet. With its emphasis on performance—an important point for both Iser and Bruner—the reader does not merely receive the text nor discover the text's main point(s); the reader and the text negotiate moving together through their intellectual *pas de deux*. This notion of meaning emerging from mutual interaction is much akin to Humberto Maturana and Francisco Varela's "coupling" (1987), to Lynn Margulis' "symbiogenesis" (1998), and to Stuart Kauffman's "co-constructing" (2000). In short, the view of story (narrative) Bruner and Iser put forth goes well beyond interpretative inquiry as this field has (itself) been interpreted and moves closer to recent developments in complexity theory.

Wolfgang Iser, in his recent book, *The range of interpretation* (2000), moves even more boldly to align literary interpretative theory with complexity theory. As the title indicates, Iser looks at interpretation theory over a range of times and genres. He moves from interpretation of the Torah, to the "hermeneutic circle," to Umberto Eco's post-modernism; and he integrates literary theory with the cognitive and complexity sciences, paying special attention to the biology of Maturana and Varela, the cybernetics of Norbert Weiner, and the anthropological/epistemological theories of Gregory Bateson and Clifford Geertz. Although he does not mention the quanta or the work it has spawned in mathematics, physics, and chemistry, the concept of the nonlinear, in the form of recursive feedback loops, is central to all Iser says. While a dense and complex work, the book's main argument is simple. As long as one assumes stability in culture and human nature, then interpretation is essentially an act of simple translation, of transposition. Drawing on Geertz, Iser (2000) says:

> The less we are inclined to define human nature in terms of certain basic qualities—let alone in terms of an assumed constancy, independent of time, place, and circumstance—the more varied will be the modifications to which the wrongly assumed constancy of human nature is subjected. Such a revision leads Geertz to this conclusion: Modern anthropology "is firm in the conviction that men unmodified by the customs of particular places do not in fact exist, have never existed, and most important, could not in the very nature of the case exist."
>
> (p. 88; in Geertz, 1973, p. 35)

The only way to deal with interpretation in a world where culture and self, text and interpreter are constantly shifting is via recursive feedback loops. That is, via an interpretative, ongoing interaction between text and translator, each one continually "dancing" with the other. Iser, drawing on Maturana and Varela's (1980) notion of autopoietic systems, especially as presented by Varela (1979), likens this network of "mutual connections," to "conversation," where "one cannot find a firm reference point" (Iser, 2000, p. 101). Using the metaphor of dance, there is no stable center for the dancers but there is a continually shifting space between (or among) the dancers as they glide or gyrate, depending on the dance.

As Iser says (2000, pp. 101, 153), and as Donna Trueit (2005a) develops, this paradigm shift—from the stable to the dynamic—moves us from an epistemology based on representation to one based on performance. An "epistemology of performance" is not one of merely demonstrating what an author or text means; it is "dancing with the text," and in that dance (in the space the dance occupies) newness "emerges" (Iser, 2000, p. 153). Emergence is, of course, a key concept in the complexity sciences (S. Johnson, 2001). Emergence, the process of producing the new, the process of creativity, comes out of performance. So an "epistemology of performance" would be one where, in a Wittgensteinian or Serrean way, one would always be playing *with* the boundaries we both need and are entrapped by. While playing *with* boundaries is an event of practical living, working with this concept, attempting to define and frame it, represents a new challenge for curriculum and complexity theorists. What would a curriculum that played with boundaries look like? How would such a curriculum be administered? Evaluated?

In the space produced by the feedback loops, the dance, or the play—this space of "the third"—there exists, I believe, "spirit." And it is spirit which education needs and sorely lacks. For in spirit, there exists—in all its awesome mystery—a vitality and in that vitality resides creativity. The *Oxford English Dictionary* (online, 2003) defines spirit as "that which gives life" to the physical or material; it is "the breath of life" (II:1a). As such, spirit is itself non-material, it is the process of giving life or vitality to our being human or metaphorically to a situation or occasion sense of being. In Christian biblical terms, Spirit (the Holy Ghost) acts as a messenger between God and humans, bringing power and creativity: it caused Elizabeth's child (John) to leap in her womb; it impregnated Mary with the child Jesus, and was the driving force behind His ministry; and it filled the disciples with the zeal to become Christian missionaries (*Oxford Annotated Bible,* 1965). In all these acts, Spirit performs, infusing life into, "actuating" (I:3c). In theological terms, spirit is considered as "the active essence or essential power of the Deity, conceived as a creative, animating, or inspiring influence" (II:6a). The non-theological notion of spirit plays off that of this last "definition" in the sense of infusing a situation or entity (team, school, organization, movement) with an animating power, essentially a power to do that shapes the quality or mode of that situation or entity.

My focus on this sense of a principal activating, animating, giving life to, endowing a situation with "moreness" (to utilize Dwayne Huebner's word; 1999, pp. 403–404), is my belief, following Whitehead, that such infusing is necessary for "keeping knowledge alive." Such a process, active in nature, is itself a process. That is, any situation (and here I focus on teaching situations) can be more than it is by infusing that situation (experience, event, occasion) with spirit, or by finding the spirit that may well lie dormant within the situation. Whitehead, with his sense of the spiritful and spiritual—"the essence of education is that it be religious" (1967b [1929], p. 14)—believes we need to find the "relational essence" (1967a [1925], p. 88) of a situation. Relational essence focuses on a situation not being reified, not being a "thing" isolated in itself (as so many school subjects are) but always in relation to the situation present. This focus on the relationality of a situation, on its process of being, is allied with complexity theory's mode of considering relationality itself as always being in process, of always forming a dynamic system. Such a system perspective means looking at any situation in terms of its horizontal interconnections to other situations and vertically in terms of its past history and future yet-to-be possibilities.

Such an approach to a situation (including the design and implementation of school curricula) draws heavily not only on Whitehead but also on Dewey, Serres, and Wittgenstein. A focus on the interaction between *passion and play* seems essential here. The concept of spirit has within it a strong sense of passion (OED, Vol. 3, pp. 12, 13, 14). Dewey talks of "plunging into a situation" (*Art as experience,* 1958b [1934], p. 53), of feeling a situation with "passion" and "affection," of being immersed, of "surrendering ourselves" to the situation in order to experience both its fullness and our own. The complexity sciences—dealing with issues from the autopoietic to the thermodynamic—assume an interaction that goes beyond the receptive. An interaction that is active. An interaction that is throbbing with vitality, that has spirit to it.

While such a passionate approach to teaching and learning is, I believe, necessary, by itself it certainly is not sufficient. A spirit filled only with passion too often enslaves the possessor within an ideology. Lest we becomes slaves to an ideology, as we have been slaves to a method (Doll, 2002a; see Chapter 8), we need a counterbalance:

play. Play here is that Wittgensteinian playing *with* boundaries (Genova, 1995, p.123.) Hence, the binding force of passion is counterbalanced with the liberating force of play. The tension between these two, an essential and productive tension, produces that "third space" where newness, creativity, generativeness reside. I see our task as curricularists and instructionists to look at the complexity sciences with an eye to seeing the spirit inherent within these sciences, a dynamic spirit featuring the interplay of *passion and play*.

12

KEEPING KNOWLEDGE ALIVE

(2005)

> The problem of keeping knowledge alive, of preventing it from becoming inert … is the central problem of all education.
>
> (Alfred North Whitehead, 1967b [1929])

This statement by Alfred North Whitehead in his short 1917 essay, "The aims of education" (p. 5), has been a challenge to educators and curricularists for almost a century. It is not usual for us in education to consider that the ideas we expound are "dead," "inert," "useless," "lifeless," "barren," and full of "mental dry rot." Yet, this is the charge and challenge Whitehead has given us educators. In the Preface to the book he states that "the whole book is a protest against dead knowledge" (p. v); and in his essay of the same name mentions the need to avoid "inert" ideas no less than seven times in the first three paragraphs. Ideas are inert when they are "disconnected," atomistic, isolated, related neither to the practicalities of life, nor to an individual's own interests, nor to the field in which they exist. Then they become monads without souls, floating through time and space. Relationality is, of course, a key theme in Whitehead's cosmology; it is what he calls the "really real" (1938, pp. 205–206) and forms the heart of his "Philosophy of organism" (1978 [1929], especially Ch. 2). Whitehead had a formula for keeping knowledge alive: the integration of the three teaching/learning modes of romance, precision, generalization (1967b [1929], Ch. 2), along with his wonderful teaching aphorisms: "Do not teach too many subjects"; "What you teach, teach thoroughly"; "Let the main ideas … be few and important"; and "Let them [the ideas] be thrown into every combination possible" (p. 2). Before elaborating on and exploring these three "stages of mental growth" and the concomitant aphorisms, I'd like to describe a bit of the educational system Alfred North Whitehead experienced at Cambridge—one he felt filled him with dead, lifeless, inert ideas.

Cambridge, the university not only of A. N. Whitehead but also of Gregory Bateson, Bertrand Russell, and Ludwig Wittgenstein—individuals who directly or vicariously were connected to the ideas of Whitehead—was a traditional, Victorian institution in 1880. Whitehead entered Trinity College, Cambridge, that fall to pursue a B.A. degree in mathematics. He had been a strong "maths" student at Sherborne, a minor but good English public school, preparing (mostly East Kent) students for the universities of Oxford or Cambridge. As was common for undergraduates in those days, Whitehead avoided as many of the university lectures he could and spent three full years with a mathematics "coach," training for the all-decisive Tripos—named not after the examination's three parts but after the three-legged stool on which the candidate sat while disputing with *his* examiners.

As Victor Lowe (1985, Ch. 6) tell us, Parts I and II of the Tripos were traditionally "sat for"—five and one-half hours per day for three days in a row—in late May of the candidate's third year. A week or so separated the Part I sitting from the Part II sitting. Part I was heavily Newton—the first three sections of Book One of his *Principia*[1]—while Part II focused essentially on the calculus, trigonometry, and analytic geometry. The candidate needed to know these areas quite completely (today we'd say "cold"), for the exam was mostly doing "riders" (intricate problems) attached to each question. Speed was of the essence, for one advanced to Part III by doing more riders successfully than one's fellow candidates. It was for speed in problem solving, "tricks" as it were, that one hired a coach and worked with him weekly for three years. As Lowe (1985) says: "The man who had to stop and think about the bookwork [Euclid, Newton, etc.] would not get far; his fingers ought to be dispatching it while he was thinking about the rider" (p. 101).

Dr. E. J. Routh, F.R.S., lead Wrangler (successful mathematics candidate) in the year Clerk Maxwell was second, was Whitehead's coach, as he had been for generations of Trinity mathematicians. His task was not to inspire his pupils with the beauty or usefulness of mathematics—for that "he would have been laughed" out of his profession—rather he was paid to drill his students "in tackling problems with precision and [in] finding the shortest [and most efficient] proofs" (p. 101). In sum, Routh was a trainer, a coach, and a good one, in teaching for the test. It is this university experience that Whitehead (1967b [1929]) said lead British university students to a "paralysis of thought" brought on by "the aimless accumulation of precise knowledge, inert and unutilized" (p. 37). As a Cambridge Don—a position Whitehead assumed after defending his thesis for Part III of the Tripos (taken seven months after the first two parts) on Clerk Maxwell's *Treatise on electricity and magnetism* (1873)—Whitehead worked hard and successfully to reform the Mathematical Tripos. In 1907 the Tripos was eliminated in mathematics, 24 years after Whitehead was fourth Wrangler (Lowe, 1985, p. 213).

---

1 Newton wrote *Principia* three times, the first edition dated 1687. The 1729 edition is the third and last. The 1972 date refers to the modern printing.

Of the triumvirate of romance, precision, generalization—the interplay of which Whitehead believed would keep knowledge alive—I'd like to begin with precision. This is the stage we understand best today. This stage forms the heart of any scientific or empirical research we do in education, and in our test oriented society is well prized. It is the stage our schools honor the most and the stage we ask teachers to develop the most. Romancing (playing with) knowledge or generalizing (abstracting) knowledge are not concepts we easily understand. While we do understand precision, "the aimless accumulation of precise knowledge" (Whitehead, 1967b [1929], p. 37), or "training" alone (p. 35), or "precision imposed" too early (p. 33) is self-defeating. Thus, the art of teaching is one of timing, of placement, and of judicious use. In his comments on precision—"The rhythm of education," 1912; "Aims of education," 1917; "The rhythmic claims of freedom and discipline," 1922—Whitehead never says he is opposed to precision, far from it. He is *not opposed* to precise knowledge, to training, or even to imposition. He *is opposed* to these done at the wrong time (too early before romance has "run its course," p. 33) or in the wrong way ("discipline when it comes should satisfy a natural craving," p. 32). When "the intermediate stage of discipline" (precision) does come for Whitehead, around age 14, it comes with a firmness, even with a ruthlessness. As Whitehead says:

> [In contrast to the area of romantic knowledge], the area of precise knowledge … can be, and should be, definitely determined. … A certain *ruthless definiteness is essential* in education. I am sure that one secret of *a successful teacher* is that he *has formulated* quite clearly in his mind *what the pupil has got to know in precise fashion.*
> (p. 36; emphasis added)

Whitehead, thus, sees the role of the teacher as one of integrating the development of personal interest—this is what the romance stage is all about—with training in the field studied. These two, interrelated, are absolutely necessary Whitehead believes if one is to move beyond "mere precision" to the generalization stage where knowledge is "utilized" (p. 3), not in the sense of simple or direct application but in a deeper sense where one can make the main ideas of a subject "one's own" (p. 2). Here one can *be creative* with the ideas. This sense of creativity sends one to Whitehead's cosmology, that for which he is so famous.

In his biography of Whitehead, Victor Lowe (1985, vol. I; 1990, vol. II) tells us repeatedly that in Whitehead's own personal teaching he followed the maxims he put forward, especially the one of needing "exact knowledge," of always "push[ing] on to definite knowledge" (Lowe, 1990, p. 58; Whitehead, 1948 [1911], p. 128). And, of course, this sense of exactness permeates Whitehead's own work in *Process and reality* (1978) when in his endeavor "to frame a coherent, logical, necessary system of general ideas in terms of which every element of our experience can be interpreted" (p. 3), he argues that "[t]he scheme should be stated with the utmost precision and definiteness" (p. 9).

I emphasize this notion of definiteness in Whitehead's precision stage, not merely to help us be aware that he is not a "soft or mushy" liberal, advocating that "anything goes" in the teaching/learning situation but rather to prepare us, as readers, for the formidable challenges Whitehead saw coming in the then vaguely envisioned post-modernist world. This challenge, as I see it, is how can we be certain, precise, definite, logical in a universe which we now realize is by its nature, by its reality, always in creative process, thus being uncertain, imprecise, indefinite, and non-logical? The answer to this question lies for Whitehead, I believe, in his concept of generalization/abstraction, and goes to the heart not only of his cosmology (including his metaphysics and theology), but also of what he feels any teacher needs to wrestle with if s/he is to be a "serious" teacher. Whitehead was a serious teacher; his craft was most important to him.

A serious teacher, though, is a playful teacher—one full of play—and so before delving into Whitehead's concept of generalization/abstraction, I'd like to comment on his first stage, that of romance. As an aside, an important one, while I am most interested in Whitehead's triune concept of romance/play, precision/definiteness, and generalization/abstraction, I do not take to his linear ordering of these groupings, to his calling them stages, nor to his assigning ages to them. Rather, I prefer to consider these three as ways or modes of teaching/learning and of the interrelating of all three continually. In this latter view, I have support from Whitehead himself who at the end of his "Rhythm in education" essay (1967b [1929]) says: "Of course, I mean throughout a distinction of emphasis, of pervasive quality—romance, precision, generalization, are all present throughout. But there is an alternation of dominance" (p. 28). And a bit later, "The romantic stage [in one subject] should persist for years after the precise stage [in another subject] has commenced" (p. 38).

For me it is not so much an alternation as a dynamic integration: all three continually interplaying among themselves.

Romance is Whitehead's word for his first stage of the teaching/learning process, or as he calls it the "first apprehension" (p. 17); whereas play is my own word—influenced as I've been by both Dewey and Wittgenstein. I believe, though, that Whitehead's concept of romance and what I have to say about play can be synthesized. Whitehead says that the romance stage concerns itself with "unexplored connexions," with "possibilities half-disclosed ... and half concealed" (p. 17). In this stage there needs to be enough freedom, freedom from set methodologies or "systematic procedures" to allow "an awakening to the *apprehension* of objects and to the *appreciation* of connections" (pp. 18–19). The essence of this stage is one of "browsing" (p. 22)—what Judith Genova (1995) borrowing from Wittgenstein, calls "playing with" (pp. 123–24). The territory which this stage, really mode of thinking, explores "is large, ill defined, and not to be controlled by any explicit boundary" (Whitehead, 1967b [1929], p. 36). This stage is important, not only as a precursor of precision but as its fountainhead: "There is no comprehension apart from romance" (p. 33). This is why precision that comes too early is so dulling. As Whitehead says, drawing on his own years of experience: "If you have much to do with the young as they emerge from school and from the university, you soon note the dulled minds of those whose education has consisted in the acquirement of inert knowledge" (p. 32).

The art to working with and within the romance mode, though, is not—as so many romantic progressives have done and still continue to do—to leave the child or learner alone to explore as s/he wishes. As Whitehead says: "This initial stage of romance requires guidance ... accordingly, a certain pointing out [by the teacher] of important facts, and of simplifying ideas, and of usual names really strengthens the natural impetus of the pupil" (p. 33).

This view of the human mind as curious and inquisitive and of the teacher's role as aiding and helping the learner transform this inquisitiveness and blossom this curiosity is very Deweyan (Dewey and Archambault, 1964). The human being, Whitehead (1967b [1929]) believes, craves to explore, to discover, to know—to investigate "curious thoughts, to shape questions, to seek for answers" (p. 32). This "general process [that humans are curious and creative] is both natural and of absorbing interest" (p. 32). But as Dewey has pointed out, this interest needs development; it needs to move from a stage dominated by "wonder" to one dominated by precision and definiteness. When this rhythm occurs, when the stage of romance (or play) has "run its course" (Whitehead, 1967b [1929], p. 33), then there is a natural movement—indeed "a craving"—to move to the next, different, more complex and challenging, stage. In this manner the desire for precision, for definiteness, for understanding beyond mere fascination, emerges naturally from (*stimulated*) *exploration*. The teacher has a definite role in stimulating this exploration. The teacher aids, helps, guides, stimulates the student in exploration. The teacher does not impose precision too early (p. 33) but guides the student in exploration as both teacher and student, cooperatively, throw ideas "into every combination possible" (p. 2). In this way, nascent, romantic, playful, interest grows into mature interest (p. 12). It is this personal interest which is the "*sine qua non*" for all further development; without which there can be no "mental development" (p. 31). The difficulty is, though, that personal interest needs careful development; but even in our best of intentions to develop that interest, we educators often kill the very process we wish to develop: "It is the unfortunate dilemma that initiative and training are both necessary, and that training is apt to kill initiative" (p. 35).

A solution to this dilemma, if there is one, I believe lies in Wittgenstein's notion of play, particularly as this has been developed by Judith Genova (1995) and M. Jayne Fleener (Fleener et al., 2004). In his works, particularly in *Philosophical investigations* (1958), Wittgenstein talks of "play." While Wittgenstein uses examples of playing as a way to talk about order and "rules" without being confined by the narrow boundaries of logic—"Now everything is different" (II, 180)—Genova sees important differences among these examples. "Playing at," especially playing at language-games, is somewhat metaphoric play—as in playing at tea or playing school. Here the rules are loosely defined by those playing. "Playing in," takes on a more formal structure, akin to playing a well-known game (or engaging in a set subject, like mathematics) with a definite structure and history. "Playing with," that which I see as the most powerful for integrating training and initiative, is where one is aware of the rules (of a game or subject) and purposefully pushes against them, maybe to test them or to extend them or to transcend/ transform them. In any event, in "playing with" rules and structures, one acquires an understanding of these at a deeper level than merely playing at or in. Creativity comes, but is certainly not guaranteed, by one exploring the boundaries of a structure. One makes a subject or bit of knowledge "one's own" (Whitehead, 1967b [1929], p. 2), as one is able to play with the subject or bit of knowledge: "inert ideas ... are [those] merely received into the mind without being utilized, or tested, or thrown into fresh combination" (p. 1). I am saying, in most simple terms, that "playing with" ideas, subjects, bits of knowledge is necessary for making said ideas, subjects, bits of knowledge, one's own.

M. Jayne Fleener, Andy Carter, and Stacy Reeder (2004) in their research have found most teachers working inside the "playing in" frame and consciously or unconsciously staying away from the "playing with" frame, one of throwing ideas into "every combination possible." In one instance, the authors saw a teacher continually wanting students to acquire the vocabulary (or language-game) of the subject (here fractions) as she saw it. The teacher did not "see," in Wittgenstein's sense, the potential for understanding, indeed a deeper understanding the students were displaying as they struggled with the very concept of what a fraction was. The teacher wanted the students to acquire the "correct" vocabulary—to play "in" the field—rather than to help them develop their nascent potential for a deeper understanding as they (unconsciously, but definitely) "played with" the subject of fractions. In focusing on the students' "mistakes," she failed to "see" what was there before her very eyes. Precision too early imposed really does make us blind to the potential existent in almost every teaching situation. Both Wittgenstein—himself an Austrian schoolteacher for eight years—and Whitehead saw this clearly.

Generalization is the "final stage," it is the "final success," a return to the exploration of romanticism (Whitehead, 1967b [1929], p. 19), to the seeing of connections, but with the power of knowledge not had in the first encounter. One is now able to focus on relationships, to see patterns among the facts studied. This new level gives the student not only knowledge but wisdom (p. 29). The reason for throwing ideas (and facts) into various combinations has been to help the student "see" relationships, interconnections, patterns. It is at this level of thought that Whitehead believes one begins to "make knowledge one's own." One can now use the knowledge one has, for one has acquired not just facts but the power of knowing itself (pp. 26–27).

There are a number of interesting aspects about this stage. One is that this stage arises only after one has been able to go beyond what one has been taught. As Whitehead says: "Your learning is useless to you till you have lost your textbooks, burnt your lecture notes, and forgotten the minutiae that you learnt by heart for the examination" (p. 26). And, in the same paragraph: "The function of a University is to enable you to shed details in favour of principles" (p. 26).

In his sixth "Dialogue" with Lucien Price (1954), Whitehead goes further and states that "static ideas," those which are dead, inert, lifeless, actually accompany "too-good teaching" (p. 63). That is, teaching, in both schools and universities, has a tendency only to impart information, thereby "congealing creative intelligence." It is, of course, not congealing creative intelligence that is Whitehead's great passion, but keeping knowledge alive, vital, and full of power.

Another aspect of Whitehead's generalization is that this mode is not purely abstract. The abstract is where imagination, relationships, creativity, patterns all intermingle. But one is never to be merely abstract or theoretical. A disciplined mind, says Whitehead, "should be both more abstract and more concrete" (1967b[1929], p. 12). His strong insistence on "utilization" (pp. 1, 3, 32, to name but a few) is characteristic of how he believed one could make knowledge one's own. Knowledge not used is "barren knowledge"; and our schools have too much of it, he believed. Whitehead, as we know, left Cambridge, England, to go to London since he was finding himself in a rut at the University (Lowe, 1985, Ch. 15). In London he accepted a position at the University of London as Lecturer in Applied Mathematics and Mechanics (Lowe, 1990, Ch. 1). The practical application of knowledge was most important to him; his was not merely an ivory tower pedagogy. In his more philosophic writings he tackles this practice/theory distinction head-on. In *Process and reality* (1978), he says:

> It is a complete mistake to ask how concrete particular fact can be built up out of universals. The answer is, "In no way." The true philosophic question is, How can concrete fact exhibit entities abstract from itself and yet participated in by its own nature?
>
> (p. 20)

The educational issue I see here is how can the facts we teach be seen to exhibit patterns of relationships, patterns removed from, or on a cognitive level above the facts, and yet found in the very nature of the concept fact? The answer, I believe, lies in the notion that a fact by itself is really nothing; it acquires its "factness" only as it enters into relationships with other facts, only as it is contextualized.

What Does Whitehead Have to Offer Teachers Today?

The pedagogical issues that Whitehead raised in the early 20th century are just as important, I believe, in the early 21st century. And the analyses he made of these issues and the solutions he suggested continue not only to be valid but are reinforced, I believe, by the writings of others during this past century. So his message, as I see it, is even stronger and more poignant now as then.

Whitehead was passionate in his opposition to the type of learning and teaching he saw going on in schools, colleges, universities. He felt the knowledge dispensed, not by "bad" teaching but by what we would usually call "good" teaching, was dead, lifeless, barren. Thus, the challenge he presents to all who read him for educational purposes is to reconsider the very act of teaching. What should this act comprise? For him, it should not be dispensation of idle facts; such barren dispensation actually works against developing creative intelligence. As he says in a quote already given from one of his "Dialogues" with Lucien Price (1954):

> I have a horror of creative intelligence congealing into too-good teaching—static ideas. ... Teachers should be acutely conscious of the deficiencies in the matter taught. ....They should be on their guard against their materials and teach their students to be on their guard against them. Once learning solidifies, all is over with it.
>
> (p. 63)

This is not advice we in education usually hand out to our pupils. Yet, without paying attention to this advice, we easily become caught up in the routine of textbooks and tests—two particular issues Whitehead felt were a detriment to learning.[2] Whitehead's comment on textbooks, the signature of the Ramists, was that "knowledge ... [of this sort] marks an educational failure" (1967b [1929], p. 29). Such knowledge then, as now, is very constricting and does dull the creative intelligence, which Whitehead believed we all possess.

Whitehead's alternative, of course, designed to keep knowledge alive and to actually develop the creative intelligence he believed the human species to posses, was to approach teaching and learning from the tripartite perspective of romance, precision, generalization. With my own penchant for alliteration, I would call these the 3 P's of teaching/learning: Play, Precision, Patterns (or Principles). To play with ideas, to be precise with one's facts, and to see these facts related to a set of patterns showing us principles is the way, I believe, of keeping knowledge alive.

At this point, I'd like to give an example: I was talking with a young math teacher about ways of teaching multiplication facts. I suggested that 12×12 could be played with, could be looked at as 6×24, or even as $6 \times 6 \times 4$ (which of course could be factored into even more combinations). He was quite excited about this and we conversed. Then I asked him if he could see a pattern (or a meta-pattern) in what we were doing—one way to do this would be to go to the general factoring of numbers, another would be to see the principle that the heart of mathematics (as Whitehead states in his very early writings) is intricate and precise relationships.

Here, unfortunately, the conversation stopped! Abstraction of general principles was not part of his mental "habitude."

We who are in teacher education have a long way to go to truly educate our future teachers, as our teachers have a long way to go to truly educate our future leaders and

---

2 Further research on the methodization movement would help educators wishing to understand how we came to consider textbook teaching and testing as the paragon of good teaching.

citizens. There is, though, a developing body of literature most complementary to the position which Whitehead lays out. Gregory Bateson, a neighbor of the Whitehead's in Grantchester, presents provocative ideas on difference, the role of perturbation in learning, and on patterning. John Dewey, of course, has a message about interest and its development that is strongly allied with Whitehead. Ludwig Wittgenstein's notions about language and play are seminal, if a bit obscure. Here Judith Genova and M. Jayne Fleener have been helpful. David Jardine and colleagues (2003) have done fine work in helping us reassess what is basic in teaching and learning, and in bringing forward the aesthetic and spiritful, important points in Whitehead that I did not address in this essay. Finally, some of my own work has thrown, I hope, a bit of light on modernity's methodization movement and its metaphysical base in a classical physics, which Whitehead saw a century ago as being outmoded. This leads to the exciting, provocative and yet still speculative movements in chaos and complexity theories, which draw much of their emphasis from Whitehead's own work. Indeed Alfred North Whitehead is a wonderful guide to anyone willing to re-look at the very foundations of teaching and learning, to question fundamental assumptions, to create the yet-to-be.

13

RESPONSE TO PROULX

MATURANA IS NOT A CONSTRUCTIVIST—
NOR IS PIAGET

(2008)

Readers of *Complicity* are most fortunate to have Jerome Proulx's (2008) paper distinguishing "Maturana and Varela's theory of cognition…from constructivist theories." This paper sits as a fine companion piece to the *Educational Theory* paper by Brent Davis and Dennis Sumara (2002), distinguishing various types of constructivism and situating complexity as an alternative to constructivism, one focusing neither exclusively nor heavily on the actions of the learner but rather on the interplay of factors or forces within a dynamic, learning situation. Proulx points out that "constructivist" (constructivism)—a word Davis and Sumara note is not part of Jean Piaget's vocabulary[1] (p. 411)—has become, in the hands of Ernst von Glasersfeld, a mantra for teachers dealing with children.

Today, if you teach children, you must be a constructivist, else you really are not a teacher. Without denying the fine contributions von Glasersfeld has made in helping us see the difficulties inherent in a *passive* epistemology—one based on "taking things in," one our schools tacitly use—Proulx points out that von Glasersfeld's "radical" epistemology is heavily subjective. He quotes von Glasersfeld:

> Radical constructivism is an attempt to develop a theory of knowing … [one concerning itself with] the experiential world of the knower. This experiential world is constituted and structured by the knower's own ways and means

---

1 While not a common part of his vocabulary, Piaget did, in the last year of his life (1980), use the words "constructivist" and "constructivism" (Piaget and Garcia, 1991, p. xii and p. 43, respectively). Davis and Sumara point out that Piaget's relation to the notion of "construction" is not immediately obvious. As a proclaimed structuralist, what Piaget asserted was, I believe, that the child constructs the structures or schemas necessary for his/her learning. How the child constructs these structures is an issue Piaget wrestled with all his life.

of perceiving and conceiving, and in this elementary sense it is always and irrevocably subjective.

(von Glasersfeld, 1992, pp. 1–2)

Proulx points out that while Maturana and Varela agree with von Glasersfeld that there is no objective "'truth' out there waiting to be grasped or discovered," they disagree with the implications inherent in his statement that "the *only* thing we have access to is our world of experience" (Varela, 1996, pp. 104–105). Rather, Maturana and Varela's frame is an interactive one, one wherein "we and the physical external environment are reciprocal." They co-define each other. Proulx quotes Varela: "*C'est le processus continu de la vie qui a modelé notre monde par ces aller et retour …*"

In introducing life (*la vie*) into this "going and returning," Proulx is, of course, bringing forth Maturana and Varela's biological frame, one different from von Glasersfeld's cognitive frame. Proulx goes on to say, "the world of *meaning is* not in us, nor in the physical world, it is *in the interaction* of both in a mutually affective relationship" (p. 21, emphasis added). As Davis and Sumara (2002) point out, this emphasis on *interaction* is a major thrust of John Dewey; and also lies at the heart of complexity science—particularly as that science has been developed by Ilya Prigogine (1997).

What fascinates me at this point is the relationship between Prigogine and Piaget, especially during the latter years of Piaget's life. In 1980, Piaget made two statements I have found heuristic in my own thinking. The first statement is: "With respect to practical actions, we must distinguish their causal aspect (the outcome that is verifiable after the fact) from their anticipation which is inferential" (Piaget and Garcia, 1991, p. 4).[2]

Piaget is here making a distinction, important at the level of *practical operations*, between a logic of verification (the "truth" of a statement—the basis for the theory of assessment that educational research uses) and what he calls operatory logic.

Operatory logic[3] can rightly be considered as the practical logic a child uses in developing his/her understanding within one of Piaget's stages of operations, as well

2 In his book *Pure immanence,* Gilles Deleuze (2005) brings forth and expresses well the *new* sense of causality that Piaget and Garcia are implying here, one that does not come from a mechanistic frame: "Causality requires that I go from something that is given to me to the idea of something that has never been given to me, that isn't even give-able in experience. … Causality is a relation according to which I go beyond the given; I say more than what is given or give-able—in short, *I infer and I believe,* I expect that…" (p. 40; emphasis added).
3 Piaget's operatory logic–not a mechanistic if/then or cause/effect logic—is, obviously, a logic of actions. It includes along with the behavioral actions themselves, anticipations, inferences, intentions. The 1991 book, that with, and finished by, Garcia, is very much concerned with reframing the (too often dichotomous) relationship between extensional (formal) logic and intensional (operatory) logic. As Garcia says, "Logic starts at the moment a child is able to anticipate a relation between actions … [and] anticipation of actions means inference" (Piaget and Garcia, 1991, p. 155). Bringing inference into the logic of a child's actions emphasizes what the child intended or thought would happen when

as the logic the child uses in moving from one stage to the next, more advanced stage. In either case, *this practical logic is one of development, not of verification.* As a logic of development—operatory—this logic involves inference. To infer is to draw conclusions, to deduce, to make connections, to see relations. Piaget calls this logic, *natural deduction*; it is "the reasoning actually used" by the child or learner. To focus on the actual reasoning the learner uses—his/her intentions—is a departure from the validity *only* frame so dominant in current schooling. The validity of an action, statement, procedure is, of course, important; but to exclude a person's intentions/anticipations/inferences from the process of learning is to turn learning into a simplistic and mimetic act.

In traditional acts of teaching what the child or learner *intends* to do is not considered, only what s/he did. For Piaget, such a non-developmental view misses the child's "constructions," his/her practical actions with all their "illogicalnesses." In a word, traditional teaching ("teaching-as-telling") actually obliterates the very actions of the learner as s/he is engaged in the *activity* of learning. Piaget's operatory logic with its focus on process/anticipation/inference is indeed based on interactions. Such a dynamic relationship, carrying in its process the power of transformation, lies at the heart of the open systems frame that both Piaget and Prigogine share.[4]

Curriculum designs and instructional strategies focusing on a learner's anticipations (what s/he intends) and bringing those intentions into *dynamic interplay* both with themselves and with the results produced by the actions would make learning far more efficient, of better quality, and would open space for the creative emergence of new ideas and procedures. Incorporating non-linearity into curriculum design and using *conversation* as a prime mode of instruction presents interesting challenges to educators. A focus on such challenges calls into question the efficacy of a sequentially ordered curriculum,[5] as well as the common teaching strategy of "teaching-as-telling." While the constructivist movement does help us see the efficacy of paying attention to the learner's frame—his/her schemas; the complexivist movement goes beyond this subjectivization to bring forth the concept and practice of transformation via *situational* self-organization. The comment about situational self-transformation leads me to the second statement of Piaget's I find fascinating: "At all levels of development there are implications between actions or

---

s/he performed his/her action. As one of the book's editors (a teacher–educator) says, "Schooling often involves an effort to eradicate … this … aspect of a child's learning process."

4 In 1975, Prigogine looking over Piaget's epistemological framework (an active, dynamic one) said that he was "in complete agreement with the basic ideas of genetic epistemology" (in Piaget and Garcia, 1991, p. 312). Rolando Garcia, in his part of the book says: "The evolution of biological and cognitive systems are both *examples* of the evolution of *open systems* in interaction with their environment" (p. 126; italics in the original).

5 Piaget's stages/schemas are indeed sequentially ordered, and hence one might infer a sequenced curriculum from such, but the movement from stage to stage with its process of dynamic equilibration is both non-linear and recursive.

meanings; then there are dialectical relations that lead the subject to go beyond what he has already acquired" (Piaget and Garcia, 1991, p. xii).

Looking at the latter part of this statement, I see Piaget saying that there are interactive relations—I would prefer the word dynamic to dialectical—*that lead* the subject, the one acting, to go beyond; to go beyond where s/he now resides and to venture into the land of the new. This process of going beyond is transformative. In Piaget's terms, it is the *elusive* process of jumping from one stage or level to the next. He never could explain this process, only show that it happens (and has its own logic, that of relations). There is a spirit of the mystical existing within this interactive process.[6] To me, this spirit is reminiscent of A.N. Whitehead's dictum: "It lies in the nature of things that the many enter into complex unity" (1978 [1929], p. 21), and with John Dewey's statements (1966a [1916], Ch. 3) concerning a sense of control, social control, which is not imposed externally but rather emerges internally from the interactions in the situation itself. This "other mode of control … a more natural mode … residing in the nature of the situations" is one where the activity, the *process of doing*, in conjunction with and shared with others doings, provides its own direction, "guiding an activity to its own end." This conjointness is also akin to the co-evolution and co-adaptation Proulx brings out so well in his discussion of Maturana and Varela.

Once one focuses on *process as conjoint with product*, process now being not merely a subservient means to a set end, then the activity of the child's or learner's actions takes on a new importance. What the child/learner *intends or anticipates* is as important as what results from his/her actions. Meaning arises from the interplay of process and product, of that intended/anticipated and that resultant. Such a focus is pointed out by Proulx (2008, p. 21)—"meaning is not in us, nor in the physical world, it is in the interaction of both in a mutually affective relationship"—and if brought to the forefront in any teaching/learning situation would, I believe, make such situations not only more enjoyable but far more effective and efficient.

---

6 A sense of the mystical does exist in this process; and it is important I believe to keep this sense elusive and ill-defined. To anthropomorphize the spirit of process—as did those proposing an *élan vital*—is to fall into the trap of turning the process into a thing or saying that within the process there is a "thing," and then of course being unable to find this material "thing."

PART 3

Modern/Post-Modern

Structures, Forms, and Organization

Introduction: Donna Trueit

Bill Doll's liberal, classical education and his in-depth study of Dewey, Piaget, Bruner, and Whitehead was the intellectual groundwork that predisposed him to recognize the import of intellectual work in architecture, art, literature, related to a concept called post-modernism. Making connections to curriculum studies, the culmination of Doll's study was his first book, *A post-modern perspective on curriculum* (1993), still in print, translated into six languages, currently studied in Canada, USA, Iran, Turkey, Israel, Korea, and Brazil and influencing widespread Chinese curriculum reform. Doll views post-modernism as an opportunity to question and explore taken for granted structures, forms, and organizing principles of modernism, which he sees as a particular form of thought related to a particular time period, characterized by: the influence of scientism; the mathematization of reality; the separation of subject and object; and the obfuscation of discourse. He uses the hyphen in "post-modern" to signify a relationship between modernism and that which has yet to emerge. Following Lyotard, the truly modern would be dynamical, always on the cusp, and therefore eluding either definition or prediction. When Doll uses the words "structures" and "forms" he has in mind not the rigid structures of Newtonian thought; but rather a more fluid or evolving arrangement. Doll does not focus on Piaget's ages and stages but rather on the transition from one mental schema to another, broader and more useful. Finally, Doll moves to Prigogine's "dissipative structures," those far from equilibrium, where the traditional laws of physics no longer hold. Here Doll finds a new vision for curriculum, one that focuses on the relational not the set.

Chapter 14 is a definition of "Modernism" written for a Sage Encyclopedia of curriculum studies. This entry encompasses a brief history of the evolution of modernism as a form of thought which begins as a revolutionary wave, always the cutting edge, but devolves, in the 1950s, to a tradition staid and outmoded.

The essay "A new sense of order," written in 1986, presages Doll's movement to complexity theory with the brief phrase "order emerges" signifying a totally new way of conceiving "organization," now linked with "transformation" instead of the static top-down hierarchies that usually inform our conception of linear order. Prigogine and Stenger's radical rethinking of chemical reactions, laws of physics, and the concept of time has implications for the way "reality" is conceived, i.e. always in flux, and enables Doll to ground his ideas about process thought in the new sciences.

How does one change paradigms? How does one relinquish utopian ideals of modernism without re-inscribing the very paradigm one aspires to move away from? Without foundations, what vision might guide our thinking in post-modern directions? In "Post-modernism's utopian vision" (1990) Doll presents four ideas that draw him (away from foundations and certainty) toward a flexible, fluid, interconnected, and relational way of thinking.

Finally in this section, recently written "Structures of the post-modern" attempts to answer questions generated by Chinese readers of Doll's 1993 book. Here he clarifies and expands upon his ideas about the unique relation between modernism and post-modernism and implications for teaching. This paper reveals his current emphasis on relations and complexity thinking.

14

MODERNISM

(2010)

Modernism, an umbrella word, covers the words modern, modernity, and even *moderné*. These words derive from the Latin *modo*, "just now." As "just now," modernism, modern, and modernity all deal with the continually current, always on the cutting edge of the present. Their histories, though, stretch back many centuries, and thus, while continually in the present, modernism and its allied words have long pasts. It is the play of the past with the present that keeps modernism always on the edge of an emerging future. Modernism can be looked at linguistically, intellectually, socially/politically, and educationally. Each view gives modernism another layer of richness and presents to us a concept that at times is *apart from* current traditions and at other times is *a part of* current traditions. This interplay of *apart from/a part of* is what gives modernism its dynamism.

Linguistically, the modern is part of that tripartite division of languages into Old, Middle, Modern. Modern language raises issues of what is linguistically acceptable or not acceptable: street language, official language; native language, dominant language; phonetic spelling, authorized spelling. Intellectually, the modern is part of the historic breaking of thought into periods: pre-modern period, modern period, post-modern period. Each of these has its own way of thinking, its own episteme. Here, the modern is frozen into a time period, approximately mid-16th/early 17th century (Copernican revolution) to the early/mid-20th century (quantum revolution). Socially/politically modernism goes back to the 17th century "wars" between the ancients and the moderns, those of a classical (and conservative) bent as opposed to those of a newer and more liberal, scientific/mathematical bent. Educationally modernism goes back to Peter Ramus (1515–1572), who first used the word curriculum in an educational sense. There is a "family resemblance" (Wittgenstein, 1958, pp. 65–67) in the curricular forms and thoughts of Ramus,

René Descartes, and Ralph Tyler. What Ramus founded in the mid-1500s has been with us for centuries (Triche and McKnight, 2004) and occupies a prominent place in schools today. The Tyler Rationale can well be considered the epitome of modernist curricular design.

The Modernist movement, in all its forms, can be bracketed in the time span between Copernicus' positing of a sun-centered universe in the 16th century along with the scientific revolution this spawned and the quantum revolution of the 20th century. By the end of World War II (in the mid-1940s) modernism and all it stood for (including its progressive phase) had died. After World War II, the advanced industrial countries of the West entered a new age, one Jean-François Lyotard labeled postmodern. This new, computerized, information dominated age both fascinated and frightened Lyotard.

Ramus' work preceded, slightly, the scientific revolution spawned by Tycho Brahe, Johannes Kepler, and Galileo Galilei, all of whom accepted and advanced the astronomical work of Nicholas Copernicus, a century earlier. Together these movements—Ramism in education (with a special interest in curriculum) and the scientific revolution—ushered in the modern age, one logically ordered, scientifically framed, Protestant in its values, commercial in its outlook. Prior to Ramus, education was a piecemeal affair, young children learning to read and write from dames (wives and mothers) and proceeding on to study as they wished with itinerant teachers. The church schools (Catholic) were a bit more formalized, with the Jesuits, in 1599—a half century after Ramus—producing their *ratio studiorum* (plan of study). Ramus was a professor and schoolmaster. As a schoolmaster he trained boys ages 8 to 16 for the university; as a professor he organized the knowledge he taught the boys into what, borrowing from John Calvin (*curriculum vita* or path of life), he called a curriculum. The word curriculum (Latin for circular path) was used by Ramus, to designate not a racetrack, but rather a course of study to follow. He laid out this path in a linear, hierarchal, and orderly manner (actually a visual chart) beginning with the most general ("that which came first") and proceeding step by step "to that which came next, and so on, down to the most particular." Ramus' charts, much akin to the bracketing done in current tennis, golf, or basketball tournaments (or to university/corporate line and flow charts from Presidents through Vice-presidents to Deans or Directors to faculty or employees) were usually dichotomized into splits of two or three. Thus "Knowledge to be Taught" would be split into the *trivium* and *quadrivium* with the *trivium* split into grammar, logic, and rhetoric and the *quadrivium* split into arithmetic, geometry, music/ethics, and physics/astronomy. These individual subjects would again be split into sub-parts: arithmetic would be split into addition, subtraction, multiplication, division. Addition would then be split into whole numbers, positive and negative integers, fractions, etc. Subtraction, multiplication, division would follow the same branching (ramification). This charting of knowledge into a visual representation (logical, orderly, hierarchal) was a great advance on previous, disorganized forms of representation, either woodcuts—

the most famous of which was the tower of knowledge with a key (the alphabet) unlocking the basement door and the flag of philosophy fluttering from the top turret—or just long memory lists given in no particular order. Ramus' sequencing of knowledge in a logical form became popular with the rising merchant class—it was both orderly and efficient. As an organized way to study, curriculum entered the Protestant universities of Leiden and Glasgow in the early 1600s.

Along with organizing knowledge in a textbook manner, Ramus made a decision that has influenced Western teaching ever since: knowledge should be taught (via direct instruction) in the same way he organized it. Today reading which follows the phonetic method is a carryover from Ramus' sense of logic. Whole word or sight recognition methods are often considered "illogical": they do not have a definite pattern. Ramus' sense of pattern—simple in its sense of order—appealed immensely to the Puritans and their "simple piety." They quickly adopted Ramus' method of organizing and his logic, based on there being one and only one true (or best) way. In Colonial America in the late 17th and early 18th centuries, Ramism—the product of "that Great Scholar and Blessed Martyr"—and all it stood for, permeated virtually every thesis done at Harvard College.

Ramus' method of organizing knowledge (a curriculum) while attacked, often quite mercilessly (common at the time), as being too simple—starting with the most general or well known and proceeding, reductively, down to the particular—was part of the larger and more general "methodization" movement which swept northern Europe and Colonial America in the 17th and 18th centuries. Francis Bacon, John Bunyan, Johann Comenius, René Descartes, Gottfried von Leibniz (not to forget Isaac Newton, alchemist and scientist) were all caught up in this movement. It has been said that by the end of the 17th century, Protestantism had its answer to Catholicism's Spirit: Method. Method—scientific, rational, normed—captured the allegiance of the "new men" (engineers, builders, industrialists) of the 18th and 19th centuries. Frederick Taylor brought it to the fore in his time and motion studies in the late 19th and early 20th century. Efficiency and scientific management became bywords of the times, including the organization of school curricula. Ralph Tyler's *Basic principles of curriculum* (1950)—(pre-) planned, sequentially ordered, scientifically assessed—comes from this lineage; and his four steps for developing a good curriculum has a strong resemblance to René Descartes' four steps in his "Discourse on the method of rightly conducting one's reason and seeking truth in the sciences" (1985).

Another aspect of modernism came from the 17th and 18th century "war" between the *ancients* and the *moderns*. This "war"—represented in the writings of Giambattista Vico (1668–1744)—was over who would control university curricula. The *ancients* (scholastics, rhetoricians, classicists) favored learning the classical languages, in particular the grand rhetoric of Cicero. The *moderns* (the new natural philosophers) favored contemporary ("now") scientific, rational, mathematical learning and the use of vernacular language. This classical/modern distinction carried well into the 19th century, particularly in the curricula of British schools, some favoring the classics and ancient languages, others favoring the sciences, mathematics, and vernacular language. In the United States, Robert Hutchins' "Great Books" program and the curriculum at the colleges he founded in Santa Fe, New Mexixo, and Annapolis, Maryland, carry vestiges of this classicism.

Over time, the *moderns* with their success in medicine and astronomical predictions, as well as their practical appeal to a rising commercial class of merchants (where employment not heredity were determiners of rank) became dominant. Their values—practical, bourgeois, progressive—became the traditional values of society. Social power shifted from those connected with the church or aristocracy to those prominent in commerce and industry. Education (and the curricula in schools) took on a practical hue. No longer was education restricted to the elite few, nor was it purely for the enjoyment of study. More and more education became associated with schooling adopting a practical, useful bent. One became schooled for commerce, industry, a trade, or profession. In this new industrial (modern) age, the engineers, planners, builders believed they would tame and improve the ways of nature—in genetic breeding and in human society. The notion of being "civilized" took on a definite white, Anglo-Saxon, male flavor. And with such civilizing came the moral duty of those civilized, to civilize, or at least control and lead, those not civilized.

Modernism now took a twist: it became *the* tradition, and as such spurred a counter (*avant-garde*) movement. This counter movement, lead by the artistic, flamboyant avant-garde—in music, dance, painting, drama, literature—along with some intellectuals on the political fringe, played modernism off against itself. In a sense modernism now defined itself (as tradition) and transcended itself. The avant-garde, favoring the cutting edge of the "*just now*," an edge continually reforming, reframing, redefining itself, took the social traditionalists (the bourgeoisie) as their enemy. They wished to shock the sensibilities of those possessing traditional authority, those who saw employment and productivity as virtues, indeed as the holy grail to lead all to a life of progress. As brilliant (and still brilliant) as are the works of Pablo Picasso, Sergei Diaghilev, Igor Stravinsky, Frank Lloyd Wright, and James Joyce (to name but a few), the modernéists were caught by that which they attacked. As avant-garde, they needed bourgeois tradition as a foil for their creativity. With the advent of pop culture in the 1950s this form of modernism died—the traditional/avant-garde distinction disappeared. This particular modernist tradition had a relatively short life of about one century—from the mid-1800s to the mid-1900s.

During this century though, modernism in both its scientific form and artistic form dominated intellectual thought, and brought with it great creativity. Scientific creativity and artistic creativity not only existed side by side but actually played off one another. Curriculum was mostly influenced by science, which in its ideological form became "scientism," a grand narrative answering all needs. In many ways Frederick Taylor's work in industry (his time and motion studies on worker productivity) became the holy grail of modern progress. Through scientific management—workers separated from and taking orders from managers—production increased as did worker's pay (albeit to a far lesser degree). Progress—defined in terms of *efficiency* and *productivity*—in the early decades of the 20th century, seemed not only assured but inevitable. Into this rich, industrial, milieu of efficiency through tight control, and productive progress through efficiency, the Progressive Education Association (PEA) was born (1919). The PEA was part of the broad political and social progressive movement, a modernist movement, which captured the hearts and minds of many Americans, from the 1890s through the 1940s. By the end of World War II, though, progressivism and the PEA, and indeed modernism itself, were "dead."

After World War II, pop culture became so diffuse (and indeed so common) that avant-garde no longer was a meaningful term. The avant-garde/traditional distinction lost its sense of definition; it referred to a time past, not a time present ("just now"). Scientific thinking now infused with the quantum, became less certain and more problematic/probabilistic, rational reason was beginning to be seen as only one form of reason, educational research became infused with the qualitative and anthropological, and society started on the road to integration. A new, computerized world came into being. No longer was there one dominant (traditional, unified, correct, all encompassing) culture; a variety of "posts"—post-modern, post-structural, post-colonial, post-patriarchal, even post-human—emerged. All these "posts" challenged the basic metanarrative foundation of modernism. In advanced, Western, industrial societies capital was replaced by knowledge as the currency of the realm. The current "information age" came into being. Nothing captures the drama and excitement around the creation of this information age better than the Macy Conferences, held in New York City in the years 1946–1953. Here were gathered some of brightest mathematicians, computer designers, psychologists, psychiatrists, anthropologists of the time. Information theory, communication theory, cybernetics, and insights into learning and mental disease came from these conferences. The systems foundations for the new sciences of chaos and complexity were also laid at this conference. A new paradigm began to emerge, a paradigm heavily tilted towards and influenced by technology, the new sciences, and the coming to age of biology. The arts—literature, music, drama, painting, architecture—which had been so dramatic, indeed flamboyant, a generation before, were not part of the Macy Conferences, nor were they part of the "measured world," which defined the mathematical/scientific/rational aspect which so engulfed intellectual thought at that time (and continues to do so today). Scientific rationality has become the dominant mode of thought; it has taken on the power Lyotard (1984) feared it would. This rationality, devoid of personal feeling, artistic expression, or aesthetic culture has become paradigmatic. For Lyotard we need to eschew this mode of thought, be incredulous toward it, especially its universalizing tendency to see all through one lens. Instead we need to look at the "now" as an ongoing (re)creation.

Interestingly, Lyotard's use of the term postmodern actually refers, not to a time after modernism, but to a modernism that is continually "re-writing" itself; "Modernity writes itself, inscribes itself on itself as perpetual re-writing" (1987). Here is Lyotard's hope for the future, a dynamic ("now") modernism, continually on the cutting edge of the current epoch. A postmodernism separate from the modern, which *freezes* the modern in a particular time period, is a postmodern which "terrorizes" all that does not fit into one, universalizing, grand narrative. For Lyotard, the postmodern (in its best sense) is really a dynamic form of the modern; it is a modern that is always "just now," it is a modern which is situated in the local, which interplays with the traditional and accepted but always moves beyond these. In a real sense it is post-modern.

The Teacher's Role in a Modern/Post-Modern Frame

Every period, movement, has its own ethos; and often that ethos is recognized after the period, movement, has passed. To take this statement at face value, though, is too simple, for in many ways a period or movement does not pass on as much as it is subsumed or extended by the next movement. In short, there is a flow between movements, which we break into linear order for our own purposes. Such linearization is far more common in the English speaking world than in the French. French intellectual thought is more fluid, integrative, relational, as is evidenced by a host of French "post" writers, often labeled post-structuralists. Hélène Cixous, Gilles Deleuze, Jacques Derrida, Julia Kristeva, Bruno Latour, Michel Serres are but a few of those who point out this relationship between language and thought. These authors provide a fine counterpoint to the analytic/linear style of analysis so common in modernist, Anglo-American philosophy.

The ethos of Modernism is complex. It is universalizing, totalizing, indicative of the grand narratives, on which Lyotard declared "war." This modernist thrust, born from the union of both the scientific revolution and the Protestant burghers (the gentlemen of commerce) of the rapidly expanding towns and cities in northern Europe, with vestiges of the Enlightenment (particularly its commitment to Reason), created an ethos the "modernés" (the avant-garde artists) were to challenge. Without the straight-jacket of this form of modernity, though, the avant-garde artists would not have been so creative. So, too, in a sense, without the work Tyler put out for others to pick up as a Rationale, the Reconceptualist movement would have taken a different form.

The point/counterpoint play of Modernism as it struggled both to define and transcend itself has yet to emerge in the curriculum field. Certainly no longer moribund, this field is still caught in either/or dichotomies rather than point/counterpoint interplays. In short, the field is not yet post-modern.

The hyphen in post-modern, to signify this interplay, is similar to Lyotard's use of "re" in his reflection on his own statements about the postmodern. A few years after writing *The postmodern condition* (1984), Lyotard suggested the phrase "(re)writing" as a useful addenda. Here he talks about the Modern, the "*just now*," always reflecting back on itself: "to make seen … what is not visible" (1987). Such a recursing, so important to chaos and complexity theories, keeps the modern always on the cutting edge, on the cusp of change. The postmodern (or better, post–modern) is but a phase in this process of modernity continually (re)writing itself. The teacher who is able to envision the "*now*" as a continual process, not as a set period in time, who is not placed in a straight-jacket by the prevailing culture of the time, who is able to bring the yet-to-be into focus, should be able to deal with curricula issues in a way in which the history, contemporariness, and emerging possibilities of a field flow together in a continually recursive manner. This challenge is Modernism's greatest legacy to contemporary curricularists.

15

PRIGOGINE

A NEW SENSE OF ORDER

(1986)

Ilya Prigogine, the 1977 Nobel Prize winner in chemistry, begins his most recent book, *Order out of chaos* (Prigogine and Stengers, 1984) with the statement: "It is hardly an exaggeration to state that one of the greatest dates in the history of mankind was April 28, 1686" (p. 1).

On that day Newton presented to the Royal Society of London his epic work, *The mathematical principles of natural philosophy* (commonly called *Principia*, 1972 [1729]),[1] in which he provided an "explanation" of movement which would include both planets and billiard balls, thus giving proof of God's grand and mathematical design. In short, he summed up all which had preceded him in science and set direction for what was to follow.

During the almost 400-year period between Copernicus's *De revolutionibus* (1976 [1543]) and Einstein's two works on relativity, written in 1905 and 1916 (see Einstein, 1961), the Newtonian paradigm was developed and applied. It governed not only science but also social science, including education. It formed the basis for early and mid-20th century thought and is the paradigm with which modernist alternative theories must compete. It forms the foundation of the measured curriculum.

The history of Western thought can be grouped into three broad paradigms, or world views (Doll, 1983; Prigogine and Stengers, 1984). The first of these is the classical-Christian view developed by Aristotle, Ptolemy, and Thomas Aquinas (see Burtt, 1955 [1932]; Lovejoy, 1936; Koyré, 1957; Aristotle, 1961; Kline, 1980). The second is the classical-scientific view summarized and guided by Newton. The third paradigm is presently in the process of being formed. It is developing out of work

---

1 Newton wrote *Principia* three times, the first edition dated 1687. The 1729 edition is the third and last. The 1972 date refers to the modern printing.

in quantum physics and is strongly influenced by the thoughts of Albert Einstein, Neils Bohr, Werner Heisenberg (1971), and now Ilya Prigogine. The emergence of this paradigm can be traced to the late 1920s and early 1930s when Einstein had a famous series of debates with Bohr and Heisenberg concerning the usefulness and validity of the quantum view versus the classical view of science (Heisenberg, 1971, Chs 5 and 6; McCormmach, 1982; Pagels, 1982, Ch. 1). Fifty years after these debates Prigogine has added new dimensions to the paradigm with his investigation of dissipative and self-organizing structures *(Being to becoming*, 1980; with Stengers, *Order out of chaos*, 1984).

In reading Prigogine's work on self-organizing chemical and biological structures one might equate these with Piaget's work on adaptive biological and cognitive structures. Both Prigogine and Piaget draw upon the theoretical biologists Waddington (1957, 1975) and Weiss (1971). One of the reasons Piaget has been so misinterpreted by American psychologists and educators is that their disciplines derive from the classical scientific paradigm of Newton, while Piaget has been on the forefront of establishing a new paradigm. As Kuhn (1970) points out, differences in paradigms are differences in worldviews, involving differences in assumptions made, questions asked, evidence taken, and methodologies used. It is virtually impossible to work across paradigms; a choice must be made.

This new paradigm, born of quantum physics but not limited to such, is very much in keeping with, and will be influenced by, the work Gould (1982) has been doing on "punctuated equilibrium" and on new forms of evolutionary theory. Gould's work, *The mismeasure of man* (1981), provides a historical connection linking the measured curriculum with Newtonian science and its assumptions. Gould sums up this connection as follows: "The social sciences have physics envy ... [worse] they have lived to practice their science according to their clouded vision of physics" (p. 262). Prigogine and Stengers (1984) add:

> We can hardly avoid stating that the way in which biological and social evolution has traditionally been interpreted represents a particularly unfortunate use of the concepts and methods borrowed from physics; unfortunate, because the area where these concepts and methods are valid was very restricted, and thus the analogies between them and social or economic phenomena are completely unjustified
>
> (p. 207)

Attempts to apply this new scientific paradigm to educational issues have been limited, and in regard to Prigogine I know of only one other attempt (Sawada and Caley, 1985). But Prigogine's work will bring this paradigm to the forefront (Atkinson, 1985; Strauss, 1985) and will contribute to a better understanding of Piaget's work. This paradigm will ultimately provide the basis for an educational model that will go beyond and stand as an alternative to the measured curriculum.

Newton and the Measured Curriculum

The clearest feature of Newton's world is its simplicity. The planets in space and billiard balls on earth are governed by the same law of gravity; every effect has a simple and direct cause; time is measured in constant units no matter where in the universe it occurs; all actions are determined by a cause which can be measured in quantifiable terms. The image we have of Newton's world is that of a mechanical clock. In fact, Newton called God a "clockmaker," and saw God as an engineer, a mathematician, and a geometer (Kline, 1980, Ch.3; Bronowski, 1978, Ch. 3).

According to Prigogine and Stengers (1984), Newton's world is best described by the following words: simple, spiritual, and uniform or universal. Of these the first is the most important: "What are the assumptions of classical science? ... Generally those centering around the basic conviction that at some level *the world is simple* and is governed by time-reversible fundamental laws" (p. 7).

This notion of simplicity is at the foundation of the reductionist movement in physical and metaphysical thought: every complex is but a collection of simples; all complexes can be reduced to simples. This is in keeping with the search from Copernicus to Galileo to Kepler to Newton for a single mathematical formula to explain God's grand design. Newton's Law of Gravity "explained" the movement of planets, the falling of apples, the height of tides. All these were put together in one formula, one law. This law is expressed in terms of an analogy with human *forte,* gravity being an abstract concept based on human pushing and pulling. The mechanical clock is based on the same analogy but with gears added for increased power. As Bronowski (1978) points out, the notion of cause–effect is a direct extension of the mechanistic, human force model Newton used. "After two hundred years then Newton's method, the method of causes and mechanisms, had become the standard method for every science. No other method was conceivable" (p. 61).

Stephen J. Gould (1981) points out that the whole field of factor analysis is based on the assumption of simple reductionism, as is the notion of a simple and single IQ number.[2] In fact, the continual "attempt to establish a unilinear classification of mental abilities" runs through the whole psychometric movement from Goddard to Spearman to Jensen (p. 159). Further, the notion of a G factor, one identifiable and measurable factor to which all intelligence can be reduced, is but an expression of Hamilton's attempt to explain "all the dynamics of a system completely ... in terms of a single function" (Prigogine and Stengers, 1984, pp. 68, 70).

In terms of curriculum and behaviorist learning theory the same simple assumptions hold: pupils learn that which is taught; the curriculum is seen as a linear "course to be run." Prigogine and Stengers (1984), like others who have criticized this Newtonian view, see it as more simplistic than wrong: "Today this (view) appears as an excessive simplification" (p. 7). In place of this simplicity, they offer a world which is complex, self-organizing, and non-predictable.

---

2 Introduction and Chapter 6, particularly.

Spiritual, the second of the terms Prigogine and Stengers use to describe Newtonism, has two meanings. The first meaning is the usual religious one. Like the classical scientists who preceded him, Newton was deeply religious.

> When I wrote my treatise about our system (*Principia*) I had an eye on such principles as might work with considering men for the belief in a Deity; and nothing can rejoice me more than to find it useful for that purpose.
>
> (Newton, 1692, cited in Kline, 1980, p. 59)

Kline (1980) states: "Newton's religious interests were the true motivation of his mathematical and scientific work." In fact, Newton wrote hundreds of religious tracts, far outnumbering his mathematical and scientific works.

In a more subtle sense of spiritual, Newton took a God's-eye view of the universe, seeing it as static, uniform, and externally controlled—"governed by a rationality that lies outside itself" (Prigogine and Stengers, 1984, p. 46). Time in this view is non-existent; to God time means nothing. There is no "arrow" to time, no sense of development or progress. This view is reflected in a quote from Giordano Bruno (16th century) which Prigogine and Stengers use to sum up the Newtonian worldview: "The universe is, therefore, one, infinite, immobile. ... It does not move itself locally. ... It does not generate itself. ... It is not corruptible [no decay]. ... It is not alterable" (p. 15).

Prigogine and Stengers (1984) go even further. In Chapter 7, "Rediscovering time," they argue that the two key concepts of Einstein's theory of relativity—time and space—are non-essential in the Newtonian framework. Commenting on the limits of this view, they assert: "Scientific rationality ... [the science of Newton] ... is incapable of understanding duration since it reduces time to a sequence of instantaneous states linked by a deterministic law" (p. 92).

This statement and the one on external control go to the very heart of the measured curriculum. Whether discussing the determinism of IQ or the averaging of grades as a series of instantaneous states, the measured curriculum in no way understands duration. Yet duration, and with it internal development, underlie Piaget's notion of stages. Coming from an Anglo-empiricist tradition, American educators and psychologists have been able to focus only on the correlational aspects of stages—the measured age aspects. But the heart of Piaget is the process of internal, transformatory development. As he says in *Biology and knowledge* (1971a [1967]) the one hypothesis which has guided him throughout his career is that "life is essentially autoregulation" (p. 26). The measured curriculum has no place for autoregulatory systems.

While Piaget asserts that autoregulation is the essence of living systems, Prigogine argues that self-regulation and transformatory change apply to chemical compositions as well. Prigogine sees internal regulation as not merely the structure of life but as the predominant structure of the universe and of reality itself.

Both Dewey's notion of experience and Piaget's notion of development have a sense of internality and duration; both are progressive and transformational, coming out of themselves and leading back into themselves, but always at higher, qualitatively different planes. Education, Dewey (1966b [1902]) says, is really "the development of experience into experience" (p. 18). In this view, there is a definite arrow to time. Both Dewey and Piaget have been misunderstood because each has come from a paradigm quite different from the Newtonian one governing the measured curriculum.

Uniformity or universality are probably the best known of the terms used by Prigogine and Stengers to describe the Newtonian paradigm. From a God's-eye view both space and time are uniform. Thus the universe can be looked at as a large grid with each square or quadrant equal to every other square or quadrant. Time neither accelerates nor decelerates, and space does not curve back on itself. Those who followed Newton, particularly the mathematician and astronomer Laplace, believed that mathematical predictability and certainty could be achieved through precise measurement. Newton held that the movement of the planets could be predicted accurately from his time to eternity, on the assumption that the planets' movements would be uniform forever. Laplace extended this to the notion of predicting all future happenings in the universe by achieving a mathematical positioning of all the atoms in the universe (Bronowski, 1978, p. 63).

While Laplace realized that such positioning was not physically possible, the concept was his ideal and framed the theory he pursued. Herein lie the foundations of determinism and objectivity in classical science—a determinism and objectivity which still frame our popular vision of science and its method. Herein also lie the roots of the assumption that IQ and standardized test scores have predictive value.

Einstein's theory of relativity shattered the notions of objectivity and predictability. But the myth remains, especially in the social sciences and education. Here these elements emerge in subtle but powerful form: in our belief that the teacher has a God's-eye view, and hence sees all objectively; that testing is both objective and predictive; and that curriculum should be uniform for all. While none of these statements is ever taken in a strictly literal sense they do form the ideal toward which the measured curriculum aspires, just as complete and mathematical objectivity and predictability formed the ideal toward which Laplace looked. This ideal underlies not only the testing movement and curriculum development, but also such mechanical devices as teaching machines. The ultimate goal is perfection within a closed system. But Prigogine, following in the footsteps of Einstein, Heisenberg, and Piaget, has shown that the universe is not closed, that it is filled with change, randomness, and indeterminacy.

> Where classical science used to emphasize permanence [closed systems] we now find change and evolution [open systems]. ... [Where Newton and others looked to the skies and found predictable trajectories] we now see strange objects: quasars, pulsars, galaxies exploding and being torn apart; stars that, we are told, collapse into "black holes" irreversibly devouring all they manage to ensnare.
>
> (Prigogine and Stengers, 1984, pp. 214–215)

In place of simplicity, spirituality, and uniformity, today we are seeing the world, the universe, and reality itself as a mixture of "the complex, the temporal, and the multiple" (Prigogine and Stengers, 1984, p. xxvii). This new view is one which demands a different paradigm—and educational model—from the one Newton and the measured curriculum have given us. We must go beyond the measured curriculum to a transformatory curriculum.

Prigogine and a New Order

In his recent works, Prigogine (1980; with Stengers, 1984) focuses on two themes: the (thermo)dynamic relationship between order and chaos; and the nature of transformatory (or becoming) change. The integration of these two themes forms Prigogine's ideas on a new order and on a new sense of order.

In classical science time is meaningless, it is reversible, it has no arrow. In classical dynamics one can move a billiard ball up and down a ramp and a watch can be moved forward and backward. All mechanical devices contain the notion of reversibility. Thermodynamics, the science of heat reactions, changed all that. As water heats up steam power is produced and work is done. This process is not reversible. The power in a steam engine used to drive a locomotive cannot be turned back into water. In fact, the condensed water from the cooled steam plus the power produced by the steam is not equal to the potential power in the original water. There is a loss in the conversion process; energy is not totally conserved. This wasted or dissipated energy is called *entropy*, after the Greek meaning of a change or a turning.

This notion of wasted energy at critical turning points contradicts the essential scientific notion that the energy of the world is constant or stable. At a deeper level it contradicts Laplace's metaphysical view of the world and the universe as basically "ideal perpetual-motion machines" (Prigogine and Stengers, 1984, p. 115). These contradictions may be dealt with in two ways. One way is to relegate thermodynamics to a lesser status, to explain its contradictions as minor aberrations in an essentially dynamic system. This reductionist view keeps a single order and deals with all variations from this order as minor fluctuations or aberrations.

The second way is to accept a multiple worldview: the laws of dynamics need not be those of thermodynamics. Prigogine and Stengers argue that the history of science has been to advocate the first way, while it should have advocated the second. Once thermodynamics is accepted as having its own (non-dynamic) laws, it is easier to envision thermodynamics and other systems such as biology as open. Without such acceptance both thermodynamics and the biological sciences (as well as education and the social sciences) are reduced to closed system terms.

In a closed system, such as hot water circulating in a house, there is no sense of transformatory change (i.e. change which leads from one state or level to another, qualitatively higher level). Rather, change leads either to chaos—water evaporates, and the furnace melts the pipes—or an external, beyond-the-system adjustment must be made (e.g. water added to the system). Newton's worldview conceived of God in just such a *deus ex machina* role: God was to adjust the clock (world) periodically.

An open system has no pre-set limits and internality is the key to change. Feedback is not cyclical, but spiral, and transformatory change is possible. Disturbed order will not necessarily lead to chaos; higher levels of reorganization are possible.

Education, as a process of intended human development, should be modeled on an open system paradigm. However, it has been plagued with the Newtonian, closed system paradigm. Manifestations of this are seen in the notion that IQ cannot be changed appreciably, that programs such as Head Start cannot make substantial differences, and that in any good test a certain percentage of individuals will always fail. While all these comments are supported by factual evidence, the evidence itself has been gathered in a framework governed by the Newtonian, closed system paradigm. Theorists such as Dewey, Piaget, and Bruner have worked on developing a new educational model, one based on an open system concept—but until the social sciences accept a new paradigm it is almost impossible for education to develop one. Work on such a model can, however, contribute to a changed paradigm.

Prigogine presents a new paradigm and with it a new sense of order which intrinsically transform chaos. In this paradigm order does not need to be imposed externally—by God, scientific laws, or teachers. Order emerges internally, through interaction.

> The classical view divided the universe between spiritual self and the physical, external world. Yet inside us … we experience change. This internal experience is in complete contrast with the view of the world as a timeless automaton. As we begin to discover the roots of time outside us, this duality tends to disappear. With the paradigm of self-organization we see a transition from disorder to order. … This is perhaps the main experience we have—every artistic or scientific creation implies a transition from disorder to order.
>
> (Prigogine, 1983, p. 92)

The concept Prigogine is advancing is that when disorder increases in a given system—biological, chemical, social—at the critical turning point (entropy) chaos does not need to ensue; sometimes, but not always, there are spontaneous self-reorganizations to higher levels of development. Hubbard (1983) states:

> The work of Belgian physical chemist and Nobel prize-winner IIya Prigogine has demonstrated how systems "suddenly" shift to higher order. In his work with open systems, he found that when perturbations caused by energy flowing through a system reach a critical size, they can drive the whole system into a new state that is more ordered, coherent, and connected.
>
> (p. 55)

This is basically the model Weiss (1971) and Waddington (1957, 1975) have proposed in their study of biological organisms. It is also the model Piaget uses in his idea of adaptation, in which he proposes that development follows an equilibrium–disequilibrium–reequilibration pattern (Doll, 1983). This model is also reminiscent of Dewey's (1958a [1929]) notion that secondary experiences reflect on the primary experiences of doing to lead to a new, higher level of experiencing.[3]

Gould (1982), in discussing punctuated evolution—the theory that evolution does not occur gradually, but in quantum spurts—adds some important dimensions to this open system paradigm: "Punctuational thinking focuses on the stability of structure, the difficulty of transformation, and the idea of change as a rapid transition between stable states" (p. 139).

Three points are key here. The first is that development is a movement from one stable state to another, higher stable state—Piaget's stage theory. The second is that making this transformation is difficult; the structures—intellectual, biological, chemical—resist change, again Piaget. The third is that transformations, when they do occur, take place rapidly.

A Transformative Curriculum

The argument has been made that the measured curriculum is a natural outgrowth of the Newtonian, closed system paradigm; and that Prigogine, along with Einstein, Bohr, Heisenberg, Piaget, and Gould, is helping to develop a new, open system paradigm. The educational model that follows would be a transformative curriculum, with the individual and his or her structures or levels of understanding being transformed. Such a change would be internal and include disequilibrium as a prime motivator, as well as the opportunity for self-regulation to work. The teacher's attitude, however, plays a key role in this process.

Bruner (1973, Ch. 13) argues that set or attitude is the most important of all curricula criteria. If teachers and administrators accept, either tacitly or openly, the Newtonian paradigm—often espoused via an emphasis on performance rather than competence (Doll, 1984)—the concepts of internality, disequilibrium, and autoregulation will be for naught. In fact, they will be more a hindrance than a help. Thus, the starting point in making the transformative curriculum work must be an acceptance of Prigogine's assertion that reality is multiple, temporal, and complex.

A multiple vision of reality means that teachers will not occupy a God's-eye role; rather, they will realize that various positions, interpretations, and procedures are legitimate. Even in arithmetic this is true. While 2 + 2 equals 4, and conceivably will do so in the future, 3426 − 1984 can be done starting from the left as well as from the right, with negatives as well as positives, and additively as well as subtractively. In

---

3 On primary experience leading toward a new level of experiencing, see Dewey's *Experience and nature* (1958a [1929]), Chapter 1.

fact, this problem can be done in at least four legitimate, logical ways. The teacher unwilling to recognize and seek out legitimate alternatives is not helping students recognize the multiple dimensions of reality.

The teacher must also recognize that development, growth, and understanding are not instantaneous, direct, and continuous, but come in punctuated spurts. Time, especially the quality of time, is a key factor. Students must have an opportunity to reflect, to try alternatives, and to disagree. Asking students to reflect on their actions, to explain why they did what they did, and to present their methodologies to open scrutiny is important. An example would be to ask students to compute 3426 − 1984 in at least two ways or to write a report on the Boston Tea Party from a Loyalist point of view.

In one of my college classes, the students use primary source materials to write papers on learning theory. Each paper is written twice, and critiqued twice—by peers and the teacher. Further, each paper is used as a springboard or introduction to the next. Thus the students collect a portfolio of papers with critical comments on each. One paper builds on another. Their work is cumulative and developmental, not episodic.

Through the process of integrating their thoughts vertically (paper after paper) and horizontally (peer comparisons) they begin to understand the complexity of the problems before them. Objectivity takes on a new dimension, as does the need for them to listen well to the arguments of others. Their own thinking and writing become more subtle and insightful. In fact, they often surprise themselves with their abilities. They also realize dramatically the difficulties inherent in grading, for a methodology like this does not lend itself to a curve, not even a skewed curve. Development is not continual and gradual; it is punctuated with plateaus, spurts, and bifurcation points. It also requires the cooperative efforts of a community (class). Development occurs more through cooperation than competition; although each has its place and role. The measured curriculum has these roles reversed.

Once an attitude in line with transformations has been set, methodologies for developing internality, disequilibrium, and self-regulation can emerge. Since all transformatory change is basically a change of personal structures, ways of looking at the world and dealing with it, opportunities must be given to reflect, to see and try alternatives, and to experiment. The curriculum must be designed to have the student "construct, unconstruct, reconstruct" (Bruner, 1973, p. 429). This doing, undoing, and redoing process is essential. Knowledge is not a copy of reality, but a process of construction (Piaget, 1971a [1967], p. 27). This is why students need to do subtraction problems in a variety of ways, and read and critique varying perspectives on learning theory. Pedagogically the wheel must be re-invented (Doll, 1981; this volume, Chapter 21).

Any curriculum which emphasizes the active and the reflective—the only way to achieve internality—must by nature run the risk of disequilibrium. The developmental model Piaget proposes is that of equilibrium–disequilibrium–

reequilibration (Furth, 1981; Doll, 1983). Disruption, or disequilibrium, is the motor which drives reorganizational behavior. "However the nonbalance arises, it produces the driving force of development" (Piaget, 1977a, p. 13).

The teacher must intentionally cause enough chaos to motivate the student to reorganize. Obviously this is a tricky task. Too much chaos will lead to disruption (Bruner, 1973, Ch. 4), while too little chaos will produce no reorganization. Just the right amount is needed. Because no pre-set formula can tell a teacher what this will be for individual students, teaching becomes an art. Behavioral objectives with their set predeterminations have no place in this art. Immense responsibility is placed on the teacher, and curricula need to be teacher manipulated, not teacher proofed.

Underlying both internality and disequilibrium (leading to reequilibration at a higher plane) is the notion or belief in self-regulation. The measured curriculum with its emphasis on the set and the predetermined finds this idea of internal regulation an anathema and an absurdity. Yet it forms the foundation of Dewey's (1966a [1916], *passim*) concept of interest, Piaget's concept of construction, Bruner's concept of competence, and Prigogine's concept of transformational change. Prigogine and Stengers (1984) discuss self-regulation in terms of "spontaneous reorganization" when a critical point has been reached (p. 165). This critical point varies from individual to individual, is not predictable, and needs both internal development and disequilibrium to be effective. At this critical point (termed "bifurcation" by Prigogine) various pathways of development are possible. Which one occurs will depend on how the individual interacts with the recognized perturbations. The teacher's task then changes from presenting perturbations to supporting reconstructions in a cooperative and caring way.

In this model of equilibrium–disequilibrium–reequilibration the teacher assumes varying roles often simultaneously. She or he is asked to have a far more complex set of skills than is required by the measured curriculum. But this is Prigogine's point. Reality is not simple, spiritual, and uniform; it is complex, temporal, and multiple. We need an educational model to fit this reality. We need a transformative, not a measured, curriculum.

16

POST-MODERNISM'S UTOPIAN VISION

(1990)

> The art born as the echo of God's laughter is the art that created the fascinating imaginative realm where no one owns the truth and everyone has the right to be understood.
>
> (Milan Kundera in Rorty, 1989)

> My liberal utopia ... would regard the realization of utopias, and the envisioning of still further utopias, as an endless process—an endless, proliferating realization of Freedom, rather than a convergence toward an already existing Truth.
>
> (Richard Rorty, 1989)

It is not usual to consider post-modernism, as a movement, as having a utopian vision. In fact, just the opposite is often stated: post-modernism is too eclectic for any stable vision to emerge. However, these two quotations—from the Frontspiece and Introduction (p. xvi) of Richard Rorty's *Contingency, irony, and solidarity* (1989)—represent, I believe, the essence of a new vision, one which is unstable but no less powerful than the one it replaces. This vision is born not from a firmly set, a priori ideology, nor from the despair which ensues when practical experience helps us become aware that such an ideology cannot be realized. Rather, this vision is born from our own collective, creative imaginations. It is a vision which recognizes its own limits—that our self-hood, language, thoughts are always contingent on particular times and places; that our vision will always be incomplete and unrealizable; further, that *this must always be so* if the process of visioning is to continue. In this post-modern act we lose the certainty modernism posited but open ourselves to a sense of community it never had—a dialogic community (Bernstein, 1983; Ruf, 1987).

Such a vision is ironic in that it is continually self-critical; it mocks itself as it strives, and it considers imperfection not as failure from a pre-established norm but as a goad to further striving. Whether this striving produces a "better" situation is open to doubt—a doubt which always needs to exist.

Before explaining this, my post-modern vision and its connections/disconnections with modernism, I would like first to comment on the paper's title, one which does not particularize a post-modern vision to any one person or group view but generalizes this vision to the universal, to all post-modernists. Stephen Toulmin (1982) comments that post-modernism is still too young to be defined in terms of "what it is", it can only be defined in terms of "what it has-just-now-ceased-to-be", modernism (p. 254). Almost a decade later this statement still holds true—the only unifying factor in the multiple versions of post-modernism is that none of them are modernist, all reject modernism. David Griffin (1988b, 1989) has helped us see, along the lines of C.P. Snow (1964), that the literary, political, philosophical view of post-modernism (which he reads as deconstructive) is quite different from the scientific-theological view (which he calls constructive). Richard Bernstein (1983, 1985, 1986) and Richard Rorty (1979, 1982, 1989) and Jerome Bruner, too, (1986b) have helped us see that Griffin's distinction, while useful, is not absolute. The Continental post-structuralist tradition which integrates art, literature, philosophy, science, social theory, and theology (into a cosmology) deconstructs not in an attempt to negate but to help us reframe our thoughts and visions in a totally different way.

This "different way" (a *tertium quid* from Piaget or Dewey's point of view) is one where truth, reality, values are not imposed by some force "out there," or pre-set, or even agreed to in advance of an experienced situation. Rather, these qualities are dialogically negotiated (or trans-acted as Dewey would say)[1] as we interact with nature and ourselves. Prigogine and Stengers (1984) call this our "new alliance" with nature, one where we cooperate not dominate. To negotiate truth, belief, value within our cultural and historical moments (and to renegotiate continually as Rorty points out in the quotation at the beginning of this chapter) need not cause us to give way to nihilism or to "rampant relativism." We can and should have standards, criteria, judgments. These stem, though, not from an "aboriginal reality ... out there" (Bruner, 1986b, p. 158) but from our own *collective and public* interactions. The utopian vision remains but it has been reframed.

While post-modernism is, as Toulmin asserts, not yet able to define itself in terms of itself, such a possibility is beginning to emerge. The various brands of post-modernism are not categorically incompatible. The union Griffin finds between a new, reenchanted science and process theology can be extended to cover the deconstruction of texts and the pragmatics of language. There is a unity here but it is a unity ever born anew; it is a unity Prigogine and other chaos theoreticians assume in their work with turbulence. Pedagogically, this means, as Piaget (1980 [1974])

---

1 On inter- and trans-action see Dewey and Bentley (1964), *Knowing and the known.*

recognized so well, there needs to be just enough disequilibrium in every situation that reequilibration can be generated. Or to quote from Jean-François Lyotard:

> The novelty of an unexpected "move," with its correlative displacement ... can supply the system with that increased performativity it forever demands and consumes. In fact it may even be said that the system can and must encourage such movement to the extent it combats its own entropy.
>
> (1984, p. 15)

Modernism, especially in its Enlightenment and social-scientific forms (the former through such philosophers as Immanuel Kant, the latter through such technocrats as Henri Saint-Simon and Auguste Comte), had a definite utopian vision. It was to produce a better world for all through correct reason and the technocratic spirit. The mystical faith of medievalism was to be replaced by the logic of Reason and the science of measurement. A "new" society was to be born—*l'ancien régime* controlled by the clergy, the military, and royalty was to be replaced by a new breed, the "scientists, artists, industrialists" (Saint-Simon, 1952 [1825], p. 78). Ancient distinctions between upper and lower classes would be blurred as a new, all-uniting, middle class (the bourgeoisie) arose. As an ideal, this vision influenced a number of working utopias in England and America during the mid-1800s. As a practical reality, however, this vision had a number of "contradictions" built into it. One of these was that the industrial revolution kept the same class distinctions but changed the titles of lords to managers, and the category of serfs to workers. Charles Dickens and Karl Marx, each in his own way, railed against these "contradictions." Still, the vision remained and continues to remain, reinforced by degrees of practical success in Western, democratic societies.

Utopia *(ou* from the Greek "no, not" plus *topas* for "place") literally means "no place." It has been modernism's visionary "no place" since Sir Thomas More (1975 [1516]) assigned the word to his imaginary island where perfection—in moral, social, and political affairs—reigned. Utopia has always been aligned with progress and perfection—an ideal never-never-land. But modernism always held out the hope that someday, somehow this utopia would be realized. The farm utopias of upstate New York and Indiana as well as those of rural England were spurred by the power of this external and all-consuming vision. Karl Marx's own "utopian perspective of a collective life process ... which would spontaneously emerge from the institutionally unmediated interaction of emancipated individuals" (Wellmer, 1985, p. 38) was as strong and unrealistic as Saint-Simon's. Both were driven by on external and absolute reality, not by a dialogic interaction among human beings living the praxis of life, nor even by the ideal of "a realm where no one owns the truth but everyone has a right to be understood." (Kundera, 1988)[2]

---

2 Quaker communities and New England town meetings were, and are, obvious exceptions to this latter statement. However, even here restrictive covenants have been placed on membership. "Everyone" has never meant *every* person.

As a "no place," the modernist utopian vision was not shattered by the realities of lived experience. Failures were considered failures of practical application, not of the vision itself. The crises which post-modernism has created—a crisis Peter McLaren analyses well in his article "Postmodernity and the death of politics" (1986)—involves the questioning, indeed the denial, that any vision has reality apart from the practical experiences of life. As McLaren says, the visionary world modernism posited "has been inexorably annihilated." In Bruner's terms, there is no "aboriginal reality … out there." Instead, "reality is socially constructed or semiotically posited" (McLaren, 1986, p. 389). Modernism's dichotomous separation of ideation from lived experience (based on Descartes' separation of *res cognitans* from *res extensa*) has allowed the ideal vision to remain no matter what the practical realities. Such a view reduces the practical to a handmaiden of theory.

What post-modernism asks us to do is to adopt a new frame. The only reality we have is the here and now, one of lived experience. We have ourselves, the universe, and our temporal moments of time. How we integrate these is not entirely our choice but our choices play a key role in making temporal moments into lived "occasions" or "events" (to use Alfred North Whitehead's terminology – 1967a [1925], 1967b [1929]). And reality is composed of these events.

At this point it might be helpful to comment that my use of the term post-modern (hyphen intended for continuity between the modern and post-modern) does *exclude* the "dystopian potentialities" McLaren asserts exist within the "character of postmodern society" (1986, p. 77). These potentialities characterized by social malaise, apathy, lack of history, privatization are indeed both "dystopian" and contemporary. I see them, however, not as part of a rapidly evolving post-modern society (one which has yet to mature) but as representations of the dying throes of modernism. Here, I agree with Charles Jencks (1988) who believes this "spirit of negation" to be a reflection not of post-modernism but of the final stage of modernism. He labels this "ultra," "high," or "late" modernism. It is modernism's avant-garde gone berserk. This distinction between late-modernism and post-modernism, between the ending of one paradigm and the beginning of another, is not merely semantic. It defines the very way we look at post-modernism: either as a form or subset of modernism, which Lyotard asserts or as a new vision, which Jencks' asserts.

For me, post-modernism is not just a fad on the fringe of the modernist movement; it represents, rather, an epochal change of "megaparadigmatic" proportions (Küng, 1988). Like all paradigmatic changes of such sweep, it will take generations for the implications inherent in this new structure to work themselves out. To aid in this process, I'd like to finish this paper by listing four implications I presently see. All are imminent, and all carry pedagogic corollaries. These are: (1) a vision built on doubt not certainty, (2) centrality of the dialogic process, (3) reinterpretation of the practical, (4) adopting an overall ecological frame or orientation.

A Vision Built on Doubt

In art, literature, science, and theology the modernist vision has been built on certainty. John Dewey developed this point in his *Quest for certainty* (1960 [1929]), as did Morris Kline, 50 years later, in his *Mathematics: The loss of certainty* (1980). The Western intellectual tradition, particularly in its Platonic–Kantian form, has both searched for and accepted the reality of certainty. Positivist and Realist thought is based on the assumption certainty exists. As Rorty says: "The metaphysician thinks that although we may not have all the answers, we have already got the criteria for the right answers: (1989, p. 76). In contrast, the ironist, she who comes from the hermeneutic tradition, maintains a vision based on doubt. Again, to quote Rorty:

> The ironist, by contrast, is a nominalist and a historicist. She thinks nothing has intrinsic nature, a real essence. … The ironist spends her time worrying about the possibility that she has been initiated into the wrong tribe, taught to play the wrong language game. … She reminds herself of her rootlessness by constantly using terms like "Weltanschauung," "perspective," "dialectic," "conceptual framework," "historical epoch."
>
> (1989, p. 75)

As the rational/metaphysical vision is based on (masculine) certainty, so the hermeneutical/ironist vision is based on (feminine) doubt. In doubt one questions, continuously, basic assumptions, procedures, obtained results. This is well represented by post-modern art which is self-mocking or by post-modern science which realizes its procedures and results are always open to reinterpretation. This sense of the self-critical and doubtful is what originally attracted Dewey to science as a methodology. But, unfortunately, this key aspect of science was soon replaced by a positivist methodology designed to produce certainty. Science turned from science into "scientism," as both Huston Smith (1982) and Paul Feyerabend (1988) remind us.

A vision based on doubt has definite pedagogical implications. One of these is to reassess, continually, one's procedures, assumptions, results—to listen to and search for the (small) voice doubt presents in every act. Another is to realize that *no one*, not even the teacher, *has the truth*. Truth is history bound and comes from present situations as these are analyzed publicly. We all need to contribute. A third is to enter into a dialogic relationship with one's peers, students, teachers. This is the procedure by which any truth is developed. A fourth is to adopt a playful attitude toward that which is most important to us, to let "the art born as the echo of God's laughter" ring in our hearts, souls, minds. Seriousness quickly overpowers our sense of alternative possibilities; it locks us in to the already tried; it limits our perspective. In this frame, the Tyler Rationale (1950) is beside the point—not so much wrong as irrelevant, a work of the metaphysicians not of the ironists.

Centrality of the Dialogic Process

As Hans-Georg Gadamer (1980) has stated, and as Richard Bernstein (1983) has emphasized, "what is most essential to our being-in-the-world is that we are dialogical" (Bernstein, 1983, p. 229). The "essence" of our being, if I may borrow the metaphysician's concept, is to be dialogical—to have interaction with others in a community. Goals, plans, purposes, procedures, judgments, evaluations all come from this sense of community. This is why the *a priori* characteristic of the Tyler Rationale is irrelevant; it neglects the dialogic nature of our being and the qualitative, developmental change which can come from that dialogic nature. While the present will indeed influence the future it need not predetermine the future.

Pedagogically, this means, as Dewey emphasized so many, many times, goals arise in and from action—they are "turning points in activity," "redirecting pivots in action" (1964 [1922], pp.71–72). They are not set (except in the most general, broad, and "fuzzy" manner) prior to action. Process becomes not a precursor to product but an all-encompassing frame in which many products, moments, or events exist. Important as these "ends" may be they are but turning points in a larger process frame.

Peter McLaren recognizes the validity and importance of this insight when he says that one of Paulo Freire's fundamental assumptions is "recognition of the world, not as a 'given' world, but as a world dynamically 'in the making'" (1986, p. 397). Such realization allows the people Freire works with "to participate consciously in the sociohistorical transformations of their society." This emphasis on the dialogical provides post-modernity, McLaren says, with a "reprieve" from the negative image it too often carries—an image that could lead to its death as a political movement. Such a reprieve is really testimony to the power of post-modernity as both an educational and political movement, one which possesses a new and unstable, utopian vision.

Reinterpreting the Practical

Almost a quarter century ago, Joseph Schwab declared the field of curriculum "moribund," an unhappy state arrived at by a "mistaken reliance on theory" (1970 [1978], p. 287). Too often, indeed almost always, educators and curricularists borrow theories from other disciplines and, without proper analysis of their applicability, use them directly as models for education. Such wholesale, unexamined borrowing produces a poor match between theory and practice. But even more important for Schwab is the fact that "theoretical constructions are, in the main, ill-fitted and inappropriate to problems of actual teaching and learning." The practical, daily problems of teaching and learning are not well served by the application of theoretical modes. He argues that theories, both in terms of the grand designs Lyotard calls metanarratives and those of lesser stature, have an idealist cast which removes them from the practical activities of lived experience. In this frame, the practical becomes a handmaiden for theory. Schwab recommends we relook at the practical, reversing

its relation to the theoretical: the practical, with its emphasis on the local and the temporal, should be the basis for curriculum. Any theory we develop should emerge from and be centered around the practical.

Once we look at the practical–theoretical distinction this way, it becomes obvious, I believe, that our approach to curriculum has been from the theoretical mode not from the practical mode. We have not focused on the practical problems Dewey urged us to, a point Rorty continually makes, nor have we developed skills for dealing with the practical. Instead, we have focused on pre-set, theoretical designs and, in a procrustean manner, have tried to fit the learner to these designs. The attention we have paid the learner has been in terms of how efficiently (quickly and accurately) the learner can achieve pre-chosen goals and techniques. We have avoided what William Pinar (1975) calls *currere,* the learner as a person, not as an object to be molded. As a person, the learner is unique with individual organizational patterns and procedures that need development, not manipulation.

Piaget, in many of his experiments with children, has given us some of this *currere* aspect—at least in regard to the child developing logical thought. Unfortunately, in our mechanistic and modernist mindset, we have overly focused on the concept of ages and its correlation with theoretical stages as we have interpreted Piaget, thus missing the practical of the child. It is the practical, in all its rich eclecticness, which makes the child not only so fascinating but which also forms the base for future growth and more sophisticated development. It is, as Piaget argued so vehemently in his concept of transformative, personal structures (1971b [1969]), a base which should not be overlooked.

The practical by its very nature is oriented with the temporal, the unique, the personal. Its focus, as Schwab points out, is on decision making—evaluating, judging under indeterminate conditions. It is one with the eclectic and the pragmatic. By focusing on the practical we are focusing on life's real activities and generalizing from these experiences what we can for future occasions. The process is ongoing; it has no end outside itself.

This practicalizing process is what Richard Rorty (1979) calls the edifying mission of philosophy, developed by the pragmatists, as opposed to the epistemological theoretical mission, developed by Immanuel Kant and his followers. Donald Schön (1983, 1987) calls this practicalizing process the art of "reflective practice," and he comments that those who do it well draw on an experiential competence not taught in professional training schools. These schools oriented themselves from the theoretical, rational–technical mode, but practical problem solving (indeed problem posing) comes from reflecting-while-doing. Here the practitioner/teacher needs to work with the client/student in an interactive manner; each needs the other, each must help articulate the nature of the problem being posed. Often the problem, be it personal or professional, lies hidden, enmeshed in the vagaries of the situation. Both teacher and student need to work together, each trying to understand the other's point-of-view, each respecting the other's "right to be understood."

Focusing on the practical and letting the theoretical emerge from the practical (not precede it) leads to the development of a new sense of community—one dialogical and ecological.

Adopting an Ecological Frame

Once we shift our focus from an "aboriginal reality out there" to a here-and-now reality, our utopian vision takes on a new frame. This frame—C.A. Bowers (1987; with Flinders, 1990) calls it "post-liberal," referring to its move beyond individualism—focuses on the ecological, communal, dialogical. It produces for us a reality which is always emerging, a "proliferating realization of the yet possible rather than a convergence toward an already existing Truth." While we construct the reality we know, we are also aware of a larger, natural frame in which our own existence is finite and tenuous. Our continued survival as a species depends on our ability to balance what we know with what we do not know. This ecological view, drawn heavily from Gregory Bateson's work with other cultures, goes beyond defining ecology as a concern for nature's "naturalness" to envisioning ecology as a way of thinking in which cooperation, balance, respect for others becomes central. Such a cosmological concept helps us realize that we are part, and only part, of a larger natural frame. This frame, or network of relations, is far more complex than the simple, mechanistic system Newton envisioned. The network appears self-generating—through information and energy exchange—not only thriving on change but actually requiring change as the source for the order it develops.

Humans and their cultures, contingent on the historicity of events, lie within not outside this network. As Bateson (1972) says: "The unit of survival is not the breeding organism, nor the family life, nor the society. ... *The unit of survival is the flexible organism-in-its-environment*" (p. 451; emphasis added). At first reading this quotation seems to articulate the obvious: our survival as a species depends on our ability to be flexible within changing conditions. But the quotation's thrust runs counter to modern thought; a closer examination shows it to contain elements key to a post-modern, utopian perspective. Three of these are (1) flexibility, (2) interdependence, (3) unity.

Utopian visions in the modernist past could remain conceptually inflexible for there were always new lands where theoretical ideologies could be put into practice. During the 17th, 18th, and even the 19th centuries, America often served as this land. In the 20th, almost 21st, century space for continual expansion is no longer available. Our visions must now be more flexible; they must accommodate others and their visions. Further, we need not only to honor others' voices, we need to listen to and learn from these voices. This is as true in teaching as it is in foreign policy. We are now an interdependent world. We will not survive—ecologically, economically, politically—unless we recognize our mutual interdependence. As teachers our task is to provide a frame for students which moves beyond the rugged individualism of the past to an envisioned cooperative communalism. Dewey made this point in his *Individualism old and new* (1962 [1929]) but it fell on modernist ears. With the economic collapse of authoritarian communism as a political movement, we may well believe that laissez-faire individualism has won the day. Such a belief, however, would be a mistake; our needs will be better met by moving beyond Cartesian bifurcations to an integrated, post-liberal vision based on unity, cooperation, interdependence. As Bowers and Flinders (1990) say:

> We think that Gregory Bateson's way of thinking, derived from his studies of communication in different cultural settings ... provides a more useful analogue than the ones that have dominated thinking in the West for the last four centuries. "The definitive relationships in the universe are not competitive but interdependent."
>
> (p. 249)

Our cosmos demonstrates a fragile but interconnected unity, an ecological network. We are *part of* not *apart from* that network. While this statement, too, borders on the obvious, it is true, as Huston Smith points out, that Cartesian rationality has encouraged us to separate ourselves from our lived world, to assume we could "rise to a God's-eye view of reality" (1982, p. 10). The arrogance inherent in this view has separated the knower from the known, producing a false, "objectivist" epistemology, one which makes the knower only a spectator. Further, and of even more import, it has separated us from ourselves and our cultures. In this separation it has been deemed acceptable for us to manipulate both our selves and our environment. In fact, our sense of *noblesse oblige* has even deemed such control and manipulation "a duty." Certainly, Frederick Taylor (1947 [1911]), the foster father of the American curriculum, considered it his duty to impose the principles of scientific management not only on industry but on all forms of American life. This was part of his and other technocrats' vision.

As we approach the 21st century it behooves us to rethink some of our most basic assumptions, formed during the Enlightenment over 300 years ago and based on the modernist worldviews of Descartes and Newton. Our own vision is a good deal more doubtful, inherently filled with problematics, rooted in dialogue and history, and continually remade as we interact playfully with ourselves and the environment of which we are but part. We have lost our sense of certainty, but in this loss we may well find a sense of ourselves.

17

STRUCTURES OF THE POST-MODERN

(2011)

The term post-modern, a conceptual term only, has evolved meanings over time and through use. It came to prominence in the late 1970s via a French intellectual, Jean-François Lyotard, who, anticipating the changes technology would bring (*The postmodern condition: A report on knowledge*, 1984), presaged that Western rationality was entering a new era. This era he called post-modern to distinguish it from the modern era—one the West, with its Eurocentric viewpoints, was just leaving. The modern era, originating in the 17th century with the rise of what we now call traditional science, and imbued with the liberal humanism of the Enlightenment, focused on forms of thought that were complete in themselves (*grands écrits*, or master narratives, Lyotard called them). He believed the coming age, the post-modern, would be suspicious of such fully formed, complete, and universalizing modes of thought. He said the new age would display "incredulity toward such master narratives"—in master narratives, all individual components fit nicely, easily, completely. A type of surrealism begins to emerge in these narratives. Marxism and Capitalism are examples of such master narratives, as is science when expanded to an "ism"—Scientism. Each of these has a certainty about itself and its methods that does not allow for doubt or questioning, especially of basic or foundational assumptions. Lyotard encourages us to question these assumptions and the projects they have spawned: We need to "'work through' ... the meanings or events that are hidden not only in its *pre*judices but also in *pro*jects, *pro*grams, *pro*spects, and the like" (Lyotard, 1987, 3).[1]

---

1   This notion of "working through" which Lyotard borrows from Sigmund Freud is too often overlooked. In his 1987 article, "Re-writing modernity," Lyotard puts forth the proposition that for him the post-modern is not so much a break with the modern as it is the working through of the meanings which are hidden within the modern. In this sense

In distinction from modernism, the *productive use of doubt* and the *interpretative art of inquiry* (or questioning) are hallmarks of post-modern thinking. Post-modern doubting does not refer to the removal of all certainty; rather it is recognition that certainty is always temporary, contingent on the situations in which we find ourselves. One might say that certainty with a large "C" does not exist, only certainty with a small "c," and that small "c" certainty is always problematic—heavily dependent upon an existent situation and always open to further exploration and questioning.[2] Pedagogically this means that a post-modern classroom would encourage students and teachers (together) to investigate a subject with depth, going *beyond knowledge and skills*.

Post-modern questioning of modernist foundations and assumptions is also prominent in art, architecture, and literature. A post-modern aesthetic challenges traditional assumptions of form by creatively and playfully combining and integrating distinct artistic genres (Jencks, 1988, 1992).[3] In the post-modern arts, space and time are treated differently—as dynamic and interactive, fluid and nonlinear. Ironically, many ancient, as well as contemporary Chinese buildings, especially the Shanghai skyscrapers, have this post-modern flavor. In China we observed the pre-modern (agriculture), the modern (industry), and the post-modern (technology) all present in the same locale. Quite fascinating.

Post-modern science similarly reconsiders space and time. The definite and measured pull of gravity, a *constant* so important to Isaac Newton's (17th century) equations, and most relevant to his time, we now see depends on whether one's feet are firmly planted on celestial earth or dangling in outer space. (Utilizing a toilet in a space station is a delicate art.) Further, few of us question whether or not $1 + 1 = 2$, everywhere and always. In base two, though, $1 + 1 = 10$, and the relational use of that base (1s and 0s) is the binary foundation of contemporary computers, which bring us into the post-modern era.

Questioning foundations and exploring taken for granted assumptions is often missing in current curriculum designs. In schools, especially American schools, it is not uncommon to teach zero as "nothing" and thus to begin our number system, *not* with 0 as the first of ten digits but with 1, hence quietly slipping 10 (a double digit) into the first ten digits (all singles). This points out that what we assume is

---

the post-modern is the modern, continually "re-writing itself." As I have said, my use of the hyphen in post-modern is designed to convey this modern/post-modern connection.

2   Incidentally here lie the roots of American pragmatist thought and its commitment to the scientific method. Science is always open to further exploration and modification. Alas, Western rationality has too often made science itself into a *grand écrit*: science as the answer to everything, with scientific research providing not so much what John Dewey called "warranted assertions," but rather issuing definitive conclusions. "Research says" is a phrase often used in this regard.

3   Charles Jencks, an architectural and cultural historian, argues that a post-modern frame honors history, eclecticism, and "multilayers of interpretation" (Jencks, 1986, 1988; Doll, 1993, Introduction).

certain and hence take for granted is really historically situational, even cultural.[4] The ability to explore these situations, indeed to "see" them in a different light, is key to developing creativity and new insights. Such *developing*, based in part on questioning what we take to be certain, is one goal of a post-modern teaching/ learning epistemology.

John Dewey, who spent much time studying the West's *Quest for certainty* (1960 [1929]), believed that seeking certainty actually *hinders* intellectual and social development. In questing after certainty, we have, as one post-modern commentator has said, "put a straightjacket" on our ways of thinking (Waters, 1986, p. 113). We have limited our goals too severely, have cut off the possibility for the new to emerge naturally, forcing the new to emerge post-curricularly, outside a school frame. Whitehead (1967a [1925]), a contemporary of John Dewey, said, almost a century ago, the way (British) schools and universities taught "produced a paralysis of thought" (p. 37). That is, knowledge acquired exclusively for passing a test is "inert, dead, and barren"; it is knowledge useful only for doing well on a test, it is not knowledge utilized in the living of life and its experiences.[5] As an antidote to such a modernist view of knowledge acquisition—full of drill, copying, memorization of inert facts, Whitehead advocates that curriculum developers choose "main ideas" for their goals, and that teachers in implementing these goals "teach a few [of these main] ideas ... thoroughly and well ... throwing [the ideas] into every combination possible" (p. 2). In saying this, Whitehead, paralleling Dewey, is advocating that goals be directions, not destination points; in encouraging the teacher to be present and active but not dominating, and in encouraging that ideas be looked at from various perspectives, the teacher *sets initial conditions* and *provides space* for the new to emerge. New ideas can emerge when there is a beginning rich in problematics and incorporating sufficient time and space for interactions, as reflective recursions, to gestate, mature, come forth, and develop. Such a developmental process—a rigorous reflection on the relations inherent in a rich situation—is key for the design and implementation of post-modern practices, those encouraging *creativity, inquiry, innovation, and social responsibility*.

A post-modern frame can be demonstrated in the following example. adding the numerals 2, 3, 4. As this is done, it is easy to see multiple ways emerging: 2 + 3 + 4, then 2 + 4 + 3, etc., leading to a simple set of six ways: a + b + c, a + c + b, b + a + c, etc. Patterning of this sort eases the elementary grade student into combinations and permutations, as well as into a beginning sense of logic—all the while providing the student with an abundance of "drill." A perturbation can then be introduced by asking the question of how one finds a seventh way to add these three numerals. Exploring

---

4   For example, we are told math in China is more analogical than digital.
5   Utilized knowledge, knowledge having a meaning for life occurs, Whitehead believes, only when one has thrown away textbooks and burned exam notes: "Your learning is useless to you till you have lost you textbooks, burnt your lecture notes, and forgotten the minutiae that you learnt by heart for the examination" (1967b [1929], p. 26).

this question opens up a whole new realm of mathematical thinking—a realm not limited to skills only but one of *using skills to explore relationships*. As an example, it is possible to envision the exercise not as 2 + 3 + 4 but as 3 + 3 + 3, which leads to multiplication (3 × 3) and demonstrates the multiplication/addition relationship. It is possible, also, to use 2 as a base numeral and hence "see" the seventh way as 3 of the 2s, plus 1, plus 2. Mathematically this can be written as (3 × 2) + 1 + 2. Taking 4 as a base numeral can lead to the subtraction/addition relationship: (2 × 4) −1 −2. All these latter ways (seventh, eighth, ninth) can also lead to an understanding of the role zero plays on a "number line" scale—zero being the founding base for the original (2 + 3 + 4) problem. Here, of course, is also the beginning of a Cartesian grid and its inherantmathematical logic.[6] An introduction to such "big" mathematical ideas is quite possible in the early elementary grades.

The preceding example also illustrates the nascent development of a pedagogical design, one encouraging students to think in terms of patterns and relationships.[7] Placing discrete operations into patterned relationships is part of what Whitehead is after in his call to "throw ideas into every combination possible." Through *multifocal* perspectives (really through the difference that occurs via such a perspective) "deep" learning occurs—one that goes beyond copying. Time and space are no longer the metrics used for creating worksheets or designing problem sets for students. Relationships and creative combinations take precedence over numbers of problems drilled or speed of accomplishment. Likewise, the language of mathematics and patterning is merged with everyday language as patterns and relationships are described, depicted, and demonstrated. In this learning, the student is acquiring the power to be creative. Really, it takes scant time for such intellectual power to emerge—only a few classroom minutes. The transformative vision it develops, though, is astounding and long lasting.

The unfortunate vision modernist thinking has encouraged teachers to use—a vision of learning occurring as a direct and immediate result of copying what one is told, thus encouraging "teaching-as-telling" and the textbookizing of knowledge—

---

6   The Cartesian grid, that of the *x* and *y* axes lying perpendicular to one another, is a fixture of high school mathematics and the solving of simple first degree (and a few second degree) equations. Metaphorically, these linear crosses represent a type of thinking that is rational, boxed, deductive. As Fleener (2002) points out such rational thinking has a strong sense of the dominant in it—good thinking is adroit, right, and (self) centered; poor thinking is gauche, wrong, and other(ed). Ambiguous (or in-the-middle) thinking, where interpretation exists, does not, as a category, exist.

7   If one were to use the numbers 3, 4, 5, instead of 2, 3, 4 in the preceding example, then the Pythagorean Theorem would come into play: in a right triangle the sum of the squares of the two sides equals the square of the hypotenuse ($3^2 + 4^2 = 5^2$). Once into Pythogoreanism, the basis of much of Plato's sense of number, one also comes into contact with mystical numerology, so fascinating to scholars in the Middle Ages (Henry, 2008), and active today with horse players and gamblers. On mythical numerology see Inna Semetsky's essay, "Simplifying complexity," in *Complicity*, Vol. 5, No. 1, July 2008 and Tony Whitson's "Response," in the same issue.

can be traced to Peter Ramus, a schoolteacher and early curriculum designer in the 16th century (Triche and McKnight, 2004; Doll, et al., 2005). In Ramus' view there was *one and only one way* to deal with any pedagogical activity—the "best practices" way he advocated. This way, Ramus said, was the "one and only way Aristotle taught." Leaving aside the accuracy of Ramus' statement (approximately 1800 years did separate the lives of these two), it is fair to say that the dichotomization of Western knowledge and thinking into either/or can be traced to Aristotle and his successors. As Dewey pointed out so many times, the either/or, right/wrong, good/bad, true/ false, quantitative/qualitative, objective/subjective split has dominated Western thought for millennia. Teachers today, in their quest for and belief in "best practices,"[8] or in asking students to give back to them what they "give" to the students, actually shuts down students' own thought processes, and the natural human ability to be creative. In some ways, schooling that teaches all students to memorize the same material in the same manner is actually a hindrance to education. Such a schooling/ education split is most unfortunate.

Aristotle's logic (drawn from Euclid's geometric methods), that which Ramus so honored and dishonored,[9] is itself based on an unfortunate split: an either/or frame that precludes a middle or "third" space (Doll and Gough, 2002; Wang, 2004). What is, IS; what is not, IS NOT; no middle exists, little interpretation (really none) is needed. Once the rules for IS are set up, Ought-To's follow in a direct, linear manner. Teachers, then, need not be interpreters or inquirers, just transmitters and enforcers—of what IS. Teachers become automatons controlled by the textbook. Such a frame has dominated not only Western logic and epistemology but Western metaphysics as well. Reality itself has been conceived as being either objective (in which case it can be scientifically "discovered") or relative, personally subjective (in which case it has no foundation other than individual whim). The awareness of quanta in the early part of the 20th century, contradicting Newton's belief that the universe is made up of set, solid, and stable, individual atoms—an important point not only for Newton but also for pedagogy's belief in, and teaching of, individual "facts"[10]—brought with it a paradigmatic change in intellectual thought (Fleener,

---

8   "Best practices" has become a shibboleth in Western cultures. David Snowden (2005), a critic of best practices, states that such practices are merely "entrenched past practices"; they attempt to impose the past on the present. Instead he suggests a curriculum that "manages for serendipity."

9   Those interested in the changes Ramus made to Aristotle's logic—changes which have influenced the West's way of *thinking*, and of thinking about pedagogy, should refer to both Meyers (2003), and Triche and McKnight (2004).

10   Pedagogical facts today, those we consider foundational to any discipline, are often considered "hard" as Newton considered the atom. Such an assumption, though, is cultural, as Barbara Shapiro points out in her *A culture of fact* (2000). Here she shows that fact has a long history, that it *emerged* (to use a complexity term) over centuries. Francis Bacon (1561–1626), as both a scientist (concerned with accuracy and verifiability) as well as legal scholar (Lord Chancellor of England) brought together law and science. He wished for "fact" to be "a matter capable of proof, preferably by multiple eyewitness testimony,"

2002). Since atoms, in a quantasized frame (*Discover* magazine, June 2007), are now seen not as solid objects (itself a frame for "solid facts") but as bundles of dynamic energy with subatomic particles of many kinds being created and dying by the millions of billions, and electrons (part of an atom's nucleus) being potentially both waves and particles, a new worldview comes into existence. Not simple stability, but *dynamic change is seen as the very structure of the universe* (Whitehead, 1967a [1925], p. 72). Such change though is not random nor is it uncontrolled; dynamic change maintains itself as an emerging, ongoing, and continually reforming structure through the very process of change itself. The pedagogic corollary to this new, post-modern, worldview is to see education as an ongoing, dynamic process, controlled not by the external force of the teacher or the textbook, but guided by, and through, its own interactions. The interactions, as a process, yield a product: *the new.* Teacher, text, student, environment, culture all play roles in this interaction but no one of them becomes dominant. The variables in any interactive situation are so many that there is no one, universal "best way." Each situation needs its own analysis and interpretation; each situation has metaphorically its own (emerging) "rules." Each situation's own rules while indigenous, are also "self-similar"—one set nested inside another, larger set, much like the flowerets of a head of broccoli are self-similar to the whole head itself. Each floweret is unique but part of a larger, cohesive whole. It is the quality of relationality that provides a part/whole structure (Smitherman, 2005). As already said, designing *a curriculum that emphasizes relationality is key to a post-modern pedagogy.*

Relationality (relations) as a "foundation" is, for critics of the post-modern, no foundation at all. They say that since there is nothing solid, only relations, no foundation exists. For them, that which is relational is always in flux, and its ambiguity should be avoided, not embraced. Post-modernists like Richard Rorty (1979, 1989), might well reply, as does Ted Aoki (2005b, p. 431), *we need a foundationless curriculum.* There is nothing solid outside ourselves, nothing but ourselves, we can "hang onto." Nor do we have ourselves, "inside," as immutable beings; there is no Cartesian "I," independent, autonomous. We are always embedded, part of the very fabric we weave as we study that which we weave, and that with which we converse. What we have is a bricolage of relations and situations, and we are part of that bricolage, in our everyday, actual relations. Educationally speaking, this viewpoint encourages us to honor and utilize relational practices and conversations—developing interactions with ourselves, our students, texts, and cultures; thereby moving beyond "teaching-as-telling" to a whole new teaching/learning epistemology (Trueit and Pratt, 2006; Pratt, 2008). This new epistemology is very much based on Gregory Bateson's

---

particularly by persons (essentially 12 juried men) of "appropriate credibility" (p. 110). "Facts" are a cultural phenomenon, born at a certain time and place of a social need—here to develop an English natural philosophy "expunged of literary, mythical, and symbolic elements" (p. 108). Facts are not so much indigenous or foundational to a discipline as they are cultural artifacts, useful to a culture, and changing as the culture changes.

notion of relational difference (1988) and on Richard Rorty's admonition to "keep the conversation going" (1979, p. 377).

In the past few decades, the "new sciences" of chaos and complexity have provided an open frame, a different "foundation,"[11] for dealing with issues of ambiguity, uncertainty, and the new possibilities that flow from these issues. A study of these issues and their educational implications can be found in Fleener, 2002; Doll et al., 2005; Davis and Sumara, 2006; Mason, 2008 and the online journal, *Complicity* (www.complexityandeducation.ualberta.ca). The important point that runs through these books and the journal is that the open frame of post-modernity with its tolerance for, and indeed use of, ambiguity and uncertainty allows creativity and imagination to emerge and flourish. Such an open frame (Prigogine and Stengers, 1984; Kauffman, 1995, 2008; Stengers, 1997) is useful not only for education—developing emerging possibility by *playing with ambiguity*—but is needed to understand the new physics of the subatomic and the astrophysical, as well as to understand the new biology dealing with evolution and the structural processing happening inside animal (including human) brains. Mathematics-oriented chaos theory with its emphasis on nonlinear recursions and physics/biology oriented complexity theory with their emphases on structural transformations present an open frame which encourages participants, players, observers to think in terms of, and work with, patterns, networks, webs.[12] Again, here lies the heart of a new, post-modern pedagogical paradigm.

Pedagogically, in the past, we have thought in terms of, and worked with, individual facts—facts too often separated from other facts. Our disciplines have been segregated, and within disciplines we have further subdivided, as Peter Ramus advocated (Triche and McKnight, 2004; Doll et al., 2005). Alternatively, to think and work in terms of patterns, networks, webs—indeed to build a living epistemology from such (Bateson, 1988; Capra, 1996)—is to encourage students to "see" not just what is there but to "see" in terms of relationships (Fleener, 2007; Doll, 2008b). No matter what the course taught, the teacher can, at any time, ask students in the class to envision another interpretation, another way of operation. As in the example above, $2 + 3 + 4$ can be worked in a variety (indeed an infinite number) of ways. A story can be read from the viewpoint not just of the main themes or characters but from the viewpoint of non-obvious themes and minor characters. A number of post-modern writers do this—works by Umberto Eco, Thomas Pynchon, or Thomas Stoppard come to mind. The important point here, pedagogically speaking, is not just a different perspective but the utilization of such a perspective to make comparisons, build relationships, create the new. In this frame, learning comes not so much from the teacher directly passing on his/her

---

11 Brent Davis, following along the lines of Ted Aoki, uses the phrase "foundationless foundations," in his "Languaging, irony, and bottomless bottoms" (*Complicity*, Special Issue, No. 1, 2009). For those interested in Complexity Theory this issue is most helpful.
12 For a study of network theory (webs), see *Complicity*, Vol. 7, No. 1, January, 2010.

"expert" knowledge to an unknowing "novice,"[13] but from all participants, teachers and students (as well as texts), building a network of relations. Such is, of course, what is happening already via the internet and is the heart of the fast growing field of information technology (Hayles, 1999; Mitchell, 2009). The challenge and the opportunity of an open, post-modern frame is to help students develop networks of relationships (maybe even to "program" those relationships), to see how adding $2 + 3 + 4$ can morph into 3×3 or into $(2 \times 3) + 1 + 2$. Such a conversing activity not only aids a student in acquiring math "facts," but aids him or her in acquiring an understanding of the very structure of mathematics itself. The same process can be used pedagogically in any subject or discipline "taught." It lies at the heart of a post-modern teaching/learning epistemology, one that is dynamic and developmental by nature.

---

13 A dramatic example of this can be found in the first chapter of Jie Yu's LSU doctoral dissertation (2011). Here her undergraduate education professor is filled with passion about the "right way" to teach, a passion which he wished to impart ("tell") to his students. The professor's passion (his telling) did not translate into Jie's practical classroom activities (her lived doings).

PART 4

Complexity Thinking

Introduction: Donna Trueit

Throughout his career Doll has been a historian of science, which has provided him with a unique perspective of the influence of science, or as he often says, scientism, calling attention to a particular conceptualization of science. He refers to the distinction Gerald Holton makes between science$_1$ and science$_2$, between science as it is practiced by scientists doing research, and the cleaned up and idealized version of science that is characterized by "method." Over the last few years, Doll has come to focus on the thinking epitomized by scientific methods, that taught in schools, which is not really thinking at all, but rather a following of prescribed steps—not really what scientists do! Indeed, the new sciences of complexity and chaos challenge the logic of reasoning which comes to a conclusion rather than dynamical reorganization. The following three essays reflect Doll's own transformation, leading to the kind of change in thinking that Edgar Morin calls a paradigmatic shift. It is a shift that for Doll involves moving from:

- criticism which looks at what is and suggests an alternative, process-oriented way to look at education;
- to a radically different epistemological position, one informed by the new sciences concerned with dynamically self-organizing systems; and
- informed as well by philosophers such as Martin Heidegger, Hans-Georg Gadamer, and Jacques Derrida, but especially by, Richard Rorty, anthropologist Gregory Bateson, and most recently, chaotician, Michel Serres.

From this new perspective one steps back to look for connections, relations and interactions that comprise a system and influence a system, understanding that the system is creative and healthier with both an abundance of interactions and richness of interactions—and importantly, that one is a part of the system. Reflexively, one ponders the effect of the system in shaping one's ideas, questioning how those same ideas might be shaped in and by other cultures. This practice introduces the idea of ambiguity to challenge modernist ideals of certainty (or Truth). A diversity of ideas will benefit the system as differences, and via feedback loops, generate new ideas. A classroom can be thought of as a learning system where teachers and students all learn. Taking his cue from Tom Kieran, Doll attempts to learn three things from each class he teaches, each presentation he observes. In this way, Doll, like two of his intellectual heroes, Serres and Aoki, works at humility as a teacher, being always a learner.

In "Recursions on complexity" we see the beginning of Doll's epistemological shift as he ponders the language/words of complex systems, wondering what the implications are of using the words: there is a difference between using words from complexity theory to throw light on aspects of modernism—but still using modernist rational thought processes—and shifting to an entirely new form of reason/logic/thought—one appropriate (like it or not) for a global, technology-oriented, non-renewable resource-gobbling world. The only way to deal with the complex issues that confront the world today, says United Nations Educational, Scientific and Cultural Organization's (UNESCO's) Edgar Morin, is a paradigmatic shift to complexity thinking.

"Complexity," a definition written for Sage Encyclopedia, is an exercise in simplicity in which Doll makes connections between the curriculum and self-organizing systems and the conditions of emergence.

Co-authored with Donna Trueit, written for presentation at IAACS in South Africa and for *Complexity theory and the politics of education* (Osberg and Biesta, 2010), "Thinking complexly" initiates a discussion of what it might mean to move beyond reductive reasoning to thinking complexly. Instead of concerning oneself with "what is" (things, *forms*) one might begin to think differently, now exploring situations by looking at connections, relations, open systems, networks, dynamics etc., as the interest of representation. Instead of using the telescope as the underlying metaphor for our practices of representation, maybe a fractal would be generative.

18

RECURSIONS ON COMPLEXITY

(1998)

> We shall not cease from exploration
> And the end of all our exploring
> Will be to arrive where we started
> And know the place for the first time.
>
> (T. S. Eliot, 1943)

Returning to my article, "Complexity in the classroom" (1989; this volume, Chapter 22) after an away period of almost a decade, I find myself seeing it, yet again, for the first time. At that time, the field of complexity was just dawning on the general consciousness: James Gleick (1987) had recently published his popular book, *Chaos: Making a new science*, Ilya Prigogine and Isabel Stengers (1984) had their earlier work translated into English as *Order out of chaos*, and both Roger Lewin (1992) and Mitchell Waldrop (1992) were investigating Complexity in the deserts and mesas of New Mexico. Stuart Kauffman (1991; with S. Johnsen, 1991) was beginning to use the word chaos[1] in his exploration of self-organization. And Katherine Hayles (1990, 1991) was making web-like connections between chaos in the sciences and in literature. As the nineties have progressed, the allied fields of chaos, complexity, and nonlinearity have virtually exploded, especially in the sciences, mathematics, and medicine. Any minimally comprehensive list of readings would run well into the hundreds of books and thousands of articles. Yet the effect on the humanities, despite Hayles' works, and on the social sciences, especially education, has been minimal. Still I believe the potential for developing nonlinear curricula and modes

---

1 The contemporary use of the word chaos first appeared in a 1975 mathematics article by T. Y. Li and J. A. Yorke, "Period three implies chaos."

of instruction continues to exist. But I realize now, more than then, the difficulties inherent in reconceptualizing curriculum and teaching in such a way as to allow nonlinearity to be a meaningful heuristic. Such a challenge challenges many of our most fundamental and "natural" worldview beliefs—those involving not only teaching but also the composition of that we call reality. Indeed to turn the potential existent in the complex into actualized realization requires a paradigmatic shift concerning nature and its ways of organization.

> A. A violent order is disorder; and
> B. A great disorder is an order.
> These two things are one.

(Wallace Stevens)[2]

Probably the most important topic, then and now, is the one I used to begin my article: the emergence of a new sense of order, or more specifically our newly found awareness of the order inherent in nature. If what Gleick calls a "new science" is about anything, it is about our new awareness of the order existent in the universe. As I state in my book (1993) and elsewhere (1998a) the sense of order we have accepted as natural is about 300 years old—starting somewhere in the scientific revolution of the 17th century—and is now seen as overly simple, linear, centered. The effect of this type of order is evident in American society through the scientific management work of Frederick Taylor (Kanigel, 1997) and in education through the Tyler Rationale (1950) and its aftermath of framing curricular and instructional goals in precise and pre-set objectives, all offered to us in behavioral terms. The carryover, of course, exists today in the usual or traditional ways we organize our lesson plans, textbook sequences, curricular guidelines, methods of instruction. The desired goals for all of these are simplicity, linearity, centeredness. Further into this article, I will make the radical proposal that having a class work on the same text, problem, or experiment, especially in one uniform way, is an inefficient way to aid students in their learning or meaning-making. However, before making an argument for such a proposition, I'd like to explore, rather broadly, the concepts of order and control (Doll, 1998a). Both are key to virtually everything we do in formal instruction; both are paradigmatic to our view of the way reality is organized.

At the cosmological level we have become aware this century that our universe is fantastically ordered, marvelously ordered beyond our wildest imaginations. However, this order is not the order we have (mistakenly) taken as natural: it is an order most complex, fractaled, and continuously developing (Argyros, 1991; Capra, 1996). We recognize this, of course, most easily in the small and strange world of what we call the quanta and in the extremely large world of the cosmological (P. Davies, 1988, 1992; Prigogine, 1997; with Stengers, 1984). Awareness of this order

---

2 "Connoisseur of chaos," 1959 [1938], p. 97.

is also apparent but far less so in our everyday world—i.e., the earth does revolve around the sun in less time each year, and the sun is slowly, very slowly "dying." In short, our universe is temporal not eternal. Thus the universe Isaac Newton saw as simple, stable, regular, we now see as complex, dynamic, arrhythmic—filled, as Prigogine and Stengers (1984) say, with strange objects, "quasars, pulsars, galaxies exploding and being torn apart" (pp. 214–215). While Albert Einstein stated firmly that "God does not play dice," we now see her as throwing loaded ones (Stewart, 1989). And we are pleased with this insight; for in a universe whose very spirit is creativity, this sort of disequilibrium is necessary to keep creativity active. Yes, this is a very different world and universe from the one Newton and his followers "saw."

In John Dewey's wonderful 1938 phrase about "[hu]mankind liking to think in terms of either/ors" (1963, p. 3), this new insight into nature—a nature which has existed "unseen" for eternity—is by no means to extol the truly random, the abysmally disordered, and the radically relative. Rather this new vision is saying that more and more we are realizing our universe to be comprised of an order that is complex, chaotic, nonlinear. What is so fascinating about this new sense of order is the way the (seemingly) random and the (simply) ordered are integrated or enfolded one into the other. Not only does order emerge from chaos, as Prigogine asserts, but chaos is itself embedded in order, as chaos theory shows. In this complex order, what we have previously taken to be a dichotomous split between randomness or disorder and order are now bound together in a dynamic (and indeed nonlinear and "chaotic") new sense of order.[3] In this union, of what we have previously seen as bifurcated, lies, I believe, a powerful heuristic for curriculum and instruction. It goes without saying that a venture into this chaotic land of the nonlinear is disturbing; I have also found it immensely rewarding. I hope you will find the rewards worth the disturbance.

As stated in the 1989 article (written on research done a few years earlier), our intent in the Friday math sessions was "to challenge [the sixth grade students] own creative and constructive powers." Particularly we used this procedure—hardly a procedure then, more trial and error than anything else—in regard to solving mathematics word problems. We had been quite unsuccessful in "teaching" such: closer reading, step-by-step analysis, choice of main ideas, increased drill on math skills had all been minimally helpful at best. Frustrated, we decided to stop teaching by direct instruction and instead to adopt a more flexible, interactive approach—one that bordered on the nonlinear. We randomly placed number and sentence fragments into a hat and asked the students, working in groups, to draw from the hat, "what they needed." Often, by randomness, too much was drawn; sometimes, by lack of

---

3 Obviously I am using the words complex, chaotic, nonlinear in synonymous ways. They are closely allied and appear together in most of the literature on new senses of order. Any difference is one only of emphasis. It seems possible to say that chaos is the mathematical framing of this new order with complexity focusing heavily on the self-organization (and cosmological) aspects, and with nonlinearity on the process of mathematical iteration by which the order is graphically seen.

perspective, too little was drawn. Each group worked on the material drawn to devise problems for other groups to solve. The overabundance or under-abundance of math facts and sentence fragments was marvelously disguised so that the solving groups had to figure out what was pertinent as well as to solve the problems themselves. This sense of play (Doll, 1980; Gough, 1994) was a strong and quite natural motivator. The fact that these students—most encased in low socioeconomic situations— scored top in the county and in the top 25 percent in the state on given exams was known to us only after the project ended. Undoubtedly this interested the editors of the journal but for us the year was a success due to the students attitudes, their commitment to work (in a playful way), and in their obvious understanding and appreciation of the structure of the number system and of varying word problems. They did indeed develop their "own creative and constructive powers."

While words and concepts such as nonlinear, self-organization, disequilibrium, and spontaneity were used and discussed in these days, a synthesis of them was not yet present. In fact, only now is such a synthesis beginning to emerge from the interlocked fields of chaos–complexity–nonlinearity (Argyros, 1991; Cohen and Stewart, 1995; Capra, 1996). Underlying this synthesis, the well-spring from which all three flow, is the assumption that the universe is filled with "creative energy" (Berry, 1988a; Argyros, 1991), or, more dramatically, that the universe in its very soul and spirit is creative. Creativity is the universe's distinguishing characteristic. Such an assumption has strong cosmological, philosophical, psychological, and theological implications. For education, particularly for the fields of curriculum and instruction, I believe this synthesis and its assumption of inherent creativity—existent in teachers and students, as well as in the universe in general—has at least three important implications. These are (1) a legitimization of teachers' (and students') own procedures, choices, actions; (2) a new foundational frame: one which supports these local actions; (3) the suggestion of a new teaching and learning "model." I'd like to comment on these in seriation.

Legitimization of Local Teaching Practices

In the modernist frame most schools adopt today, teachers are caught in a double-bind: they are responsible for delivering the curriculum but the curriculum is not of their devising nor is the mode of instruction. From teacher education courses, through in-service training and evaluation, teachers are taught to accept others forms of curriculum and modes of instruction. Such prescribing effectively limits the teachers own local modes of practice and removes creativity almost completely from the model teaching act. Thus, teachers are seen as automatons delivering someone else's standardized curriculum in a uniform manner.[4] As John Dewey

4 Ironically those teachers given rewards for outstanding teaching are almost invariably those who have deviated from the standardized norm and designed curricula and instructional modes to fit the needs of their local classrooms.

(1966a [1916]) has said: "Nothing has brought pedagogical theory into greater disrepute than ... handing out to teachers recipes and models to be followed in teaching" (p. 170).

Breaking this pattern of universalizing uniformity—a pattern not present in either law or medicine—is extremely difficult and it is to the teaching profession's merit that so many teachers do struggle to develop their own local practices. The chaos–complexity–nonlinearity synthesis with its strong emphasis on local conditions and non-uniform development does encourage a questioning of the straight-jacket in which we—teacher educators, textbook writers, supervisors and evaluators, administrative bureaucrats—have placed teachers. The time has clearly come to legitimate, honor, and help teachers develop their own local practices.

A Chaotic Structure

The structure which supports the legitimization of teachers' own local practices is an interesting one, quite unusual even oxymoronic to those not imbued with a post-modernist or complexity/chaos theory mindset. From a modernist perspective, chaos–order, randomness–structure, flexibility–setness are all dichotomous either-ors. One chooses or exists in either of the dichotomies but not in both. In the chaos–complexity–nonlinearity synthesis developing however, the reality of nature is that both exist, each intertwined, embedded, dependent on the other. Simple graphing of chaos equations shows this pattern (Stewart, 1989; Doll, 1993; Ott and Spano, 1995). Further, creativity seems to reside or activate itself best in the area or process where there is interplay between stability and flexibility. Prigogine (with Stengers, 1984) call this area "far-from-equilibrium," while at the Santa Fe Institute for the study of complexity (Kauffman, 1993, 1995; G. Johnson, 1996) it is named near or on "the edge of chaos." Whatever the name used, the place or process where chaos is happening is dynamic, interactive, alive. In those fields where chaos is taken seriously the "effects" are revolutionary.

A New Model (?)

Despite the growing popularity of the chaos–complexity–nonlinearity synthesis and its startling insights in many fields, the question of its long-term viability and of the development of teaching–learning "models" from it is still problematic.[5] And to call such an open-system process—deterministic yet unpredictable—a "model" is to challenge the very concept of model. It is also to challenge our evolving concept of the post-modern. Still for all these caveats, a teaching–learning structure is emerging from the synthesis.

---

5 It should be noted, however, that the popularity of the Caines' work (1994, 1997; Caine et al., 1995, 1999) does indicate the eagerness of the educational community to find a new structure.

The heart of the structure lies in the concept of creativity and in the belief that everywhere the cosmos is in the process of creating. If creativity is a natural state and function—of humans as well as of all nature—then how do we as educators develop a curriculum and modes of instruction based on creativity? This is a challenge all curricularists—theorists, designers, implementers—committed to the viability of this synthesis need to address.

Answers to this challenge need to come at the local level, of course. However, a few observations—some already made—might serve as guiding beacons:

- The creative process being described by the synthesis is open-ended, dynamic, emergent. So should be the curriculum. A pre-set curriculum will kill the very existence of the creativity inherent in this process.
- The process is iterative or recursive, dependent in its existence on dialogic, feedback loops.
- The process is bounded and directional, always leading toward more complexity, that which Dewey called *growth*. Local constraints and direction are essential. It might be worth considering my suggestion (1993) of developing a curriculum around the 4 R's of richness, recursion, relations, rigor.

The process fuels itself by the essential and generative tension between diversity and integration. To have all students do the same problem, text, exercise in the same uniform manner is an inefficient way to teach and a poor way to learn.

19

COMPLEXITY

(2008)

Complexity theory, along with fractal geometry and chaos theory, is one of the New Sciences, coming to prominence in the latter part of the 20th century. These three fields contribute to our new awareness that nature in its organization is complex, fractaled, and turbulent. This is quite different from the past (modernist) view that nature is simple, linear, and stable in form and organization. Isaac Newton, in the 17th century, believed nature to be "pleased with simplicity" and "conformable to herself." Charles Darwin (1964 [1859]) brought forward a different view, one wherein nature is capricious or random in its development. "Chance caught on a wing" is the way one scientist has phrased evolutionary development. In their study of nature, contemporary scientists, using the mathematical tools of nonlinear dynamics and the power of supercomputers, posit that nature is in form *self-organizing* and that the disorder we see in the cosmos, universe, and world is really an "orderly disorder." Models of this "stable" disorder are found in avalanches, economic systems, evolutionary development, galactic births and deaths, human bodily and social systems, population dynamics—to name but a few. What looks and appears disorderly is really a new type of order, an order emerging from (and even embedded within) disorder. The implications for education are immense and radical. Up to the present day, education, in its forms of curriculum design and instructional strategies, has been premised on a simple design, directly transferable. To think of learning, not as a passive, receivable act—the mind as a *tabula rasa* imprinted by teaching—but as an interactive, dynamic, and self-organizing process, challenges past (and even present) methods of syllabi design, lesson plans, and instructional strategies.

Self-Organization and Emergence

Self-organization, whether in computer simulations, ecological, environmental, information processing models, or social interactions is the defining characteristic of all complexity research and study. Whereas imposed organization—be it institutional (including education), political, or religious/philosophical (God as progenitor of the West's *Great chain of being* (Lovejoy, 1936))—is always top-down, self-organization *emerges from* an interactive base of particulars. Life itself, at the cellular, species/human, social levels is an example of such a self-organizing system. As particulars or events interact they do (under certain conditions) form a system: an interactive, dynamic, creating system. Complex networks arise from simpler networks, as in evolutionary theory; or conversely, simple, unifying networks emerge from complex interactions, as in galactic order, human bodily systems, or population dynamics.

"Self-organization" refers not to an individual self becoming consciously organized, but rather to a dynamical system—sometimes large, sometimes small—organizing (even transforming) itself in particular phases of its development. Such a system, often labeled anti-chaotic, existent in all natural sciences but most prominent in the biological/living sciences, maintains its stability even as the interactions within itself and between itself and its environment proliferate. Complex *adaptive* systems is another phrase used here, to indicate the system's overall ability to maintain order as events or particulars within the system experience change. Bodily immune systems or neurological systems are examples of this—as cells both die and regenerate, the system maintains its overall harmonious functioning. At a *critical* point, though—far-from-equilibrium or the system's center, out near "the edge of chaos"—a small perturbation or occurrence leads to a major, transformative change. In this view, chaos is embedded within complexity. Evolution here is not simply the result of random/chance occurrences but is rather a natural, interactional, complex process. Organization emerges, freely and spontaneously—"order for free"— from what seems to be chaos. For those complexity theorists studying evolutionary development, "natural selection" is not the one and only way species evolve. Rather, development is stochastic, combining elements of randomization with those of natural emergence. Such emergence (arising more *from* than *toward*) is sporadic, spontaneous, and unpredictable (although deterministic, at least in a probabilistic sense).

The educational implications of this emergent/self-organizing process are numerous and radical; most significant is the recognition of order emerging from interactions—it need not be imposed. In fact, imposition may well be a hindrance to development. If development is indeed a stochastic process—interactions among elements/events themselves interacting with random external events—then the educational design of curricula, teaching strategies, syllabi or lesson plans need to be rethought. At the very least, flexibility needs to be built into the structure of curricular design and teaching strategies. Even better would be syllabi or lesson plans that emerge; a real challenge to any educator. "Teachable moments" would now be not a surprise but expected. Here, the abilities a teacher needs to possess go beyond the skills and methods usually offered in teacher preparation or school mentoring courses/situations. Further, to guide a situation toward a far-from-equilibrium situation—away from stability, toward "the edge of chaos," without going over that edge into an abyss—requires a sense of feeling for the situation not present in current teacher-centered (or even student-centered) designs. Situations become their own managers and guides, with teachers (and students) playing important but non-dominating roles. Ambiguity, uncertainty, imbalance, chance, probability all take on importance as issues, not to avoid, but to utilize.

All the foregoing represents a major shift in curricular design, instructional strategies, and teacher-preparation courses/experiences. This shift is away from *goals pre-set*, experiences pre-chosen to mirror those goals, experiences organized to achieve the pre-set goals chosen, and assessment as to how the pre-set have or have not been achieved. The shift is toward a curriculum *rich* in problematics, *recursive* in its (nonlinear) organization, *relational* in its structure, and *rigorous* in its application.

20

THINKING COMPLEXLY

(2010)[1]

We live in a universe of complexity. By our very human nature, and through the use of language, we impose limitations on that complexity. The reduction of complexity has been a key element in classical Western thought from Kepler and Galileo to the present, yielding great scientific advancements; we suggest, however, that in our current diversified, globalized, technologically oriented era, reduction as a habit of thought is no longer as useful as it once was. In our view, complexity theory encourages us to recognize the limitations of human thought and also enables us to acknowledge unseen possibilities, inherent in any situation, as creative potential. Shifting one's attitude from "reducing" complexity to "embracing" what is always already present in relations and interactions may lead to thinking complexly, abiding happily with mystery.

We take as our premise that historically all Western human intellectual practices limit complexity as these practices are framed by and communicated through language. We understand, as did Gregory Bateson, that humans can never be more than humans; our capacity to comprehend complexity and the complex world in which we live is limited: by our biology and genetics, by our history and environment. Limited as we humans are, we do reflect, recurse, review, and renew our actions, interactions, and discursive practices. It is precisely these activities that make a new discursive practice, that of thinking complexly, possible.[2]

---

1 Co-authored with Donna Trueit.
2 In his essay entitled "Hume", Gilles Deleuze (*Pure immanence*, 2005) explains Hume's displacement of metaphysics in terms of the relations of man to God and the environment. Relations, explains Deleuze, constitute *human nature*. "Causality [one of four types of relations along with association, contiguity, and resemblance] is a relation according to which I go beyond the given; I say more than what is given or giveable—in short, *I infer and I believe*, I expect that …" (pp. 39–40).

Discursive practices—culturally accepted and reinforced ways of thinking, speaking, writing, and non-linguistic forms of representation such as painting, architecture, town planning— are an organization of "visible and describable" signs (Reiss, 1982, p. 9). These practices produce and reproduce a culture. Concepts such as "schooling," "teaching," "learning," "knowledge," and "education," those that affect policies, practices, and politics of the last 500 years, have all developed within a modernist *episteme*.[3]

The use of language in discursive practices is not neutral; it is political and powerful in that it advances certain frames of reference and denies or limits others. Often the political aspects of language use are *occulted*, as Reiss points out in describing how 17th century literature was quite "consciously instituted by the French monarchy as a political tool … Louis XIV and [Jean-Baptiste] Colbert used what they instituted as proper literature, the canon, to help achieve the setting-in-place of a particular political system." Louis XIV's agenda was "to bolster internal and external policy," "to inculcate values desirable to Louis," and to "license writers to control publication"; these direct political actions are forgotten over time (occulted), but continue to exert a powerful effect because they have been institutionalized, becoming *ideological* (Bertonneau, 1986, p. 10).

The visible and describable signs that Reiss talks about in a modernist *episteme* are those viewed as though seen through a telescope, a decontextualized, universalized view called "objectivity" (1982, pp. 34–37). In this modernist view, *signs* (viewed objects), converted to *conceptualizations* (words), are ordered/organized to make sense as they coincide with a natural, theological order. Objectivity is characteristic of a modernist discursive practice and a hallmark of modernist science. It is *epistemic* in the sense that it informed ideas about knowledge in Western cultures and therefore has deeply influenced ideas about education.

A transformation of discursive practices occurs in the historical moment when its limits have been reached; for example, when it is recognized that the (absent, but enunciating) subject is the producer of discourse, when the subject's view is recognized to be perspectival (not universal), when order can be seen as a system of relations ranging from simple to complex and still evolving. This moment "poses tremendous difficulties for the notion of scientificity … [and] makes necessary the abandonment of assumptions generated in the period before" (Bertonneau, 1986,

---

3   *Episteme* is Foucault's term for the body of ideas which shape the perception of knowledge in a particular historical period: "The 'sciences of man' are part of the modern *episteme* in the same way as chemistry or medicine or any other such science; or again, in the same way as grammar and natural history were part of the Classical episteme" (Foucault, 1970 [1966], p. 365). We suggest that prior to the intellectual ferment of the late 19th century, the modernist *episteme* was heavily influenced by the theological view that God created the world and everything in it—a closed, deterministic system. In this view, the world began with God as the head of a *Great chain of being* (Lovejoy, 1936) and ended with the simplest life forms. *Order* within this closed system is hierarchical; similarly, modernist discursive practices encourage social relations that are top-down in keeping with "natural" order.

p. 10). The presence of the (previously occulted) subject in scientific discourse, and then in other types of discourse, renders objectivity obsolete. Similarly, the presence of the subject calls to question the subject/object, Self/Other relation: the emergence of the "individual," a concept which did not exist in the Middle Ages. The *modern* subject is "the constituting individual subject organizing the social order" (p. 9), an autonomous, independent Self. For us, the new found importance of relations and interactions in complex systems signals the limits of the concept of *individualism*. And through science, the limits of *order*, previously conceived as "natural" theologically defined, and then as mechanical, sequential, and linearly defined by Newton, are disrupted by quantum physics.

Drawing on Reiss's ideas about the disintegration and subsequent (re)formation of a discursive era and Rorty's (in Niznik and Sanders, 1996) notion of shifting metaphors (that structure meaning) we adopt the idea of complexity as an organizing principle of a new *discursive practice* (reasoning, thinking, speaking) and extend these ideas to include and focus on the importance of social interactions, *Being*-in-relation. We believe that *embracing* a complexity perspective—in *all* of its complexity— may enable us to "see" possibilities as yet unseen in the policies, practices, and politics of schooling and education.

Reiss's point about the transition and transformation of one discursive practice into another is that it happens not as a rejection of the past practice, but as an outgrowth. It is precisely because of modernist discursive practices that we develop the cognitive skills to be able to see the limitations of this practice: we reflect, recurse, review, and renew our actions and interactions. Through these actions and interactions we see a process of change beginning, and drawing on principles from complexity theory (metaphorically and practically) we hope this change will lead to a better socio/political world.

We recognize that as a word "complexity" has a number of meanings and subtle distinctions. As Paul Cilliers (2000) and others have pointed out, complexity and complicated are of different genres. That which is complicated can be taken apart, reduced to simples; the whole is equal to the sum of its parts. This is not possible with complexity; complex relations cannot be reduced to simple actions, a complex whole is indeed a whole, greater than the sum of its parts (if one were to think of a complex whole having parts—which by its very nature it does not).[4] Too often, one mistakes the complex for the complicated and hence tacitly assumes reduction is useful and valid.

A common use of *complexity* refers to situations that are confusing, hard to understand, full of many unrelated, competing factors. Trying to deal with such

---

4   Regarding reduction, Cilliers (2000) puts forth statements we consider worth noting. He believes chaos theory, particularly deterministic chaos, to be of little help in understanding "the dynamics of complex systems"; such a theory, although useful in modeling nature, is really "part of the modernist paradigm" (p. ix). He does, though, believe complex systems can be modeled using connectionist theory. The art here is "to conserve the complexity of the system itself"; hence "a complex system cannot be 'reduced' to a simple one" (p. 24). Embracing complexity "conserves the complexity of the system itself."

situations in an ordered way is itself trying. For many, the hope here is that concepts drawn from complexity theory might bring order to a complicated mess. Indeed such concepts can be heuristic (i.e. shifting a focus from individual elements to a system of interconnected relationships).

Complexity as used in the complexity sciences deals with interactive, dynamic systems that under *specific and limited* conditions are able to transform themselves (Prigogine and Stengers, 1984: Kauffman, 1995, 2000, 2008; Prigogine, 1997). These systems, chemical and biological, not mechanical, are nonreversible and have a developmental arrow to them.[5] While these open systems[6] are not reducible (a human being cannot be reduced to sperm and ovum), they are often simple but definitely defined in their constituent elements with complexity emerging not from the elements themselves but from the interaction of the elements.

We (authors of this chapter) use *complexity* as a word that signifies a dynamical self-organizing process within which we are embedded, embodied, emboldened. As part of the dynamical process of our engagement in this world, we are constantly reorganizing/changing. We take this fluidity/flow to characterize, as well, a way of thinking/speaking that no longer relies on foundations and facts as the static building blocks of past intellectual thought; rather, drawing on principles derived from complexity science, we are encouraged to think of *emergence* as the ongoing flow of our awareness and appreciation of *being*-in-relation to others, the environment, the cosmos. We see these relations as systemic, networked, and patterned.

Educational Implications of Thinking Complexly

As educators we strive for creating a "better" or "good" society even as we are suspicious about the very act we advocate,[7] conscious of the influence of the ideology, a cultural unconsciousness that informs our striving. Our suspicion arises from a concern about limiting the diversity and differences which, through the process of interaction, energize the system. We wish to honor diversity and difference and believe this is best done by embracing not limiting the complexity found in relationships, life, situations. Ultimately we believe our faith should lie not in our personal ability to control through prediction, but believe it should lie in what Dwayne Huebner (1999) labels the call of "moreness." "Moreness" has a spirit to it, a spirit which asks us to realize our own finitude, our own ignorance, and calls

---

5   Prigogine explores the issue of time's directionality, its "arrow," in his 1997 and 2003 books. Time's arrow is, of course, a key assumption for complexity theory and has been a distinguishing feature of Western thinking since Darwin.

6   Prigogine (1961) asserts that closed systems "exchange energy but no matter" (they transfer) while open systems "exchange both energy and matter" (they transform). It is this transfer/transformation distinction that we believe educators need to consider (Doll, 1993, p. ix and *passim*).

7   Peter Meyers (2003) believes teachers should be skeptical of their advocacy: "To be a teacher requires a radically critical orientation towards one's own activity" (p. 41). A teacher does not just transmit information: s/he professes, indeed proclaims, an ethic.

us to "transcend the known, the expected, even the ego and the self" (p. 403). It is the source of hope, a hope that whatever our limitations we can be more than we are. In this spirit of hope, we *embrace* complexity, calling for a new discursive practice; one which focuses not on the nodes (things in themselves) existent in this world but on their relations to the world we live in, and the world which is yet to come. Huebner believes it is "trivial" to think of education in terms of learning *things*—of learning names, objects, procedures, rules, skills. While all these are important to living life, he believes education is more than these and advocates we think of *education as a journey* into the land of the unknown, taken by ourselves but with others (p. 405).[8]

We suggest that principles derived from complexity theory may inform a discursive practice that we call "thinking complexly." For us this discursive practice, still developing, slowly being articulated, encourages us (the authors) to begin to move beyond the telescopic, objective seeing of modernism. We begin to see differently working with this interrelated constellation of features, focusing on relations and interactions, being recursive, playing with and exploring differences, attending to intuition and abiding with mystery and ambiguity, happily relinquishing certainty.

Relations

We use the word "relations" paying attention to C. S. Peirce (1992) and Giles Deleuze (2005) assuming, as they tell us, that relations are not "natural"; relations are habits of thought, associations that organize and order thoughts in particular ways. The discourse of modernism is characterized by linear, cause and effect ordering and a disregard of potentialities. We are suggesting that linearity toward certain ends is a habit we can change and that thinking otherwise is possible. We believe complexity as a frame offers a fine opportunity for developing this thinking.

From our perspective, one is always embedded in a network of relations. Our *Being* then, as Martin Heidegger (2002, 2008) reminds us, is always in relation, we are always "be-coming." We are as nodes in networks (Mitchell, 2009, Part Four), interconnected to other nodes within other networks: people within cultures, cultures within humanity, humanity within an ecosystem, our ecosystem within our universe, our universe within a cosmos, ever evolving. Our sense of Being develops through interactions among these nodes in networks and networks within networks. This developmental process, arising from interactions, leads, unpredictably (since we

---

8 Compiler of Dwayne Huebner's essays (Vicki Hillis, editor), William Pinar (1999), makes a point similar to Huebner about the triviality of learning. Drawing on the work of many who have contrasted study with instruction or learning, especially Alan Block's (2004) interpretation of the writings of Joseph Schwab, Pinar (2006) talks of "The Lost World of Study," of "Study as a Prayerful Act," and ends his essay (Ch. 7, p. 120) with the conjecture "If we have a future, it will come to us through study" (not through school learning).

can never know how these interactions are going to "play out"), to creation of the new.[9] We believe that limiting these relationships moves us way from "conserving the complexity of the system itself." Instead we advocate working with the system's complexity, open to that which can not yet be seen, that which has yet to emerge. In working *with* complexity we begin by acknowledging the limitations of our perceptions, cultural consciousness and language. Because we cannot know or perceive all, we believe that ambiguity, uncertainty, and an openness to unpredictability must be part of our thinking and teaching.

We suggest thinking in terms of the *relation of relations*, of building a network of relations: vertically (historically) and horizontally (present circumstances) (Pinar, 2009a, 8).[10] In demonstrating his 4 R's, William Doll often presents an example of a network of relations. He illustrates learning beyond atomistic, discrete facts, transgressing disciplinary boundaries, to provide openings for students to engage reflexively. Doll begins with an obviously simple example of kindergarten/grade 1 arithmetic, using six poker chips, each red on one side, white on the other. With these young students he talks about addition and simultaneously plants a seed for algebraic thinking:

red chip + red chip + red chip + white chip + white chip + white chip = 6 chips;

or, abstracting to the letters themselves, the following combinations can be made:

$$r + r + r + w + w + w$$
$$r + w + r + w + r + w$$
$$3r + 3w$$

From this experience, Doll develops an introduction to permutations and combinations:

$$r + r + r + r + w + w$$
$$r + r + w + w + r + r$$
$$4r + 2w$$
$$2(2r + w)$$

---

9   Mitchell comments that "humans and mustard plants each have about 25,000 genes," with the biological complexity between these organisms arising from the "complexity in the *interactions* among the genes (2009, p. 233; emphasis in original). How this biological complexity emerges is a question unanswered and maybe unanswerable: the *mysterium tremendum* of life.

10 Appreciating Pinar's point about knowing a field in terms of its history and culture, we see these as two axes (horizontal and vertical) of a field's multiple dimensions, suggesting additionally that looking for points of transformation, patterns, global connections, and environmental impact are also necessary.

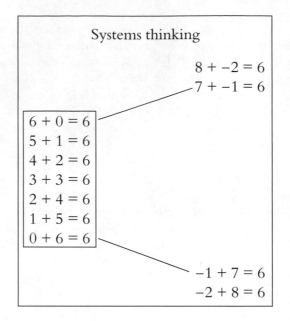

Systems thinking

$$8 + -2 = 6$$
$$7 + -1 = 6$$

$$6 + 0 = 6$$
$$5 + 1 = 6$$
$$4 + 2 = 6$$
$$3 + 3 = 6$$
$$2 + 4 = 6$$
$$1 + 5 = 6$$
$$0 + 6 = 6$$

$$-1 + 7 = 6$$
$$-2 + 8 = 6$$

FIGURE 20.1 Systems thinking: outside the box

Moving beyond kindergarten/grade 1 students, Doll suggests grouping the numbers into closed and open systems (see Figure 20.1), thereby showing the relation of addition to subtraction, and of positive to negative integers. Mathematics as logical relations begins to emerge.

Looking at the column of numbers on the left in Figure 20.1, one sees patterns of ascending and descending numbers. The numbers on the right are ways of extending the pattern which leads into subtraction as well as "negative numbers." Each is an extension of addition; a relationship is made among all three, instead of each being a separate function.

Building on the idea of patterns, Doll moves the poker chips into a "bowling pin" formation to introduce first the idea of a different sense of order:

X

XX

XXX

Then, since the bowling pin formation resembles Pascal's triangle (Figure 20.2), Doll points out a relation to the distributive principles of algebra:

Looking at Pascal's triangle, Doll asks the students to find, within the triangle, the pattern that reveals the Fibonacci sequence (Figure 20.3): the numbers are 1, 1, 2, 3, 5, 8, 13, 21...

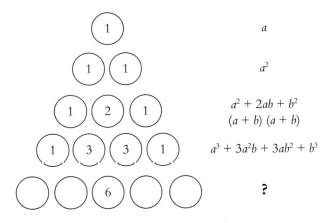

FIGURE 20.2 Visualizing distributive principles of algebra in Pascal's triangle

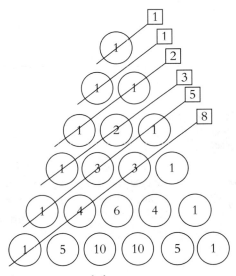

FIGURE 20.3 Fibonacci sequence revealed

Within the triangle, on the diagonal, the Fibonacci sequence is revealed. So what, one might ask?—and students often do! Why does one need to understand anything about the Fibonacci sequence? Doll seems to be making what might be termed a series of "Serres-ian" leaps.[11] The Fibonacci sequence is, however, a series of numbers that has a connection with the golden ratio, the mystical value of *phi* in

---

11 Bruno Latour notes that Serres's (Serres and Latour, 1995) "method" takes epistemological leaps: "To take Lucretius, to leap over the philosophers who discount him by saying he's obsolete, and to bring him to the hypotheses that are current in physics …" (p. 54). Serres points out that Lucretius is only obsolete when time is conceived as linear (p. 57).

Greek mathematics and the ratio on which Greek architecture was founded. The ratio of numbers in the sequence settles into the number that is the golden ratio, defined as the number which is equal to its own reciprocal plus 1; for example:

$$\frac{1}{1} = 1 \qquad \frac{5}{3} = 1.66 \qquad \frac{21}{13} = 1.615$$

$$\frac{2}{1} = 2 \qquad \frac{8}{5} = 1.6 \qquad \frac{34}{21} = 1.619$$

$$\frac{3}{2} = 1.5 \qquad \frac{13}{8} = 1.625 \qquad \frac{55}{34} = 1.618$$

$$x = \frac{1}{x} + 1 \rightarrow x = 1.618033\ldots$$

Says Mario Livio (2003):

> Some of the greatest mathematical minds of all ages, from Pythagoras and Euclid in ancient Greece, through the medieval Italian mathematician Leonardo of Pisa, aka "Fibonacci," and the Renaissance astronomer Johannes Kepler, to present-day scientific figures such as Oxford physicist Roger Penrose, have spent endless hours over this simple ratio and its properties.
>
> (p. 6)

In this presentation, Doll illustrates a number of important lessons for teaching that may come from this type of inquiry. He points to: the limitations of teaching addition and subtraction as discrete functions; the fluid way that one might introduce one concept flowing out of another, such as the relations between positive and negative integers; ways to think of mathematics in terms of systems, and (dis) orderly arrangements (arranging the poker chips in bowling ball formation), providing a springboard for further thinking (yielding the connection to the Fibonacci sequence). He is indicating, too, that teachers need to know their disciplines (subjects) well enough to understand the artificial disciplinary boundaries that de-contextualize them. Finally, in bringing forward a connection of the Fibonacci sequence to the golden mean, an underlying connection of the relationship of mathematics to art, aesthetics, and even contemporary ideas about beauty can be made. [12] The golden ratio is the pervasive value of proportion that underlies Western culture's appreciation of beauty. [13] It is, as

---

12 The phrase *je ne sais quoi* was used in 1628 to express the inexpressible as an objective, describable *something* (Reiss, 1982, p. 39); subsequently, aesthetics emerged as a field in the 1700s, dealing with beauty and its relation to the sublime ("almost heavenly ... of the highest moral or spiritual value," Encarta). Phi, the golden ratio, was already embedded in this sense of such inexpressible beauty related to the spiritual.

13 A Google search of "golden ratio" and "beauty" will bring forward sites that relate classical proportions of a sunflower, the Parthenon, daVinci's Andruvian man, and a "beautiful face"— all displaying the proportions of *phi*. See www.intmath.com/Numbers/mathOfBeauty.php

Reiss describes, an occulted practice, one now a part of the cultural "consciousness that conforms to the dominant socio-cultural practice, to the way in which the socio-cultural environment is organized" (Bertonneau, 1986, p. 10).

> Beauty is truth, truth beauty—that is all
> Ye know on earth, and all ye need to know.
> (John Keats, 2007 [1819])

At this point, it would seem students should be able to reflect, asking themselves how their sense of beauty has been influenced by mathematical thinking, and whether or not they agree with this idea. How do other cultures come to understand beauty?

Reiss, an admitted post-modernist, describes as "post-structural" the deconstruction of occulted discursive structures of modernism that brings to recognition the limits that lead to discursive transformation; for Lyotard, a self-acclaimed modernist, these limits signal modernism in the act of its always ongoing transformation (1987, p. 3). For Doll, inquiry that brings forward these kinds of connections is rich, rigorous, recursive—and most of all, *relational.*

Recursion

Complexivists Brent Davis and Dennis Sumara (personal communication) use the idea of recursion—going back and looking at what you have seen for a second, yet first, time—in their teaching of literature. It is in this second, yet first, seeing that the richness of a situation begins to emerge; and as we become more aware of our participation in the situation, recursion turns into *recursive reflection.* Usually the act of reading is taught in a linear manner: words, phrases, sentences, paragraphs, chapters, books.[14] Alternatively, Dennis and Brent adopted the use of "stickies" when having school students read a story. On the stickies, or in notebooks, the students write a short note about the word, phrase, idea that attracts their attention. In *recursive* fashion, at a later time, the students read again the story *and* the stickies. This act of "seeing again, for the first time" occurs as the students read not only the story again but also read their stickies. In effect, they reflect on their original reflections. Such *reflection on reflection* opens up a whole new world of thinking, that of *Reflexivity.* In this recursive (or layering) process, one comes to understand better not only the story, but also one's self reading the story. One is studying self as well as text. Such activity goes well beyond "learning."

---

14 Jerome Bruner (personal contact) has mentioned that he reads a book beginning with the last chapter, followed by the first chapter, and then choosing any intermediate chapters he deems worthy or interesting. A variation on this would be to read a book by choosing words from the index. Each method emphasizes the reader as an interpreter not consumer of the book.

Exploring Difference

It is Gregory Bateson who develops an epistemology of education based on the concept of difference (Bateson, 1988 [1979]; Berman, 1981, Ch. 7), arguing that we learn through exploring and playing with difference. It is Tom Kieran, though, speaking of "embracing complexity" at the first Complexity Science and Educational Research (CSER) conference in Alberta (2003) who came forth with a practical and powerful classroom activity. Tom presents to the class a math problem and when a student proffers an answer and receives the usual praise/questions, Tom then asks "Now does anyone in the class *see another way* to do this?" This recursive question-upon-an-answer process moves the discourse beyond a right/wrong frame to an exploratory one. In this exploration the new can come forth; indeed the focus is on bringing forth the new. Here difference is used "*to find the difference that makes a difference*" (Bateson, 1988 [1979], Ch. 4, Criteria 2).

Intuition

Intuition, coming from the Latin *in-tuit* (to look upon or into) is defined by the 2003 OED as "the ability to understand something instinctively, without the need for conscious reasoning" (p. 909). For Dewey (1997 [1910]) this art of looking into (discriminating) is "perhaps the most untaught of all" (p. 37). Teaching to intuit (to look into) cannot really be taught at all, for the word today also carries a strong sense of *feeling*, a precognitive act. To the degree that *feelings are only feelings*, they indeed cannot be taught since teaching is a cognitive act. To the degree, though, that "feelings are not just felt" (Dewey, 1958a [1929], p. 258) but actually "direct one's behavior" (p. 299), they lead us into a new land, that of concept and rational reflection (Semetsky, 2004, p. 445).

Dewey begins his famous five-step analysis of the "scientific method," not with the collection of data but with "a felt difficulty" (1997 [1910], p. 72). While it is obvious that one cannot collect data without discerning what data to collect, it is also true, we believe, that the purpose for which the data is collected, the feeling for the situation and its complexities is too often overlooked. To *feel* a situation, to sense it at a pre-conscious level, to intuit its possibilities and parameters (or solution, if the situation contains a problem) requires one to be attuned to the situation, to listen to it, to be immersed in it, even to converse with it.

Educationally this means that while one cannot "teach" intuition as way of thinking, as a discursive practice, one can through curriculum and instruction provide opportunities for students to explore, to speculate, to intuit. At the design stage—of a curriculum, of teaching units, or of lesson plans—there should be enough problematics embedded in the design and the goals should have just enough *fuzziness* to them that the students will be encouraged to speculate. At the instruction stage, the teacher should listen not only to the students and their speculations but also to the situation in which they (students and instructor) are embedded. We know of none who do this better at the classroom level than David Jardine and members of the Galileo Project. See for instance their book, *Curriculum in abundance* (2006).

Ambiguity

Max Black, in his book *Perplexities* (1990), devotes a chapter to the notion of ambiguity. He relates a story from the teaching of a philosophy/literature seminar with M. H. Abrams. Author unidentified, they gave the students eight lines from one of Wordsworth's Lucy poems to interpret:

> A slumber did my spirit seal,
> I had no human fears:
> She seem'd a thing that could not feel
> The touch of earthly years.
> No motion she has now, no force
> She neither hears nor sees
> Roll'd round in earth's diurnal course
> With rocks and stones and trees!

The responses as to what this poem "meant" were astonishing to each professor. The issue of "she" in the poem became a focal point. Responses as to who "she" was and the "meaning" of the poem seemed to both Black and Abrams to lack "common sense," to be "illogical," to show a poor sense of literary interpretation, and to indulge in flights of imaginative fancy. Cliques formed to argue their various cases of interpretation: different *certainties* of interpretation prevailed. Much "one eyed" reason was evident. As Black pondered this unexpected turn of events, he brought forth, for seminar study, interpretations from acknowledged scholars as to the "meaning" of Wordsworth's Lucy poems. Again, "one eyed" reason or "single vision" prevailed, only this time with more sophistication.[15] Ambiguity was not in existence; scholars and students both argued for *one and only one* interpretation, albeit differing ones. Certainty and a sense of "rightness" prevailed; inquiry and doubt did not.

As Black reflects on this case of "the slumber poem" (p. 182), he makes, throughout the chapter, a number of points. One is that while "the triumph of modern physics would have been impossible unless scientists had firmly believed that behind the flux and confusion of phenomena there are unique causal chains awaiting discovery," contemporary science has "finally been compelled to abandon this belief in causal determinism" (p. 175). Another is that "arbitrary choice" (really what both students

---

15 "One eyed reason" comes from A. N. Whitehead (1967a, p. 59) in his assessment of the 18th century's singular focus on scientific reason. "Single vision" comes from William Blake's famous statement "May God us keep from Single vision and Newton's Sleep" (Letter to Thomas Butts, 1980 [1802]). Blake's own vision—"fourfold in my supreme delight" refers to the mystical spirituality he finds in nature. Whitehead would likely agree.

and scholars were doing—"judgment first, investigation second") "is really not a defensible procedure" (p. 191). Nor is it really possible to adopt, at least for a rationalist such as Black, either a policy of *vive les différences* or one of a *cherchez le sens unique parce qu'il existé*. This latter though, Black says, does encourage "close reading," even if it does not remove the ambiguities.

Throughout the chapter, 21 pages long, it is possible to see Black struggling with what he calls "radical ambiguities." Preferring certainty, he would like to eliminate ambiguity, but finds, after reflecting on both student and scholar interpretations, that in regard to artistic works, "radical ambiguity cannot ultimately be eliminated." Further, and in a more general sense, he concludes by saying, "I would like to suggest that the persistence of incompatible readings (interpretations) is not necessarily a bad thing," and we should not be alarmed or feel uncomfortable about "a variety of perspectival views" (pp. 194–195). In short he is, although he never quite says this, on the verge of advocating a new discursive practice.

In describing his struggle in accepting ambiguity as a legitimate intellectual practice, Black, as an analytic philosopher, considers A. P. Rossiter's view on ambiguity "unappealing." For us though, Rossiter's comment states well the complexivist case for needing to include ambiguity as an important concept in *thinking complexly*: "The whole is *only* fully experienced when both opposites [differences] are held and included in a 'two-eyed' view; and all 'one-eyed' simplifications are not only falsifications; they amount to a denial of some part of the *mystery* of things" (A. P. Rossiter quoted in Black, 1990, p. 51; emphasis added)

While the art of thinking complexly as we see it focuses on relations and being-in-relation, it is necessary, for us to not simply *see* relations (following Bateson, Whitehead, and Wittgenstein, to see, utilize, play with relations between and among relations) but for us to interact with others with these ideas in mind. In calling for change, we must also be the change we want to see.

Focusing On the Political

So far we have argued that in our "diversified, globalized, technologically oriented" society, the post-modern one in which we live, new discursive practices are needed. We have argued that embracing, not reducing, complexity is a useful way to bring forth such practices. Further, we have tacitly (or not so tacitly) suggested that reducing complexity not only destroys the fabric of a complex system but actually situates us in the modernist episteme we are trying to escape. In making this argument we have not so far explicitly paid attention to the political, a point the book's editors and we consider most important: all educational acts are political, "serving the interests of some while denying the interests of others." We agree that all acts of education involving teaching are by nature political, we also believe the new discursive practices we have listed lessen the hierarchal gap existent in the modernist educational episteme in which we are now caught. Thus, our contention is that by embracing complexity we may be able to do political acts (teaching) that are, if not universally fair, at least moving in the direction of equitability.

Trueit and Pratt

At the IAACS conference (Finland), Donna Trueit and Sarah Smitherman Pratt (2006) presented their theorizing of complex discursive practices working with pre-service teachers. They begin with the observation that pre-service teachers are very good students who often assume that they know how to teach because of their previous years of schooling—thus reproducing the culture of schooling. Their presentation, "Complex conversations in education: Moving away from teaching-as-telling" outlines their efforts in "methods courses" to shift pre-service teachers ideas of teaching away from the methodized curriculum used since the times of Peter Ramus (late 16th century). It was Ramus who argued for a "one best way" to present a topic: indeed he says that in regard to teaching there is a "one and only way" (Ong, 1983, p. 251; Triche and McKnight, 2004, p. 40; Doll et al., 2005, p. 25). This notion of one, universal way has existed for centuries, emerging in recent times as "best practices," and dominating the literature and student expectations in pre-service education students' Methods Courses (Smitherman Pratt, 2006; Buckreis, 2010). In Ramus' model, which fits the sense of *natural* order in his time, the teacher is the expert knower, the student is the receiving non-knower, or at best, novice. The flow of knowledge is direct, linear, one-way. The political frame is one which plays on the knowledge/ability gap, elevating the teacher and his/her authority, reducing the student to a receiver only and thus aborting his/her own sense of being.

Trueit and Pratt present the notion of "complex conversations" as a new (relational) discursive practice based on the idea that *inter*actions in classrooms (rather than a one-way flow) can be the place to effect political change. The interactions they propose have a dynamical, self-organizing order, visualized as fractals (as opposed to a Ramus-styled, organizational flow chart). They take these ideas from complexity theory to be important to classroom interactions: relations are patterned, holding across scales; feedback processes cause instability; instability leads to systems branching off in new directions, resulting in new forms of order; and solutions of non-linear equations result in a collection of values rather than one exact answer. This last idea, a "collection of values," seems significant and relevant in a diversified world and gets away from a universalized, unified sense of the "good." The class experiences and develops a tolerance for ambiguity, what Ted Aoki (2005b) calls "a tensioned space of both and/not and" (p. 318). While this conversation is "open [it is] not empty," where "the meaningfulness of one understanding comes into view illuminated by the whole context; and the meaningful of the whole comes into view illuminated by a part … a bridging of two worlds by a bridge which is not a bridge" (p. 318). Dynamism of this system is drawn from hermeneutic listening, "a new way of *seeing* made possible by *listening* to the other" (Bronwyn Davies, 1995, p. 168; emphasis added). In their inquiries, exploring together *questions for which the answer is not known*, students and teacher together consider alternatives, question assumptions, look and listen for—and play with—differences and develop each their own critical interpretation and creative ability. In this process of interaction, students gradually transition from being students to becoming teachers for whom there is more than one best way.

Aoki

In his first year of teaching Japanese–Canadians in a one-room school outside Calgary as World War II in the Pacific was still raging, Ted Aoki (2005b) found himself assigned to use a basic reading text: *We work and play*. Dutifully he had his students read the text word by word, slowly acquiring a social skill. Only years later did he realize that embedded in this text was a definite social ethic. He was teaching not just a social skill, he was also "teaching an ethic" (p. 357), one that honored not his heritage nor those of his students but rather one that promoted northern European, Protestant values about the separation of work and play—we work, then we play.

   In realizing that he was teaching not just an instrumental skill but also a cultural ethic, Ted moves beyond teaching *How* (the frame for almost all university "methods" courses) to teaching *What* (a political question, too often hidden due to an overemphasis on *How*).

Pinar

Socio-cultural-political issues have been a hallmark of William Pinar's writings for over three decades. His focus has been on subjectivities, an exploration of the socio-historical, political forces that shape lived experiences. Education, including school education, plays a large role in our framing of ideas about self. Unfortunately, in the US, the curriculum of state "social" schooling does not generally encourage an exploration of relations between our selves and our experiences in relation to subject matters. Thus we become disenfranchised from the society in which we live. We have at best half-lives. In reference to this chapter, we would frame William's social/political work in terms of *Being*-in-relation: "selves" perceived as connected to the society and the world (sensually, intellectually, experientially) in which we live. In *The worldliness of a cosmopolitan education* (2009a), Pinar asks us as readers to consider "the cultivation of humanity" via "reflective citizenship" (p. 143).

   Whatever relation one wishes to take regarding complexity and its attributes we believe the issue of understanding "localism … as part of a larger world of differences'" (p. 143) is of prime importance. Regretfully this is a focus few have taken. One of Pinar's many contributions to this issue is to bring forth the notion that "global justice requires social labor"; that "political action requires the subject to 'dwell totally in the antagonisms of the moment, that is … [to] embrace antagonism as a process'" (p. 146). While we prefer to think of the positivesness of a dynamic tension, instead of the negativeness of antagonism, the issue underlying both is the relation of the local and the global. To deal with this issue we need, as we have asserted, a new set of discursive practices

Meyers

In his article, "Method and civic education" (2003), Peter Alexander Meyers, traces the history of the *methodization* movement from Peter Ramus in the late 16th century to the present day (this volume, Chapter 8). This movement—organized around "a few clear and distinct formal steps" (Descartes, 1985 [1637]) leading you to "where you want to go," absolves the teacher of responsibility, of "developing a living relationship with students," and hence deprives the student (at least in democratic societies) of his or her birthright to be a participating citizen (2003, p. 7). To quote Meyers:

> Method tends radically to reduce … experience and to cover over the inherent pluralism of knowledge. Method aims to deliver some one thing to students. But … to know is a process constituted by necessarily different and often cognitively irreconcilable parts. Democratic education must not only present this plurality but foster it as well.
>
> (2003, p.7)

Plurality of thought is necessary for the making of judgments, a factor key in the operation of a democratic society. Good decisions are neither given nor found, they are made, by committed citizens working together. As Meyers says, "the plural character of knowing creates a space of possibility," (2003, p. 7) not only for the new to emerge but for character to develop. Character is formed by people, here students and teachers, working together. This "living relationship between teacher and student … is mediated by the matters they undertake to consider *together*" (2003, p. 7, emphasis added). In this living, experiential relationship, this considering together, more than knowledge is acquired, so is teacher–student reciprocal respect. Character comes forth. Equity may or may not be reduced but mutual respect is increased. The modernist class relationship of superior expert and inferior subject, a discursive practice accepted and perpetuated by both disappears.

In a democratic society, the political purpose of education, especially liberal education, is the development of character, of judgment, of responsibility, of respect for "other." In the complex, diversified, globalized, technologically oriented society in which we live, we believe a new set of discursive practices are needed, ones which develop, embrace, work with, relate to the complexity we find.

> We need to stop thinking of words as representations and to start thinking of them as nodes in the [relational] network which binds the organism together with its environment.[16]
>
> (Richard Rorty, in Niznik and Sanders, 1996)

---

16 We have substituted *relational* for *causal* in this quotation.

PART 5

Reflections on Teaching

Introduction: Donna Trueit

Doll is a pragmatist and his views reflect his humanist roots,[1] believing that people can solve problems by coming together, conversing, creating, determined to work for communal good. His own classes, those he teaches, are conducted with these ideals in mind. This view assumes that there is a common good, that it emerges out of interactions, and there is direction to change conceived in this manner. The good is that people begin to think and the direction is that you can't go back.

Five of the following essays are specifically about teacher education and reflect several key themes helpful for teachers working with curriculum. William Doll found the idea of Koch's curve, a fractal snowflake, appealing and generative as a way of talking to teachers about "infinity bounded."[2] Metaphorically, Koch's curve illustrates the freedom teachers might have in working with curriculum if they conceived "curriculum" not literally, as a document to be followed in a step-by-step manner, but rather as a guide. The idea is simple but not reductive. Through the analogy of infinity bounded, Doll encourages teachers to recognize, in addition to the complexities of classroom situations, their freedom to work

---

1 "The English equivalent 'humanist' makes its appearance in the late 16th century with a similar meaning. Only in the 19th century, however, and probably for the first time in Germany in 1809, is the attribute transformed into a substantive: *humanism*, standing for 'devotion to the literature of ancient Greece and Rome, and the humane values that may be derived from them'" (Nicholas Mann, "The origins of humanism," *Cambridge companion to humanism*, Jill Kraye, editor [Cambridge University Press, 1996], pp. 1–2).

2 William Doll presented the idea of infinity bounded in relation to Koch's curve a number of times; however, Sarah Smitherman Pratt subsequently developed and expanded these ideas, illustrated in a brilliant PowerPoint presentation for a LSU graduate seminar.

with the curriculum. This metaphor is emancipatory, perhaps even revolutionary. Teachers need not feel oppressed by the curriculum which often places impossible demands upon them.

In "The educational need to re-invent the wheel," although he does not use the words "mimesis" and "poiesis," Doll points to the cultural tensions between reproduction and creative, evolutionary change. Schooling that emphasizes copying and memorization is not educative. It serves to reproduce existing social structures. The cumulative view of knowledge, as that which is memorized, is criticized by Dewey and Piaget who both call for thinking—re-inventing—as learning. Doll provides a practical example referring to students in an elementary mathematics classroom.

"Complexity in the classroom," a rather remarkable essay, describes the success of a mathematics class in California in terms of self-organization from chaos and complexity theory. Bill tells this story:

> The class (sixth grade) was a mixture of students, many from a low socio-economic status with little interest in school tasks. Ron's challenge, and he enlisted Sam's and my help with it, was to prepare his students to solve arithmetic problems. This was a district mandate. We three tried the usual method of asking the students to read the problem carefully, think about how to solve it, and then solve. This produced no improvement what so ever. Sam then suggested we turn the problems, challenging ones designed by Ron, over to the students. Let them disengage the facts from the problems and then restructure the problem, using these facts, or adding to or subtracting facts from the problems. In short, they played with the problem in a structural manner. Although I did not see it at the time, the problems were rich in content, relational in structure, and rigorous in nature. The students "had a ball," to use a colloquialism. They worked in groups restructuring the problem Ron had assigned, then giving the new problem to another group to solve. Some new problems could not be solved as information was lacking, others had extraneous information, still others required assumptions be made. Finally as a group we would look at the original problem Ron had given and one of the new problems a group had devised. The excitement and enthusiasm in the class was electric—all became involved.

"Reflections on teaching: developing the non-linear" developed out of William Doll's discussions with his graduate students, two who worked with him in what might be called a math methods course for practicing teachers. The two students, one Korean, the other Chinese, had never seen pedagogy enacted in the way Doll does it. Their discussion pressed Doll to articulate ideas that he had not expressed before. The bonus in this article is having the students' reflections on the experience of him and the class.

Chapter 24 deals with the subject of classroom management. Criticizing once again the pressure on pre-service teachers to control their classes, Doll traces ideas of control in education to the scientifically efficient management style of Frederick Taylor, a friend of Charles Eliot, president of Harvard University (1869–1909). Drawing on John Dewey, who wrote disparagingly about social control long before Michel Foucault's illuminating studies, Doll posits that instead of external control (imposed, external), schooling needs to be oriented to guiding students in their development of self-organization (internal control). Dewey's concept of growth depends upon both perturbation (the disruption of habits of thought?) and interactions between student and teacher in the context of a situation, leading to development of the natural capacities of the student.

Accepting that we live in a complex and chaotic universe, can we not see our way to bring dynamical change, a new sense of order, and the art of interpretation to curriculum? In "Looking forward" Doll elaborates on these themes.

The final chapter in the book is the Da Xia Lecture of 2010, a distinguished lecture open to the entire university. Previous speakers have been, among others, Jacques Derrida, Jürgen Habermas, and Richard Rorty. In his lecture, Doll draws upon Michel Serres' concept of wisdom to bring forward what he feels is a misguided direction among those who feel that Dewey stands for a child-centered curriculum. Not at all, says Doll. Dewey stands for the development of practical wisdom which involves making moral choices in everyday situations, choices for the good. The emphasis on practical wisdom, seen in Serres and Dewey, can also seen in Confucius, claims Doll, which helps to explain Dewey's affinity for China and Eastern philosophy and more recently the appeal of Doll's approach to curriculum for Chinese curriculum reformers.

21

THE EDUCATIONAL NEED TO RE-INVENT THE WHEEL

(1981)

> ... real comprehension implies reinvention by the subject.
>
> (Jean Piaget)

One of the most treasured and respected of educational maxims is the one which states that the teacher does not have the learner re-invent the wheel. Rather the teacher's task is to give each student, or have each student memorize, the techniques and methods society has developed—particularly those developed by the various disciplines of knowledge. This knowledge is then used as a base for further exploration and development. This pattern is used from the primary grades through college, with more giving being done in the elementary grades than in college. But in both, "giving" is dominant.

There is a long history to this tradition; not only has it dominated American curriculum thought for all the present century, with brief digressions into a process approach during the progressive and open-educations eras, but it is the dominant method of applied science. Isaac Newton is reputed to have said, "If I have seen afar, it is because I have stood on the shoulders of giants." And Thomas Kuhn (1962) points out in his book, *The structure of scientific revolutions*, virtually all "normal" science is predicated on this cumulative approach.[1] Being able to take up where others leave off is a hallmark of the scientific approach. From this approach many advances developed: scientific progress is cumulative.

However, as Kuhn also points out there is a price paid for this cumulative progress. The average scientist is locked into one particular paradigm or way of thinking. His training has prepared him to carry forward the paradigm in which he has been

---

1 See Kuhn (1962) Chapter 3, especially the remarks on p. 24.

initiated, but it has not prepared him to question that paradigm. The history of his field, the assumptions on which the paradigm is based, its strengths and weaknesses are not part of the scientist's education (p. 47). Thus the scientist of normal training and work is well learned in carrying forward and developing a particular view of his field. What he is not well learned in is questioning the basic assumptions of that view, of integrating or comparing that view with others, or of breaking outside that view to a broader, more integrative and complex framework. In short the usual scientist's view is more tunneled than it is ecological, more narrow and focused than broad based and integrative.

As we all well know from our present vantage point this paradigm approach to science has created for us in America a tremendous number of technological advancements and just as tremendous a number of social problems. The balance is an uneasy one. As we also know this scientific or *scientistic* way of viewing is the one education has adopted since Herbert Spencer first posited science as, "The knowledge of most worth"; John Dewey and Jean Piaget have long objected to applying this particular paradigmatic or cumulative view of development to human learning; and lately they have been joined by Jerome Bruner and most recently by Urie Bronfenbrenner and John Goodlad.

Dewey, of course, is famous for his objection to the giving of knowledge. As he says in one memorable quote:

> No thought, no idea, can possibly be conveyed as an idea from one person to another. When it is told, it is, to the one to whom it is told, another fact, not an idea. ... What he (the person) directly gets cannot be an idea. Only by wrestling with the conditions of the problem at first hand, seeking and finding his own way out, does he think.
>
> (1966a [1916], pp. 159–160)

Thinking then is different from learning. In learning one can copy, follow someone else's formula or paradigm, maybe even extend it a bit; but the more the pattern is extended into new areas the more there is need for a new and different act, that of thought. Here Dewey identified thinking with active reconstruction, reinvention, if you will.

Piaget elaborates and develops this notion of re-invention even more than Dewey did. In a remarkable little book, *To understand is to invent*, Piaget (1974 [1948]) argues that "for a child to understand something, he must re-invent it," if we are to help form individuals "who are capable of production and creativity and not simply repetition." Thus, in rather simple terms our task as teachers is to aid the student in re-inventing that which we already know, for "that which we allow him to discover by himself will remain with him ... for all the rest of his life," (p. 20)[2] while that

---

2   See also Piaget, 1972 (p. 23).

which we impart, or give, to him will pass as quickly as a weekend or a summer vacation.

This distinction between a doing which is active and a receiving which is passive—and when we teachers give the students receive—is brought out nicely by Bruner (1959) in his article, "Learning and thinking." There he argues that thinking in terms of organizing, combining, abstracting, synthesizing, is one of the unique characteristics of the human being. Being able to think well should be the ultimate reward of learning. But the irony is that in giving too much to the student, imparting too much, we are depriving him of the learning which will lead to thinking. This learning is not the *narrow* learning of copying and repetition, but the *broader* learning of manipulation and re-invention. Thus it is through active discovery that the human powers of thinking are developed. These powers will remain dormant and underdeveloped if learning is passive, receptive, and repetitious, but they will blossom where learning is active, manipulative, and inventive. The teacher's task is not to impart all he, she, or society knows, but to help the learner grow in the development of his or her own powers of thought. There is a very real educational need to have the learner re-invent the wheel.

For the past three years [1979–1981] we at Oswego (State University of New York at Oswego) have been working on a structural arithmetic curriculum designed to help the students re-invent the wheels or, more precisely, develop their own powers of thought. Before describing this curriculum project let me mention two concepts which *are not* part of the project. When we say re-invent we do *not mean* that the learner will: 1) do whatever he or she wishes, or 2) re-invent all wheels. What we do mean is that the overall thrust will so combine giving and doing (both active and reflective doing) that the intellectual powers of the learner will be of primary concern. As much as this sounds like a truism, just as much is it *not* a part of the usual school curriculum. As Bruner has said, "We may be systematically depriving our students of this reward (of thinking) as far as school learning is concerned" (1959, p. 187).

The task of devising a curriculum which would foster thinking has been formidable. We have tried to integrate the structures of the learner, here primary grade children. Our guide maxim has been: "The task of teaching a subject to a child at any particular age is one of representing the structure of that subject in terms of the child's way of viewing things" (Bruner, 1973, p. 413).

As a general guide this statement by Bruner is fine, but as an operational reality it leaves much to be worked out. The structures of arithmetic, such things as reversibility, identity, equality, are the very logical structures primary grade children do not yet possess. Here Piaget is very right: children at certain ages cannot be taught any subject no matter how inventive and clever is the teaching. The basic intellectual structures upon which arithmetic is based, something as key as place value, are just not formed in the average primary grade child. Thus it is only now, in the month of May, that our third graders are beginning to understand place value in a way which allows them to work the system in a creative and inventive manner. Yet the usual school curriculum asks that place value be taught in the second grade.

On the other hand, once children have acquired structural learning, learning which Bruner would say is generic or abstract, having within it Piaget's "real comprehension," they can transfer and transform knowledge almost at will. An example would be the ease with which our third graders, last week, moved from two-digit place value to two-position combinations, from 56 or 65 to AB or BA; from three-digit place value to six-position combinations and permutations, from 123, 132 etc. to ABC, ACB, BAC, BCA, CAB, CBA. They then moved to four-item permutations (24 possible combinations) and five-item permutations (120 possible combinations). A few even saw the pattern which was used to produce these logical possibilities. This sort of transfer and transformation is natural though, at least in a structural framework, for the basic structure underlying place value and combinations—permutations is the same. The art to teaching for this sort of transfer and transformation requires a knowledge of both the field's structure and the learner's structure, as well as a sense of timing, that in the individual's own re-invention he or she is able to take the qualitative leaps it took humankind hundreds or thousands of years to make.

The day-in and day-out practicality of the structural arithmetic curriculum centers around the seeing of relationships among numbers, and the organizing of those relationships into systems. Thus in the first and second grades there is a strong emphasis on what teachers normally call "number families" $(3 + 5, 5 + 3, 8 - 5, 8 - 3$, etc.). This relational concept is also applied to multiplication/division, to addition/multiplication, and to odd/even. In the third grade, relationships are then expanded to help the student do multiplication via the process of doubling or halving $(8 \times 7$ can be done as $2(4 \times 7)$ or $28 + 28$, as 16×7 can be done as $56 + 56)$. This doubling-halving process is then combined to produce work with the identity element for multiplication. Right now our third grade children are comfortable and skillful with doing 12×15 as 6×30 (halving one number, doubling the other). Most of the present experimental group can do, mentally, two-digit multiplication or division by one digit, and a few are able to do two digit by two digit multiplication. That is, 36×12 can be done mentally as $12 \times 12 \times 3$, or 144×3, or even $288 + 144$.

It is exciting to watch third grade children do complex equations, but it is far more exciting to watch the enthusiastic openness and skillful dexterity they possess as they tackle new and different situations. The curriculum project is now in its third year. The most advanced group, third graders, has remained together for three years as an experimental group, counterbalanced by a three-year control group.

While all statistical results are not yet in, the experimental group has been performing significantly better than the control group on national achievement and cognitive abilities tests, given each fall and spring. We have, however, done multiple case studies for the testing of competence, those basic abilities underlying performance. Here we have questioned the third grade children individually and in-depth, on the procedures they used in doing problem or exercise assignments. We have done this with a broad range of individual interviews on work material drawn from both the experimental and control groups. Clear, procedural differences have emerged from the two groups. As one researcher remarked, "the knowledge the children in the experimental group have is their own knowledge, while those in the control group are always trying to follow the teacher." For the experimental group re-invention has paid off in terms of confidence, innovation, and intellectual sophistication. These children are quite willing to tackle most any problem or exercise, and to figure out a solution. The control group is much more constrained. Here the children, almost regardless of ability, are fearful and inept at venturing beyond the bounds of what they have been taught. If the material is new they will venture such remarks as: "I've not been taught," "We can't do that," "I don't know how." In short, one group has been trained in a narrow view of learning where learning is equated with copying, while the other group has been trained in a broader, more inventive, framework where learning is the springboard to thinking. It is this latter view of learning which Dewey, Piaget, Bruner and others advocate as the end of education—the furtherance of thinking which leads to more thinking.

Summary

In this article I have argued for the need to have the learner re-invent the wheel. I have presented my case theoretically and practically. Further I have argued that with a judicious mixing of the given and the discovered, and with an emphasis on structure, it is quite possible, over a three-year span of time, to end up with students who can perform more efficiently than those trained in the normal modes of curriculum. Finally I have attempted to point out that curricular failings are not the result of teacher incompetence—the teachers usually teach as well, if not better than we teach them to teach. Rather the basic failings are deeply ingrained in the fabric of our society. We have adopted a scientific model which has been well suited to the production of technological objects. But it has not been well suited to the development of human thought processes. We need to pay more attention than we have to Dewey's (1998) distinction between the scientist and the teacher (p. 242). The scientist needs to know the field, the teacher needs to know both the field and the learner; further he must know how to help the learner know that field in such a way that the learner can operate in the field without the aid of the teacher. The educational model we have been using is not designed to accomplish this task.

22

COMPLEXITY IN THE CLASSROOM

(1989)

To say that tomorrow's world will be complex is to utter the obvious, even the trite. However, I do not use the word *complex* in its usual sense of *more confusion, more decisions* to make, or *more factors* to analyze. Rather, I wish to use it in the sense that it is used in "complexity theory"—a movement in contemporary physics, biology, and mathematics that is encouraging us to look at complexity as a subject in its own right. This movement is changing our views of the origin of the universe, of the way life develops, and of the order we find in both mathematics and nature. Shortly, complexity theory may well have as strong an influence on our views about teaching and learning as it is now having on our understanding of the basic structures of the physical sciences and mathematics.

In Hans Küng's (1988) terms, we are in the midst of an epochal or megaparadigm change, one many label as a move from the abstract formality of modernism to the eclectic creativity of post-modernism (Jencks, 1986; Griffin, 1988a, 1988b). The change is giving us a new perspective on reality, on how we conceive of order, and on how we solve problems. It is this aspect of post-modernism—the possibility of solving problems aided by the insights of complexity theory—that encouraged me to spend a school year (1987–1988) working weekly in a sixth-grade mathematics class. Friday morning math took on a new dimension for these students whose teacher, with a visiting instructor, taught them using insights from *complexity theory*.

Order and Control

The teacher, Ron Scott, is a former Air Force officer. He is disciplined and runs an ordered classroom. Further, he is committed to helping students acquire their own

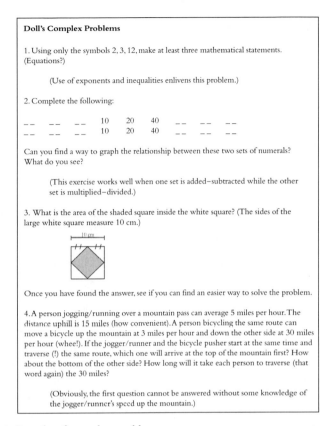

Doll's Complex Problems

1. Using only the symbols 2, 3, 12, make at least three mathematical statements. (Equations?)

    (Use of exponents and inequalities enlivens this problem.)

2. Complete the following:

| __ | __ | __ | 10 | 20 | 40 | __ | __ | __ |
| __ | __ | __ | 10 | 20 | 40 | __ | __ | __ |

Can you find a way to graph the relationship between these two sets of numerals? What do you see?

    (This exercise works well when one set is added–subtracted while the other set is multiplied–divided.)

3. What is the area of the shaded square inside the white square? (The sides of the large white square measure 10 cm.)

Once you have found the answer, see if you can find an easier way to solve the problem.

4. A person jogging/running over a mountain pass can average 5 miles per hour. The distance uphill is 15 miles (how convenient). A person bicycling the same route can move a bicycle up the mountain at 3 miles per hour and down the other side at 30 miles per hour (whee!). If the jogger/runner and the bicycle pusher start at the same time and traverse (!) the same route, which one will arrive at the top of the mountain first? How about the bottom of the other side? How long will it take each person to traverse (that word again) the 30 miles?

    (Obviously, the first question cannot be answered without some knowledge of the jogger/runner's speed up the mountain.)

FIGURE 22.1 Sample of complex problems

sense of order and control—over their lives, themselves, their studies. This sense was sorely wanting in most of the students in his class. Ron quickly recognized that the overly simple and linear style of presentation in the mathematics texts the school district used did not help the students develop this order or control. Like most mathematics texts, these encouraged memorization, not understanding; the working of set algorithms, not the creative utilization of patterns. Ron realized that his own mathematical understanding—stronger than he knew when we began— was based on a knowledge of numerical structure his father had helped him develop when he was a youth. He was also aware that his own way of solving problems and working with numbers was more complex and varied but no less ordered than the methods prescribed in the texts. In his own way, Ron was already moving toward a practical theory of complexity.

We met with students weekly, on Friday mornings for 45 minutes to an hour. We divided them into groups of two or four and asked them to solve problems that Ron devised—problems that were loosely tied to work they had been doing in science or math class (see Figure 22.1). Our intent was to challenge their own creative and constructive powers; hence the problems were hard, interesting, humorous. They were not the routine drills that filled the textbooks.[1]

Mathematical Chaos Theory

Complexity theory is of recent origin. While no precise date can be set for its inception—indeed to do so would be to oversimplify complexity—a number of occurrences converged in the early- and mid-1970s that gave shape to the theory. One such occurrence was the development of nonlinear mathematics, which, with the aid of powerful computers, allowed mathematicians and other scientists to study directly the complex actions of flags fluttering, smoke curling, water cascading, and cream droplets mixing turbulently in coffee. All of these have high degrees of randomness in them; their patterns are neither fully predictable nor repetitious. The study of these patterns, called *mathematical chaos theory*, is a major force in virtually every science today. It is even emerging, Gleick (1987) argues, as its own interdisciplinary science. This science is, of course, the science of complexity, the science of process.

Nonlinear Patterning

What is fascinating about mathematical chaos is not that disorder is present in it but that the disorder present is patterned. Disorder is thus embedded within order—as Paul Davies says, chaos "has some underlying order in its manifestation" (1988, p. 51). To speak, then, of chaotic patterning or ordered chaos is not to speak in contradictions; it is to speak of a newly discovered order, one in which randomness, unpredictability, and indeterminacy are essential features. This type of order is different from that found in teachers' guides or curriculum syllabi.

I will not go into the details of chaotic or nonlinear patterning here. Those interested might begin with Gleick's *Chaos* (1987), Davies' *The cosmic blueprint* (1988), or Prigogine and Stengers' *Order out of chaos* (1984). I will, though, pick one illustration from chaos theory and show how this guided Ron and me in our work with the students.

Figure 22.2 is a graphic picture of computer data simulating turbulence in long-term weather patterns; it resembles a butterfly's wings or an owl's mask. Although the pattern of the data is random, never following exactly the same line twice, its randomness is patterned; boundaries clearly exist—otherwise the butterfly would have no "wings," the owl no "eyes." The looping back of the data produces the "attractor" area. Ron and I borrowed two features from the chaotic order presented here: (1) boundaries and (2) an "attractor" area.

---

1 The sixth grade class described in this article was the top-scoring class in mathematics in the Riverside, California, Unified School District in 1987–1988. These results on the California Achievement Profile put the class in the top 25 percent in the state and in the top 3 percent among "schools serving students with similar backgrounds" (that is, same economic and social categories).

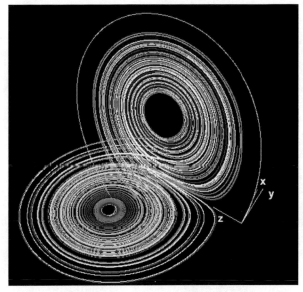

FIGURE 22.2 The Lorenz "butterfly", retrieved from http://en.wikipedia.org/wiki/
File:Lorenz_R028.png

More Dancing, Less Marching

The concepts of boundaries and attractors within disorder provided a metaphorical
basis for us to use as we considered how to interact with the students: we decided
to give them flexibility in their intellectual and social organization—they solved
the problems in their way and in their time. The patterns that emerged were both
disorderly and coherent. Randomness was present in the way they approached their
work—they skipped from problem to problem, they left problems unfinished, they
interjected social comments into their conversation; they also did all the problems
on the page, they went back to the unfinished ones, they put boundaries on their
social conversation. Whether an observer saw randomness or progressive order
depended on whether that observer was in the class for a few minutes or for the
whole class period.

While I was worried about the lack of linear order, about the direct challenge
the students were giving to the "time-on-task" maxim, I became aware that over
the period of the 45 to 60 minutes a new type of order was emerging—progressive,
constructive, personal, interactive. Interest during the class was extraordinarily high,
answers emerged from a variety of directions, those who were quiet often raised key
questions, and Ron and I virtually never had to admonish students "to finish." While
the process seemed disorderly from a segmented view, it had a unity found only by
looking at the *whole* class during the *entire* period.

While this insight seems obvious, it runs counter to the reductionist, particularist,
and atomistic view that has generally been applied both to science and to teaching.

The "new physics" (P. Davies, 1983; Kitchener, 1988) is taking a more holistic, time-oriented approach to nature and in doing so is seeing factors in development not seen before. An example from medicine is that the healthy heart beats with a touch of irregularity—chaos. The perfectly balanced heart beat, rhythmical in all respects, occurs a few hours before death and, while not a cause of death, is a sign of its approach. "The healthy heart dances, while the dying organ can merely march" (Browne, 1989). I am quite convinced we must re-order our curriculum and instructional methods to promote more dancing and less marching. Both have an order, but one is lively, the other monotonously deadly.

Self-Organization

Another occurrence in the 1970s that has shaped, and is shaping, complexity theory is the concept of self-organization. Self-organization has long been recognized in the biological sciences but not in the physical sciences. As stepchildren, the biological sciences have sublimated their methodologies to those of physics and chemistry. Recently, however, Browne (1989; see also Prigogine and Stengers, 1984) has applied the concept of self-organization to the chemistry of gases, and a number of physicists have applied it to theories about the universe's origin— particularly the "big bang" theory (P. Davies 1983, 1988). Unfortunately, except for Jean Piaget's work, self-organization has not played a role in curriculum theory or development.

Spontaneous Occurrence

In his study of self-organization, Prigogine has shown that it possesses a number of specific characteristics, all of which were useful to Ron and me in teaching the students and in designing a problem-solving environment for them. One of these features is that self-organization occurs suddenly and spontaneously—almost, it seems, out of nowhere. Students "see" at one moment that which they could not see before. As teachers, our task was the tricky one of combining flexible time with directed time in the right proportion to allow and encourage this restructuring to occur. While we cannot specify what this proportion should be, for it varied in our work, we can assert it was essential for us to mix flexible time with directed time.

Occurrence Through Disequilibrium

A second feature of self-organization is its occurrence only when there is a difficulty to overcome—Prigogine calls these "far-from-equilibrium" situations. It is at this time and under these conditions that internal reorganization takes place. Piaget, himself a biologist, called this *disequilibrium* and made the concept central to his equilibrium–disequilibrium–re-equilibration model of development: "However the nonbalance arises, it is the driving force of development. ... Without the nonbalance there would not be 'increasing re-equilibration'" (1977a, p. 13).

It is unfortunate that American educators and curricularists in their early enthusiasm for Piaget paid more attention to his concept of stages and their characteristics than to his concept of how one moves from stage to stage. This latter concept he outlined clearly in such works as *Behavior and evolution* (1978 [1976]), *The development of thought* (1977a), and *Adaptation and intelligence* (1980 [1974]). By the time these "biological" works of Piaget appeared, in the late seventies and early eighties, America's love affair with Piaget had passed its peak, and these works were neglected.

For Ron and me, the concept of self-organization through disequilibrium meant we had to organize the Friday curriculum and our presentation of it in such a manner that we had enough of a "burr" to stimulate the students into rethinking their habitual methods but not so much of a burr that reorganization would fall apart or not be attempted. Maintaining this dynamic tension between challenge and comfort was one of the skills we had to perfect. One device we used was to ask the students to pick out or "unpack" the facts in a problem and then to make up new problems using these facts. A variation on this was to have the students change or rearrange these facts. This device, which proved popular, provided the students with insights into the structure of both the original problem and the ones they constructed.

One conclusion I have developed from this is that problem solving may well hinge on this factor of understanding the structure of the problem; closer reading and strong math skills may be helpful, but they are tangential to the idea of knowing the problem's structure. Too rarely do we teach a problem's structure or even the structure of the operation used to solve the problem. Our methods, if not structureless, at least hide that structure from view.

Occurrence At Critical Junctures

The third of Prigogine's (1988) characteristics of self-organization revolves around time. He argues that we usually (and incorrectly) look at time in quantitative and cumulative terms, not as we should in qualitative and developmental terms. For him there are critical junctures in periods of development—"bifurcation points"—when reorganization occurs. To find these critical junctures, Ron and I had to analyze time not in terms of amount spent but in terms of the insights developed by the students. This orientation kept the class lively and accounts, I believe, for the quick passage of time in the class. In almost every 45- to 60-minute segment we wished for "more time."

In retrospect, one aspect of self-organization we might have utilized better was that of the forced grouping of students. We placed them into groups of twos and fours because of my belief in the role cooperation and communication play in reorganization. Now I see we could have had cooperation and communication in a more varied, less forced mode. We should have *allowed* interaction and verbalization to occur, *not forced it*. Learning occurs on a number of levels and in a variety of manners—this is the nature of complexity. Oliver (Oliver and Gershman, 1989) makes this point nicely in his distinction between "grounded" and "technical" knowing.

The Application of Fractals

A third occurrence—the last I will deal with in this article—that converged to form complexity theory is of even more recent origin. The discovery and application of fractals (measuring nature's irregularities by using complex numbers) can be tied quite directly to Benoit Mandelbrot's book, *The fractal geometry of nature* (1982). Nature is, of course, highly irregular in many—indeed most—aspects of its structure (coastlines, cloud shapes, star clusters). However, the mathematics we have used to describe and measure nature's irregularity has been highly regular—straight lines, smooth curves, the arithmetic of whole numbers. Our mathematics has thus *approximated* and *abstracted* nature—that is, we use leap years, except for the centennial years not divisible by 400, to compensate for the irregular time of the earth's yearly transit around the sun. The earth does not make this transit in 365 days; not even in 365 days, 5 hours, and 48 minutes. In fact, we cannot measure the transit in such regular terms. Mandelbrot's contribution has been to deal with nature's irregularities in irregular terms.

Figure 22.3, beautiful in its seeming (but random) symmetry, is a computer-generated pattern of a series of numbers—numbers that are squared and added in an $(a, a^2, a + a^2, (a + a^2)^2, \ldots)$ sequence. If one does this with a whole number such as two (for example, 2, 4, 6, 36, 42, 1764 …) the pattern is purely cumulative, growing ever larger. However, if one uses complex numbers—those involving a real number and the root of a negative (i.e., $3 + \sqrt{-2}$)—then strange, unusual, and seemingly symmetrical patterns appear. Some of those patterns, generated by the doubling-adding sequence done thousands of times on a computer, will cluster (like stars) around a certain area or a certain number—an "attractor" area or number. These form the dark spots or blobs in the figure—the "Mandelbrot set," it is called. Other sequences spiral around, gradually or quickly, moving off into higher denominations. The combination of these makes the overall pattern. No quadrant is exactly the same, yet the overall effect of the flames, tendrils, whorls, and filigrees is one of organization in a new sense—complex, chaotic, random organization.

The curricular and instructional task for Ron and me was not to have the students generate chaotic symmetry with computers (although this could be done with advanced classes and advanced equipment) but to help them see that complexity and simplicity are related to each other in such a manner that from

FIGURE 22.3 Mandelbrot spiral cleft fractal, retrieved from http://www.en.wikipedia. org/wiki/Wikipedia:Featured_picture_candidates/Mandelbrot_Spiral_Cleft_2

simplicity—squaring and adding—complexity can be generated. We believed this would prepare the students not only for the complex world of the future but also for their own work in high school, when the study of complexity might well be part of their science or mathematics curriculum. The device we used was disarmingly simple—generating a set of numbers through doubling (5, 10, 20, 40, 80, etc.) and through halving. Continuing this set was fine practice in mental arithmetic, and it would easily go on to five digits every time we tried it—with, of course, a different first, or seed, number. It is through the halving process that complexity appeared— that is,

$$5, \quad 2\tfrac{1}{2}, \quad 1\tfrac{1}{4}, \quad \tfrac{5}{8}, \quad \tfrac{5}{16}, \quad \tfrac{5}{32}, \quad \tfrac{5}{64} \cdots$$

This pattern was obviously a challenge for the students. Complexity became even more apparent when we asked the students to put all the foregoing numbers into fourths. The pattern became,

$$\tfrac{20}{4}, \quad \tfrac{10}{4}, \quad \tfrac{5}{4}, \quad \tfrac{2\tfrac{1}{2}}{4}, \quad \tfrac{1\tfrac{1}{4}}{4}, \quad \tfrac{\tfrac{5}{8}}{4}, \quad \tfrac{\tfrac{5}{16}}{4} \cdots$$

Connecting these two together one can see the following:

Halving					Doubling					
$\frac{5}{32}$	$\frac{5}{16}$	$\frac{5}{8}$	$\frac{5}{4}$	$\frac{5}{2}$	5	10	20	40	80	...

Fourths					
$\frac{5/8}{4}$	$\frac{5/4}{4}$	$\frac{5/2}{4}$	$\frac{5}{4}$	$\frac{10}{4}$	5

The students easily saw that $\frac{5}{4}$ in both rows was the same, but a new and exciting world opened when they proved that $\frac{5}{16} = \frac{5/4}{4} = 1\frac{1}{4}$. A deeper understanding of fractions began to emerge. Further, the exercise itself is rich with connections and interconnections. Doing a variety of these exercises, letting the students make up their own patterns, provided excellent drill and substantive insights into the nature of fractions and their relations with whole numbers.

The Complexity of Tomorrow's World

Complexity theory is new. Ron and I used it only on Fridays and only in mathematics problem solving. However, it gave us, along with challenges and complications, insights into teaching and learning we did not have when we began. Some general principles of the theory are universally adaptable and applicable to any subject. The entwining of chaos with order occurs universally and can be seen in all student learning. Self-organization is a feature of all nature, and certainly is evident in students' developing their own creative powers. To see how complexity can emerge from simplicity requires only that we study and teach our subjects—at any level—with depth, not superficially.

As our insights toward complexity deepened and developed, our teaching practices allowed, even encouraged, the students to develop their own appreciation of the irregular but beautiful patterns inherent in both mathematics and nature. The complexity of tomorrow's world is one we hope they will approach not with fear but with awe.

23

REFLECTIONS ON TEACHING

DEVELOPING THE NON-LINEAR

(1999)

When I entered graduate school, to study education in a formal and serious manner, ultimately to become a curriculum theorist, I was already a seasoned but naive teacher. I had two decades of successful teaching, administrating, conference and workshop presenting. My naivety came from my non-recognition that what success I did have—even a Saturday morning TV show with junior high students discussing "great books"—was a personal success only. I did not realize that *my* practices, *my* activities, *my* personality were localized. I believed others could adopt that which I demonstrated. Worse yet, I believed they should so adopt.

Graduate school was a revelation for me. It helped me realize both the arrogance and impossibility of my position. Reading John Dewey aided me in realizing that meaningful learning does not come by imposing one's methods and values on others. Each of us must come and indeed does come to learning through her or his own experiential frame. It is the development of this experiential frame which is so important—doing one's own activities and then reflecting on them. For Dewey this is the development of experience into an experience,[1] having experience lead itself further, into other experiences—"to make one experience freely available in other experiences" (1966a [1916], p. 339). Others, notably Harry Beilin (Beilin and Pufall, 1992), placing this development of experience in a Piagetian frame

---

1 The terminology here of differentiating experience from an experience is my terminology, attempting to deal with the distinction Dewey makes in both *Experience and education* (1963 [1938]), Chapters 2 and 3, and in *Democracy and education* (1966a [1916]), Chapter 11 and *passim*, concerning his distinction between experience that is "educative" and that which is "miseducative" or between experience with "retrospect and outlook" and that without such.

have called it a "hermeneutics of action" (p. 1), [2] an action that goes beyond a mere doing to a reflective doing. Such doing, rational in its core, can be done only by the person involved, all the other—we as teachers—can do is to provide an environment which is comfortable for such reflective doing. Once we set up such an environment and invite others into dialogue with it, "all has been done which a second party can do" (Dewey, 1966a [1916], p. 160). Now, each of us must do our own reflective thinking, we hope in concert with others' kind and constructive aid and critique.

While in graduate school I realized the arrogance, naivety, and folly of my attempted impositions on adults, mostly through the workshop models I offered for others to "copy." I also realized that in dealing with school students, I operated quite differently. I gave them the freedom, encouragement, and guidance to develop their own experiences. I allowed, encouraged (did I force?) them to play with the subjects we were studying. Such play was well received. Through play we, together— conjointly to use Dewey's word—explored school subjects and their structures. Usually this happened in mathematics but sometimes spread over into other areas, notably social studies. This rich exploration led us down all sorts of alleyways and by- paths, and, thereby, we discovered the beauties, intricacies, complexities of language, literature, mathematics, science, and social studies, all beautiful in their pristine forms. It is we, in our methodologies, who have anesthetized these subjects and rendered them, as Alfred North Whitehead (1967b [1929]) says, "dead" and "inert" (p. v.). Later, I (Doll, 1993, 1998b) would call this beauty a subject's richness (even its spirit) but at that time I only enjoyed the play. My students and I were alive with our "being" in the subjects we studied.

Dewey helped me in my desire to explore a subject's intricacies through the act of play, as he spoke out against using teaching to fit everyone with a uniform mode of learning. As he says (1966a [1916]),

> To suppose that students, whether in the primary school or in the university, can be supplied with models of method to be followed in acquiring and expounding a subject is to fall into a self-deception that has lamentable consequences … [for] imposing an alleged uniform general method upon everybody breeds mediocrity in all but the very exceptional.
>
> (pp. 172–173)

---

2 The actual phrase Beilin uses is "a logical hermeneutics of action," in keeping with Piaget's interest in the logical–mathematical. However, in his next phrase, Beilin states that the logical for Piaget, in his "new theory"—that developed in the latter years of his life—shifted "from an emphasis on logical necessity to that of possibility." For this reason, and because Beilin's whole emphasis in his essay and book is on Piaget's shift in his thinking about logic—away from "truth-table (propositional) logic" to a more hermeneutically oriented logic, I have chosen to use the phrase "a hermeneutics of action." It is this concept of action (hermeneutical) which I believe allies with Dewey's concept of habit (reflective). Both are necessary, I believe, for the development of experience, as opposed to having an experience.

Here is a sense of the plural and varietal that I feel is natural to both teaching and learning but which up to that time I had never expressed or reflected on in a conscious way.

After doctoral graduation I was in a dilemma. How could I help others, particularly classroom teachers, develop their own teaching styles which emphasized Dewey's concept of an experience (1963 [1938]) or my own of exploration and play? I could demonstrate such individually in classrooms, obviously to little lasting effect, but I could not develop a methodology of experience (1972, 1973) nor one of play (1980), except on paper. I did work with schools and I did teach (large) classes. But in all cases, and even with the successes I had, I was plagued by the very admonition Dewey warned against—imposing a model or method for all to follow. I was not able to develop what I later (1993) called an open systems theory, one which encouraged teachers to take their own directions and yet provided a frame for their operations. I was caught in the land of the "either/ors" (Dewey, 1963 [1938], p. 3)—either dogmatically prescriptive or unrestrainably loose. I could not find that alternative which Dewey himself sought so much, where both frame and flexibility, structure and spontaneity, intersected and interacted (Kauffman, 1995; Doll, 1998a).

Two experiences, instructive in their negativity, stand out as I reflect back on my early years as an education professor. In my first year of teaching at the college level (1971), due to the illness of the assigned instructor I was asked to take over a three-week summer curriculum course (250 masters students). This was my first graduate level course, it was with practiced teachers, the lecture hall was daunting, and I was scared. Worse, I quickly found I did not like the synoptic text chosen. In fact, I did not like any synoptic text—none had a "spirit" to them, the spirit of being (Doll, 1998b). So I chose primary sources from authors then riling the educational field—Bruner, Goodman, Holt, Illich, Kozol, Piaget, Vygotsky (temporarily I had forgotten play but was into Piaget's sense of disequilibrium as a necessary stimulus to thought)—and asked the teachers, in groups, to present their views on the works they chose and to apply these thoughts to their classrooms. My course did not go well: the teachers presented book reports only, descriptions at best, and found applying the thoughts of these authors to their classes daunting and often impossible. Needless to say, the negativity they found in both the authors' works and in my reactions to their reportish presentations did not endear them to the works read or to me. One reviewer commented that all she (or he) received from this course was instruction in how "not to teach."

I did not leave the profession, I am still in it, but I did spend more time administrating—and seemed mildly successful at this. A dozen or so years later, I found myself directing a teacher education program at a small southern California university and still working on the idea of trying to find ways to have life breathed into my own and my students' classes. Toward this end, I tried to utilize play, disequilibrium, and experience. Over the years I had truly become a much better university teacher—combining work at the theoretical level with practical experience in the schools, where I taught weekly (Doll, 1989). My classes with teachers were now much more "spiritful," and discussions went on in class with vigor and verve. I had discovered Donald Schön's (1983, 1987) interpretation of Dewey and from them both fashioned my own teaching creed (this volume, Chapter 8), emphasizing reflection, relations, and responsibilities of both student and teacher.

This creed gave me a frame both to expound my theories and to use when working with either teachers or students. It very much expressed where I was coming from with its emphasis on inquiry, mutuality, exploration, openness, and reflection. Again, play, disequilibrium, and an experience remained in the background, tacit observers to our classroom discussions.

Against this rather idyllic frame is placed my second memorable failed experience at helping teachers develop what I now call teaching in a nonlinear mode. One night, our class was especially exciting. A young man had such a rich presentation that of the five points on his outline only two were "covered" as the ending hour drew near. If one uses Jim Garrison's (1998) felicitous phrase, "texts are tools for thought," this night had been a success—we had used well the tools the presenter gave. His frame was quite different however; he had five points written in a linear fashion and he kept us another 45 minutes while he went through them all. Regretfully, the drive home that night was filled not with the excitement of reflective, even playful and imaginative, thought but with the frustration of time lost. The more he gave, the less we received.[3] Ironic but I fear not that unusual in our didactic way of teaching.[4]

This experience, while discouraging, was not defeating. I admired the young man's creativeness in presenting a situation rich enough for us, as a class, to generate animated and fruitful discussions for so long. I also realized the powerful hold that "closure" had upon him and indeed upon many in the class. The concept of education as an open system, a process or system that leads itself into itself—one that Dewey espoused as "having no end beyond itself" (1966a [1916], p. 50)—requires us to rethink and indeed reframe some of our most fundamental pedagogical assumptions and habits. In later years, reflecting on closure and control (Doll, 1998a), I came to a deeper understanding of why Ralph Tyler's curriculum guidelines (1950) captured so many for so long and why they spurred the movements they did. The pre-setness of all the procedures in Tyler's "rationale"—goals, experiences, organization of experiences, assessment—does indeed provide both control and closure (Doll, 1993;

---

3 It was Edward L. Thorndike who formulated the Law of Exercise: more drill equals better connections (learning). But even Thorndike realized this was too simple and became aware an inverse effect could occur: too much exercise (or drill on a subject/idea) leads to diminished not increased learning. The issue of the "right amount" of presentation is one that has not been studied in education. For Thorndike see Joncich, 1962, p. 25; for some comments on the "right amount" see Doll, 1993, p. 176.

4 I am aware that in European usage, the word didactic is often synonymous with curriculum or teaching—a fair interpretation from the dictionary and from history (*The great didactic* by Johann Amos Comenius, 1896 [1632]). However, I am also aware that in America the word often means pedantic and it is that to which I am referring.

Kliebard, 1995). Developing an alternative to these procedures, one that has form and shape to it, indeed structure, but that is flexible, open, dynamic is a challenge. I have been working on an alternative for at least two decades, and I still approach this task with trepidation.

My inaugural thoughts concerning a system—recursive, stochastic—began in southern California via my introduction to the writings of both A. N. Whitehead and Ilya Prigogine. Pedagogically it is Whitehead who taught me to look consciously for that which I already felt—or *prehended* to use his word—namely the spirit or life of a subject. And, his admonition to throw ideas into every combination possible provides me with justification and substantiation for what I called exploration and play (this volume, Chapter 12).

My introduction to Ilya Prigogine (1980, 1997; with Stengers, 1984) was really a reintroduction. Piaget (1985) had already introduced me to him in Piaget's own work on equilibration—"cognitive equilibria are quite different from mechanical equilibrium … they are closer to those dynamic steady-state conditions [referred to by Prigogine] that maintain a functional and structural order in an open-system" (p. 10). It was David Depew and Bruce Weber (1984) who encouraged me to look closely at the (educational) implications of order in an open, dynamic system. Such order I soon found was being labeled by mathematicians, philosophers, scientists as "chaotic order"; an unusual, almost contradictory order—at least to us raised in the modernist tradition (Kahn, 1998). It is not contradictory though: chaotic or complex order is an order which maintains itself over change. That is, as change occurs there is often (but not always) a pattern to it—a complex or fractaled pattern. It is the search for this pattern which "chaoticians" do; and it is this unusual or chaotic sense of patterning which seems to permeate the universe in which we live (Stewart, 1989; Lorenz, 1995).

In the union of Whitehead (on whom Prigogine draws) and Prigogine (whom Whitehead presages) I began to find my own sense of the foundation I needed to guide me in my attempts to help others develop their own experiential frame or sense of *becoming* to use Prigogine's term. Becoming is being that moves beyond being, away from the centered state of equilibrium to the exciting, dynamic, and perilous state of far-from-equilibrium. This state opens each of us up to the potential that exists: within life, ourselves, and the creative spirit which infuses the universe. Such a state also exists within the primordial nature of the school subjects we teach. There is an aliveness to both these subjects and ourselves (as creative creatures) if we are but willing to explore this realm far-from-equilibrium and near the edge of chaos. Out here dynamic, transformative, and power change can and does occur.

Journeying in this land is perilous however, as it is easy to step over the edge into the abyss of totally disordered chaos. Lest this happen, I recommend we approach curriculum in this land via the 3 S's of *science, story, spirit* (Doll, 1998b). I suggest our curriculum designs and pedagogic methods of instruction keep all the logical rigor of *science* that have developed over the centuries, but infuse this science with the personalness and culturalness of *story* which we have had for millennia, but recently seem to have lost. Finally I encourage us to infuse both science with the life and vitality of spirit—the very breath of being. This is my answer to Whitehead's challenge (1967b [1929]) that we keep knowledge alive to keep it from becoming inert (p. 5). A curriculum (and with it modes of instruction) based on nonlinearity seems a way to approach this challenge.

Needless to say, this sense of developing the nonlinear did not occur to me full-blown in the winds of southern California, but rather, has come to me slowly after a decade of study with colleagues and students at Louisiana State University. While nonlinearity in teaching and curriculum design is what I wish to talk about in the rest of the article, such a dynamic and emergent approach is itself embedded in the broader synthesis of open or self-organizing systems thinking that is occurring in the fields of chaos/complexity/nonlinearity. Anyone wishing to break the grip that Tyler's model has had on us, not only in his form but in that espoused by Frederick Taylor, the English Puritans, Peter Ramus, and René Descartes—a lineage that stretches back 400 years (this volume, Chapter 8)—must, I believe, look to the concept of open, emergent, dynamical, self-organizing systems (P. Davies, 1988, 1992; Stewart, 1989; Argyros, 1991; Kauffman, 1993, 1995; Lorenz, 1995; Bak, 1996; Capra, 1996).

My own approach to the post-modern has been eclectic. Founded on the constellation unity of chaos/complexity/nonlinearity, it is infused with the art and architecture representations of Charles Jencks (1986, 1988, 1992); with the humanism of Jacques Derrida (1994, 1995); and with the playful, profound, and ironic sense of literature and history Michel Serres (1983, Serres and Latour 1995 [1990]) brings to all he explores.

Finally, my approach is permeated with the eco-evolutionary theories of contemporary biology (Lovelock, 1979, 1991; Maturana and Varela, 1987; Margulis and Sagan, 1995). Last but certainly not least in influence are the theo-cosmological theories of both A.N. Whitehead (1978 [1929]) and Thomas Berry (1988a, 1988b, 1992, 1995).

The nonlinear can be looked at in a number of ways: as all third-order and many second-order mathematical equations, as graphic descriptions of the fractaled universe in which we live, as recursive patterns which show a beautiful, curved, and almost symmetrical order. The linear, on the other hand, is the geometry of the straight line. Two illustrations show this difference (see Figures 23.1 and 23.2).

The straight line graph we all know from first year algebra. It has strong predictive power, for the x, y relationship stays stable. It is this stability of proportionality between the x and the y which causes the line to be straight and allows the linear to be so predictable. The beauty of the Julia set comes from a simple mathematical equation, probably something no more complex than $f(x) = k(x) \, [1-x]$. But not all entries into this equation will produce such recursive beauty: the relationship between the variables needs to be quite precise and yet this precision can be determined only after the fact. It cannot be predicted in advance; we see the pattern emerging only as it emerges.

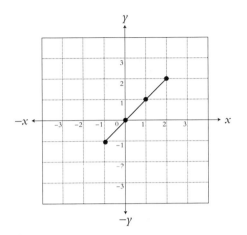

FIGURE 23.1 Line graph

FIGURE 23.2 Julia set (revised formula 04) retrieved from http://en.wikipedia.org/wiki/
File:Julia_set(Rev_formula_04).gif

Metaphorically the foregoing means that we can have a pre-set curriculum where all the stimuli or questions, and right answers, are decided in advance (as our lesson plans encourage us to do); or we can have an emerging curriculum which proceeds dialectically in the interaction between teacher and students, text and both teacher and students, students and students. Another visual might help here. Let us consider the curriculum and its implementation in terms of the familiar x, y grid of Cartesian mathematics with the traditional x-stimulus (question) and y- response (answer) frame.

	Stimulus X — Response Y
P	stimulus_1 — response_1
R	stimulus_2 — response_2
E	stimulus_3 — response_3
S	stimulus_4 — response_4
E	stimulus_5 — response_5
T	stimulus_6 — response_6

FIGURE 23.3 Traditional, linear stimulus–response teaching model

Figure 23.3 is a visualization of what I'd call our usual teaching model. We, as teachers, pre-choose the stimuli to be presented (#s 1–6) and expect the students to reply with the correct (also pre-chosen) responses (#s 1–6). As teachers we "know" the correct answers to the questions we've asked. Exploration is excluded, or is treated as an extra, an enrichment. This system is quite closed; we even talk of keeping our students "on task" or "on the right track." The tracks are #s 1–6, both questions and answers. The progression is linear and preset, s–r, s–r, s–r, etc. The proportional relationship between the stimuli (questions) and the responses (answers) remains stable throughout—essentially one correct answer. Often the student "sees" the questions and answers as isolated bits of information, atomistic in their being.[5] We learn our math facts this way, as isolated bits of information not as parts of an emerging pattern. The same might be said of our science, grammar, and social studies facts. Here learning is no more than the accumulation of bits of information, and the "brighter" students are those who can recall (or regurgitate) the most facts in the shortest amount of time. Larger themes, patterns, abstractions, heuristics do not emerge; none of what Whitehead (1967b [1929]) calls "the power of ideas, the beauty of ideas, the structure of ideas" (p. 12). Sadly, only inert facts exist.

A non-linear frame, using the same *x–y* /stimulus–response frame, might look like Figure 23.4.

These two modes differ in that the linear mode comes from pre-set determinations and controlled proportionality while the mode emerges from dialogic interactions and has an exponential and/or tangential proportionality. It is not a line but a matrix or sphere or web which is built. In the linear mode both stimuli (questions) and responses (answers) are determined in advance. The learner's activity is "to guess the

5 One teacher, reflecting on this truth, said in her journal: "When I moved to teaching middle school, I thought I had to start on page 1 of the text and go as far as I could in 9½ months. I have found this leaves everyone. ... Bored? Ignorant? I'm not sure what term to use! But I do know this does not achieve any real educational goals. It is simply a battle toward an unknown and unattained (unattainable) end which my students have no desire to reach!" Lynn Bourgeois (1998).

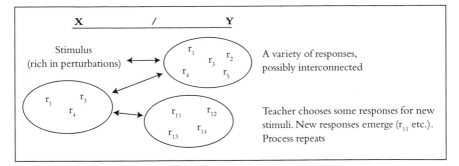

FIGURE 23.4 Schematic of nonlinear stimulus–response

right answers," to glean in advance what the teacher wants. This game the students play well, even in the elementary grades. In the mode, the teacher "plants a seed" (a phrase applicable both to agriculture and chaos mathematics), a seed rich in problematics or possible interpretations/analyses/procedures. From the multiplicity of responses given, the teacher chooses some for further exploration (the curriculum now begins to develop or emerge) and encourages dialogic relationships among the responses given. Over time, and developmental time becomes crucial in this dialogic/process mode, a matrix/sphere/web of relations develops. The field or area of study in its multiple facets, various perspectives, and interrelated connections begins to emerge. While a student, or students working together, may well pursue particular aspects of a subject, through interactions all begin to interconnect their own particulars with those of others. In this manner a holistic image emerges. Whereas the linear mode is often associated with a reductionist methodology, a non-linear mode is associated with a holistic, matrixical methodology.[6]

Using the foregoing as a background, I'd like to provide two examples of teaching, one at the graduate level, one at the undergraduate level. Both examples occurred in spring semester classes and are paired examples with a graduate assistants participating. Jeong Suk from Korea participated in the first set of classes—graduate and undergraduate, Hongyu Wang from China is participating in the second set

---

6 I realize, of course, that what I am proposing here under the post-modern banner is a type of meta-narrative, that which Lyotard's (1984) said all post-modernists should eschew or at least be "incredulous toward" (p. xxiii). This famous statement about the post-modern and its supposed antifoundationalism seems to me to be a well needed warning for all in the field. But it also seems to me that the debate this has stirred comes essentially from those literary, philosophical, and cultural circles still mired in modernism or at least struggling to get out of this mire. In contrast, there is emerging, I believe, a new open systems, foundational paradigm drawing heavily on Whitehead's view of process. This view brings with it a new and very different concept of meta-narrative coming from the biological sciences, complexity theory, and holistic forms of cognition. For insights into this new, open and emergent, foundationalism, see works by Berman (1981, 1989), Thompson (1989), Varela et al. (1993), Margulis and Sagan (1995), Capra (1996).

(ongoing as I write). I believe their cultural perspectives are particularly valuable and so I've asked them to write their reflections at the end of mine. The graduate class, in principles and practices of elementary education, is for teachers in a master's program; the undergraduate class in the teaching of mathematics to elementary school children is for teachers-to-be seeking certification. Jeong Suk and Hongyu were both teaching assistants who had the opportunity of watching me wrestle with a frame at both the theoretical and practical levels.

One of my practical wrestles has been with the issue of using a syllabus—that which, with its pre-set readings, assignments, papers, discussions, "drives a course." Rather than be trapped in the rigidity of this system, framed linearly well before the first student walks into the classroom, I have chosen for the past two spring semesters to not issue a syllabus to the graduate students—to those teachers enrolled, usually as master's candidates. Instead I have drawn on the "chaotic" concepts of rich initial beginnings, recursions, flexible but bounded interrelations, and the rigors of multiple perspectives. I announce the readings—provocative in content—randomly assign small groups, give the students the charge of choosing their learnings from the material set out, and require periodic journal submissions. There are, of course, other ways to limit the controlling force of a set syllabus, so that emergence, spontaneity, choice, reflection, might be active, but this frame is the one I have chosen twice. Generally it seems to work quite well: texts are read as "tools for thinking," issues are pondered/debated, experiences in the school classroom do undergo modification and development, and a sense of communal being is fostered. In future classes I may well modify this participatory structure but it is hard for me now to envision my ever going back to the pre-set, rigid, and linear structure I knew in the past.

Part way through my second attempt at this mode, I find two, previously unforeseen features standing out: (1) attitude, (2) meaning making. There is no doubt that all who participate or even observe in these classes find a spirit present. It is not easy to be definitional with this spirit but it has joy, frustration, hope, excitement—an abundance of life—in it. As individuals, as a group we do wrestle. In the first semester of this class, a student actually brought in the Old Testament Bible and read to us (Genesis, 32:24) of Jacob's wrestling with God (or an angel of God—this, too, was debated/pondered). So far there seems to be good evidence—journals, reflective papers, talkings, classroom practices—of the teachers getting "good holds" on this grapple. They are reading, writing, thinking broadly, deeply, experientially. I attribute this attitude or spirit to our conjoint creation of an environment whereby we can all engage meaningfully in a manner that is both free and constrained. Following John Dewey (1963 [1938]), Richard Bernstein (1992), and Stuart Kauffman (1995), I find the "both/and" of freedom and constraint to be most important.[7]

---

7 Dewey begins his *Experience and education* (1963 [1938]) with the assertion that "[hu] mankind likes to think in terms of either/ors" (p. 3). I believe that slowly, and due in part to chaos theory and its sense of integrating what we have previously separated, we

The second unexpected feature has been the ease with which the teachers have made meaning from the texts, discussions, journals, and personal reflections. Working at a level where theoretical and often perturbing thought meshes with practical activity has not always been easy in my courses. Jerome Bruner (1996) insightfully states that meaning is made only when ideas "descend" into habits and practices (p. 152). The concept of ideas descending to permeate our being, as reflective and thoughtful habits and practices—quite distinct from mechanical or unthoughtful habits/practices—is very Deweyan (1966a [1916], pp. 339–340 and *passim*). Such descent or permeation is often missing, I find, in our linearly structured courses. But through the process of recursion, meaning making has emerged easily in both classes. It is indeed a usual activity. A strong connection has been forged between the theoretically oriented discussions on Tuesday nights and the weekday classroom practices the teachers develop. Truly an experiential frame is being built. Not only are theoretical–practical interconnections being made but the teachers' usual practices, through the process of equilibration, are being transformed. The teachers are challenging themselves to transcend their current states of being, not only in the classroom but in life itself. What is happening to them is also happening to me; this is exciting.

The mathematics education course—for those prospective teachers seeking certification—has been both easier and more frustrating. Its purpose is to help these prospective teachers handle the teaching of mathematics to elementary school children and youth. Many teacher preparation programs call such a course a "methods" course. In our attempt to have students develop their own experiential frame, we shy away from such a designation. Instead we call it a curricular disciplines course, partly to honor the discipline and structure of mathematics and partly to raise the concepts of curriculum and instruction to a discipline level. There is indeed a history, philosophy, and pedagogy to each.

The course has been easier in that we, as a class, have a well-defined discipline on which to draw. Understanding the nature and structure of mathematics with at least a degree of depth is one of the goals in such a curricular discipline. Mathematics can, we believe, be looked at as a curricular discipline—integrating the structures of the field with the structures of the learner's thinking. Integrating these two is a fascinating, albeit frustrating, challenge—one combining the linear, atomistic presentations of school textbook mathematics with the associative thinking of children and youth. Our intent in the course is to have the prospective teachers think deeply about the structures of both mathematics and the learning patterns of children—i.e. how the inherent logic and abstractness of mathematics can be personalized and localized for the concretely oriented learner. As Jeong Suk has said:

---

are beginning to develop an epistemology that is based on a frame other than this *bête noire* of Dewey's. I have begun my own development of a "both/and" epistemology in my "Curriculum and concepts of control" (1998a) in which I draw heavily on Bateson (1988 [1979]), Bernstein (1992), and Kauffman (1995).

one of the goals of the course is "to help the students understand the contents in a deep [and I'd say structured] way."

The frustrating aspect of the course is not only that it is categorically difficult to mesh the linear and atomistic presentation of school textbook mathematics with the learner's patterns of thought but that the prospective teachers have little experience doing such. They do not generally have the reservoir of tacit knowledge and practices to draw on that experienced teachers do. Coming in direct contact with children and their ways of thinking—two prospective teachers to a group of five or six children—in order to recognize patterns in children's thought has brought these prospective teachers face to face with the nonlinearity of such thought. It has also brought them to a dramatic and frustrating awareness of the misfit between the linear and atomistic structures of textbooks and curricular guidelines, and the nonlinear and holistic structures of children's and youths' thinking. But with this frustration has come a new sense of awareness, a sense that is not merely cognitive but one Morris Berman (1981) calls "participatory" and one Donald Oliver (1990) calls "grounded." Again, returning to Jeong Suk's observations, a depth of reflection and understanding has developed in this course with a shift occurring from "how much contents are imported into the course to how students properly interplay with the contents."[8] Such playing with contents, "putting ideas into every combination possible," is, I believe, crucial to any understanding which is to be deep and meaningful, to the development of a consciousness which goes beyond the receptory to the participatory.

After a quarter century of wrestling with the "art of teaching" I feel I have found, for myself at least, a way to make Dewey's theory of experience practical. It involves an aesthetic and intuitive (Garrison, 1997) sense of what is pedagogically exciting. Many teachers have this sense and it is one they—with our help and encouragement—should honor and develop. This can be done by "playing" or dialoguing with ideas, combinations, relationships—both logical and personal. Such reflective dialoguing with text, self, others helps frame an environment in which experience can grow and develop. As experience emerges into an experience, life is breathed into the subject(s). The process has a spirit to it, one that is truly and often "chaotically" creative.

Jeong Suk's Reflections

I graduated from Seoul National University of Education which is the specialized university for elementary school education is Seoul, the capital of Korea. Since receiving a master's degree in elementary mathematics education in 1996, I have been a doctoral student at LSU to pursue in-depth study in mathematics education.

---

8 It is interesting to note that the Third International Math and Science Study (TIMSS Report, 1996) condemns American math teaching for trying to teach too much in too shallow a manner.

The two courses I participated in during the spring of 1997 were fascinating for me as I was able to observe a close relationship between theory and practice. The two different courses led me to conceive theory in practice and of practice in theory. A post-modern perspective on curriculum and instruction was new for me, since my cultural and academic orientation had been more geared towards a closed modern perspective. Participation in the two courses shed light in understanding how a post-modern perspective makes various aspects intermingle towards meaning-making, including the connections between teacher and student, student and student, person and material, person and curriculum, history and culture, past and present, present and future, spirit and structure of mathematics.

In the master's course, we did not have a syllabus at one level, making initial confusion and chaos. But we developed a syllabus at another level through vivid interactions both in small groups and in the whole group. For instance, the issues which we as a classroom community wrestled with in one day were revisited in our next classes in a deep and structured way, based on our enthusiastic preparation of the issues. We experienced the process of recursion throughout the course. If I use the terms of stimulus and response, the first stimulus and some responses slide under the second stimulus. Again, the second stimulus and some variate responses slide under the third stimulus. In this way, the last response contains the whole process interconnected through the whole semester, helping us develop rich understanding.

In the Mathematics Education course, the prospective teachers at first expressed a similar embarrassment and uneasiness. But as time went on, they actively participated in classroom discussion and implemented their experience of mathematics and its teaching into elementary school classrooms. This undergraduate class was very different from the methodology courses to teach mathematics I had experienced, which usually focused on transmitting desirable teaching models. The difference started from the fact that the teacher (Dr Doll) and students mutually appropriated each other's contributions. The teacher did not attempt to transmit a good teaching model, but tried to help students reflect on their own mathematical thinking and their students'. The topics discussed in the class emerged from both the teacher and the students through their "authentic" interactions. The nonlinear teaching approach in the class, I think, helped the students construct their own teaching style by participating in the class discussion and by reflecting on various views of teaching mathematics. It is in this sense I think that the art of teaching lies in emergent meaning and that the power of teaching is in continuous reflection based up inter-subjectivity through discourse.

Learning about teaching and creating a desirable classroom teaching practice are not either/or propositions, but exist on a continuum that requires continuous creation of knowledge through reflection, openness towards knowing, and multiple perspectives. As I understand it, a teaching approach in which I was a participant–observer provided such a continuum for both prospective and experienced teachers.

Hongyu's Reflections

As a person coming from China (I finished my bachelor's and master's degree in education from Chinese universities), I am often amazed by an open, uncertain yet transformative space that nonlinear teaching can create in the classroom. As both a participant and an observer in Dr Doll's two classes in the spring of 1998, I have experienced the creative spirit of the nonlinear teaching in which curriculum structure is continuously co-emergent with personal and communal explorations by both the teacher and students. In this teaching mode, the teacher is open to students' own becoming and emergence, and the curriculum itself is engaged in a continuous process of transformation and re-creation.

The notion of linear teaching is grounded on behaviorism which is not deeply rooted in China, so this notion is somewhat a Western concept. However, the didactic mode of teaching embedded in this linearity is not so different from the systematic transmission teaching model, dominant in Chinese schooling practices. Interesting enough, the transmission from the teacher to students of a systematic pre-set core knowledge packaged by outside experts is often conducted in a disconnected way since knowledge structure is imposed upon students who rarely have any significant chance to make it meaningful to themselves. As a result, what students learn from the class is often isolated, atomic facts in a closed, static system.

The nonlinear teaching mode shows a different picture. It offers an open system in which interconnected knowledge and meaning-makings are constantly built and rebuilt by a dynamic interplay between the structure of students' thinking and the curriculum structure. In the undergraduate course, the patternness of mathematics is the focus of the class. But students approach this patternness through their reflections upon their own mathematics thinking. When the "seed," rich in multiplicity and complexity, is thrown in the classroom by the teacher, students come up with various responses. Further explorations are built upon these responses by playing with different ways of patterning together, and reformulation of this patternness happens along the road (Dr Doll calls it "recurricularization"). Through constant reflections and dialogic interactions, students keep going back to the initial question but with new understandings; as a result, new connections are made and a mathematics matrix is constructed and reconstructed.

In this way, the process of teaching and learning is still systematic, but at a new level—the system is not set in advance but constructed in an ongoing process in which complex and multilayered connections between students and texts, the teacher and texts, students and teachers, and students and students are constantly transformed and continuously generative to new structures. This sense of holism and wholeness also reminds me of Chinese holistic ways of thinking and being, but it is a more complex holism based upon individuality and dynamic interconnections. Moreover this wholeness allows and even encourages the existence of "redundancy" to be dissipated for new change.

Another salient feature of nonlinear teaching which often strikes me is its narrativeness. Because of this cultural and personal narrativeness, nonlinear teaching becomes a highly localized and contextualized process in which creativeness and imagination are called upon to situate pedagogical strategies. At both the undergraduate and graduate levels, students who are either prospective teachers or in-service teachers bring their experiences of both teaching and life into the classroom and share their stories together. While the input of students is unpredictable, the interactions between the teacher and students and among students frame a stimulating background for further discussions and inquiry. In a flexible and supportive classroom atmosphere, students become willing to share their frustrations and unsuccessful attempts to figure a way out together.

There is a fair amount of tension and anxiety aroused among students in encountering the nonlinear both in the class and in their own teaching practices. While coping with an initial uneasiness in the class, students, especially at the graduate level, become more and more enthusiastic about exploring the nonlinear in their own classrooms. The fear of "out-of-control" is indeed a great challenge for them, but the excitement about the possibility the nonlinear can open up leads them to rigorously search for their own ways of incorporating more flexibility and creativity in their teaching.

Upon my reflections on nonlinear teaching, I believe no general formula or a pre-established model can be offered to develop the nonlinear in the classroom, but it is precisely within this uncertain and emergent space that nonlinear teaching plays its transformative and creative roles by exploring culturally, socially, (auto) biographically, and temporally–spatially situated strategies.

24

CLASSROOM MANAGEMENT

(2000)

Classroom management, indeed management in general, is usually not associated with disturbance. Disturbance is to be avoided, not advocated. *Ma*nagement has to do with control—centralized control—and disturbance dissipates that control; hence to be avoided. "Do not lose control of the classroom" is the number one fiat given beginning classroom teachers. The loss of control is the novice teacher's greatest fear. But what does this loss of control mean ? What does control mean? The dictionary I have at hand (*American Heritage Dictionary of the English Language*, 1969, pp. 290–291) says for control: (1) to exercise authority or dominating influence over; direct; regulate; (2) to hold in restraint; to check. John Dewey devoted a whole chapter to control in his *Democracy and education* (1966a [1916]). Presaging my dictionary definition, he says: "control subordinates a person's natural impulses to another's end," and the term thus used has "a flavor of coercion or compulsion about it" (p. 24). Indeed, if control—what I have elsewhere (1998a, p. 298) called "the ghost in the curriculum"—is exercising a dominating influence over, is holding in restraint, is subordinating a person's natural impulses, and has a flavor of coercion about it, then how can learning that is good, deep, meaningful take place in such an atmosphere ? Wrestling with this question may well provide us with reason to rethink the whole notion of classroom management as centralized control. It may not be oxymoronic to think of a term like "dissipated control." Maybe a case can be made for a sense of control that is non-centralized; a sense of control based on "*just the right amount* of disturbance."

The concept of control within the teaching framework is as old as is the use of curriculum as an educational term—back to the Protestant Reformation (Doll, 1998a). Its contemporary American roots, however, are usually traced to the "scientific management" movement (Taylor, 1947 [1911]; Rice, 1969a [1914];

Callahan, 1962; Kliebard, 1975; Kanigel, 1997; Doll, 1993), begun when Frederick Taylor did his first time-and-motion studies at Bethlehem Steel in the 1890s. In this study (1947 [1911]), the concept of control is quite evident in the four principles which Taylor believed management and workers were to attend: (1) a science for each element of a man's work to replace the old rule-of-thumb method, (2) a scientific selection and training of the men to do the work, lest these men be left to their own methods, (3) attention given to insuring that all the work be done in accord with the scientific principles developed, (4) an equal division of responsibility drawn between management and workers (pp. 36–39). This latter point Taylor considered the most important, one "requiring further explanation." Management is to plan out fully, "in writing and in detail," one day in advance, the work each man is to do. These orders are to specify "what is to be done, how it is to be done, and the exact time allowed for doing it" (p. 39). Workers are to follow, in exact detail, the orders given. Here then is Taylor's "equal division of responsibility"—one group is responsible for planning, the other group for following. That this dichotomous, planning–following model has strongly influenced American curriculum and instruction is an assertion that needs hardly be made. Nonetheless, the wording from a contemporary textbook—*Classroom management strategies: Gaining and maintaining students' cooperation* (Cangelosi, 1993)—is instructive:

> *The goals you establish for your students to achieve; how you plan*, prepare, and conduct *[their] learning activities; how you evaluate your students' achievements; how you organize* and manage *the classroom setting*; and *the manner in which you communicate* with students and their parents *will* be major *influences* on how much of your *students'* time is spent cooperatively engaged in *learning activities.* Of course *other factors*, many of which *are out of your control*, will also influence how well your students cooperate. ... *But dwelling on causes outside of your control* will *not* be *a productive* means *for you to* begin *increasing students' time on-task.*
>
> (p. 12; emphasis added)

The correlation between the 1911 statement and the 1993 statement is obvious. What may not be so obvious is that both statements emphasize a sense of cooperation. Taylor truly believed that his methods were those of shared and cooperative responsibility, the classroom management book uses the word cooperation in its title and does talk of the students being "cooperatively engaged in learning activities." What sort of cooperation, though, emerges when one person has a dominating influence over others? When one holds others in restraint?

Is there another way to deal with (or "manage") a classroom of learners? Indeed, is there another way to conceive of control? John Dewey said yes to both! In his chapter on control (1966a [1916], Ch. 3), Dewey, as one might expect, attacks the dualism of external/internal control. He finds both impositional, one directly, the other indirectly (as imitation of a pattern already set). Both require outside authority, neither develops a person's natural impulses. So Dewey mentions, but only mentions, a different form of control—one that is "more important," "permanent," "intellectual not personal" (pp. 27 and 33). Today with our interest in and development of chaos/ complexity theory such control might well be called dissipative control, emergent control, self-organizing control. Dewey, a presager of such contemporary, post-modern thoughts and words, relied for himself on the concepts of interaction and development. He talks of this "other mode of control," as a "guiding of activity [by activity] to its own end" (p. 24). This guiding resides not unilaterally with the teacher nor with the students but instead "resides in the nature of the situations" themselves (p. 39). That is, the control resides in the interactions (teacher–students, students–students, people–texts, history–present, present–future hopes, etc.) existent in the situations as they be.

For Dewey (1990 [1902]) the issue is not whether the child or the curriculum is dominant—he uses the phrase "child versus curriculum" to describe this unfortunate social frame—but how the child *and* the curriculum are interactive. "The child and the curriculum are simply two limits which define a single process" (p. 189). In more contemporary, post-modern terms, the structure of control actually emerges from these interactions—interactions which need "just the right amount" of perturbations (Dewey called them problems) to be active and alive. For Dewey, the beginning of all learning has to start with the "natural capacities of the individual" but these capacities need "assisting through cooperation," if they are to progress beyond mere impulses and undeveloped potentialities (p. 23). This, as well as I can phrase it, represents Dewey's concept of growth, a growth which develops over time through social interaction. Growth is a *reflective* process, subservient to no end beyond itself.

Can this same social/intellectual process model be applied to classroom management? Again, Dewey said, yes! In at least one place he uses the analogy of a boat and a boatsman [boatsperson]:

> The teacher is a guide and director; he steers the boat, but the energy that propels it must come from those who are learning. The more a teacher is aware of the past experiences of students, of their hopes, desires, chief interests, the better will be understood the forces at work that need to be directed and utilized for the formation of reflective habits.
>
> (1963 [1938], p. 36)

Two issues stand out here, I believe. One is that Dewey does indeed posit a general goal or direction—he pre-sets such—that of reflective habits. Reflective habits are the primary goal Dewey posits for all education, these habits are necessary for an American style democracy. The second issue is that this general goal achieves its specificity, its details, through a time-developmental process of cooperative interaction—the boatsperson steers but the energy he (or she) steers comes from the boat itself, from the dynamic interaction of "the forces at work" in the present situation. A combinatory dynamic is at work here. The teacher does steer but does so by tapping into the creative energy existent in the classroom. Metaphorically, no one is merely taken for a ride, nor is anyone along just for the ride; the specific development of each situation—its own growth—is the result of the alive and dynamic interaction of "the forces at work" in the situation. Lest the boat sink or capsize, such a process-development, reflective-habit, social-interaction frame requires a very special form of community. Dewey chose to entitle his major educational work, *Democracy and education* (1966a [1916]).

Stuart Kauffman, a preeminent complexity theorist, posits that such a "communitarian" frame (my word, not his)—one allowing for and indeed operating from a dynamic blend of stability and flexibility (1995, p. 188)—can indeed produce naturally all sorts of miracles: order, life, social justice.[1] In simple terms, his argument is that under *the right conditions* order arises naturally from an interaction of forces. This order is neither through random chance nor imposed by a more superior force. It emerges as a consequence but unpredictable interaction of forces, that which chaos mathematics likes to call deterministic but unpredictable or which Gregory Bateson (1988 [1979]) called the "Great Stochastic Process." We "see" this process (or at least the results of the process) in mathematical simulations of complex systems, in the formation of life itself, in the social arrangement we call democracy. The key to this emergence is the unique combination of constraining structural stability (mathematical equations, DNA codes, forms of society) and the liberating forces of flexibility operating within and challenging these structures. It is the dynamic interplay of these forces—not the exclusive dominance of any one—which produces the spontaneous emergence of order, growth, development, learning. A new sense of control, that which I am calling dissipative control, is a new concept coming out of the new sciences.

Is a different form of control—one that as Dewey says, is a "more important," "permanent," sense of control, that which I call dissipative control, worth considering for classroom management which up to now has been extremely centralized in its conceptualization and application? Whether one calls it systems, networks, or communities, the frame Kauffman and others are studying is that

---

1 Details of Stuart Kauffman's work on complexity theory, nonlinear dynamics, network systems can be found in *The origins of order* (1993), and *At home in the universe* (1995); see also a short article, "Antichaos and adaptation" (1991). Secondary sources of his work can be found in George Johnson's, *Fire in the mind* (1996) and Fritjof Capra's *The web of life* (1996). But Kauffman is not alone in this field as a look at the bibliographies of any of these works shows. Business management theorists lead by Tom Peters—*Thriving on chaos* (1987), *Liberation management* (1992)—have also picked up the concepts. David Parker and Ralph Stacey have a book on *Chaos, management and economics* (1994) as does Tony Watson, *In search of management: Culture, chaos and control in managerial work* (1994). In the field of educational administration, Spencer Maxcy (1995) has a book: *Democracy, chaos and the new school order*. In short, the concept of a new sense of control, that which I am calling dissipative, is current in the year 2000.

of a group, self-developing or self-organizing. The key to such organization—dissipative organization, if I may use such a phrase—is to set up (mathematically, socially) or find (biologically, ecologically, cosmologically) frames demonstrating "just the right amount of disturbance." As Piaget (Doll 1983, 1993) knew so well, in an equilibrium–disequilibrium–reequilibration frame, it is *just the right amount* of disequilibrium which "drives" the developmental process.

Dewey knew this, too, with his continual insistence that school curricula be built around "problems," themselves the outgrowth of the "hopes, desires, and interests" of students. The development of experience into more experience, of unrefined experience into sophisticated, mature experience (*Experience and nature*, 1958a [1929]; *Experience and education*, 1963 [1938]), is the result of a process built around the notion of a problematic—that which is "asking" to be explored (more explored than solved). Obviously the teacher (boatsperson) plays an important role here but this role is not a dominating one; it is one of guiding, helping develop, suggesting of a general direction for the creative energy which resides in the situation both to come forward and to be shaped (by all in the situation).

Stuart Kauffman, neither a Deweyan, Piagetian, nor educator—but heuristic in his own right as a complexity theorist—posits that self-organizing systems develop or emerge when "just the right amount" includes (a) a critical, active mass, (b) only a few operating connections at any given time, and (c) a simple set of operating rules (1995, Ch. 4). Such a frame works as he experiments with mathematical iterations which produce order from randomness, is a hypothesis about the evolutionary origins of life on this planet, and a speculation about the structure of social democratic groups. Using Kaufmann's frame as a metaphor for the structure and dynamics of classrooms, I see his "(a)" as the collection of a viable, active group of learner-students, teacher included, his "(b)" as the emergence of varying, interconnected, dynamic foci (the "aliveness" of situations as it were), and his "(c)" as the few basic procedures needed for having the energy generated by these interactive situations be iteratively or matrixically connected. Use of this frame does of course pretty well destroy the usual rubrics of classroom management—the centralizing of control with the teacher, the use of linear lesson plans, the detail of advanced organizers or syllabi, rules of conduct, and traditional evaluations. Control is dissipated into the group, community, network, system, and indeed frames itself. Lesson plans are nonlinear and for me, recursive, depending on the interactions developing within the situations. Details dealing with organization, conduct, evaluation are all the result of reflections on occurrences rather than on pre-set formulae or procedures to be followed.

As of this writing (2000), I have tried implementing such a "management" system—akin somewhat to Lucent Technologies' "Mission from above, Methods from below" (Petzinger, 1997)—only with university graduate and undergraduate classes. Work with schools in the K–12 range is most informal and only beginning—i.e. through the pre-service teachers in our Holmes teacher education program and through the graduate teachers taking my elementary curriculum course. I hope in time to have some data on how this new sense of control works in their classes. In the meantime, the difference seen with these university students is amazing. The biggest change I make is in providing flexibility within a structured network, through which in-depth study of issues emerges. A number of shifting and interconnected foci or attractors emerge from the group and these are studied (recursively) over time from a number of varying perspectives. The aliveness or "spirit" of the classes operating in this manner is truly exciting. Meaningful issues (in curriculum construction, in mathematics, in teaching, in the living of life) are raised and their complexity studied. A curriculum matrix, not a linear sequencing, is being built, and this construction is the result of our group interactions (this volume, Chapters 19 and 22). As boatsperson I do steer, I steer or guide the creative energy we generate, an energy which propels our learning. 'Tis most fascinating to watch us navigate our way along the river of life and learning.

25

LOOKING FORWARD

(2006)

May God us keep, from single vision and Newton's sleep.

(William Blake , 1980 [1802])

We live in a rainbow of chaos.

(Paul Cézanne, 2006)

It is hard to believe that a scant decade and a half ago, Newton's Dream of a universe stable and secure, "consonant with Herself," guided by the universal law of gravity—would be shattered in the *fin de siècle* decade beginning in the 1990s. It was a most post-modern decade.[1] In that decade, we came to realize that the universe in which we live is expanding at an accelerating rate. It is true that in the 1920s Edwin Hubble had shown us that our universe was not so constant as Newton had believed, that it was expanding, but wishing to hold onto the Dream, we and our metaphysical assumptions paid little attention. At least, we did not revise our metaphysics; it still formed the foundation for our epistemology, including the way we taught. From the 1920s on we have averaged grades, set out our curricula in pre-set units, assumed a stable IQ, and taught from a centralized focus (what the teacher or text "knew").

The sense of a universe expanding at an accelerating rate has made us aware that Newton's Dream is no longer. Gravity is not the only force in the universe; nor, perhaps, the prime one. Gravity is not holding our universe together; other forces (are they dark forces?) are also at work. Indeed, we live, as Ilya Prigogine (with Isabelle Stengers, 1984) has said, in a most complex and chaotic universe, one filled

---

1 Supporting material for this essay can be found in Doll et al. (2005).

with shooting stars, black holes, great turbulence. Should it follow then that we have a "chaotic curriculum"? What an anathema! Yet, we must find a way to deal with our new "reality," develop a new metaphysics, look to a new future and see what is yet-to-be-seen.

Chaos does not need to be seen in dichotomous terms. This is a modernist frame— one we have been trying to leave behind. As I have said (Doll, 1993), chaos in ancient terms was the name for the rich material from whence came the world in which we live. Chaos was dark, deep, fecund, rich in the material that forms the universe: it was the "messy primordial source from which all being and organization sprang" (p. 86). Only with the rise of modernism, with its insistence on an either/or reality (chaos or order), did we separate chaos and order. Chaos, in the post-modern sense, much influenced by new directions in mathematics (chaos mathematics), harkens to the more ancient, pre-modern frame. Here chaos is no more than a *type* of order, a complex order, one we can trace deterministically but not predict from. That is, once an incident has occurred (a new planet, a new situation) we can look back and see "causes"—a modernist habit of thought— but the complexity of a situation is such that we cannot predict the future with any accuracy, certainly not with long-term accuracy. Not only is certainty an impossibility, there too many factors in play—we now realize that a small disturbance can, over time, result in large changes: metaphorically, a butterfly flapping its wings in Brazil can cause a typhoon in Japan—but also *prediction* is virtually impossible. Change, *dynamic* change (Fleener, 2002), needs to be our foundation. Newton's Dream of a stable universe has indeed been shattered.

So what does dynamical change mean for teaching, learning, curriculum, and instruction in the future? It means a number of *things* (my, it is hard to escape Newton's hard, massy, particles). I would suggest here three, from many one might develop.

First and foremost is the acceptance of change as a fundamental foundation (again, language of the modern rules our thoughts). With change as fundamental comes the realization that our curriculum and methods of instruction need to accept that the learner develops not just incrementally over time but actually undergoes some sort of transformation. A student who can read, or one who can understand the abstractions on which mathematics is based, is not the same student who previously did not possess these skills. What a student does can and indeed should be seen as transformative, not just as incremental. The "grades" a student receives in his senior year of college or university are far more important than the ones he receives in his or her freshman year. Even the work a student does at the end of a semester is more important than the work s/he does at the beginning of a semester. We need then to look not merely at grade point averages but at the work done, at the situations in themselves.

Secondly (if there is to be an ordering), to recognize situations in themselves (John Dewey tried so hard to have us realize the importance of each and every situation—the very foundation of American pragmatism) means we need to embrace (yes, embrace) complexity. With the complex comes a sense of the nonlinear. To teach in a nonlinear manner is a major challenge.[2] It means at least to teach in a way that honors conversation, difference, interaction. These three—conversation, difference, interaction—have been brought forth dramatically in the work of the great Chilean biologists, Humberto Maturana and Francisco Varela.[3] What they have said about visual perception and animal/human interaction is still reverberating in the complexity community. After reading these two authors, it is most hard to believe that we still accept the maxim that what we teach well will be learned well. Yet we proceed as though a well "taught" lesson is a well "learned" lesson—too simple, too ignoring of the situation at hand.[4]

Thirdly, not lastly nor finally, is the issue of interpretation. If one gives up the issue of centralized certainty—certainty found in texts, past practices, teacher's knowledge, etc.—what we have left is the art of interpretation. This art (hermeneutical in nature) coming from a desire to have some control, however slight, over a situation, requires us to honor interaction (listening to both students and situations), to utilize difference (seeing it as a positive for learning—no sense of self without an understanding of other), and to recognize that relationships (and patterns) are what A.N. Whitehead (1978 [1929]) calls, the "really real" (p. 23)

Developing all, even *any*, of these frames into practical operations is a challenge not easily met. We are so caught in a modernist frame that to think outside this box is a major struggle—as my small quips have pointed out. Let me, though, present a few activities I and others have developed over the years.[5] At the university level a seminar syllabus might be open-ended, starting with a seed from the teacher and then (with consultation from others in the seminar) opening to a plethora of ideas, which are then (with help from the teacher) drawn into a matrix of connections. In this manner, learning goes both deep and broad. With larger university or college classes, one might encourage students to utilize the internet to ferret out information on a given topic and then not merely to present that information to others but to *analyze* (and ask others to analyze) the *assumptions* underlying the information. At the school level (K–12) one might ask members of the class to

2　Teaching in a nonlinear manner is an important theme in the 4 C's book of Doll et al. (2005)—too complex to outline here.

3　The major works here are *Autopoiesis and cognition* (1980) and *The tree of knowledge* (1987). For a penetrating analysis of the arguments presented in these works see N. Kathryn Hayles, *How we became posthuman* (1999).

4　I am reminded here of the medical joke about the doctor who performed a magnificent operation, marred only by "the death of the patient." On a non-joke level one is reminded of the Swiss Air pilots who crashed with all lives lost off the coast of Nova Scotia in 2002 or the coal miners in West Virginia (2006) who died by "following the book." The whole issue of developing methods which are situational not universal is one we need to wrestle within our 21st century world.

5　Much of what I am to say here comes from work in the LSU Curriculum Theory Project and its graduates who have gone on to make their own contributions.

come up with alternative ways of solving a math problem, interpreting a story, designing an experiment, or evaluating a "fact." In all of these, one is working from Gregory Bateson's sense that it is "difference which makes a difference."[6]

It is indeed a strange and marvelous world we have yet to bring into existence (a strong Maturana and Varela point). As we so do, I encourage us to heed Milan Kundera's words: "There exists a fascinating imaginative realm, born of the echo of God's laughter where no one owns the truth and everyone has the right to be understood" (Milan Kundera, 1988).

---

6 Gregory Bateson's works are many. They are certainly highlighted in the 4 C's book, in Katherine Hayles book, and comments/analyses exist on my website: http://educ-calvin2. lsu.edu/~wdoll/

26

DA XIA LECTURE

THE WISDOM OF JOHN DEWEY

(2011)

The fear of a unitary solution makes for the beginning of wisdom.
(Michel Serres, 1991[1983])

There is wisdom in what Michel Serres says; wisdom, a word seldom used in Western thought today. Not only does French philosopher, social critic, and chaotician, Michel Serres argue *against* a unitary solution to a problem, he also states that in Western thought the concept of a unitary solution has been dominant, even rampant. The "rightness" tradition in Western thought has replaced its tradition of wisdom. Serres begins his quote with the remark that "Wisdom provides the yardstick of moderation," a quality espoused by the ancient Greek philosophers Plato and Aristotle, but rarely practiced by their followers. Certainly moderation was not part of imperial Rome and the stamp it put on Western religion and thought (1991[1983]). Nor has moderation been part of the Western political tradition of world colonization and domination in the centuries since. Today all of us are paying a dear price for the immoderation Western powers have exercised. Current world political and economic tragedies attest to this.

In the last decade of the 20th century, when Serres wrote *The troubadour of knowledge* (1997 [1991]), his hope was "that science [the West's shining star] could learn a tolerant wisdom that the other instances of power were never really able to learn and [thus] prevent a united, madly logical, rationally tragic world" (p. 122). With these words, worth reading over—a madly logical, rationally tragic world— Serres indicts all Western, rational thought (along with its "scientism"), and its pandering after certainty, not wisdom. It is hard to trace when Western thought turned from honoring wisdom to pandering after certainty. The Hebrew Old Testament of the Bible talks much of wisdom, even developing what has come to be called a wisdom–literature, from the biblical books of Job, Proverbs, Ecclesiastes (OED online, *s.v.* wisdom, definition 5). King Solomon is honored in both Jewish and Western literature for his wisdom. In fact, the book of Proverbs and other wisdom writings (10th to 6th centuries BCE) form a core of Jewish thought. Even the ancient Greeks, for all their exaltation of reason and the certainty it brings, had within their culture the Homeric stories of wisdom and folly. In his book, *The end of certainty* (1997), Ilya Prigogine talks of Homer's Achilles (8th century BCE) and his desire for god-like perfection, a type of certainty. Achilles' quest leads him to abandon the virtues and vicissitudes of humanity. His rage in not acquiring what he wants leads to his death, the disgrace of the Greeks fighting on Trojan soil, and the destruction of Troy itself (p. 186). Odysseus, the other main figure in Homer's tales of the Trojan War, chooses the vicissitudes of *humanity*. After 20 years of wandering and the tempting possibility of living forever in ideal bliss as the lover of Calypso, Odysseus returns to his home and hearth. In a sense, Odysseus chooses life; Achilles unwittingly "chooses" death. Humans in Western literature can, on occasion, display wisdom; ancient gods never do, for wisdom requires humility.[1]

John Dewey, in his *Quest for certainty* (1960 [1929]), puts forward the proposition that humans fear uncertainty, they wish to *feel* secure; certainty—whether real or imagined— provides this feeling. The Christian religion with its emphasis on eternal life helps provide this feeling, as does the belief that nature itself is mathematically designed, and hence humanly discoverable through mathematical reasoning. René Descartes (early/mid-17th century), a pillar of Western, rational, analytic thought, believed he had *the* "Method of Rightly Conducting One's Reason and Seeking Truth in the Sciences" (1950 [1637]). This method, and its *power*, was based on "long chains of mathematical reasoning," reinforced by Descartes' faith that God would not deceive one who reasoned as well as Descartes felt he had (p. 27). Serres (1983) ridicules Descartes by comparing him to a chess player who has God helping him with his moves (p. 27), hence his certainty of always winning, of having ultimate *power* of understanding the inner workings of Nature. This "mathematization of nature," with its concomitant belief in a perfect, stable, all knowing God, was a feature of the West's "scientific revolution" in the 16th and 17th centuries. Such a measurement mentality, Alfred Crosby (1998) points out, surfaced around the early 13th century with the introduction of mechanical clocks, became an obsession by the time of, and with, Descartes, and reached its solidifying form in Isaac Newton's *Mathematical principles of nature* (1962, 1972 [1729]).[2]

---

1   Prigogine (1997), citing Carl Rubino, says, "The wisdom of the *Iliad,* a bitter lesson that Achilles, its hero learns too late, is that such perfection can be gained only at the cost of one's humanity" (p. 186).

2   Prigogine (1997) refers his readers to Stephen Toulmin's *Cosmopolis* (1990) "to clarify the circumstances that lead Descartes on this quest ... the pursuit of certainty" (pp. 184–185).

> May God us keep, from single vision, and Newton's sleep.
>
> (William Blake, 1980[1802])

John Dewey (1960 [1929]) offers an interesting insight into the West's "single vision," into its search for rational certainty. He says, "modern philosophy inherited the framework of Greek ideas about the nature of knowledge" (its splitting of knowledge into the ideal/rational and the practical/experiential). "But it inherited them through the medium of Hebraic and [especially] Christian religion" (p. 51). The result was the scientific revolution of the 16th and 17th centuries, with its emphasis on experimentation (an emphasis Dewey made a feature of his pragmatist philosophy), encapsulated within a religious tradition. The moral righteousness of religion enveloped the probability assertions of scientific experimentalism. The activities of science took on a new aura, that of religious certainty. In a word, Science replaced God; or more correctly the "warranted assertions" that scientists could make became clothed in the righteous certainty of religion. In A.N. Whitehead's felicitous phrase, reason (thinking) now became "one-eyed" (1967a [1925], p. 59); it could not look back on itself, actively reflect, question its fundamental assumptions, or lead us to a new world, one not "madly logical, rationally tragic." The procedures adopted by Western science and exported to a willingly accepting world became, ironically, rigid and sacrosanct. This Dewey never wanted, this he always decried.

Wisdom is not a word Dewey uses often but when he does, as in "Philosophy and democracy" (1970a [1919]), he brings forth his hope for the future, a hope that led him away from Western societies to look at those of China and Russia. As is well known, democracy for Dewey is not the political, representative democracy practiced in many Western countries; rather it is a form of associated living, a "social hope" enacted through "disciplined" inquiry and "serious" reflective thought (p. 843). Like life itself, democracy is always in transformation.

Before examining Dewey's concept of wisdom, I'd like to look at the word in English, and at Michel Serres' ruminations on it in his *Conversations with Bruno Latour* (Serres and Latour, 1995 [1990]). In English, the word "wisdom" (OED online, 2010; *Oxford English Dictionary*, 2nd edition, 1989) has a long history, going back more than 1,000 years. It is strongly connected with wise, often spelled *wisedome* or *wisedam*. As "the capacity of judging rightly," or displaying "soundness of judgement in the choice of means and ends," it is opposite to "folly" (Definition 1a.). More interesting in the dictionary definitions, I believe, is the notion that wisdom is separate from knowledge: "Knowledge and Wisdom, far from being one, Have ofttimes no connexion," for "Knowledge is proud … . Wisdom is humble" (William Cowper, 1785, pp. vi, 88 and 97). Alfred Lord Tennyson presents this distinction: "Knowledge is earthly of the mind, But Wisdom heavenly of the soul" (1850, pp. cxiv, 22). Knowledge is of earthly science, logic, reason; wisdom is of human ideals, aesthetics, morality. The word *right* has different meanings in each genre: in knowledge it refers to correctness, in wisdom it refers to goodness.

There is no record of Michel Serres every having read William Cowper's poem, *The task* (1785),[3] but Cowper's distinction between knowledge (proud in its learning) and wisdom (humble in its knowing) presages Serres' concerns about knowledge that exists without humility. Knowledge focuses on the *What* and *Is*. To know is to be aware of what an object is. Great as knowledge is, it can *kill*: abort new knowledge, and of greater import, lead to violence.[4] Knowledge, especially scientific knowledge—which after World War II exploded in domain after domain, quickly becoming, as Jerome Bruner (1986a) says "our paradigmatic way of thinking" (p. 13)—o'er leaps itself when it is not moderated with humility. Our strength as humans, as teachers, Serres says, lives in recognizing our limitations as humans. Wisdom involves weakness: "Wisdom and Weakness go together" (Serres and Latour, 1995 [1990], p. 186). The Christian God demonstrated his strength not through his power to do, but through enduring human suffering. Serres wonders, "In all the animal kingdom what animal is more dangerous to his fellow creatures and the Earth than the arrogant adult human male who has succeeded [as did Achilles] in competitive life?" (Serres and Latour, 1995 [1990], p. 186). For Serres, the greatest sin ever committed by man was the twice successful bombing of Hiroshima. This atrocity turned him away from science, with its emphasis on knowledge, to the humanities with its emphasis on moral values. The relation between "science and violence," between the power scientific thinking has acquired and the violence it has spawned, has occupied Serres since the "universal noise of Hiroshima" (p. 16). He says, "Hiroshima remains the sole object of my philosophy"; its problematic can be found "on every page of my books" (p. 15). It was not the quantity of destruction, great as this was, that was so devastating, but the rational ("good") reasons given for its necessity. Ends and means were so separated that a good end (the end of the war) justified any means (total annihilation). As one general is reputed to have said, "it was necessary to destroy, in order to preserve." Here is logical rationality gone mad. Since this time, the end of World War II, "man" has acquired a new sense of *power*: a power to create and a power to destroy—all planetary life. Serres says: "We are the masters of the Earth, and we are constructing a world that is almost universally miserable and that is becoming the objective, founding *given* of our future" (p. 177); a future

---

3   William Cowper, son of a Herefordshire clergyman, was a much admired 18th century poet, a forerunner of the Romantic poets of England. Given to despair and madness, he wrote much of God and His love. As a scholar, Cowper did his own translation of Homer's *Iliad* from the Greek into English. *The task: A poem in six books* is generally considered his masterpiece.

4   "To know is to kill," and "Man is the wolf of science," are two of Serres' more startling statements in his essay, "Knowledge in the classical age" (1983). Each is open to varied interpretations, as is Serres' wont. Reflection on each, though, brings forth insights not immediately recognized. The second statement makes Serres' point that it is man, not science, which is the wolf.

we will pass on to our children and their children. It is the "founding given." As we in the West have acquired power to conquer, we find ourselves conquered by power. We are slaves to our own creations: "Our new mastery ... limits our freedom." "No sooner is it announced that something is *possible* than ... it is almost as quickly considered *desirable,* and by the next day it is *necessary*" (p. 171; emphasis in original).[5] Ultimately the United States dropped those atomic bombs because they *could* drop them. The power to do (power from technology) became separated from the wisdom of humanity. Serres believes that since the development of the atomic bomb—able to annihilate the whole planet and hence all life—it has "become urgent to rethink scientific optimism," particularly "the relationship between science and violence" (pp. 15–16). As the power of science increases, so does the power of violence increase. Each reinforces the other.

This is not to say Serres rejects science, far from it; rather he wishes to reform our relation to science and its methods, which, even if moderated, are still the West's shining star. If science can acquire a "tolerant wisdom the other instances of power were never really able to learn," then "a madly logical, rationally tragic world" might be avoided (1997 [1991]). To quote Serres:

> Knowledge is certainly excellent, but in the same way cold is: when it remains cool. Science assuredly, is just and useful, but the way heat is: if it remains mild. Who denies the utility of flame and ice? Science is good, who denies it, and ever, I am sure, one thousand times better than a thousand other things that are also good, *but if it claims that it is the only good and the whole good,* and if it behaves as if this were the case, then it enters into a dynamic of madness.
>
> (p. 122; emphasis added)

And,

> It would be dangerous if the hard sciences came to pass themselves off as the only way of thinking.

And,

> What does the rigor or the depth of a theorem matter if it ends up killing men, or making an excessive power weigh on them.
>
> (p. 122)

The reformation of science, really of our *thinking* about science and its way of thinking, brings Serres to call for a new education (pedagogy), one able to encourage

---

5   Looking ahead to Dewey's distinction between *desired* and *desirable,* I believe the translator might better have chosen desired instead of desirable.

the creation of a new person, a hybrid, a new hero, "'*le Tiers Instruit*'—'the Instructed Third,' or 'the Troubadour of Knowledge'"(p. 183). Serres goes on:

> The troubadour of knowledge, who is of both science and letters, has some chance of instituting the age of adulthood for which we hope. He is admittedly a rationalist, but he does not believe that all the requirements of reason are met by science. He tempers one with the other. Likewise, he never sees the social sciences as exhausting the content transmitted by the humanities—far from it. So, for him there is as much rigor in a myth or a work of literature as in a theorem or an experiment and, inversely, as much myth in these as in literature.
>
> (p. 183)

Serres' hero is indeed a new (*hu*)*man*, quite unlike the industrial *man* Auguste Comte, Claude Henri de Rouvroy, Pierre Laplace, saw emerging 200 years ago, an "engineer, builder, planner" (Doll, 1993, p. 21), a rational technocrat who in his quantification, his "measurement of reality" has given the Western world a model it has emulated. As a "third instructed," Serres' hero understands the need not simply to balance scientific measurement with humanistic insight but, more, to interplay these two to create a "third." A third person, instructed by a new, third curriculum. At the end of *Troubadour* (1997 [1991]), Serres has a two-line aphorism (p. 166):

> Reborn, he knows, he takes pity.
> Finally, he can teach.

The Troubadour, reborn of new understanding, knows that scientific thought left alone leads to violence; it must be tempered with the wisdom and morality of the humanities. Understanding the pitiful situation we have created, "this sage who knows but is capable of pity" can now teach (Serres and Latour, 1995 [1990], p. 188). One of the many "knowledges" the Troubadour has acquired is that our world needs a new morality, one based on wisdom: a wisdom which "will weave the warp of the rediscovered humanities to the woof of expert exactitude"—the sciences (p. 184). This new morality is based on our responsibility for the new power we have created with our ever increasing technological advances, a power over the life and death of ourselves and of the planet on which we live. This new morality deals with our human responsibility for all we have created. As such it is universal, applying to all of us, personally and collectively. Ethics, a word often used interchangeably with morals or morality is more relative: "perhaps ethics depend on cultures and places and are relative, like customs. Ethics are aligned with ideology" (p. 192). What we consider to be ethical varies from culture to culture, from time to time. Always, though, ethical choices are made according to the cultural rules and regulations in place, at a time. Morality, more universal as it deals with human responsibility, refers to the personal choices, decisions humans make.[6] Emphasis on responsibility is important for Serres. Having created technologies with their awesome power of controlling human and planetary life and death, we personally and collectively are responsible for the moral use of these technologies—to provide a better, less violent life for all that exists.

Serres (Serres and Latour, 1995 [1990]) begins his Fifth Conversation with Latour (on Wisdom), with the remark that the word *sapiens*, as in *homo sapiens*—man the knowledgeable or wise—comes from the Greek *sage*. It "derives from a verb that means having taste, subtly sensing flavors and aromas" (p. 167). In short, *discerning* subtle differences. The wise person, in displaying wisdom, is able to discern, and with that discernment is able to make moral decisions. Discernment is a quality we need to foster in our contemporary world, in our school curricula. To have discernment as a guiding light in school curricula is not to remove our modernist emphasis on right/wrong or the following of rules; it is, rather, to place this emphasis in a broader, moral context. A context of discernment is one where the situation at hand is the primary focus. Choices, decisions, are made within this situational context. Responsibility now shifts from the ethical one of following cultural rules set by others to choices one makes as a person. Wisdom adopts a practical hue; it is the morality of everyday living.

As practical morality, wisdom necessarily entails acknowledgment of evil. If there is no sense of, recognition of, evil, then there is no morality, only blind adherence to an ideology. Too often this is an ideology based on power. Morality, based on rational choice, is practical reason in action. As rational choice, it involves discerning the difference between good and evil. Looked at objectively, scientifically, we see that evil is always with us. It cannot be eradicated. It has existed since humans first acquired the ability to reason; it is universal. Once we look at evil scientifically, that is objectively, we will see, Serres believes, that as we have attacked the evils of poverty, famine, destruction, terrorism, we have, ironically, only increased these evils. Our Western wars on poverty, crime, terrorism, coming, as they do, from a single-sighted vision—reason unmitigated by humility and pity—"is always lost because we and the enemy find renewed force in the relationship" (p. 195). Each, ironically, reinforces the other; as we try to eliminate evil, we increase its presence. Serres provides an alternative: instead of fighting against —"disease, germs, violence"—it may be better to find a "symbiotic" relationship, a relationship where we *work with* instead of against. Fighting to eliminate or conquer provides winners and losers, or really, as Serres points out ("Knowledge in the classical age," 1983), greater and lesser losers. Instead of developing an antagonistic relationship, one where all are losers,

6   The distinction between morality and ethics is a subtle one, often not made. Dictionary definitions tend to conflate the two, using each as a synonym for the other. Reading the many definitions for each word though does reveal a pattern: "Morals define personal character, while ethics stress a social system in which those morals are applied. In other words, ethics point to standards or codes of behavior expected by the group to which the individual belongs." Retrieved December 14, 2010, from http://www.wisegeek.com/what-is-the-difference-between-ethics-and-morals.htm

Serres suggests it might be better to develop a symbiotic relationship, taking the bacteria in curdled milk and turning it into "delicious cheeses" (p. 195), or genetically mutating cancerous cells to productive, healthy ones. Such a transformative thrust, Serres believes, lies at the heart of a new curriculum, one designed to encourage the emergence of *le tiers instruit* (the third instructed).

John Dewey does not use the metaphorical language Michel Serres does but he definitely agrees with Serres on the need of a new curriculum, a third-curriculum, a transformative curriculum. It is fair to say that transformation as a concept lies at the heart of Dewey's educational philosophy: "the real problem of intellectual education is the transformation of natural powers [those we all possess, child and adult] into expert, tested powers" (1971 [1933], p. 84). Transformational change has been my study in my years as a Dewey student. By no means do I claim to be a Dewey scholar, as I am still much a learner. As for connections between Dewey's concept of wisdom and the Wisdom traditions of China, I would do both you and myself a disservice by attempting more than a cursory connection. Instead, I will present what I hope is a fair reading of Dewey's comments about transformation and wisdom. In so doing, I bring forth what I believe are unfortunate, albeit easily made, misinterpretations of Dewey writings, made by many Western educators. I say here "easily made" misinterpretations, for Dewey's writing is not always clear. Oliver Wendell Holmes Jr., the great American jurist and fan of Dewey, said upon reading Dewey's magnum opus, *Experience and nature* (1958a [1929]), "it seemed to me to have a feeling of intimacy with the universe. ... So methought God would have spoken had He been inarticulate but keenly desirous to tell you how it was" (in Menand, 2002, p. 437).

I start with a well known quote from *The child and the curriculum* (1966b [1902]). This quote progressive educators have rallied around for decades: "How, then, stands the case of Child vs. Curriculum? ... The case is of Child" (pp. 30–31). Progressive educators internationally, including the 1920's Chinese educational reform movement, have taken these two statements to develop what has become known as a "child-centered curriculum." This is an unfortunate interpretation, one Dewey tried unsuccessfully to counter in his 1938 address to the Progressive Education Association (1963 [1938], Ch. 1).

Dewey's curriculum is not a centered one, at least in the sense of a center being a place, a fixed, static focus. Dewey's focus is on the process of transformation. As a *process*, it is a changing curriculum one where the child (or learner) and curriculum are each transformed as they interact with one another. Earlier in this essay Dewey says:

> The child and the curriculum are simply two limits which define a single process. Just as two points define a straight line, so the present standpoint of the child and the facts and truths of studies define instruction. It is *continuous reconstruction*, moving from the child's present experience out into that represented by the organized bodies of truth that we call studies.
>
> (1990 [1902], p. 189; emphasis added)

He continues:

> The child's present experience is in no way self-explanatory. It is not final, but too often progressive educators, the world over, confine their gaze to what the child here and now puts forth, without realizing these are only signs of possible growth tendencies.
>
> (p. 191)

Probably Dewey's strongest comment against a child-centered education comes from his later reflection on his Chicago Laboratory School: "Contrary to an impression about the school which has prevailed since it was founded and which many visitors carried away with them at the time … is the idea … that it must be child-centered. … The school was 'community centered'" (in Mayhew and Edwards, 1966 [1936], p. 465).

I propose that the purpose of education for Dewey is to have the child's (learner's) tendencies grow toward the "good." Indeed the child's (or learner's) nascent powers are to be shaped toward a moral end. This shaping (or maturing), though, is not to be done by the teacher, nor by any outside, impositional force; rather it is to foster the individual's own development. Dewey did not believe in forcing learners to learn, did not believe it could happen in any meaningful or lasting way. As he says: "There is a strong temptation to assume that presenting subject matter in its perfected form provides a royal road to learning," hence saving the immature "time and energy … and needless error," allowing learners to begin their own learning from "where competent inquirers have left off" (1966a [1916], p. 220). In reality, what happens, though, is the teacher places "intellectual blinders" on the learner. In this case, the teacher is not helping students develop their own thinking, their own moral choices, but rather restricting "their vision to the one path the teacher's mind happens to approve" (p. 175). Wisdom begins with the fear of a unitary solution.

Wisdom, says Dewey, is "a moral term … it refers to a choice about something to be done" (1970a [1919], p. 844). It is not simply knowledge, it is more than knowledge: "It is an intellectualized wish, an aspiration subjected to rational discriminations and tests, a *social hope* reduced to a working program of action, a prophecy of the future, but one disciplined by serious thought," reflective thought (p. 843). Wisdom for Dewey, as for Serres, and for Confucius, I believe, is practical wisdom; it is making moral choices in everyday life situations, not simply a judgment but a decision about how to go forward. It means being attentive to the *situation*, being able to discern (intuit, feel, perceive) both consequences and possible pitfalls.[7] It occurs when we reflect on past actions and possible future actions. There is, in terms I use as a complexity theorist, a recursive process to our thought. It

---

7   I see this process of discernment akin to Bateson's notion of looking for the difference that makes a difference. Taking it a step further, discernment is not for the purpose of creating either/or distinctions—and stopping there—but rather to be able to understand

is common to align Dewey with what is often called in educational circles, the "scientific method," a five-step, linear process of defining a problem, assembling data, developing hypotheses, looking for alternative possibilities, testing the results of the action chosen. What is too often overlooked in this process is that (1) it is too linear and rigid, leading, Dewey believed, to pedagogical theory's disrepute (1966a [1916], p. 170); and (2) preceding any problem identification there needs to be a "feeling" for the situation in which the problem is located. This "feeling" has an aesthetic, even a moral quality to it; it is nurtured by aesthetic discrimination, brought to the fore by the realization that every choice is a moral choice about right actions. This wisdom aspect of Dewey has been overlooked for too long by those of us trained in Western, one-eyed reason.

As a practical activity, wisdom guides our recognizing and bringing to fruition, the "social hope" of a better society, transforming "that desired into that desirable" (Dewey, 1939a, p. 31).[8] This transformation occurs as we choose, act, reflect in a never-ending process. For Dewey, this transformative process occurs as we are attentive to the situation in which we are enmeshed. His "attentiveness" though is Western, even very American. He says (1958b [1934]), we must "plunge into" the situation, experiencing it "aesthetically," be "absorbed" by it, "feel" it, intuit the possibilities and pitfalls in it, actually-almost "surrendering ourselves to it": "[It is not easy] to understand the intimate union of doing and undergoing ... the esthetic or undergoing phase of experience ... involves surrender. But adequate yielding of the self is possible only through a controlled activity that may well be intense" (pp. 48–56, *passim*).

This being absorbed into a situation, feeling it aesthetically, morally, actually-almost surrendering ourselves to it is not a unilateral act nor an act of resignation, for then Dewey says, as we are actually-almost absorbed into the situation, "we must summon energy and pitch it at a responsive, key" (p. 53). In short, we need to be so attuned to the situation that its problematics, potentialities, pitfalls energize us for further action. We grow through our challenges and how we respond to those challenges. Simply, our school curricula need to be rich with challenges (Doll, 1993, Ch. 7).

One of Dewey's interesting thoughts, to me at least, is the notion that "inquiry can develop its own ongoing course of logical standards ... to which *further* inquiry shall submit." In short, external standards, rules, ethics are not needed, for inquiry is a "self-corrective process" (1966c [1938], p. 5), of choosing, acting, reacting, and choosing again. This is, though, a problematic to be pursued at another time.

I'd like to close this lecture by commenting on a statement by Alfred North Whitehead, a contemporary of John Dewey. The quotation can be found in Lucien

---

a situation in greater depth, nuance, richness, and therefore to be able to think about future possibilities and implications/ramifications of one's choices and actions.

8   This phrasing is my own but reflects Dewey's intent written in many essays. The one referred to here, from his "Theory of valuation" (1939a), expresses this relation well.

Price's *Dialogues of Alfred North Whitehead* (1954), a book written a few years after Whitehead's death. It reads, "If you want to understand Confucius, read John Dewey. And if you want to understand John Dewey, read Confucius" (p. 176). This is an unusual comment since at first blush it seems to put together in a praising fashion two people who lived centuries apart, in different intellectual times, with different cultural backgrounds. In reality, the remark is meant to show that over the centuries and across cultures there has been a tendency to elevate facts over questions. Whitehead states that Confucius believed "simple facts ought to suffice," there being no need to "ask questions about the ultimacies under those facts." Dewey, while himself a questioner, spawned an educational movement (based on American pragmatist thought)[9] that Whitehead saw as degenerating into the same "simple facts ought to suffice." Whitehead saw a fact-oriented culture as static and superficial. For creativity and imagination to emerge in a culture, it is necessary, Whitehead asserts, to pay attention to the ultimacies underlying facts, to ask "superfluous" and "silly questions" about the facts, for in "the 'silly questions' is the first intimation of some totally novel development" (p. 177). Accepting the value of silly questions, necessary for "keeping knowledge alive" (Doll, 2005a; this volume, Chapter 12), as well as accepting his important notion of honoring *process*, Whitehead's own reading of China, Confucius, and even of Dewey was, unfortunately, superficial.[10] Dewey's view of China and its future, and of Confucius and his wisdom is far more insightful, even if written almost a century ago. About Confucius he comments, Confucianism "magnifies the importance of art, of culture, of humanity, of learning and moral effort" (1970b [1922], p. 207), all areas dear to Dewey's heart. In regard to China in the 1920s and its future, Dewey shows a deep appreciation for Chinese traditions and thought, including the values in *feng-shui*. He notes that this tradition could be looked upon as a mythical superstition hindering what the West calls *progress* as it impeded the building of railroads and development of mining. Looked at more deeply, though, one sees "that the doctrine of Feng-shui is a remarkable exhibition of piety toward nature … and conservation" (p. 207). Dewey then goes on to place this conservatism against the West's, especially America's, sense of

---

9 Whitehead, commenting in the 1940s, worried about China's pandering after "20th century American ideas," and wondered if their own culture had the resources to help them "develop in their own way" (Price, 1954, p. 315). Would not Whitehead be most surprised at 21st century China!

10 I wish in no way wish to deprecate Whitehead and the contributions he has made to intellectual and educational thought. Alive ideas, creativity, process thinking, relations (not things) being the really real, have all been inspirations for my own thinking about "teaching good" (Doll, 2006). He has been one of my guiding lights. Rather I make this statement to encourage others to read Whitehead and to point out that in the area of understanding the virtues and values of Chinese thought, no one from the West has greater insights on China than John Dewey. All who read his comments on China and its traditions will be enlightened.

progress, and questions whether the concept of progress, so prevalent in the early 20th century had been and would continue to be good for the world.

In so doing, Dewey's thoughts on capitalism, China, Confucius, and progress, bring me back to Serres and his worry about the "madly logical, rationally tragic world" Western thought has spawned. It may well be that our Western vision has been too narrowly focused, not fearful enough of its own "rightness." We in the West need to adopt a broader, more complex vision.

REFERENCES

Advances in Chemical Physics. (2007). Special issue on Ilya Prigogine. S. A. Rice, (Ed.),Vol.135. Hoboken, NJ:Wiley.

American Heritage Dictionary of the English language. (1969).William Morris (Ed.). NewYork: American Heritage.

Aoki,T. (2005a).Teaching as indwelling between two curriculum worlds. In William F. Pinar and Rita L. Irwin (Eds.), *Curriculum in a new key:The collected works of Ted T.Aoki* (pp. 159–165). Mahwah, NJ: Erlbaum. (Original publication 1986, reprinted 1991.)

Aoki, T. (2005b). *Curriculum in a new key. The collected works of Ted. T. Aoki.* W. Pinar and R. Irwin (Eds.). Mahwah, NJ: Erlbaum.

Argyros,A. (1991). *A blessed rage for order.* Ann Arbor, MI: University of Michigan Press.

Aristotle. (1961). *Aristotle's physics.* R. Hope (Trans.). Lincoln, NE: University of Nebraska Press.

Arnstine, D. G. (1964). The language and values of programmed instruction: Part 2, *The Educational Forum 28*(3), 337–346.

Atkinson, D. (1985). Evolutionary process from chaos to order. *Los Angeles Times,* June 8, Part II, p. 2. Retrieved from http://articles.latimes.com/1985-06-08/local/me-7243_1_hydrogen-atoms-order-evolution

Bak, P. (1996). *How nature works.* NewYork: Springer-Verlag.

Bateson, G. (1972). *Steps to an ecology of mind.* NewYork: Ballantine.

Bateson, G. (1988). *Mind and nature.* NewYork: Bantam Books. (Original publication, 1979.)

Bateson, G., and Bateson, M. C. (1987). *Angels fear.* NewYork: Macmillan.

Beilin, H., and Pufall, P. (1992). *Piaget's theory.* Hillside, NJ: Erlbaum.

Berman, M. (1981). *The reenchantment of the world.* Ithaca, NY: Cornell University Press.

Berman, M. (1989). *Coming to our senses.* NewYork: Simon and Schuster.

Bernstein, R. (1983). *Beyond objectivism and relativism.* Philadelphia, PA: University of Pennsylvania Press.

Bernstein, R. (1985). *Habermas and modernity.* Cambridge, MA: MIT Press.

Bernstein, R. (1986). *Philosophical profiles.* Philadelphia, PA: University of Pennsylvania Press.

Bernstein, R. (1992). *The new constellation.* Cambridge, MA: MIT Press.

Berry, T. (1988a). *Creative energy*. San Francisco, CA: Sierra Club Books.

Berry, T. (1988b). *The dream of the earth*. San Francisco, CA: Sierra Club Books.

Berry, T. (1992). *The universe story*. San Francisco, CA: Harper.

Berry, T. (1995). *Befriending the earth*. Mystic, CN: 23rd Publications.

Bertonneau, T. (1986). Discourse and disocculation: An interview with Timothy Reiss. *Paroles Gelées, UCLA French Studies 4*, 4–13.

Biesta, G. J. J. (2010). "This is my truth, tell me yours." Deconstructive pragmatism as a philosophy for education. *Educational Philosophy and Theory 42*(7), 710–727.

Biesta, G. J. J., and Burbules, N. (2003). *Pragmatism and educational research*. Lanham, MD: Rowman and Littlefield.

Black, M. (1990). *Perplexities*. Ithaca, NY: Cornell University Press.

Blake, W. (1980). Letter to Thomas Butt, 22 November 1802. In G. Keynes (Ed.), *The letters of William Blake* (3rd edition, revised). New York: Oxford. (Original publication, 1802.)

Blake, W. (1991). *Songs of innocence and experience*. A. Lincoln (Ed.), Princeton, NJ: Princeton University Press. (Original publication, 1789.)

Block, A. (2004). *Talmud, curriculum, and the practical*. New York: Lang.

Bloom, B. S. (1956). *Taxonomy of educational objectives: Handbook I, The cognitive domain*. New York: McKay.

Bourgeois, L. (1998). Journal entry for EDCI 7824, LSU, Spring, 1998.

Bowers, C. A. (1993). *Critical essays*. New York: Teachers College Press.

Bowers, C. A. (1995). *Educating for an ecologically sustainable culture*. Albany, NY: SUNY Press.

Bowers, C. A. 1987. *Elements of a post-liberal theory of education*. New York: Teachers College Press.

Bowers, C. A., and Flinders, D. (1990). *Responsive teaching*. New York: Teachers College Press.

Bronowski, J. (1978). *The common sense of science*. Cambridge, MA: Harvard University Press.

Browne, M. W. (1989). In heartbeat, predictability is worse than chaos. *New York Times*, January 17, Section C, page 9: http://www.nytimes.com/1989/01/17/science/in-heartbeat-predictability-is-worse-than-chaos.html. Retrieved, January 17, 1989.

Bruner, J. (1959). Learning and thinking. *Harvard Educational Review 29*(3), 184–193.

Bruner, J. (1960). *The process of education*. Cambridge, MA: Harvard University Press.

Bruner, J. (1961). The act of discovery. *Harvard Educational Review, 31*(1), 21–32.

Bruner, J. (1973). *Beyond the information given*. J. M. Anglin (Ed.). New York: W. W. Norton.

Bruner, J. (1986a). Two modes of thought. In *Actual minds, possible worlds*, (pp. 11–43). Cambridge, MA: Harvard University Press.

Bruner, J. (1986b). *Actual minds, possible worlds*. Cambridge, MA: Harvard University Press.

Bruner, J. (1996). *The culture of education*. Cambridge, MA: Harvard University Press.

Bruner, J., Jolly, A., and Sylva, K. (Eds.) (1976). *Play: Its role in development and evolution*. New York: Basic Books.

Buckreis, S. (2010). Reflections on teaching: Dwelling in a third space. Doctoral Dissertation, Louisiana State University and Agricultural and Mechanical College.

Burtt, E. A. (1955). *The metaphysical foundations of modern physical science*. New York: Doubleday, Anchor Books. (Original publication, 1932.)

Caine, R. N., and Caine, G. (1994). *Making connections: Teaching and the human brain*, (revised). Menlo Park, CA: Addison-Wesley.

Caine, R. N., and Caine, G. (1997). *Education on the edge of possibility*. Alexandria, VA: ASCD.

Caine, G., Caine. R. N., and Crowell, S. (1995). *Mindshifts*, (revised 1999). Tucson, AZ: Zephyr Press.

Callahan, R. E. (1962). *Education and the cult of efficiency*. Chicago, IL: University of Chicago Press.

Cangelosi, J. S. (1993). *Classroom management strategies: Gaining and maintaining students' cooperation*, (2nd edition), New York: Longman.

Capra, F. (1996). *The web of life. A new scientific understanding of living systems.* New York: Anchor/Doubleday Books.

Cézanne, P. (2006). http://www.gardendigest.com/complex.htm#Quotes

Chomsky, N. (1964). Formal discussion. In U. Bellugi and R. Brown (Eds.), *The acquisition of language* (pp. 36–42). Chicago, IL: University of Chicago Press.

Chomsky, N. (1966). *Topics in the theory of generative grammar.* The Hague: Mouton.

Chomsky, N. (1968). *Language and mind* (enlarged edition). New York: Harcourt, Brace, Jovanovich.

Chomsky, N. (1975). *Reflections on language.* New York: Pantheon Books.

Chomsky, N. (1977). *Language and responsibility.* New York: Pantheon Books.

Cilliers, P. (2000). *Complexity and postmodernism.* London: Routledge.

Cohen, J. and Stewart, I. (1995). *The collapse of chaos. Discovering simplicity in a complex world.* New York: Penguin Books.

Comenius, J. (1896). *The great didactic of Johann Amos Comenius*, M. W. Keatinge (Trans.), London: Adam and Charles Black. (Original publication, 1632.)

Copernicus, N. (1976). *De revolutionibus*, A. M. Duncan (Trans.), New York: Barnes and Noble. (Original publication, 1543.)

Cowper, W. (1785). *The task: A poem in six books.* http://www.ccel.org/c/cowper/works/task.html. Retrieved December 8, 2010.

Craig, H. (1952). *The enchanted glass.* London: Henderson & Spalding. (Original publication, 1935.)

Crosby, A. W. (1998). *The measure of reality: Quantification and Western society, 1250–1600.* Cambridge: Cambridge University Press.

Crowley, D., and Mitchell, D. (1994). Communications in Canada: Enduring themes, emerging issues. In Terry Goldie, Carmen Lambert and Rowland Lorimer (Eds.), *Canada: Theoretical discourse* (pp. 133–152). Montreal: Association for Canadian Studies.

Dante. (1915). *The divine comedy.* H. Johnson (Trans.), New Haven, CT: Yale University Press. (Original Italian publication, early 14th century.)

Darwin, C. (1964). *The origin of species.* Cambridge, MA: Harvard University Press. (Original publication, 1859.)

Davies, B. (1995). *Poststructuralist theory and classroom practice.* Geelong, Victoria: Deakin University.

Davies, P. (1983). *God and the new physics.* New York: Simon and Schuster.

Davies, P. (1988). *The cosmic blueprint: New discoveries in nature's creative ability to order the universe.* New York: Simon and Schuster.

Davies, P. (1992). *The mind of God.* New York: Simon and Schuster.

Davies, P. (1995). *Are we alone?* New York: Basic Books.

Davis, B. (2009) Languaging, irony, and bottomless bottoms. *Complicity, 6*(1), 34–8.

Davis, B., and Sumara, D. (2002). Constructivist discourses and the field of education: Problems and possibilities. *Educational Theory, 52*(4), 409–428.

Davis, B., and Sumara, D. (2006). *Complexity and education: Inquiries into learning, teaching, and research.* Mahweh, NJ: Erlbaum

Deleuze, G. (2005). *Pure immanence: Essays on a life.* A. Boyman (Trans.), New York: Zone.

Depew, D., and Weber, B. (1984). *Evolution at a crossroads.* Cambridge, MA: MIT Press.

Derrida, J. (1994). *Specters of Marx.* P. Kamuf (Trans.), New York: Routledge. (Original French publication, 1993.)

Derrida. J. (1995). *The gift of death*. D. Wills (Trans.), Chicago, IL: University of Chicago Press. (Original French publication, 1992.)

Descartes, R. (1950). *Discourse on method*. L. LaFleur (Trans.), New York: Liberal Arts (Original French publication, 1637.)

Descartes, R. (1985). Discourse on the method of rightly conducting one's reason and seeking truth in the sciences. In J. Cottingham, R. Stoothhoff, and D. Murdoch (Eds.), R. Stoothoff (Trans.), *The philosophical writings of Descartes, Vol. 1* (pp. 111–151), Cambridge: Cambridge University Press.

Dewey, J. (1939a). Theory of valuation. *International encyclopedia of unified science, II*(4). Chicago, IL: University of Chicago Press.

Dewey, J. (1939b). Experience, knowledge and value: A rejoinder. In P. A. Schilpp (Ed.), *The Philosophy of John Dewey*. Menasha, WI: Banta.

Dewey, J. (1957). *Human nature and conduct*. New York: The Modern Library. (Original publication, 1922.)

Dewey, J. (1958a). *Experience and nature* (2nd. edition). Mineola, NY: Dover Publications. (Original publication, 1929.)

Dewey, J. (1958b). *Art as experience*. New York: Capricorn. (Original publication, 1934.)

Dewey, J. (1960). *The quest for certainty*. New York: Capricorn Books. (Original publication, 1929.)

Dewey, J. (1962). *Individualism old and new*. New York: Capricorn Books. (Original publication, 1929.)

Dewey, J. (1963). *Experience and education*. New York: Collier Books. (Original publication, 1938.)

Dewey, J. (1964). The nature of aims. In R. Archambault (Ed.), *John Dewey on education* (pp. 70–80). New York: The Modern Library. (Original publication, 1922.)

Dewey, J. (1966a). *Democracy and education*. New York: Free Press. (Original publication, 1916.)

Dewey, J. (1966b). *The child and the curriculum*. Chicago, IL: University of Chicago Press. (Original publication, 1902.)

Dewey, J. (1966c). *Logic: A theory of inquiry*. New York: Holt, Rinehart and Winston. (Original publication, 1938.)

Dewey, J. (1966d). *Reconstruction in philosophy* (enlarged edition), Boston, MA: Beacon Press. (Original publication, 1948.)

Dewey, J. (1970a). Philosophy and democracy. In J. Ratner (Ed.), *Characters and events* Vol. II (pp. 841–855). New York: Octagon Books. (Original publication 1919.)

Dewey, J. (1970b). The Chinese philosophy of Life. In J. Ratner (Ed.), *Characters and events*. Vol. I (pp. 199–210). New York: Octagon Books. (Original publication 1922.)

Dewey, J. (1971). *How we think* (revised edition). Chicago, IL: Henry Regnery. (Original publication, 1933.)

Dewey, J. (1980). *Art as experience*. New York: Penguin. (Original publication, 1934.)

Dewey, J. (1990). *The school and society and The child and the curriculum*. Chicago, IL: The University of Chicago Press. (Original publications, 1900, 1902.)

Dewey, J. (1997). *How we think*. Mineola, NY: Dover Publications. (Original publication, 1910.)

Dewey, J. (1998). *The essential Dewey: Pragmatism, education, democracy*, Vol. I. L. Hickman and T. Alexander (Eds.) Bloomington, IN: Indiana University Press.

Dewey, J., and Archambault, R. D. (1964). *John Dewey on education: Selected writings*. Chicago, il: University of Chicago Press.

Dewey, J. and Bentley, A. (1964). *John Dewey and Arthur F. Bentley. A philosophical correspondence, 1932–1951*. Piscataway, NJ: Rutgers University Press.

Doll, W. E., Jr. (1972). A methodology of experience, Part I. *Educational theory 22*(3), 309–324.

Doll, W. E., Jr. (1973). A methodology of experience, Part II. *Educational theory 23*(1), 56–73.

Doll, W. E., Jr. (1977). The role of contrast in the development of competence. In A. Molnar and J. Zahorik (Eds.), *Curriculum theory* (pp. 50–63). Washington, DC: Association for Supervision and Curriculum Development.

Doll, W. E., Jr. (1979). A structural view of curriculum. *Theory into Practice 18*(5), 336–348.

Doll, W. E., Jr. (1980). Play and mastery: A structuralist view. *Journal of Curriculum Theorizing 5*(4), 209–226.

Doll, W. E., Jr. (1981). The educational need to re-invent the wheel. *Educational Leadership 39*(2), 26–40.

Doll, W. E., Jr. (1983). Curriculum and change: Piaget's organismic origins. *Journal of Curriculum Theorizing 5*(2) 4–61.

Doll, W. E., Jr. (1984). Developing competence. In E. Short (Ed.), *Competence* (pp. 123–138). Lanham, MD: University Press of America.

Doll, W. E., Jr. (1986). Prigogine: A new sense of order, a new curriculum. *Theory into Practice 25*(1), 10–16.

Doll, W. E., Jr. (1989). Complexity in the classroom. *Educational Leadership 7*(1), 65–70.

Doll, W. E., Jr. (1993). *A post-modern perspective on curriculum*. New York: Teachers College Press.

Doll, W. E., Jr. (1998a). Curriculum and concepts of control. In W. Pinar (Ed.), *Curriculum: Toward new identities* (pp. 295–323). New York: Garland.

Doll, W. E., Jr. (1998b). The spirit of education. *Early Childhood Education 31*, 3–7.

Doll, W. E., Jr. (1990). Post-modernism's utopian vision. *Education and Society 9*(1), 54–60.

Doll, W. E., Jr. (2000). Classroom management. In D. Gabbard (Ed.), *Power, knowledge and education in the global economy* (pp. 69–77). Mahweh, NJ: Erlbaum.

Doll, W. E., Jr. (2002a) Beyond methods: Teaching as an aesthetic and spiritful quest. In E. Mirochnik and D. Sherman (Eds.), *Passion and pedagogy* (pp. 127–151). New York: Lang.

Doll, W. E., Jr. (2002b). Ghosts in the curriculum. In W. Doll and N. Gough (Eds.), *Curriculum visions*. New York: Lang.

Doll, W. E., Jr. (2003). Modes of thought. In *Proceedings of the 2003 Complexity Science and Educational Research Conference*, October 16–18, Edmonton Alberta, pp. 1–10. http://www.complexityandeducation.ualberta.ca/conferences/2003/Documents/CSER_Doll.pdf . Retrieved November 22, 2011.

Doll, W. E., Jr. (2005a). Keeping knowledge alive. *Journal of Educational Research and Development 1*(1), 27–42.

Doll, W. E., Jr. (2005b). The culture of method. In W. Doll, M. J. Fleener, D. Trueit, and J. St. Julien (Eds.), *Chaos, complexity, curriculum and culture: A conversation* (pp. 21–75). New York: Lang.

Doll, W. E., Jr. (2006). Teaching good: An alternative to good teaching. Presentation at Oklahoma State University, February 6, 2006.

Doll, W. E., Jr. (2008a). The arrow of time. Class notes for EDCI 7922, Curriculum and the Concept of Time. http://calvin.ednet.lsu.edu/%7Ewdoll/ Retreived January 4, 2012.

Doll, W. E., Jr. (2008b). Complexity and the culture of curriculum. *Educational Philosophy and Theory 40*(1), 181–203.

Doll, W. E., Jr. (2009). Chaos and complexity theories. *SAGE encyclopedia of social and cultural foundations of education*. Thousand Oaks, CA: SAGE.

Doll, W. E., Jr. and Gough, N. (Eds.), (2002). *Curriculum visions*. New York: Peter Lang

Doll, W., Fleener, M. J., Trueit, D., and St. Julien, J. (Eds.), (2005). *Chaos, complexity, curriculum, and culture: A conversation*. New York: Lang.

Eddington, A. (1928). *The nature of the physical world.* New York: Macmillan.

Einstein, A. (1961). *The special and the general theory of relativity.* New York: Crown.

Eisner, E. W. (1967a). Educational objectives: Help or hindrance? *School Review 75*(3), 250–260.

Eisner, E. W. (1967b). A response to my critics. *School Review, 75*(3), 277–282.

Eliot, T. S. (1943). Little Gidding, in Eliot's *Four quartets.* New York: Harcourt Brace.

Feyerabend, P. (1988). *Against method.* New York: Verso.

Fleener, M. J. (2002). *Curriculum dynamics.* New York: Peter Lang.

Fleener, M. J. (2007). Curriculum dynamics: Seeing with soft eyes. Paper presented to the International Conference on the Reform of Classroom Teaching. Shanghai, PRC. May 2007.

Fleener, M. J., Carter, A., and Reeder, S. (2004). Language games in the mathematics classroom: Learning a way of life. *Journal of Curriculum Theorizing 36*(4), 445–468.

Foucault, M. (1970). *The order of things.* New York: Pantheon Books. (Original French publication, 1966.)

Furth, H. (1981). *Piaget and knowledge* (2nd edition). Chicago, IL: University of Chicago.

Gadamer, H.-G. (1980). *Dialogue and dialectic,* P. C. Smith (Trans.). New Haven, CT: Yale University Press.

Gadamer, H. G. (1993). *Truth and method* (revised 2nd edition). J. Weinsheimer and D. Marshall (Trans.). New York: Continuum. (Original German publication, 1960.)

Gagne, R. (1965). The analysis of instructional objectives for the design of instruction. In R. Glaser (Ed.), *Teaching machines and programmed learning, II: Data and directions.* Washington, DC: Department of Audio-visual Instruction, NEA.

Garrison, J. (1997). *Dewey and Eros.* New York: Teachers College Press

Garrison, J. (1998). Personal correspondence, January 23, 1998.

Geertz, C. (1973). *The interpretation of culture.* New York: Basic Books.

Genova, J. (1995). *Wittgenstein: A new way of seeing.* New York: Routledge.

Glasersfeld, E. von (1992). Aspects of radical constructivism and its educational recommendations. http://www.vonglasersfeld.com/191. Retrieved November 22, 2011.

Gleick, J. (1987). *Chaos: Making a new science.* New York: Viking Press.

Gough, N. (1994). Playing at catastrophe: Ecopolitical education after poststructuralism. *Educational Theory 44*(2), 189–210.

Gould, S. J. (1981). *The mismeasure of man.* New York: W. W. Norton.

Gould, S. J. (1982). Punctuated equilibrium. *New Scientist 94,* 137–141.

Gould, S. J. (1990). An earful of jaw. *Natural History 99*(3), 12–23.

Green, C. (2007). Toward a school of their own, Part 1. http://video.google.com/videoplay?docid=1488007330440945673. Retrieved February 2, 2008.

Greene, M. (1995). *Releasing the imagination.* San Francisco, CA: Jossey-Bass.

Griffin, D. (1988a). *The reenchantment of science.* Albany, NY: SUNY Press.

Griffin, D. (1988b). *Spirituality and society.* Albany, NY: SUNY Press.

Griffin, D. (1989). *God and religion in the postmodern world.* Albany, NY: SUNY Press.

Guttchen, R. (1969). The logic of practice. *Studies in Philosophy and Education 7*(1), 28–43.

Haber, S. (1964). *Efficiency and uplift.* Chicago: University of Chicago Press.

Hall, G., and Jones, H. (1976). *Competency-based education: A process for the improvement of education.* Englewood Cliffs, NJ: Prentice Hall.

Hamilton, D. (1989). *Toward a theory of schooling.* London: Falmer.

Hamilton, D. (1992). Comenius and the new world order. *Comenius 46,* 157–171.

Hamilton, D. (2003). Instruction in the making: Peter Ramus and the beginnings of modern schooling. Paper presented at (2003) American Educational Research Association.

Haroutounian, S. (1979). Essay review of Jean Piaget's *Biology and knowledge*. *Harvard Educational Review 49*(1), 93–100.

Hayles, N. K. (1983). *The cosmic web*. Ithaca, NY: Cornell University Press.

Hayles, N. K. (1990). *Chaos bound*. Ithaca, NY: Cornell University Press.

Hayles, N. K. (1991). *Chaos and order*. Chicago, IL. University of Chicago Press.

Hayles, N. K. (1999). *How we became posthuman*. Chicago, IL: University of Chicago Press.

Heidegger, M. (1977). The question concerning technology. In W. Lovitt (Trans. and Ed.), *The question concerning technology and other essays*. New York: Harper Collins. (Original German publication, 1954.)

Heidegger, M. (2002). *Time and being*. J. Stambaugh (Trans.). Chicago, IL: University of Chicago Press. (Original German publication, 1972.)

Heidegger, M. (2008). *Being and time*. J. Macquarrie and E. Robinson (Trans.). New York: HarperOne. (Original German publication, 1962.)

Heisenberg, W. (1971). *Physics and beyond*. A. J. Pomerans (Trans.). New York: Harper and Row.

Hendley, B. (2006). Philosophers as educators, revisited. *Process Papers*, No. 10, 28–40.

Henry, J. (2008). *The scientific revolution and the origins of modern science,* 3rd edition. New York: Palgrave.

Hlebowitsh, P. (1999). The burdens of the new curricularist. *Curriculum Inquiry*, 29(3) 343-354.

Holy Bible (1963). King James Version. London: Nonesuch Press (Original publication, 1611.)

Hubbard, B. (1983). The future of futurism. *Futurist, 17*(2), 52–59.

Huebner, D. (1999). *The lure of the transcendent*. V. Hillis (Ed.). Mahweh, NJ: Erlbaum.

Iser, W. (2000). *The range of interpretation*. New York: Columbia University Press.

Jackson, P. (1998). *Dewey and the lessons of art*. New Haven, CT: Yale University Press

Jackson, P. (2002). *John Dewey and the philosopher's task*. New York: Teachers College Press.

James, W. (1956). Is life worth living? In *The will to believe* (pp. 32–62). New York: Dover Publications. (Original publication, 1897.)

Janik, A., and Toulmin, S. (1973). *Wittgenstein's Vienna*. New York: Simon and Schuster.

Jardine, D., Clifford, P. and Friesen, S. (2003). *Back to the basics of teaching and learning: Thinking the world together*. Mahwah, NJ: Erlbaum.

Jardine, D., Friesen, S., and Clifford, P. (2006). *Curriculum in abundance*. Mahweh, NJ: Erlbaum.

Jay, M. (1993). *Force fields: Between intellectual history and cultural critique*. New York: Routledge.

Jencks, C. (1986). *What is post-modernism?* New York: St. Martin's Press.

Jencks, C. (1988). *What is post-modernism?* (enlarged, revised 2nd edition). New York: St. Martin's Press.

Jencks, C. (1992). *The post-modern reader*. New York: St. Martin's Press.

Johnson, G. (1996). *Fire in the mind: Science, faith, and the search for order*. New York: Alfred A. Knopf.

Johnson, S. (2001). *Emergence*. New York: Scribner.

Joncich, G. (Ed.). (1962). *Psychology and the science of education: Selected writings of Edward L. Thorndike*. (Classics in Education, No. 12). New York: Teachers College Press.

Kahn, R. (1998). Exploring chaos. Doctoral dissertation, University of Missouri, Kansas City.

Kanigel, R. (1997). *The one best way: Frederick Winslow Taylor and the enigma of efficiency*. New York: Viking.

Kauffman, S. (1991). Antichaos and adaptation. *Scientific American 265*, 78–84.

Kauffman, S. (1993). *The origins of order*. New York: Oxford University Press.

Kauffman, S. (1995). *At home in the universe: The search for the laws of self-organization and complexity*. New York: Oxford University Press.

Kauffman, S. (2000). *Investigations*. New York: Oxford University Press.

Kauffman, S. (2008). *Reinventing the sacred*. New York: Basic Books.

Kauffman, S., and Johnsen, S. (1991). Coevolution to the edge of chaos. *Journal of Theoretical Biology 149*(4), 467–505.

Keats, J. (2007). Ode to a Grecian urn. In J. Barnard (Ed.), *John Keats, selected poems* (p. 192). London: Penguin Group. (Original publication, 1819.)

Kierkegaard, S. (1983). Fear and trembling. In H. Tong and E. Hong (Trans. and Eds.), *Kierkegaard's writings*, Vol. 6. Princeton, NJ: Princeton University Press. (Original Danish publication, 1843.)

Kitchener, R. (1988). *The world view of contemporary physics.* Albany, NY: State University of New York Press.

Kliebard, H. (1971) The Tyler rationale: A reappraisal. *School Review, 78*(2), 259–272.

Kliebard, H. (1975). The rise of scientific curriculum making and its aftermath. *Curriculum Theory Network, 5*(1), 27–37.

Kliebard, H. (1995). The Tyler rationale revisited. *Journal of Curriculum Studies, 27*(1), 81–88.

Kline, M. (1980). *Mathematics: The loss of certainty.* New York: Oxford University Press.

Koyré, A. (1957). *From the closed world to the infinite universe.* Baltimore, MD: The Johns Hopkins Press.

Krathwohl, D. R., Bloom, B. S., and Masia, B. B. (1964). *Taxonomy of educational objectives: Handbook II, The affective domain.* New York: McKay.

Kuhn, T. S. (1957). *The Copernican revolution.* Cambridge, MA: Harvard University Press.

Kuhn, T. S. (1962). *The structure of scientific revolutions.* Chicago, IL: The University of Chicago Press.

Kuhn, T. S. (1970). *The structure of scientific revolutions,* 2nd edition, enlarged. Chicago, IL: University of Chicago Press.

Kuhn, T. S. (1977). *The essential tension.* Chicago, IL: University of Chicago Press.

Kundera, M. (1988). *The art of the novel.* L. Asher (Trans.). New York: Grove Press.

Küng, H. (1988). *Theology for a third millennium.* P. Heinegg (Trans.). New York: Doubleday Press.

LaCapra, D. (2004). *History in transit: Experience, identity, critical theory.* Ithaca, NY: Cornell University Press.

Latour, B. (2004). *Making things public: Atmospheres of democracy.* P. Weibel (Trans.). Cambridge, MA: The MIT Press.

Latour, B. (2007). *We have never been modern.* C. Porter (Trans.). Cambridge, MA: Harvard University Press. (Original French publication, 1991.)

Lehrer, J. (2008) *Annals of science,* The Eureka Hunt. Reprinted in *The New Yorker,* July 28, 40–45.

Leibniz, G.W. (1951). On the method of universality, in *Leibniz, selections.* P. Weiner, (Ed.) New York: Scribner & Sons. (Original essay publication, 1674)

Lewin, R. (1992). *Complexity: Life at the edge of chaos.* New York: Macmillan Publishing Company.

Li, T. Y., and Yorke, J. (1975). Period three implies chaos. *American Mathematics Monthly 82,* 985–992.

Livio, M. (2003). *The golden ratio: The story of phi.* New York: Broadway Books.

Lorenz, E. (1995). *The essence of chaos.* Seattle, WA: University of Washington Press.

Lovejoy, A. (1936). *The great chain of being.* New York: Harper.

Lovelock, J. (1979). *Gaia.* New York: Oxford University Press.

Lovelock, J. (1991). *Healing Gaia.* New York: Harmony Books.

Lowe, V. (1985). *Alfred North Whitehead: The man and his work,* Vol. I. Baltimore, MD: The Johns Hopkins University Press.

Lowe, V. (1990). *Alfred North Whitehead: The man and his work*, Vol. II, J.B. Schneewind, (Ed.). Baltimore, MD: The Johns Hopkins University Press.

Lyotard, J.-F. (1984). *The postmodern condition: A report on knowledge*. G. Bennington and B. Massumi (Trans.). Minneapolis, MN: University of Minnesota Press. (Original French publication, 1979.)

Lyotard, J.-F. (1987). Re-writing modernity. *SubStance, 16*(3), 3–9.

Macdonald, J. B. (1965). Myths about instructions. *Educational Leadership, 22*(7), 571–576.

Mager, R. F. (1962). *Preparing objectives for programmed instruction*. Palo Alto, CA: Fearon.

Mandelbrot, B. (1982). *The fractal nature of geometry*. San Francisco, CA: W.H. Freeman.

Margulis, L. (1998). *The symbiotic planet*. London: Weidenfield and Nicholson.

Margulis, L., and Sagan, D. (1995). *What is life?* New York: Simon and Schuster.

Mason, M. (2008). What is complexity theory and what are its implications for educational change? *Educational Philosophy and Theory 40*(1), 35–49.

Maturana, H., and Varela, F. (1980). *Autopoiesis and cognition*. Dordrecht: Reidel.

Maturana, H., and Varela, F. (1987). *The tree of knowledge*, R. Paolucci (Trans.). Boston, MA: Shambhala. (Revised edition, 1992.)

Maxcy, S. (1995). *Democracy, chaos, and the new school order*. Thousand Oaks, CA: Corwin.

Maxwell, C. (1873). *Treatise on electricity and magnetism*. Oxford: Oxford University Press.

Mayhew, K., and Edwards, A. (1966). *The Dewey school. The laboratory school of the University of Chicago, 1896–1903*. New York: Atherton Press. (Original publication 1936.)

McCormmach, R. (1982). *Night thoughts of a classical physicist*. Cambridge, MA: Harvard University Press.

McKnight, D. (1997). Errand into the wilderness: Thematic analysis of the Puritan influence on American education. Doctoral dissertation, Louisiana State University and Agricultural and Mechanical College.

McLaren, Peter. (1986). Postmodernity and the death of politics. *Educational Theory, 36*(4), 389–401.

Menand, L. (2002). *The metaphysical club*. New York: Farrar, Straus and Giroux.

Meyers, P. A. (2003). Method and civic education. *Humanitas, 16*(2), 4–47.

Mill, J. S. (1965). *A system of logic*. New York: Bobbs-Merrill. (Original publication 1843.)

Miller, P. (1939). *The New England mind*. New York: Macmillan.

Mitchell, M. (2009). *Complexity: A guided tour*. New York: Oxford University Press.

Monod, J. (1971). *Chance and necessity*. New York: Alfred A. Knopf. (Original French publication, 1970.)

More, Sir Thomas (1975). *Utopia*. R. M. Adams (Trans.). New York: Norton. (Original publication 1516.)

Mosès, S. (2009). *The angel of history: Rosenzweig, Benjamin, Scholem*. B. Harshav (Trans.). Stanford, CA: Stanford University Press. (Original publication, 1992.)

Newton, I. (1952). *Opticks* (4th edition). New York: Dover Publications. (Original publication 1730.)

Newton, I. (1962). *Philosophia naturalis principia mathematica* (3rd edition). F. Cajori (Trans.). Berkeley, CA: University of California Press. (Original publication, 1729.)

Newton, I. (1972). *The mathematical principles of natural philosophy* (3rd edition). A. Koyre and I. B. Cohen (Eds.). Cambridge, MA: Harvard University Press. (Original work published 1729.)

Niznik, J., and Sanders, J. (Eds.) (1996). *Debating the state of philosophy: Habermas, Rorty, & Kolakowski*. Westport, CT: Praeger.

Noddings, N. (1974). Competence theories and the science of education. *Educational Theory, 24*(4), 356–364.

Noddings, N. (1980). Competence. Paper presented to the Curriculum Inquiry Conference, Pennsylvania. State University, May 18–20, 1980.

Nusselder, A. (2009). *Interface fantasy: A Lacanian cyborg ontology*. Cambridge, MA: The MIT Press.

Oliver, D. (1990). Grounded knowing: A postmodern perspective on teaching and learning. *Educational Leadership, 48*, 64–69.

Oliver, D., and Gershman, K. (1989). *Education, modernity, and fractured meaning*. Albany, NY: State University of New York Press.

Olson, D. (1970). *Cognitive development*. New York: Academic Press.

Ong, W. (1971). *Rhetoric, romance, and technology of the word: studies in the interaction of expression and culture*. Ithaca, NY: Cornell University Press.

Ong, W. (1983). *Ramus, method, and the decay of dialogue*. Cambridge, MA: Harvard University Press. (Original publication, 1958.)

Osberg, D., and Biesta, G. J. J. (2010). *Complexity theory and the politics of education*. Rotterdam: Sense Publishers.

Ott, E., and Spano, M. (1995). Controlling chaos. *Physics Today. 48*(5), 34–40.

Otto, R. (1923). *The idea of the holy*. J. Harvey (Trans.). Oxford: Oxford University Press. (Original German publication, 1917.)

Oxford Annotated Bible with the Apocrypha. (1965). New York: Oxford University Press.

Oxford English Dictionary (1989). 2nd edition. J. A. Simpson and E. S. C. Weiner (Eds.). Oxford: Oxford University Press.

Pagels, H. (1982). *The cosmic code*. New York: Simon and Schuster.

Parker, D., and Stacey, R. (1994). *Chaos, management and economics: The implications of non-linear thinking*. London: Institute of Economic Affairs.

Peirce, C. S. (1992). *Reasoning and the logic of things: The Cambridge conferences lectures of 1898*. K. Ketner and H. Putnam (Eds.). Cambridge, MA: Harvard University Press.

Peters, R. S. (1968). *Ethics and education*. London, UK: Allen and Unwin.

Peters, T. (1987). *Thriving on chaos: Handbook for a management revolution*. New York: Alfred A. Knopf.

Peters, T. (1992). *Liberation management: Necessary disorganization for the nanosecond nineties*. New York: Alfred A. Knopf.

Petzinger, T., Jr. (1997). The front lines. *Wall Street Journal*, March, 7.

Piaget, J. (1971a). *Biology and knowledge*. B. Walsh (Trans.). Chicago, IL: University of Chicago Press. (Original French publication, 1967.)

Piaget, J. (1971b). *Science of education and the psychology of the child*. D. Coltman (Trans.). New York: Viking. (Original French publication, 1969.)

Piaget, J. (1972). Some aspects of operation. In M. W. Piers (Ed.), *Play and development* (pp. 15–27). New York: Norton.

Piaget, J. (1974). *To understand is to invent*. G. A. Roberts (Trans.). New York: Viking Press. (Original French publication, 1948.)

Piaget, J. (1976). *Piaget sampler*. S. F. Campbell (Ed.). New York: Wiley.

Piaget, J. (1977a). *The development of thought: Equilibration of cognitive structures*. A. Rosen (Trans.). New York: Viking.

Piaget, J. (1977b). *The essential Piaget*. H. Gruber and J. Voneche (Eds.). New York: Basic Books.

Piaget, J. (1978). *Behavior and evolution*. D. Nicholson-Smith (Trans.). New York: Pantheon Books. (Original French publication, 1976.)

Piaget, J. (1980). *Adaptation and intelligence*. S. Eames (Trans.). Chicago, IL: University of Chicago Press. (Original French publication, 1974.)

Piaget, J. (1985). *Equilibration of cognitive structures*. Chicago, IL: University of Chicago Press.

Piaget, J., and Garcia, R. (1989). *Psychogenesis and the history of science*. H. Feider (Trans.). New York: Columbia University Press.

Piaget, J., and Garcia, R. (1991). *Toward a logic of meanings*. P. M. Davidson and J. Easley (Eds.). Hillside, NJ: Erlbaum.

Pinar, W. F. (Ed.), (1975). *Curriculum theorizing: The reconceptualists*. Berkeley, CA: McCutchan.

Pinar, W. F. (Ed.), (1998). *Curriculum: Toward new identities*. New York: Garland.

Pinar, W. F. (Ed.), (1999). *The lure of the transcendent*. Mahwah, NJ: Erlbaum.

Pinar, W. F. (2006). *The synoptic text today and other essays: Curriculum development after the reconceptualization*. New York: Peter Lang.

Pinar, W. F. (2009a). *The worldliness of a cosmopolitan education*. New York: Routledge.

Pinar, W. F. (2009b). The primacy of the particular. In Leonard Waks and Edmund C. Short (Eds.), *Leaders in curriculum studies: Intellectual self-portraits* (pp. 143–152). Rotterdam and Tapei: Sense Publishers.

Pinar, W. F. (2012). *What is curriculum theory?* (2nd edition). New York: Routledge.

Pinar, W. F., Reynolds, W. M., Slattery, P., Taubman, P. M., (Eds.), (1995). *Understanding curriculum: An introduction to historical and contemporary curriculum discourses*. New York: Peter Lang.

Popham, W. J. (1967). *Educational criterion measures*. Inglewood, CA: Southwest Regional Laboratory for Educational Research and Development.

Popham, W. J. (1969). Objectives and instruction. In R. Stake (Ed.), *Instructional objectives*. AERA Monograph Series on Curriculum Evaluation, Vol. 3. Chicago, IL: Rand McNally.

Pratt, S. (2008). Bifurcations are not always exclusive. *Complicity* 5(1), 125-128.

Price, L. (1954). *Dialogues of Alfred North Whitehead*. Boston, MA: Little, Brown.

Prigogine, I. (1961). *Introduction to the thermodynamics of irreversible processes* (2nd rev. ed.). New York: John Wiley, Interscience.

Prigogine, I. (1980). *From being to becoming: Time and complexity in the physical sciences*. San Francisco, CA: W. H. Freeman.

Prigogine, I. (1983). Interview. *Omni*, (May) 84–92; 120–121.

Prigogine, I. (1988). Reconceptualization of time. In R. Kitchener (Ed.), *The worldview of contemporary physics*. Albany, NY: SUNY Press.

Prigogine, I. (1997). *The end of certainty: Time, chaos, and the new laws of nature*. New York: Free Press.

Prigogine, I. (2003). *Is future given*. Singapore: World Scientific Press.

Prigogine, I., and Stengers, I. (1984). *Order out of chaos: Man's new dialogue with nature*. New York: Bantam.

Proulx, J. (2008). Some differences between Maturana and Varela's theory of cognition and constructivism. *Complicity* 5(1), 11–26.

Quinn, M. E. (1997). Faith and its crises. Doctoral dissertation, Louisiana State University and Agricultural and Mechanical College.

Reiss, T. (1982). *The discourse of modernism*. Ithaca, NY: Cornell University Press.

Rice, J. M. (1969a). *Scientific management in education*. New York: Arno Press. (Original publication, 1914.)

Rice, J. M. (1969b). *Public school systems in the United States*. New York: Arno Press. (Original publication, 1893.)

Rorty, R. (1979). *Philosophy and the mirror of nature*. Princeton, NJ: Princeton University Press.

Rorty, R. (1982). *Consequences of pragmatism*. Minneapolis, MN: University of Minnesota Press.

Rorty, R. (1989). *Contingency, irony, and solidarity*. Cambridge: Cambridge University Press.

Ruf, H. (1987). Moral problems and religious mysteries. *Dialogue and Alliance, 1*(3), 77–92.

Rumble, P. (1994). Stylistic contamination in the "Trilogia della vita": The case of "Il fiore delle mille e una notte." In P. Rumble and B. Testa (Eds.), *Pier Paolo Pasolini: Contemporary perspectives* (pp. 210–231). Toronto: University of Toronto Press.

Ryans, D. G., and Krathwohl, D. R. (1965). Stating objectives appropriately for program, for curriculum, and for instructional materials development. *Journal of Teacher Education, 16*(1), 83–92.

Saint-Simon, Henri Comte de (1952). *Henri Comte de Saint-Simon (1760–1825): Selected writings.* F. M. H. Markham (Ed. and Trans.), New York: Macmillan. (Original publication, 1825.)

Santayana, G. (1968). *The German mind.* New York: Crowell. (Original publication, 1915.)

Sawada, D., and Caley, M. (1985). Dissipative structures. *Educational Researcher, 14* (3), 13–19.

Schilpp, P. A. (Ed.) (1989). *The philosophy of John Dewey.* Menasha, WI: Banta. (Original publication, 1939).

Schön, D. (1983). *The reflective practitioner.* New York: Basic Books.

Schön, D. (1987). *Educating the reflective practitioner.* San Francisco, CA: Jossey-Bass.

Schwab, J. J. (1969). *College curriculum and student protest.* Chicago, IL: The University of Chicago Press.

Schwab, J. J. (1970). *The practical: A language for curriculum.* National Education Association Center for the Study of Instruction. Reprinted in I. Westbury and N. J. Wilkof (Eds.), *Science, curriculum, and liberal education* (1978) (pp. 287–321). Chicago, IL: University of Chicago Press.

Selden, S. (1999). *Inheriting shame.* New York: Teachers College Press.

Semetsky, I. (2004). The role of intuition in thinking and learning: Deleuze and the pragmatic legacy. *Educational Philosophy and Theory, 36*(4), 433–454.

Semetsky, I. (2008). Simplifying complexity. *Complicity, 5*(1), 63–79.

Serres, M. (1983). *Hermes, literature, science, philosophy.* J. Harari and D. Bell (Eds.). Baltimore, MD: The Johns Hopkins University Press. (Original French essays published 1968–1980.)

Serres, M. (1991). *Rome: The book of foundations.* F. McCarren (Trans.). Stanford, CA: Stanford University Press. (Original French publication, 1983.)

Serres, M. (1997). *The troubadour of knowledge.* S. Glaser (Trans.). Ann Arbor, MI: University of Michigan Press. (Original French publication, 1991.)

Serres, M., and Latour, B. (1995). *Conversations on science, culture, and time.* R. Lapidus (Trans.). Ann Arbor, MI: University of Michigan Press. (Original French publication, 1990.)

Shapiro, B. (2000). *A culture of fact: England 1550–1720.* Ithaca, NY: Cornell University Press.

Short, E., and Waks, L. (Eds.) (2009). *Leaders in curriculum studies.* Rotterdam and Taipei: Sense Publishers.

Silberman, C. (1970). *Crisis in the classroom: The remaking of American education.* New York: Random House.

Smith, H. (1982). *Beyond the postmodern mind.* New York: Crossroads.

Smitherman, S. (2005). Chaos and complexity theories: Wholes and holes. In *Chaos, complexity, curriculum and culture,* W. Doll, M. J. Fleener, D. Trueit, and J. St. Julien (Eds.). New York: Lang. pp. 153–180.

Smitherman Pratt. S. (2006). Reflections on teaching a mathematics education course. Doctoral dissertation, Louisiana State University.

Snow, C. P. (1964). *The two cultures: And a second look.* Cambridge: Cambridge University Press.

Snowden, D. (2005). Managing for serendipity. http://www.cognitive-edge.com/ceresources/articles/39_Managing_for_Serendipity_final.pdf Retrieved January. 4, 2012

Spencer, H. (1929). What knowledge is of most worth? In Hergert O. Spencer (Ed.), *Education: Intellectual, moral, and physical* (pp. 1-87). New York: D. Appleton. (Original publication, 1859.)

Stengers, I. (1997). *Power and invention: Situating science.* Minneapolis, MN: University of Minnesota Press.

Stevens, W. (1959). Connoisseur of chaos. In *Poems.* New York: Vintage Books. (Original publication, 1938.)

Stewart, I. (1989). *Does God play dice? The mathematics of chaos.* Cambridge, MA: Blackwell Publishers.

Stone, A. (2007). The secret life of atoms. *Discover* (June), 52–54.

Stoppard, T. (1968). *Rosencranz and Guildenstern are dead.* New York: Grove Press.

Strauss, S. (1985). Trying to join biology, physics a sticky problem. *Toronto Globe and Mail,* May 14, p. 20.

Taylor, F. W. (1947). *Scientific management.* New York: Harper. (Original work published 1911.)

Tennyson, Alfred Lord. (1850). In memoriam A. H. H. http://www.online-literature.com/tennyson/718/. Retrieved November 22, 2011.

Thompson, W. I. (1989). *Imaginary landscape.* New York: St. Martin's Press.

Tillich, P. (1957). *Dynamics of faith.* New York: Harper.

TIMSS Report (1996). *A splintered vision: An investigation of U.S. science and mathematics education.* East Lansing, MI: US National Research Center Publication.

Toulmin, S. (1982). *Return to cosmology.* Berkeley, CA: University of California Press.

Toulmin, S. (1990). *Cosmopolis.* New York: Free Press.

Triche, S. (2002). Reconceiving curriculum: An historical approach. Doctoral dissertation, Louisiana State University and Agricultural and Mechanical College.

Triche, S., and McKnight, D. (2004). The quest for method: The legacy of Peter Ramus. *History of Education 33*(1), 39–54.

Trueit, D. (2004). A pragmatist approach to inquiry: Recuperation of the poetic. In *Proceedings of the 2004 Complexity Science and Educational Research Conference,* September 30–October 3, Chaffey's Locks, Canada, pp. 241–252. http://www.complexityandeducation.ualberta.ca/conferences/2004/proceedings.htm. Retrieved January 3, 2012

Trueit, D. (2005a). Watercourses: Poiesis and the play of conversation. In William E. Doll, Jr, M. Jayne Fleener, Donna Trueit, and John St. Julian (Eds.), *Chaos, complexity, curriculum and culture: A conversation* (pp. 77–99). New York: Peter Lang.

Trueit, D. (2005b). Complexifying the poetic: Toward a poiesis of curriculum. Doctoral dissertation, Louisiana State University and Agricultural and Mechanical College.

Trueit, D. (2007). Beyond teaching as telling. Paper presentation, First International Forum on Teaching Reform, Pudong Shanghai, PRC.

Trueit, D., and Pratt, S. (2006). Complex conversations in education: Moving away from teaching-as-telling. Paper presented at Second IAACS Tri-Annual Conference, Tampere, Finland.

Trueit, D., Wang, H., Doll, W. E. Jr., and Pinar, W. F. (Eds.), (2003). *The internationalization of curriculum studies.* New York: Peter Lang.

Tyler, L. (1969). A case history: Formulation of objectives from a psychoanalytic frame-work. In W. J. Popham, E. W. Eisner, H. J. Sullivan, and L. L. Tyler (Eds.), *Instructional objectives.* AERA Monograph Series on Curriculum Evaluation, No. 3. Chicago, IL: Rand McNally.

Tyler, R. (1950). *Basic principles of curriculum and instruction.* Chicago, IL: University of Chicago Press.

Tyler, R. (1964). Some persistent questions on the defining of objectives. In C. Lindvall (Ed.), *Defining educational objectives.* Pittsburgh, PA: University of Pittsburgh Press.

Uljens, M. (2003). The idea of a university theory of education—an impossible but necessary project? In Lars Løvlie, Klaus Peter Mortensen and Sven Erik Nordenbo (Eds.), *Educating humanity: Bildung in postmodernity* (pp. 37–59). Oxford: Blackwell.

Varela, F. (1979). *Principles of biological autonomy.* New York: Elsevier North Holland.

Varela, F. (1996). *Invitation aux sciences cognitives.* Paris: Éditions du Seuil.

Varela, F., Thompson, E., and Rosch, E. (1993). *The embodied mind.* Cambridge, MA: The MIT Press.

Vico, G. (1988). *On the most ancient wisdom of the Italians.* L. Palmer (Trans.). Ithaca, NY: Cornell University Press. (Original publication, 1710.)

Waddington, C. H. (1957). *The strategy of the genes.* New York: Macmillan.

Waddington, C. H. (1975). *The evolution of an evolutionist.* Ithaca, NY: Cornell University Press.

Waks, L. (2008). *Leaders in the philosophy of education.* Rotterdam and Taipei: Sense Publishers.

Waldrop, M. M. (1992). *Complexity: The emerging science at the edge of order and chaos.* New York: Simon and Schuster.

Wang, H. (2004). *The call from the stranger on a journey home: Curriculum in a third space.* New York: Peter Lang.

Waters, B. (1986). Ministry and the university in a postmodern world. *Religion and Intellectual Life, 4*(1), 113–122.

Watson, A. J. (2007). *Marginal man: The dark vision of Harold Innis.* Toronto: University of Toronto Press.

Watson, T. J. (1994). *In search of management: Culture, chaos and control in managerial work.* London: Routledge.

Weiss, P. (1971). *Within the gates of science and beyond.* New York: Hafner.

Wellmer, A. (1985). Reason, utopia, and enlightenment. In R. J. Bernstein (Ed.), *Habermas and modernity,* (pp. 35–66). Cambridge, MA: The MIT Press.

Wertheim, M. (1995). *Pythagoras' trousers.* New York: Times Books.

White, M. (1973). *Science and sentiment in America.* New York: Oxford University Press.

White, R. W. (1959). Motivation reconsidered: The concept of competence. *Psychological Review, 66,* 297–333.

Whitehead, A. N. (1938). *Modes of thought.* New York: Macmillan.

Whitehead, A. N. (1948). *Essays in science and philosophy.* New York: Philosophical Library. (Reprint of 1911 essay.)

Whitehead, A. N. (1967a). *Science and the modern world.* New York: The Free Press. (Original publication, 1925.)

Whitehead, A. N. (1967b). *The aims of education and other essays.* New York: The Free Press. (Original publication, 1929.)

Whitehead, A. N. (1978). *Process and reality: An essay in cosmology.* D. R. Griffin and D. Sherburne (Eds.), Corrected edition. New York: The Free Press. (Original publication 1929.)

Whitson, T. (2008) Response to Semetsky. *Complicity, 5*(1), 81–106.

Wittgenstein, L. (1958). *Philosophical investigations.* G. E. M. Anscombe (Trans.), 3rd edition, New York: Macmillan.

Wraga, W. G. (1999). Extracting sun-beams out of cucumbers: The retreat from practice in reconceptualized curriculum studies. *Educational Researcher, 28*(1) 4–13.

Yu, Jie (2011). Reflections on En-Teaching: Heidegger, Dewey, and Lao Tsu. Doctoral dissertation, Louisiana State University.

INDEX

Edwards Brothers Malloy
Thorofare, NJ USA
May 18, 2012